Lecture Notes in Computer Science 1019
Edited by G. Goos, J. Hartmanis and J. van Leeuwen

Springer
Berlin
Heidelberg
New York
Barcelona
Budapest
Hong Kong
London
Milan
Paris
Santa Clara
Singapore
Tokyo

E. Brinksma W.R. Cleaveland K.G. Larsen
T. Margaria B. Steffen (Eds.)

Tools and Algorithms for the Construction and Analysis of Systems

First International Workshop, TACAS '95
Aarhus, Denmark, May 19-20, 1995
Selected Papers

Springer

Series Editors

Gerhard Goos, Karlsruhe University, Germany

Juris Hartmanis, Cornell University, NY, USA

Jan van Leeuwen, Utrecht University, The Netherlands

Volume Editors

Ed Brinksma
Department of Computer Science, University of Twente
PO Box 217, 7500 AE Enschede, The Netherlands

W. Rance Cleaveland
Department of Computer Science, North Carolina State University
Raleigh, NC 27695-8206, USA

Kim Guldstrand Larsen
Aalborg University Center, Dept. of Mathematics and Computer Science
Fredrik Bajersvej 7, DK-9220 Aalborg, Denmark

Tiziana Margaria
Bernhard Steffen
Fakultät für Mathematik und Informatik, Universität Passau
Postfach 2540, D-94030 Passau, Germany

Cataloging-in-Publication data applied for

Die Deutsche Bibliothek - CIP-Einheitsaufnahme

Tools and algorithms for the construction and analysis of systems : first international workshop ; selected papers / TACAS '95, Aarhus, Denmark, May 19 - 20, 1995. E. Brinksma ... (ed.). - Berlin ; Heidelberg ; New York ; Barcelona ; Budapest ; Hong Kong ; London ; Milan ; Paris ; Tokyo : Springer, 1995
(Lecture notes in computer science ; Vol. 1019)
ISBN 3-540-60630-0
NE: Brinksma, Ed [Hrsg.]; TACAS <1, 1995, Århus>; GT

CR Subject Classification (1991): F.3, D.2.4, D.2.2, C.2.4

ISBN 3-540-60630-0 Springer-Verlag Berlin Heidelberg New York

Typesetting: Camera-ready by author
SPIN 10512295 06/3142 – 5 4 3 2 1 0 Printed on acid-free paper

Foreword

This volume contains 12 selected papers of the first workshop on *Tools and Algorithms for the Construction and Analysis of Systems*, TACAS'95, which took place at the University of Aarhus (Denmark), May 19-20. TACAS brought together 46 researchers interested in the development and application of tools and algorithms for specification, verification, analysis and construction of distributed systems. The overall goal of the workshop was to compare the various methods and the degree to which they are supported by interacting or fully automatic tools.

During the two days 23 presentations selected from 32 submissions were given, covering a variety of topics including refinement–based and compositional verification, construction techniques, analysis and verification via theorem–proving, process algebras, temporal and modal logics, techniques for real–time, hybrid and probabilistic systems, and approaches for value–passing systems. In addition special sessions for tool demonstration were held, showing surprising performance even in cases where worst case complexity estimations hardly allowed any optimism.

TACAS was hosted by BRICS, the center of the Danish National Research Foundation at the Computer Science Departments of Aarhus and Aalborg Universities, and the local organization was in the hands of Uffe H. Engberg, Kim G. Larsen, Birger Nielsen, and Arne Skou, who were supported by the experienced TAPSOFT'95 organizers Peter D. Mosses and Karen K. Møller. This combination guaranteed a perfect and enjoyable event.

Finally, we would like to thank all the referees who assisted us in the paper selection: L. Aceto, F. Andersen, V. Braun, E.H. Eertink, A. Geser, S. Graf, L. Heerink, A. Ingólfsdóttir, W. T. M. Kars, J-P. Katoen, K. J. Kristoffersen, R. Langerak, G. Lüttgen, T. Margaria, A. Nymeyer, J. Tretmans, C. Weise, W. Yi.

The Editors

Contents

Combining Model Checking and Deduction for I/O-Automata

Olaf Müller *‡, Tobias Nipkow †‡

ABSTRACT We propose a combination of model checking and interactive theorem proving where the theorem prover is used to represent finite and infinite state systems, reason about them compositionally and reduce them to small finite systems by verified abstractions. As an example we verify a version of the Alternating Bit Protocol with unbounded lossy and duplicating channels: the channels are abstracted by interactive proof and the resulting finite state system is model checked.

1 Introduction

The purpose of this paper is to combine the two major paradigms for the verification of distributed systems: *model checking* and *theorem proving.* The advantages of each approach are well known: model checking is automatic but limited to finite state processes, theorem proving requires user interaction but can deal with arbitrary processes. Recently attempts have been made to combine the strength of both methods by using the deductive machinery of theorem provers to reduce "large" correctness problems to ones that are small enough for model checking. The key idea is *abstraction* whereby the state space is partitioned to obtain a smaller automaton which is amenable to model checking. Of course the abstraction has to be sound w.r.t. the property we want to check: if the abstracted automaton satisfies the property so should the original automaton.

In our approach the theorem prover provides a common representation language and tools for

- both finite and infinite state systems,
- checking the soundness of abstractions,
- reasoning about systems in a compositional manner.

*Research supported by DFG, *Leibniz Programm.*

†Research supported by ESPRIT BRA 6453, *Types.*

‡Institut für Informatik, Technische Universität München, 80290 München, Germany. Email: {Mueller,Nipkow}@Informatik.TU-Muenchen.De

Our work is based on Lynch and Tuttle's *Input/Output-Automata* (*IOA*) [14] as model of distributed processes which have been embedded in the theorem prover Isabelle/HOL [15]. We are interested in verifying safety properties of IOA. These safety properties are not expressed by temporal logic formulae but again by IOA. Hence we need to check that the traces of one IOA C (the implementation) are included in the traces of another IOA A (the specification). Assuming that C is infinite or at least too large to check $traces(C) \subseteq traces(A)$ automatically, we define an intermediate automaton B which is an abstraction of C and should satisfy $traces(C) \subseteq traces(B) \subseteq traces(A)$. Thus we achieve the following division of labor: $traces(C) \subseteq traces(B)$, i.e. the soundness of the abstraction, is proved interactively in Isabelle; $traces(B) \subseteq traces(A)$ is verified automatically by a model checker; finally, transitivity of $\subseteq$ yields the desired $traces(C) \subseteq traces(A)$.

The distinguishing feature of our approach is the ability to reason about the soundness of arbitrary abstractions because we have the meta-theory of IOA at our disposal. Assuming that the theorem prover and the formalization of IOA in it are correct, the only remaining source of errors is the model checker which is treated like an oracle by the theorem prover. Note that this includes the interface between model checker and theorem prover, which is particularly critical because we need to ensure that the theorem prover formalizes exactly the logic the model checker is based on.

The rest of the paper illustrates this approach using a particular example, namely an implementation of the Alternating Bit Protocol using unbounded channels. This is in contrast to pure model checking approaches where the channels are always of a fixed capacity (usually 1). The key to the success of our approach is the fact that channels may lose and duplicate, but not reorder messages. Thus is is possible to "compactify" channels without altering their behaviour by collapsing all adjacent identical messages. This is what our abstraction from C to B does. The full picture looks like this:

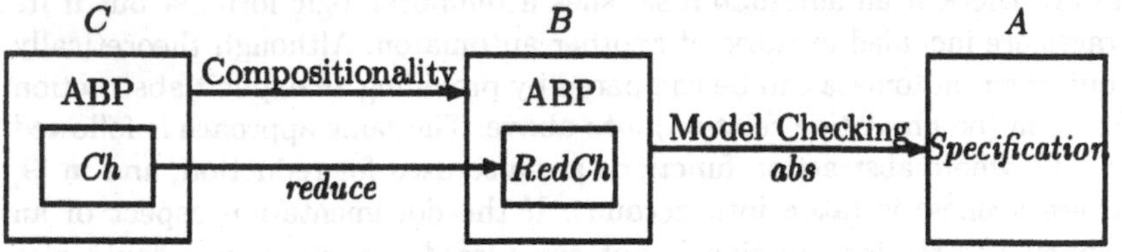

FIGURE 1. Integration Scheme

The implementation C contains unbounded channels *Ch* which are abstracted/ compactified by a function *reduce*. It is shown interactively that *reduce* is indeed an abstraction function, i.e. $traces(Ch) \subseteq traces(RedCh)$. B is the same as C except that collapsing channels are used. Compositionality proves that C must be an implementation of B, i.e. $traces(C) \subseteq traces(B)$. Although *RedCh* is not a finite state system, it behaves like one if used in the context of the ABP because at any one time there are at most two different messages on each channel. Thus B is a finite state system. Note however, that we never need to prove this explicitly: It is merely an intuition which is later confirmed by the model checker when it is given a description of B and A together with an abstraction function *abs* between them. The model checker explores the full state space of B verifying transition by transition that *abs* is indeed an abstraction. It is only the successful termination of the model checker which tells us that B is finite.

1.1 Related work

Our paper is closely related to the work by Hungar [11] who embeds a subset of OCCAM in the theorem prover LAMBDA and combines it with an external model checker. The key difference is that Hungar relies much more on unformalized meta-theory than we do: he axiomatizes OCCAM's proof rules instead of deriving them from a semantics, and does not verify the soundness of his data abstractions.

The literature on abstraction for model checking is already quite extensive (see for example, [4, 8, 5]). The general idea is to compute an abstract program given a concrete one together with an abstraction function/relation. The approach of Clarke et al. is in principle also applicable to infinite concrete systems. However, since they compute an approximation to the real abstract program, the result is not necessarily finite state. Nevertheless it would be interesting to rephrase their ideas in terms of IOA and apply them to our example. In this case we would not give B explicitly but would compute (via the rewriting machinery of the theorem prover) a (hopefully finite state) approximation of it.

Our work differs from most approaches to model checking because we do not check if an automaton satisfies a temporal logic formula but if its traces are included in those of another automaton. Although theoretically equivalent, automata can be compared by providing an explicit abstraction function (or simulation relation), *abs* above. The same approach is followed in [12] where abstraction functions are also used for reduction, and in [9] where liveness is taken into account. If the documentation aspect of an explicit abstraction function is not considered important, one could also use a model checker which searches for an abstraction function using, for example, the techniques of [6], although this is bound to be less efficient.

Finally there is the result by Abdulla and Jonsson [1] that certain properties of finite state systems communicating via unbounded lossy channels are decidable, which they apply to the Alternating Bit Protocol. However, in our work the channels can both lose and duplicate messages, hence their result does not apply directly.

2 I/O-Automata in Isabelle/HOL

Isabelle notation. Set comprehension has the shape $\{e.\ P\}$, where e is an expression and P a predicate. Tuples are written between angle brackets, e.g. $<s, a, t>$, and are nested pairs with projection functions *fst* and *snd*. If f is a function of type $\tau_1 \rightarrow \tau_2 \rightarrow \tau_3$, application is written $f(x, y)$ rather than $f\ x\ y$. Conditional expressions are written $if(A, B, C)$. The empty list is written $[\,]$, and "cons" is written infix: $h :: tl$. Function composition is another infix, e.g. $f \circ g$.

2.1 I/O Automata

An IOA is a finite or infinite state automaton with labelled transitions. I/O automata, initially introduced by Lynch and Tuttle [14], are still under development, and the formalization we used represents only a fragment of the theory one can find in recent papers [7]. For example, we do not deal with fairness or time constraints. The details of the formalization can be found in a previous paper [15], so that we give only a brief sketch of the essential definitions inside Isabelle/HOL.

An action signature is described by the type

$$(\alpha)\mathit{signature} \equiv (\alpha)\mathit{set} \times (\alpha)\mathit{set} \times (\alpha)\mathit{set}.$$

The first, second and third components of an action signature S may be extracted with *inputs*, *outputs*, and *internals*. Furthermore, $\mathit{actions}(S) = \mathit{inputs}(S) \cup \mathit{outputs}(S) \cup \mathit{internals}(S)$, and $\mathit{externals}(S) = \mathit{inputs}(S) \cup \mathit{outputs}(S)$. Action signatures have to satisfy the following condition:

$$\begin{aligned}
&\mathit{is_asig}(\mathit{triple}) \equiv \\
&\quad (\mathit{inputs}(\mathit{triple}) \cap \mathit{outputs}(\mathit{triple}) = \{\}) \wedge \\
&\quad (\mathit{outputs}(\mathit{triple}) \cap \mathit{internals}(\mathit{triple}) = \{\}) \wedge \\
&\quad (\mathit{inputs}(\mathit{triple}) \cap \mathit{internals}(\mathit{triple}) = \{\})
\end{aligned}$$

An IOA is a triple with type defined by

$$(\alpha, \sigma)\mathit{ioa} \equiv (\alpha)\mathit{signature} \times (\sigma)\mathit{set} \times (\sigma \times \alpha \times \sigma)\mathit{set}$$

and it is further required that the first member of the triple be an action signature, the second be a non-empty set of start states and the third be an input-enabled state transition relation:

$$\begin{aligned}
&\mathit{IOA}(<\mathit{asig}, \mathit{starts}, \mathit{trans}>) \equiv \\
&\quad \mathit{is_asig}(\mathit{asig}) \wedge \mathit{starts} \neq \{\} \wedge \mathit{is_state_trans}(\mathit{asig}, \mathit{trans}).
\end{aligned}$$

The property of being an input-enabled state transition relation is defined as follows:

$$\mathit{is\_state\_trans}(\mathit{asig}, R) \equiv$$

$$(\forall\text{<}s,a,t\text{>} \in R.\ a \in actions(asig)) \wedge$$
$$(\forall a \in inputs(asig).\forall s.\exists t.\ \text{<}s,a,t\text{>} \in R)$$

The projections from an IOA are *asig_of*, *starts_of*, and *trans_of*. The actions of an IOA are defined $acts \equiv actions \circ asig\_of$.

An *execution-fragment* of an IOA A is a finite or infinite sequence that consists of alternating states and actions. In Isabelle it is represented as a pair of sequences: an infinite *state sequence* of type $nat \to state$ and an *action sequence* of type $nat \to (action)option$. Here the *option* datatype is defined as $(\alpha)option = None \mid Some(\alpha)$ using an ML-like notation. A finite sequence in this representation ends with an infinite number of consecutive *Nones*. Using this representation, a step of an execution-fragment $\text{<}as, ss\text{>}$ is $\text{<}ss(i), a, ss(i+1)\text{>}$ if $as(i) = Some(a)$. Formally:

$$is\_execution\_fragment(A, \text{<}as, ss\text{>}) \equiv$$
$$\forall n\ a.\quad (as(n) = None \supset ss(Suc(n)) = ss(n)) \wedge$$
$$(as(n) = Some(a) \supset \text{<}ss(n), a, ss(Suc(n))\text{>} \in trans\_of(A))$$

An *execution* of A is an execution-fragment of A that begins in a start state of A. If we filter the action sequence of an execution of A so that it has only external actions, we obtain a *trace* of A. The traces of A are defined by

$$traces(A) \equiv$$
$$\{filter(\lambda a.a \in externals(asig\_of(A)), as)\ .$$
$$\exists ss.\ \text{<}as, ss\text{>} \in executions(A)\}$$

where *filter* replaces $Some(a)$ by *None* if a is not an external action.

2.2 Composition and Refinement

I/O automata provide a notion of parallel composition. In Isabelle this mechanism is realized by a binary operator $\|$. The definition simply reflects the fact that each component performs its locally defined transition if the relevant action is part of its action signature, otherwise it performs no transition.

$$A \parallel B \equiv$$
$$\text{<}asig\_comp(asig\_of(A), asig\_of(B)),$$
$$\{\text{<}u,v\text{>}\ .\ u \in starts\_of(A) \wedge v \in starts\_of(B)\},$$
$$\{\text{<}s, act, t\text{>}\ .\ (act \in acts(A) \vee act \in acts(B)) \wedge$$
$$if(act \in acts(A), \text{<}fst(s), act, fst(t)\text{>} \in trans\_of(A),$$
$$fst(s) = fst(t)) \wedge$$
$$if(act \in acts(B), \text{<}snd(s), act, snd(t)\text{>} \in trans\_of(B),$$
$$snd(s) = snd(t))\}\text{>}$$

where an action signature composition is needed:

$$\begin{aligned}&\mathit{asig\_comp}(S_1,S_2) \equiv\\ &\quad <(\mathit{inputs}(S_1)\cup \mathit{inputs}(S_2)) - (\mathit{outputs}(S_1)\cup \mathit{outputs}(S_2)),\\ &\quad \mathit{outputs}(S_1)\cup \mathit{outputs}(S_2), \mathit{internals}(S_1)\cup \mathit{internals}(S_2)>\end{aligned}$$

Action signature composition presumes compatibility of actions, which is defined by

$$\begin{aligned}&\mathit{compatible}(S_1,S_2) \equiv\\ &\quad (\mathit{outputs}(S_1)\cap \mathit{outputs}(S_2) = \{\}) \wedge\\ &\quad (\mathit{actions}(S_1)\cap \mathit{internals}(S_2) = \{\}) \wedge\\ &\quad (\mathit{actions}(S_2)\cap \mathit{internals}(S_1) = \{\})\end{aligned}$$

and is trivially extended to compatibility of automata.

For the aim of refinement, we make use of abstraction functions which Lynch and Tuttle call "weak possibility mappings". The set of these maps is described by the following predicate, which takes a function f (from concrete states to abstract states), a concrete automaton C, and an abstract automaton A.

$$\begin{aligned}&\mathit{is\_weak\_pmap}(f,C,A) \equiv\\ &\quad (\forall s_0 \in \mathit{starts\_of}(C).\ f(s_0) \in \mathit{starts\_of}(A)) \wedge\\ &\quad (\forall s\ t\ a.\ \mathit{reachable}(C,s) \wedge <s,a,t> \in \mathit{trans\_of}(C)\\ &\quad \supset \mathit{if}(a \in \mathit{externals}(\mathit{asig\_of}(C)), <f(s),a,f(t)> \in \mathit{trans\_of}(A),\\ &\qquad f(s) = f(t)))\end{aligned}$$

The following theorem proved in Isabelle states that the existence of an abstraction function from C to A implies that the traces of C are contained in those of A.

$$\begin{aligned}&\mathit{IOA}(C) \wedge \mathit{IOA}(A) \wedge\\ &\mathit{externals}(\mathit{asig\_of}(C)) = \mathit{externals}(\mathit{asig\_of}(A)) \wedge\\ &\mathit{is\_weak\_pmap}(f,C,A)\\ &\supset \mathit{traces}(C) \subseteq \mathit{traces}(A)\end{aligned}$$

2.3 Renaming

As in [13] we define an operation for renaming actions. The motivation for this is modularity: name clashes can be avoided and generic components can be plugged into different environments.

$$\mathit{rename} : (\alpha,\sigma)\mathit{ioa} \to (\beta \to (\alpha)\mathit{option}) \to (\beta,\sigma)\mathit{ioa}$$

In contrast to [13] we define the action renaming function with type $\beta \to (\alpha)\mathit{option}$ instead of $\alpha \to \beta$. Therefore it does not have to be injective, which facilitates reasoning about such functions.

$$
\begin{aligned}
&rename(A, f) \equiv \\
&<<\{act\ .\ \exists act'.\ f(act) = Some(act') \land act' \in inputs(asig\_of(A))\ \}, \\
&\quad \{act\ .\ \exists act'.\ f(act) = Some(act') \land act' \in outputs(asig\_of(A))\ \}, \\
&\quad \{act\ .\ \exists act'.\ f(act) = Some(act') \land act' \in internals(asig\_of(A))\}>, \\
&\ starts\_of(A), \\
&\ \{<s, act, t>\ .\ \exists act'.\ f(act) = Some(act') \land <s, act', t> \in trans\_of(A)\}>
\end{aligned}
$$

3 Specification

The Alternating Bit Protocol [3] is designed to ensure that messages are delivered in order, from a sender to a receiver, in the presence of channels that can lose and duplicate messages. This FIFO-communication can be specified by a simple queue and therefore a single automaton *Spec*. As we are aiming for a finite state system, we have to consider an additional point: The sender buffer of the implementation will not be able to store an unbounded number of incoming messages. Restricting the number of input actions to yield a finite sender buffer is not allowed because of the input-enabledness of IOA.

What we really need is an assumption about the behaviour of the environment, namely that it will only send the next message if requested to do so by an explicit action *Next* issued by the system. In the IOA-model this can be expressed by including an environment IOA which embodies this assumption. Therefore the specification is a parallel composition of two processes:

$$Specification \equiv Env \parallel Spec$$

and the interaction between them is shown in Fig. 2. The two components *Env* and *Spec* are described in the following subsections.

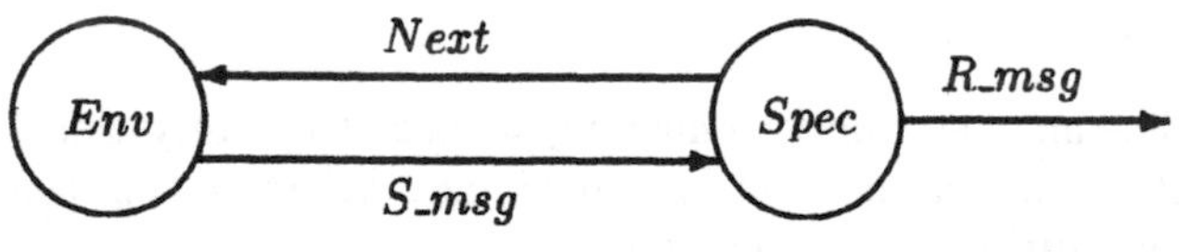

FIGURE 2. The Specification

3.1 The Environment

Env models the assumption that the environment only outputs *S_msg* when allowed to do so by *Next*. The state of *Env* is a single boolean variable *send_next*, initially true, which is set to true by every incoming *Next*. *S_msg* is enabled only if *send_next* is true and sets *send_next* to false as a result:

Next	input	$S\_msg(m)$	output
post:	$send\_next'$	pre:	$send\_next$
		post:	$\neg send\_next'$

where we use the following format to describe transition relations:

action	(input | output | internal)
pre:	P
post:	Q

Predicate P is the constraint on the state s that must hold for the transition to apply. If it is true, it is omitted. Predicate Q relates the state components before and after the transition; we refer to the state components after the transition by decorating their names with a $'$. If no state component changes, post is omitted.

3.2 The Specification

The state of the IOA *Spec* is a message queue q, initially empty, modelled with the type $(\mu)list$, where the parameter μ represents the message type. The only actions performed in the abstract system are: $S\_msg(m)$, putting message m at the end of q, $R\_msg(m)$, taking message m from the head of q, and *Next*, signaling the world outside to send the next message. Formally:

Next	output	$S\_msg(m)$	input	$R\_msg(m)$	output
pre:	*true*	post:	$q' = q@[m]$	pre:	$q = m :: rst$
				post:	$q' = rst$

4 Implementation

The system being proved correct also contains the component *Env* described in the previous section.

$$Implementation \equiv Env \parallel Impl$$

Impl represents the Alternating Bit Protocol and is itself a parallel composition of 4 processes:

$$Impl \equiv Sender \parallel S\_Ch \parallel Receiver \parallel R\_Ch$$

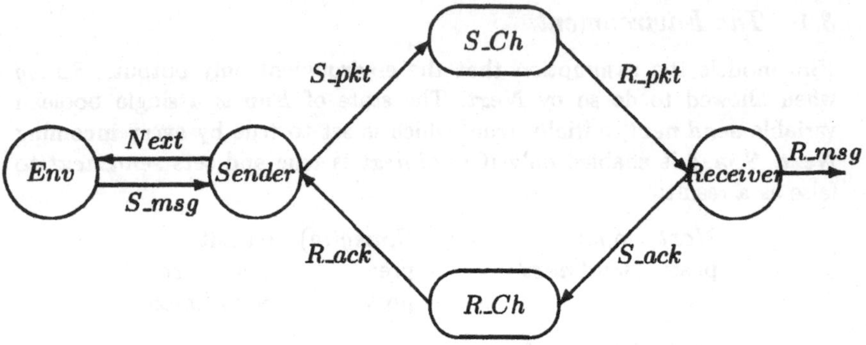

FIGURE 3. The Implementation

a sender, a receiver, and proprietary channels for both. The "dataflow" in the system is depicted in Fig. 3

Messages are transmitted from the sender to the receiver with a single header bit as packets of type *bool* $\times\, \mu$. The type of system actions, (μ)*action*, is described in Isabelle by the following ML-style datatype:

$$(\mu)action \equiv Next \mid S\_msg(\mu) \mid R\_msg(\mu) \mid S\_pkt(bool, \mu) \mid R\_pkt(bool, \mu) \mid S\_ack(bool) \mid R\_ack(bool)$$

4.1 The Sender

The state of the process *Sender* is a pair:

Field	Type	Initial Value
message:	(μ)*option*	*None*
header:	*bool*	*true*

The Sender makes the following transitions:

Next	output
pre:	$message = None$
$S\_msg(m)$	input
post:	$message' = Some(m) \wedge header' = header$
$S\_pkt(b, m)$	output
pre:	$message = Some(m) \wedge b = header$
$R\_ack(b)$	input
post:	**if** $b = header$
	then $message' = None \wedge header' = \neg header$
	else $message' = message \wedge header' = header$

Note that the presence of *Env*, i.e. the fact that the sender can control the flow of incoming messages via *Next*, enables us to get by with a buffer of length 1 (modelled by (μ)*option*) in the sender; *Next* is only sent if the buffer is empty, i.e. $message = None$.

4.2 The Receiver

The state of the process *Receiver* is also a pair, differing from the Sender only in the initial value of the header variable:

Field	Type	Initial Value
message:	$(\mu)option$	*None*
header:	*bool*	*false*

The Receiver makes the following transitions:

$R\_msg(m)$	output
pre:	$message = Some(m)$
post:	$message' = None \wedge header' = header$
$R\_pkt(b, m)$	input
post:	**if** $b \neq header \wedge message = None$
	then $message' = Some(m) \wedge header' = \neg header$
	else $message' = message \wedge header' = header$
$S\_ack(b)$	output
pre:	$b = header$

Note that *R_pkt* does not change the state unless $message = None$. This ensures that the receiver has passed the last message on via *R_msg* before accepting a new one. Alternatively, one could add the precondition $message = None$ to *S_ack* which would preclude the sender getting an acknowledgment and sending a new message before the receiver has actually passed the old one on.

4.3 The Channels

The channels, *R_Ch* and *S_Ch*, have very similar functionality. Roughly speaking, messages are added to a queue by an input action and removed from it by the corresponding output action. In addition, there can be no change at all in order to model the possibility of losing messages, in case of the adding action, and of duplicating messages, in case of the removing action. The only differences between the channels are the type of the messages delivered, packets for *S_Ch* and booleans for *R_Ch*, and the specific names for input and output actions, *S_pkt* and *R_pkt* or *S_ack* and *R_ack*, respectively. Therefore both channels can be designed as instances of a generic channel using the renaming function described in section 2.

This is done by introducing a new datatype $(\alpha)act \equiv S(\alpha) \mid R(\alpha)$ of abstract actions and defining an IOA *Ch* with a single state component $q : (\alpha)list$ by the following transition relation:

$S(a)$	input	$R(a)$	output
post:	$q' = q \vee q' = q@[a]$	pre:	$q \neq [\,] \wedge a = hd(q)$
		post:	$q' = q \vee q' = tl(q)$

In Isabelle we use a set comprehension format to describe transition relations. In the case of Ch it looks like this:

$$\begin{array}{llll} Ch\_trans \equiv \{<s, act, s'> . & \textbf{case } act \textbf{ of} & & \\ & S(a) & \Rightarrow & s' = s \vee s' = s@[a] \\ & R(a) & \Rightarrow & s \neq [\,] \wedge a = hd(s) \wedge \\ & & & (s' = s \vee s' = tl(s)) \,\} \end{array}$$

An automatic translation of the pre/post style into the set comprehension format is possible and desirable but not the focus of our research.

The concrete channels are obtained from the abstract channel by the function calls $rename(Ch, S\_acts)$ and $rename(Ch, R\_acts)$, where

$$\begin{array}{lcl} S\_acts & : & (\mu)action \rightarrow (bool \times \mu)\ act\ option \\ R\_acts & : & (bool)action \rightarrow (bool)\ act\ option \end{array}$$

map the concrete actions to the corresponding abstract actions. For example S_acts is defined by the rules $S\_acts(S\_pkt(b, m)) = Some(S(<b, m>))$, $S\_acts(R\_pkt(b, m)) = Some(R(<b, m>))$ and $S\_acts(act) = None$ for all other actions act.

5 Abstraction

What we are aiming for is a finite-state description of the Alternating Bit Protocol that is refined by the given implementation described in the previous section. To achieve this, we have to remove two obstacles:

1. The channel queues have to be finite.
2. The message alphabet has to be finite.

5.1 *Finite Channels*

Our attention is focused on this requirement. We define an abstract version $RedCh$ of Ch and an abstraction function $reduce$ from Ch to $RedCh$ and prove $is\_weak\_pmap(reduce, Ch, RedCh)$. The idea is based on the observation that at most two different messages are held in each channel. This is easily explained: each message is repeatedly sent to S_Ch, until the corresponding acknowledgment arrives. Once we switch to the next message, S_Ch can only contain copies of the previous message. Hence, S_Ch's queue is always of the form old^*new^*. The same is true for R_Ch. Thus, if all adjacent identical messages are merged, the channels have size at most 2. Fortunately, this reasoning never needs to be formalized but is implicitly performed by the model checker.

Refinement of Channels

A compacting channel *RedCh* is obtained from *Ch* if new messages are only added provided they differ from the last one added. Thus *RedCh* is identical to *Ch* except for action *S*:

$$\begin{array}{ll} S(a) & \textbf{input} \\ \textbf{post:} & q' = q \lor \ \textbf{if}\ a \neq hd(reverse(q)) \lor q = [\,] \\ & \qquad\qquad \textbf{then}\ q' = q@[a] \\ & \qquad\qquad \textbf{else}\ q' = q \end{array}$$

By renaming *RedCh* we obtain the collapsed versions of *R_Ch* and *S_Ch*, called *R_RedCh* and *S_RedCh*. Notice that the description is a priori not finite, as q is an unbounded list. Finiteness is only implied by the context, i.e. the behaviour of the protocol.

With the definition of an abstraction function *reduce*

$$\begin{array}{lll} reduce([\,]) & \equiv & [\,] \\ reduce(x :: xs) & \equiv & \textbf{case}\ xs\ \textbf{of} \\ & & \quad [\,] \ \Rightarrow\ [x] \\ & & \quad y :: ys \ \Rightarrow\ if(x = y, reduce(xs), x :: reduce(xs)) \end{array}$$

we get the following refinement goal:

$$is\_weak\_pmap(reduce, Ch, RedCh)$$

The proof of this obligation is rather straightforward, proceeding by case analysis on the type of actions. Using some lemmata on how *reduce* behaves when combined with operators like @ or *tl*, most cases are automatically solved by the conditional and contextual rewriting of Isabelle. Finally, using the meta-theorem

$$\begin{array}{l} is\_weak\_pmap(abs, C, A) \\ \supset is\_weak\_pmap(abs, rename(C, f), rename(A, f)) \end{array}$$

we get the appropriate refinement results for the concrete channels *S_Ch*, *R_Ch* and their collapsed versions *S_RedCh* and *R_RedCh*.

Compositionality

In order to extend this refinement result from the channels to the whole system, we have to prove some compositionality theorems for refinements. Lynch and Tuttle [13] established the required lemma on the level of trace inclusions. We decided, however, to prove it on the level of abstraction functions for reasons of simplicity.

$$\begin{array}{l} IOA(C_1) \wedge IOA(C_2) \wedge IOA(A_1) \wedge IOA(A_2) \wedge \\ externals(asig\_of(C_1)) = externals(asig\_of(A_1)) \wedge \\ externals(asig\_of(C_2)) = externals(asig\_of(A_2)) \wedge \\ compatible(C_1, C_2) \wedge compatible(A_1, A_2) \wedge \\ is\_weak\_pmap(f, C_1, A_1) \wedge is\_weak\_pmap(g, C_2, A_2) \\ \supset is\_weak\_pmap(\lambda{<}c_1, c_2{>}.{<}f(c_1), g(c_2){>}, C_1 \parallel C_2, A_1 \parallel A_2) \end{array}$$

Unfortunately, trace inclusion does not imply the existence of an abstraction function. Hence the above theorem is not as general as the corresponding one about traces, in particular since $is\_weak\_pmap(id, A, A)$ only holds if A has no internal actions. We intend to formalize and prove compositionality on the trace level in the near future.

Performing the proofs of abstraction and compositionality in Isabelle, we encountered a mismatch between the time required for the refinement proof and that required for the compatibility checks. Nearly half the time (1.5 min on a SPARC station 10) was needed to establish that no component causes a name clash of input/output actions. These checks, although automated, are expensive if performed by a theorem prover. Partly this is caused by our decision to have *rename* translate action names in the opposite direction one would expect (see section 2.3), something we may need to rethink.

5.2 Finite Message Alphabet

The second requirement, the problem of abstracting out data from a data-independent program has already been addressed by Wolper [17]. In his paper he shows how to reduce an infinite data domain to a small finite one if data independence is guaranteed and the properties to be checked are expressible in propositional temporal logic. In [2] and [16] this method is applied to the Alternating Bit Protocol. There, only three different message values are needed to verify the protocol's functional correctness.

Basically, a program is data-independent if its behaviour does not depend on the specific data it operates upon. A sufficient condition for a program described by an IOA to be data independent is that everywhere in the automaton the transitions are independent of the value of messages being transmitted. An inspection of our description of the protocol shows that it satisfies the condition.

In contrast to [2] our specification is not given as a collection of temporal formulae, but in terms of I/O automata. Thus, the methods above are not directly applicable to our formalization and until now, we have not investigated how to transfer them formally into our setting. However, it is intuitively plausible that Wolper's theory of data-independence holds generally, independently of the respective formalization. That is why we analogously restricted our model checking algorithm to deal with only three different message values.

A formal treatment of data-abstraction in Isabelle/HOL needs a modification of the way we model data. Currently the diversity of data is modelled by polymorphic types[1]. But since types are a meta-level notion and cannot be talked about (e.g. quantified) in HOL, even formalizing data independence seems to be impossible. Using object-level sets instead of polymorphism would cure this problem but is likely to complicate the theory.

6 Model Checking

The task of the model checker is to verify that B, the implementation with collapsing channels refines A, the specification. It is done by a generic ML-function *check*

$$check(actions, internal, startsB, nextsB, startA, transA, abs)$$

where $actions : (\alpha)list$ is the list of all actions, $internal : \alpha \to bool$ recognizes internal actions of B, $startsB : (\sigma)list$ is the list of start states of B, $nextsB : \sigma \to \alpha \to (\sigma)list$ produces the list of successor states in B, $startsA : \tau \to bool$ recognizes start states of A, $transA : \tau \to \alpha \to \tau \to bool$ recognizes transitions of A, and $abs : \sigma \to \tau$ is the abstraction function.

It is easy to translate Isabelle's predicative description of A's transitions automatically into an ML-function *transA*. For *nextsB* this is only possible if the predicates have a certain recognizable form, for example disjunctions of assignments of values to the state components. Otherwise how are we to compute the set of next states satisfying an arbitrary predicate? If σ, the state space of B (as opposed to the set of reachable states!) is infinite, this is impossible. That is the main reason why we need to specify B, i.e. *RedCh* explicitly; otherwise we could have described *RedCh* implicitly in terms of *Ch* and *reduce*.

The abstraction function *abs* is given by

$$abs(s) \equiv$$
$$l(R.message)@if(R.header = S.header, l(S.message), tl(l(S.message))$$

where $l : (\alpha)option \to (\alpha)list$ is defined by the equations $l(Some(x)) = [x]$ and $l(None) = []$. To distinguish between components of the receiver state and the sender state that have the same field names, we use a 'dotted identifier' notation, e.g. *S.header* and *R.header*.

It is also possible to generate *abs* automatically as a set of corresponding state pairs as done in [10]. This would not allow the explicit documentation of *abs*, but it would mean a step forward towards fully automatic support — the major advantage of model checking.

[1] It is not true that a polymorphic IOA is automatically data independent: HOL-formulae may contain the polymorphic equality "=" which destroys data independence.

check itself realizes the predicate *is_weak_pmap*(*abs*, B, A) by simply performing full state space exploration. Beginning with *startsB* the algorithm examines all reachable states, checking for every transition $<s_1, a, s_2>$ $\in$ *trans_of*(B) that either $<abs(s_1), a, abs(s_2)> \in$ *trans_of*(A) (if a is external) or $abs(s_1) = abs(s_2)$ (if a is internal).

At the moment the ML-code for the different arguments of *check* is still generated manually. However, we intend to automate this, subject to the restrictions on B described above. It should also be noted that *check* is just a prototype which should be replaced by some optimized model checker, for example the one described in [9].

Acknowledgements. We are grateful to Stephan Merz for providing useful comments on a draft of this paper.

7 References

[1] P. Abdulla and B. Jonsson. Verifying programs with unreliable channels. In *Proc. 8th IEEE Symp. Logic in Computer Science*, pages 160–170. IEEE Press, 1993.

[2] S. Aggarwal, C. Courcoubetis, and P. Wolper. Adding liveness properties to coupled finite-state machines. *ACM Transactions on Programming Languages and Systems*, 12(2):303–339, 1990.

[3] K. Bartlett, R. Scantlebury, and P. Wilkinson. A note on reliable full-duplex transmission over half-duplex lines. *Communications of the ACM*, 12(5):260–261, 1969.

[4] E. M. Clarke, O. Grumberg, and D. E. Long. Model checking and abstraction. In *Proc. 19th ACM Symp. Principles of Programming Languages*, pages 343–354. ACM Press, 1992.

[5] D. Dams, O. Grumberg, and R. Gerth. Abstract interpretation of reactive systems: Abstractions preserving ∀CTL*, ∃CTL* and CTL*. In E.-R. Olderog, editor, *Programming Concepts, Methods and Calculi (PROCOMET)*, pages 573–593. North-Holland, 1994.

[6] J.-C. Fernandez and L. Mounier. "On the Fly" verification of behavioural equivalences and preorders. In K. G. Larsen, editor, *Proc. 3rd Workshop Computer Aided Verification*, volume 575 of *Lect. Notes in Comp. Sci.*, pages 181–191. Springer-Verlag, 1992.

[7] R. Gawlick, R. Segala, J. Sogaard-Andersen, and N. Lynch. Liveness in timed and untimed systems. Technical Report MIT/LCS/TR-587, Laboratory for Computer Science, MIT, Cambridge, MA., December 1993. Extended abstract in Proceedings ICALP'94.

[8] S. Graf and C. Loiseaux. A tool for symbolic program verification and abstraction. In C. Courcoubetis, editor, *Computer Aided Verification*, volume 697 of *Lect. Notes in Comp. Sci.*, pages 71–84. Springer-Verlag, 1993.

[9] P. Herrmann, T. Kraatz, H. Krumm, and M. Stange. Automated verification of refinements of concurrent and distributed systems. Technical Report 541, Fachbereich Informatik, Universität Dortmund, 1994.

[10] P. Herrmann and H. Krumm. Report on analysis and verification techniques. Technical Report 485, Fachbereich Informatik, Universität Dortmund, 1993.

[11] H. Hungar. Combining model checking and theorem proving to verify parallel processes. In C. Courcoubetis, editor, *Computer Aided Verification*, volume 697 of *Lect. Notes in Comp. Sci.*, pages 154–165. Springer-Verlag, 1993.

[12] R. Kurshan. Reducibility in analysis of coordination. In K. Varaiya, editor, *Discrete Event Systems: Models and Applications*, volume 103 of *Lecture Notes in Control and Information Science*, pages 19–39. Springer-Verlag, 1987.

[13] N. Lynch and M. Tuttle. Hierarchical correctness proofs for distributed algorithms. Technical Report MIT/LCS/TR-387, Laboratory for Computer Science, MIT, Cambridge, MA., 1987.

[14] N. Lynch and M. Tuttle. An introduction to Input/Output automata. *CWI Quarterly*, 2(3):219–246, 1989.

[15] T. Nipkow and K. Slind. I/O automata in Isabelle/HOL. In *Proc. TYPES Workshop 1994*, Lect. Notes in Comp. Sci. Springer-Verlag, 1995.

[16] K. Sabnani. An algorithmic technique for protocol verification. *IEEE Transactions on Communications*, 36(8):924–930, 1988.

[17] P. Wolper. Expressing interesting properties of programs in propositional temporal logic. In *Proc. 13th ACM Symp. Principles of Programming Languages*, pages 184–193. ACM Press, 1986.

A Constraint Oriented Proof Methodology Based on Modal Transition Systems

Kim G. Larsen*
Bernhard Steffen†
Carsten Weise‡

ABSTRACT We present a constraint-oriented state-based proof methodology for concurrent software systems which exploits compositionality and abstraction for the reduction of the verification problem under investigation. Formal basis for this methodology are Modal Transition Systems allowing loose state-based specifications, which can be refined by successively adding constraints. Key concepts of our method are *projective views*, *separation of proof obligations*, *Skolemization* and *abstraction*. Central to the method is the use of *Parametrized* Modal Transition Systems. The method easily transfers to real-time systems, where the main problem are parameters in timing constraints.

1 Introduction

The use of formal methods and in particular formal verification of concurrent systems, interactive or fully automatic, is still limited to very specific problem classes. For state-based methods this is mainly due to the state explosion problem: the state graph of a concurrent systems grows exponentially with the number of its parallel components – and with the number of clocks in the real-time case –, leading to an unmanageable size for most practically relevant systems. Consequently, several techniques have been developed to tackle this problem. Here we focus on the four main streams and do not discuss the flood of very specific heuristics. Most elegant and ambitious are *compositional* methods (e.g. [ASW94, CLM89, GS90][1]), which due to the nature of parallel compositions are unfortunately rarely applicable. *Partial order* methods try to avoid the state explosion problem by

---

*University of Aalborg, BRICS, kgl@iesd.auc.dk
†University of Passau, steffen@fmi.uni-passau.de
‡University of Technology Aachen, carsten@informatik.rwth-aachen.de

[1] In contrast to the first reference, the subsequent two papers address compositional reduction of systems rather than compositional verification.

suppressing unnecessary interleavings of actions [GW91, Val93, GP93]. Although extremely successful in special cases, these methods do not work in general. In practice, ***Binary Decision Diagram***-based codings of the state graph are successfully applied to an interesting class of systems, see e.g. [Br86, BCMDH90, EFT91]. These codings of the state graph do not explode directly, but they may explode during verification, and it is not yet fully clear when this happens. All these techniques can be accompanied by ***abstraction***: depending on the particular property under investigation, systems may be dramatically reduced by suppressing details that are irrelevant for verification, see e.g. [CC77, CGL92, GL93]. Summarizing, all these methods cover very specific cases, and there is no hope for a uniform approach. Thus more application specific approaches are required, extending the practicality of formal methods.

We present a constraint-oriented state-based proof methodology for concurrent software systems which exploits compositionality and abstraction for the reduction of the verification problem under investigation. Formal basis for this methodology are Modal Transition Systems (MTS) [LT88] allowing loose state-based specifications, which can be refined by successively adding constraints. In particular, this allows extremely fine-granular specifications, which are characteristic for our approach: each aspect of a system component is specified by a number of independent constraints, one for each parameter configuration. This leads to a usually infinite number of extremely simple constraints which must all be satisfied by a corresponding component implementation. Beside exploiting compositionality in the standard (vertical) fashion, this extreme component decomposition also supports a horizontally compositional approach, which does not only separate proof obligations for subcomponents or subproperties but also for the various parameter instantiations. This is the key for the success of the following three step reduction, which may reduce even a verification problem for infinite state systems to a small number of automatically verifiable problems about finite state systems:

- *Separating the Proof Obligations.* Sections 4 and 5 present a proof principle justifying the separation and specialization of the various proof obligations, which prepare the ground for the subsequent reduction steps.

- *Skolemization.* The separation of the first step leaves us with problems smaller in size but larger in number. Due to the nature of their origin, these problems often fall into a small number of equivalence classes requiring only one prototypical proof each.

- *Abstraction.* After the first two reduction steps there may still be problems with infinite state graphs. However, the extreme specialization of the problem supports the power of abstract interpretation, which finally may reduce all the proof obligations to finite ones.

Our proof methodology is not complete, i.e., there is neither a guarantee for the possibility of a finite state reduction nor a straightforward method for finding the right amount of separation for the success of the succeeding steps or the adequate abstraction for the final verification. Still, as should be clear from the examples in the paper, there is a large class of problems and systems, where the method can be applied quite straightforwardly. Of course, the more complex the system structure the more involved will be the required search of appropriate granularity and abstraction.

Whereas complex data dependencies may exclude any possibility of 'horizontal' decomposition, our approach elegantly extends to real time systems, even over a dense time domain. In fact, this extension does not affect the possibility of a finite state reduction. For the real-time case, the basis are Timed Modal Transition Systems (TMS) [CGL93], where (weak) refinement is decidable. The TMS tool EPSILON (see again [CGL93]) can be used to find the refinements on demand.

However, in this paper *parametrized* timed modal transition systems are used. Parameters may appear either in actions (so-called *parametrized actions*) or in timing constraints. Due to infinite parameter sets, specifications may in general have an infinite number of actions. Our method however aims at reducing this set of actions to a (small) finite one, such that automatic analysis of the transition systems is possible. The method does not apply to timing parameters, although we will demonstrate how to reduce them in our particular examples. The main problem with timing parameters is that existing tools cannot deal with both, parameters and refinement.

We demonstrate our methodology by two examples: an extremely simple problem of pipelined buffers, and a specification and verification problem of a Remote Procedure Call (RPC) posed by Broy and Lamport ([BL93]). The method is explained step by step by applying it first to the simple example and afterwards to the RPC problem in order to indicate that the methods scales up. Both problems have untimed and timed versions including even parameters in the timing constraints. The specific constellation, however, allows us to capture these parameters.

The next section recalls the basic theory of Modal Transition Systems, which we use for system specification. Thereafter we describe the RPC problem. The following sections explain our method in detail. Section 4 presents our notion of projective views and discusses the first reduction step. The subsequent two sections are devoted to the second and third reduction step, while Section 7 shows how to extend our method to real time systems over a dense time domain. Finally, Section 8 summarizes our conclusion and directions to future work.

2 Modal Transition Systems

In this section we give a brief introduction to the existing theory of modal transition systems. We assume familiarity with CCS. For more elaborate introductions and proofs we refer the reader to [LT88, HL89, Lar90].

When specifying reactive systems by traditional Process Algebras like e.g. CCS [Mil89], one defines the set of action transitions that can be performed (or observed) in a given system state. In this approach, any valid implementation *must* be able to perform the specified actions, which often constrains the set of possible implementations unnecessarily. One way of improving this situation within the framework of operational specification is to allow specifications where one can explicitly distinguish between transitions that are *admissible* (or allowed) and those that are *required*. This distinction allows a much more flexible specification and a much more generous notion of implementation, and therefore improves the practicality of the operational approach. Technically, this is made precise through the following notion of *modal transition systems*:

Definition 2.1. *A modal transition system is a structure* $S = (\Sigma, A, \rightarrow_\Box, \rightarrow_\Diamond)$*, where* Σ *is a set of states,* A *is a set of actions and* $\rightarrow_\Box, \rightarrow_\Diamond \subseteq \Sigma \times A \times \Sigma$ *are transition relations, satisfying the consistency condition* $\rightarrow_\Box \subseteq \rightarrow_\Diamond$. □

Intuitively, the requirement $\rightarrow_\Box \subseteq \rightarrow_\Diamond$ expresses that anything which is required should also be allowed hence ensuring the consistency of modal specifications. When the relations $\rightarrow_\Box$ and $\rightarrow_\Diamond$ coincide, the above definition reduces to the traditional notion of labelled transition systems.

Syntactically, we represent modal transition systems by means of a slightly extended version of CCS. The only change in the syntax is the introduction of two prefix constructs $a_\Box.P$ and $a_\Diamond.P$ with the following semantics: $a_\Diamond.P \xrightarrow{a}_\Diamond P$, $a_\Box.P \xrightarrow{a}_\Box P$ and $a_\Box.P \xrightarrow{a}_\Diamond P$. The semantics for the other constructs follow the lines of CCS in the sense that each rule has a version for $\rightarrow_\Box$ and $\rightarrow_\Diamond$ respectively. We will call this version of CCS *modal* CCS.

As usual, we consider a design process as a sequence of *refinement steps* reducing the number of possible implementations. Intuitively, our notion of when a specification S refines another (weaker) specification T is based on the following simple observation. Any behavioural aspect *allowed* by S should also be allowed by T; and dually, any behavioural aspect which is already guaranteed by the weaker specification T must also be guaranteed by S. Using the derivation relations $\rightarrow_\Box$ and $\rightarrow_\Diamond$ this may be formalized by the following notion of *refinement*:

Definition 2.2. *A refinement* $\mathcal{R}$ *is a binary relation on* Σ *such that whenever* $S\,\mathcal{R}\,T$ *and* $a \in A$ *then the following holds:*

1. *Whenever* $S \xrightarrow{a}_\Diamond S'$*, then* $T \xrightarrow{a}_\Diamond T'$ *for some* T' *with* $S'\,\mathcal{R}\,T'$*,*

2. *Whenever* $T \xrightarrow{a}_{\Box} T'$, *then* $S \xrightarrow{a}_{\Box} S'$ *for some* S' *with* $S' \mathcal{R} T'$.

S is said to be a refinement of T in case (S, T) *is contained in some refinement* $\mathcal{R}$. *We write* $S \triangleleft T$ *in this case.* □

Note that when applied to traditional labelled transition systems (where $\rightarrow = \rightarrow_{\Box} = \rightarrow_{\Diamond}$) this defines the well-known bisimulation equivalence [Par81, Mil89]. – Using standard techniques, one straightforwardly establishes that $\triangleleft$ is a preorder preserving all modal CCS operators.

$\triangleleft$ allows *loose* specifications. This important property can be best explained by looking at the 'weakest' specification $\mathcal{U}$ constantly allowing any action, but never requiring anything to happen. Operationally, $\mathcal{U}$ is completely defined by $\mathcal{U} \xrightarrow{a}_{\Diamond} \mathcal{U}$ for all actions a. It is easily verified that $S \triangleleft \mathcal{U}$ for any modal specification S.

Intuitively, S and T are *independent* if they are not contradictory, i.e. any action required by one is not constraint by the other. The following formal definition is due to the fact that for S and T to be *independent* all 'simultaneously' reachable processes S' and T' must be independent too:

Definition 2.3. *An independence relation* $\mathcal{R}$ *is a binary relation on* Σ *such that whenever* $S \mathcal{R} T$ *and* $a \in A$ *then the following holds:*

1. *Whenever* $S \xrightarrow{a}_{\Box} S'$, *there is a unique* T' *such that* $T \xrightarrow{a}_{\Diamond} T'$ *and* $S' \mathcal{R} T'$,
2. *Whenever* $T \xrightarrow{a}_{\Box} T'$, *there is a unique* S' *such that* $S \xrightarrow{a}_{\Diamond} S'$ *and* $S' \mathcal{R} T'$,
3. *Whenever* $S \xrightarrow{a}_{\Diamond} S'$ *and* $T \xrightarrow{a}_{\Diamond} T'$ *then* $S' \mathcal{R} T'$.

S and T are said to be independent *in case* (S, T) *is contained in some independence relation* $\mathcal{R}$. □

Note in particular that two specifications are independent if none of them requires any actions. Independence is important, as it allows to define conjunction on modal transition systems by:

$$\frac{S \xrightarrow{a}_{\Box} S' \quad T \xrightarrow{a}_{\Diamond} T'}{S \wedge T \xrightarrow{a}_{\Box} S' \wedge T'} \qquad \frac{S \xrightarrow{a}_{\Diamond} S' \quad T \xrightarrow{a}_{\Box} T'}{S \wedge T \xrightarrow{a}_{\Box} S' \wedge T'}$$

$$\frac{S \xrightarrow{a}_{\Diamond} S' \quad T \xrightarrow{a}_{\Diamond} T'}{S \wedge T \xrightarrow{a}_{\Diamond} S' \wedge T'}$$

Of course, $S \wedge T$ is always a well-defined modal specifications (i.e. any required transition is also allowed), and in fact, for independent arguments S and T it defines their *logical* conjunction:

Theorem 2.4. Let S and T be independent modal specifications. Then $S \wedge T \lhd S$ and $S \wedge T \lhd T$. Moreover, if $R \lhd S$ and $R \lhd T$ then $R \lhd S \wedge T$.

In order to compare specifications at different levels of abstraction, it is important to abstract from transitions resulting from internal communication.

This can be done as usual: For a given modal transition system $S = (\Sigma, A \cup \{\tau\}, \rightarrow_\Box, \rightarrow_\Diamond)$ we derive the modal transition system $S_\varepsilon = (\Sigma, A \cup \{\varepsilon\}, \Rightarrow_\Box, \Rightarrow_\Diamond)$, where $\stackrel{\varepsilon}{\Rightarrow}_\Box$ is the reflexive and transitive closure of $\stackrel{\tau}{\rightarrow}_\Box$, and where $T \stackrel{a}{\Rightarrow}_\Box T', a \neq \varepsilon$, means that there exist T'', T''' such that

$$T \stackrel{\varepsilon}{\Rightarrow}_\Box T'' \stackrel{a}{\rightarrow}_\Box T''' \stackrel{\varepsilon}{\Rightarrow}_\Box T'$$

The relation $\Rightarrow_\Diamond$ is defined in a similar manner.

The notion of *weak refinement* can now be introduced as follows: S weakly refines T in S, $S \trianglelefteq T$, iff there exists a refinement relation on S_ε containing S and T.

Weak refinement $\trianglelefteq$ essentially enjoys the same pleasant properties as $\lhd$: it is a preorder preserved by all modal CCS operators except + [HL89] (including restriction, relabelling and hiding). Moreover, for ordinary labelled transition systems weak refinement reduces to the usual notion of weak bisimulation ($\approx$).

In our examples, we will deal with weak refinement and (in general) infinite action sets. In the context of weak refinement, forbidding internal τ-actions in a constraint is a severe and unnatural restriction. We therefore consider only ***saturated*** versions of specifications, which ***always*** allow τ-steps by having τ-may-loops at each of their states. Note that each process S can easily be saturated by adding τ-loops. Moreover, a process S and its saturated version S^+ are mutual weak refinements of each other:

$$S \trianglelefteq S^+ \quad \text{and} \quad S^+ \trianglelefteq S$$

Thus they are substitutive in the context of parallel composition and hiding. The restriction to saturated specifications, therefore, does not cause any limitation in our setting.

The use of saturated transition systems has a major technical advantage: the definitions of conjunction and independence work for weak refinement in the same way as before for strong refinement. This is not true in the general case, which requires tedious adaptations.

Thus let us assume in the following that all transitions systems are saturated. This guarantees the validity of some important rules:

Proposition 2.5. *Assume a (possible infinite) index set I, a subset $J \subseteq I$, a set L of actions, two families of modal transition systems $S_i, T_i (i \in I)$ and a modal transition system T. Let the families S_i, T_i be pairwise independent, as well as the processes $(S_i \mid T)$. Then the following laws for conjunctions hold:*

1. ***Adding constraints refines a specification:***

$$\bigwedge_{i \in I} S_i \trianglelefteq \bigwedge_{j \in J} S_j$$

2. ***Conjunction is preserved by refinement:***

$$\forall i \in I.(S_i \trianglelefteq T_i) \text{ implies } \bigwedge_{i \in I} S_i \trianglelefteq \bigwedge_{i \in I} T_i$$

3. ***Conjunction distributes over parallel composition:***

$$(\bigwedge_{i \in I} S_i) \| T \trianglelefteq \bigwedge_{i \in I} (S_i \| T) \quad \text{and} \quad \bigwedge_{i \in I} (S_i \| T) \trianglelefteq (\bigwedge_{i \in I} S_i) \| T$$

4. ***Conjunction distributes over restriction:***

$$(\bigwedge_{i \in I} S_i) \setminus L \trianglelefteq \bigwedge_{i \in I} (S_i \setminus L) \quad \text{and} \quad \bigwedge_{i \in I} (S_i \setminus L) \trianglelefteq (\bigwedge_{i \in I} S_i) \setminus L$$

The proofs for all these claims are straightforward. As an example, we give a proof for the left hand side of the third part.

Starting from $(\bigwedge_{i \in I} S_i) \mid T$ it is immediate for any $j \in I$ that

$$(\bigwedge_{i \in I} S_i) \mid T \triangleleft S_j \mid T$$

holds. As this is independent of j, we directly find that $(\bigwedge_{i \in I} S_i) \mid T$ is a refinement of the conjunction $\bigwedge_{i \in I} (S_i \mid T)$. □

In our examples, certain patterns of modal transition systems will be found frequently. Assuming an action set $\mathtt{Act}$ and subsets α, β and γ, Fig. 1 depicts two of these patterns, which will be used in our examples. We use the following "abbreviations" for these transition systems:

$$\mathbf{AG}_\beta \neg \alpha \tag{1.1}$$

for the left hand side transition system and

$$\mathbf{AG}_{\mathtt{Act}} ([\alpha]\, \mathbf{AG}_\gamma \neg \beta) \tag{1.2}$$

for the right hand side system.

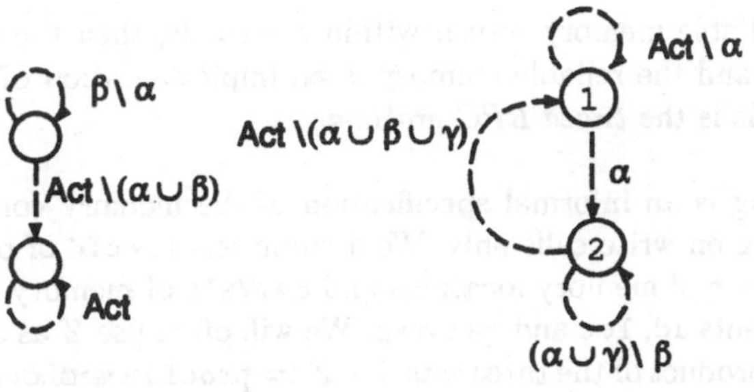

FIGURE 1. Typical Patterns of Modal Transition Systems

The intuition behind these transition system is "as long as only actions from β are taken, no actions from α may be allowed"[2] and "after an action from α has been taken, no actions from β are allowed as long as we only traverse actions from γ". The given "abbreviations" are in fact formulae of a parameterized version of CTL. As we cannot discuss the relationship between CTL and modal transition systems here, the interested reader is referred to [CES83] for standard CTL and to [Ste93] to learn about an extension of CTL which is powerful enough to capture the considered modal transition systems.

3 The Remote Procedure Call Problem

We demonstrate our method by applying it to a specification problem given by Broy and Lamport. Due to space limitations we can only present part of the problem.

The original problem consists of a *memory component* and an *RPC mechanism*. The memory component accepts read and writes from several processes, and returns the requested values (none in case of write) or raises an exception. The only exception here is *memory failure*, i.e. the memory could not read from/write to the hardware. A component in which exceptions do never occur is called a *reliable memory*.

The processes are connected to the memory component via an RPC (Remote Procedure Call) mechanism. The RPC mechanism simply forwards calls from the processes to the memory, and returns from the memory to the processes. The RPC should be transparent to the user, i.e. the composition of the memory component and the RPC should be an implementation of the memory. This is what we will call the *untimed RPC problem*.

In the real-time case, the time to forward calls and returns by the RPC should be no more than δ. Further an exception should be raised if a call to the RPC does not return within $2\delta + \varepsilon$ seconds. We will prove that if all

[2] Actions outside β can be regarded as ways to *escape* the 'universal' proof obligation.

calls to a reliable memory return within ε seconds, then the composition of the RPC and the reliable memory is an implementation of the reliable memory. This is the *timed RPC problem.*

The following is an informal specification of the memory component M, concentrating on write calls only. We assume sets `procId` of process identifiers, `memLocs` of memory locations and `memVals` of memory values, with typical elements `id`, `loc` and `val` resp. We will often use Z as an abbreviation for the product of the three sets, i.e. $Z :=$ `procId`$\times$`memLocs`$\times$`memVals`, with typical element $z \in Z$.

The events occurring in the memory component are described by *parameterized actions*, taking arguments from `procId`, `memLocs` and `memVals`. The actions of M are:

- `mWr(id, loc, val)` : write-call from process `id` of value `val` to location `loc`
- `write(id, loc, val)` : atomic write of value `val` to location `loc` initiated by process `id`
- $\overline{\texttt{mRetWr}}$`(id)` : send return from a write-request to process `id`
- $\overline{\texttt{mFail}}$`(id)` : signal memory failure to process `id`

The I/O-behaviour of the memory component M is given in Fig. 2.

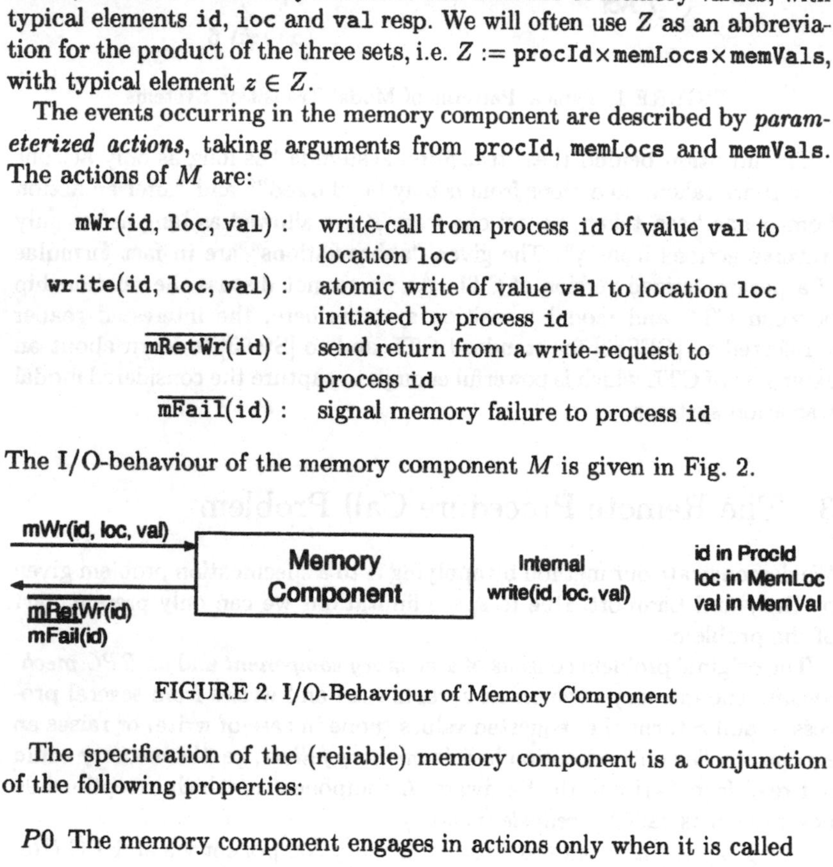

FIGURE 2. I/O-Behaviour of Memory Component

The specification of the (reliable) memory component is a conjunction of the following properties:

*P*0 The memory component engages in actions only when it is called

*P*1 Each write operation (successful or not) performs a sequence of zero or more atomic writes of the correct value to the correct location at some time between the call and return. For a successful write operation, there must be at least one atomic write.

*P*2 A memory failure is never raised.

Clearly, the memory component M is specified by the conjunction of $P0$ and $P1$, while the reliable memory M_R is the conjunction of the M and $P2$. Note that for fixed `id` the last property can be easily specified by

$$\mathbf{AG}_{\mathtt{Act}} \neg \{ \overline{\mathtt{mFail(id)}} \}$$

The RPC R simply hands calls and returns (including the memory failure exception) through. These are the actions of the RPC:

`rWr(id, loc, val)`	:	remote write of value `val` to location `loc` issued by process `id`
$\overline{\mathtt{rRetWr}}$`(id)`	:	return from remote write issued by process `id`
$\overline{\mathtt{rFail}}$`(id)`	:	RPC returns an exception from a call issued by process `id`
$\overline{\mathtt{mWr}}$`(id, loc, val)`	:	send a write of value `val` to location `loc` initiated by process `id`
`mRetWr(id)`	:	return from a write initiated by process `id`
`mFail(id)`	:	memory component raised a memory failure

The I/O-behaviour of the combined components can be depicted as in Fig. 3:

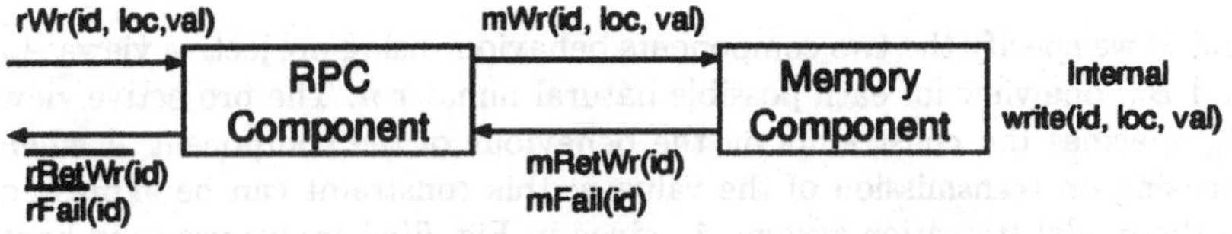

FIGURE 3. Combination of RPC and Memory

In the next sections, we will explain our method directly using a much simpler example. At the end of each section we show how our method transfers to the RPC problem. We start with the untimed case.

4 Projective Views

In the following, we present, motivate and clarify our proof methodology by means of a minimal example, which is just sufficient to explain the various phenomena.

Consider the parallel system in Fig. 4. Here two parameterized, disposable component media (supposed to transmit natural numbers) A and B are composed in parallel yielding a pipeline. Informally, the component A is supposed to input a natural number on port a, then output this number on port b after which it will terminate. The behaviour of B is similar. Using modal transition systems, the parallel system may be expressed as follows:

$$\Big(\underbrace{a_\Box x.\overline{b_\Box} x}_{A} \mid \underbrace{b_\Box x.\overline{c_\Box} x}_{B}\Big)\setminus\{b\}$$

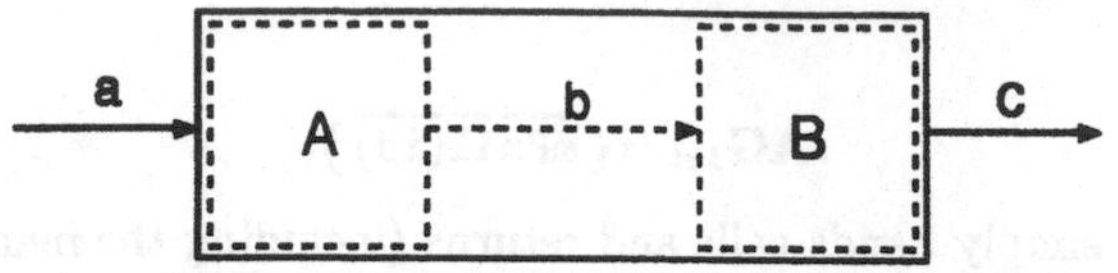

FIGURE 4. A Pipe Line of Two Disposable Media

The behaviour of A and B are given by the two infinite–width transition systems of Fig. 5. However, rather than using these direct specifications of A

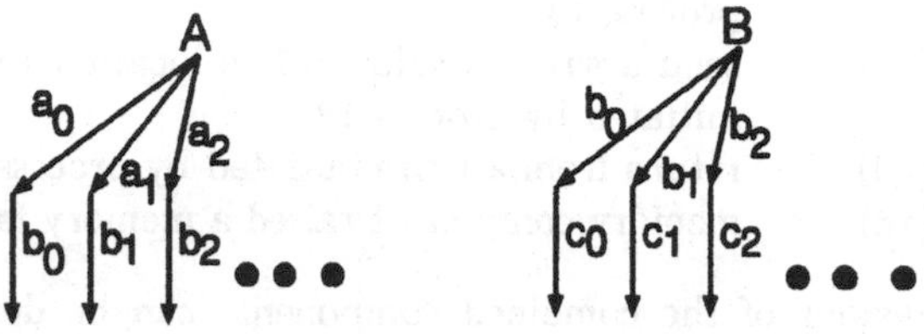

FIGURE 5. Behaviour of A and B.

and B we specify the two components behaviour using projective views A_n and B_n; one view for each possible natural number n. The projective view A_n specifies the *constraints* on the behaviour of the component A when focusing on transmission of the value n; this constraint can be expressed as the modal transition system A_n given in Fig. 6(where we use solid lines for must- and dotted lines for may-transition).

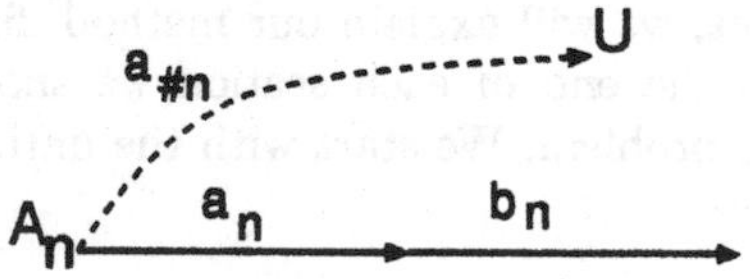

FIGURE 6. Projective View A_n

Here $a_{\neq n}$ denotes all labels of the form a_m where $m \neq n$; also $\mathcal{U}$ denotes the universal modal transition system constantly allowing all actions. Note that this 'n-th view' imposes no constraint on the behaviour of A when transporting values different from n. The complete specification of the component A is the conjunction of all projective views[3] A_n. In fact it is easy to establish the following facts:

$$A \trianglelefteq \bigwedge_n A_n \quad \text{and} \quad \bigwedge_n A_n \trianglelefteq A \tag{1.3}$$

[3]Note that all the projective views of A are pairwise independent.

where A refers to the (infinite) transition system of Fig. 5. Obviously, we may obtain similar projective views B_n for component B.

Let us now consider the problem of verifying that the overall system $\Big(A \mid B\Big)\backslash\{b\}$ is observationally equivalent to the system $C = a_{\Box}x.\overline{c_{\Box}}x$ (i.e. a slightly different disposable media). As A, B and C are standard transitions systems, i.e., everything allowed is also required, this problem is equivalent to showing

$$\Big(A \mid B\Big)\backslash\{b\} \trianglelefteq C$$

Thus (1.3), together with the observation that also C may be expressed as a conjunction of an infinite number of constraints C_n, leaves us with the following refinement problem:

$$\Big(\bigwedge_n A_n \mid \bigwedge_n B_n\Big)\backslash\{b\} \trianglelefteq \bigwedge_n C_n \tag{1.4}$$

4.1 Application to the RPC problem

We give modal transition systems for the specification of properties $P0$, $P1$ and $P2$ of the memory component. Therefore we split $P1$ into two properties $P1a$, $P1b$ meaning

- $P1a$ A write-call from process `id` cannot return unless an atomic write is performed.

- $P1b$ As long as a write-call from process `id` has not returned, no atomic write to a wrong location or of a false value occurs

The labels in the following specifications are sets of actions (called *abstracted actions*). A single action is a shorthand for the set containing this and only this action. For the other sets, we use the usual set-theoretic connectives, and a dot-notation, where a parametrized action with dots as parameters means "the set of all actions where the dotted position is replaced by all legal values for the parameter", e.g. for a fixed $\mathtt{id} \in \mathtt{procId}$, $\mathtt{mWr(id,.,.)}$ is the set $\{\mathtt{mWr(id,loc,val)} \mid \mathtt{loc} \in \mathtt{memLocs}, \mathtt{val} \in \mathtt{memVals}\}$.

The properties $P1a$ and $P1b$ are easily expressed by the following abbreviations of modal transition systems:

$$\mathbf{AG}_{\mathtt{Act}}\Big([\mathtt{mWr(id,.,.)}]\,\mathbf{AG}_{\mathtt{Act}\backslash\mathtt{write(id,.,.)}}\,\neg\{\overline{\mathtt{mRetWr(id)}}\}\Big)$$
$$\mathbf{AG}_{\mathtt{Act}}\Big([\mathtt{mWr(id,loc,val)}]\,\mathbf{AG}_{\mathtt{Act}\backslash\mathtt{write(id,loc,val)}}\,\neg\{\overline{\mathtt{mRetWr(id)}}\}\Big)$$

Our specification assumes that calls from different processes are handled concurrently. As calls from different processes do not interfere, no actions parametrized with an identifier other than `id` is constrained in the specifications of calls from process `id`. This is modelled by allowing all actions with an identifier different from the fixed id in any state. Instead of adding to each state a loop where all these actions are allowed, we draw boxes meaning "a state with a loop for all non-id actions". By this the conjunction of the specifications for all processes is the same as their parallel composition.

The modal transition systems which specify the properties for a fixed value id are given in Fig. 7.

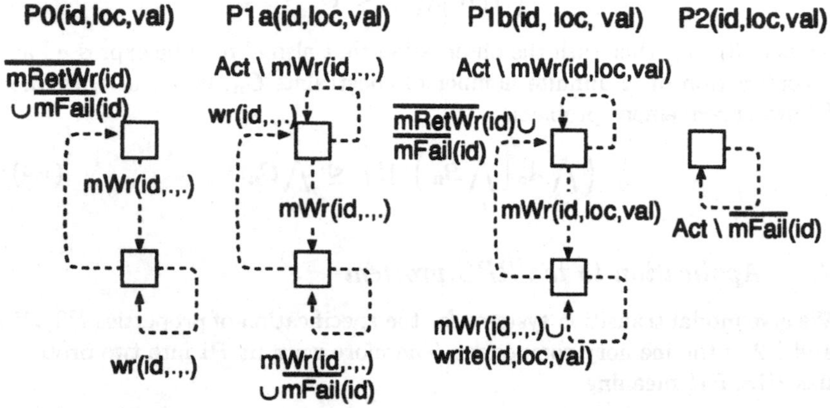

FIGURE 7. MTS for properties $P0$, $P1a$, $P1b$ and $P2$

The transition systems for $P1a, P1b$ and $P2$ are the expansions of the "abbreviated" transition systems (cf. Fig. 1), while the transition system for $P0$ was defined directly. Note that only $P1b$ really depends on loc and val, and that the properties $P0, P1a, P1b$ and $P2$ are the conjunctions of the above modal specifications over all $z \in Z$.

Let $M(z)$ be the conjunction $P0(z) \wedge P1a(z) \wedge P1b(z)$, and $M_R(z) = M(z) \wedge P2(z)$. The memory component M is the conjunction of $M(z)$ over all $z \in Z$.

Let Act be the set of all actions. For two sets $R \subseteq$ Act (*return set*) and $T \subseteq$ Act (*tolerance set*), a state s and actions $a_1, \ldots, a_m \in$ Act. Then we use the following *macro state* for the specification of the RPC:

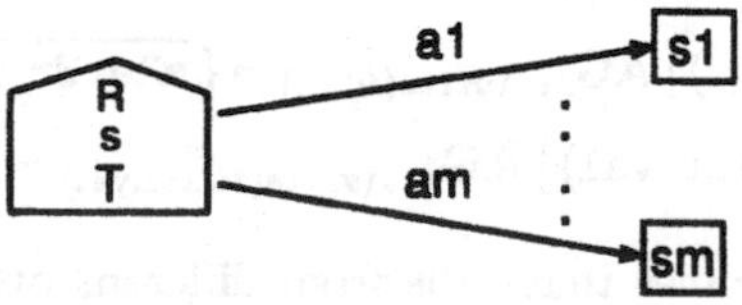

Here the edges leaving the "macro state" can be either may- or must-transition.

For a given transition system with start state s_0 and an auxiliary state s' not already in the transition system, this is meant to expand to

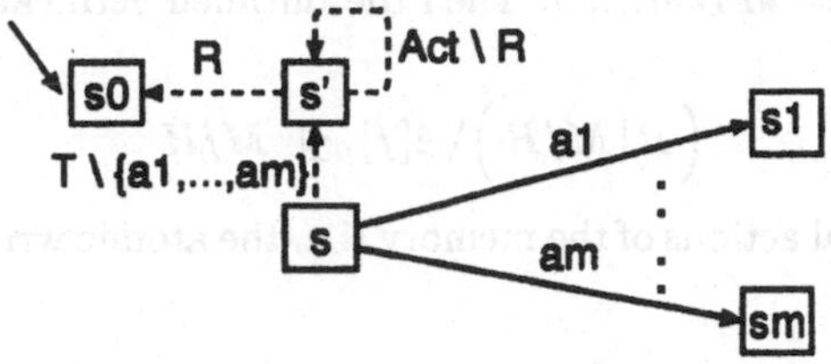

i.e. state s tolerates any action from T. If the behaviour of a tolerated action is already specified by an outgoing edge, nothing new happens. Otherwise, the system goes to the auxiliary state s', where it accepts any action until a return action (from R) occurs. Return actions take the system back to the start state.
There are two main projective views of the RPC. In the first view, a write is handed through and a return received from the memory. In the second view, instead of a return a memory failure is received. These two views R_1(`id, loc, val`) and R_2(`id, loc, val`) are given in the following picture:

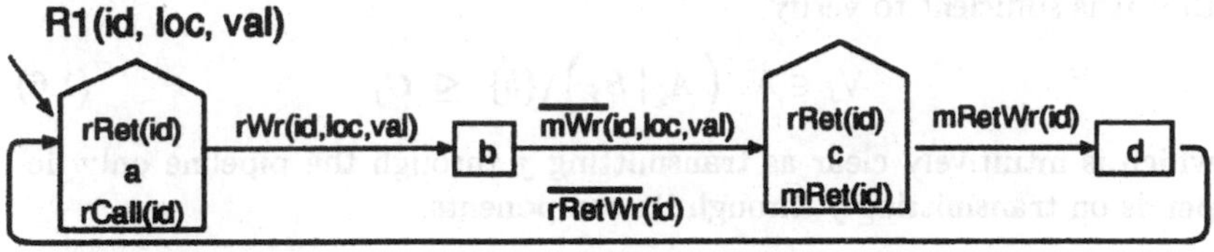

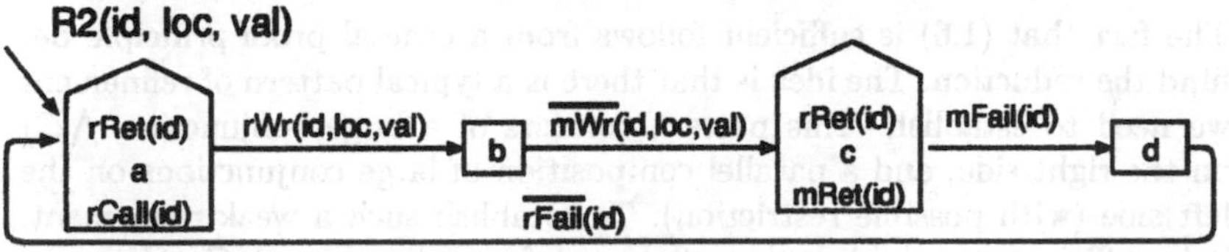

The sets in the macro states are defined as follows:

```
rCall(id)  :=  rWr(id,.,.)
 rRet(id)  :=  rRetWr(id) ∪ rFail(id)
 mRet(id)  :=  mRetWr(id) ∪ mFail(id)
```

While it is natural to use must-transitions in this specification, the lack of must-transitions in the memory component allows us to weaken these must transitions to may transitions without affecting the correctness of a successful proof. This guarantees the well-definedness of conjunction, as all our specifications are now independent.

Let $R(z) := R_1(z) \wedge R_2(z)$. The untimed specification of the RPC R is the conjunction of $R(z)$ over all z.

Let f be a relabelling mapping all actions of the RPC to the appropriate actions of the memory component, and $A := \texttt{rWr}(.,.,.) \cup \texttt{rRetWr}(.) \cup \texttt{rFail}(.)$ and $H := \texttt{write}(.,.,.)$. Then the untimed verification problem is

$$\Big(R \,|\, M/H\Big)\backslash A[f] \;\trianglelefteq\; M/H \tag{1.5}$$

where the internal actions of the memory (i.e. the atomic writes) are hidden.

5 Sufficient Proof Condition

As a conjunction is a refinement of every of its components (cf. Prop. 2.5), the proof of (1.4) can be reduced to the verification of

$$\Big(\bigwedge_{i\in N} A_i \,|\, \bigwedge_{i\in N} B_i\Big)\backslash\{b\} \;\trianglelefteq\; C_j$$

for each natural j. Note that this is even a necessary condition for our claim.

This reduction alone would not gain much. Here however it turns out that it is sufficient to verify

$$\forall j \in N.\; \Big(A_j \,|\, B_j\Big)\backslash\{b\} \;\trianglelefteq\; C_j \tag{1.6}$$

which is intuitively clear as transmitting j through the pipeline only depends on transmitting j through its components.

The fact that (1.6) is sufficient follows from a general proof principle behind the reduction. The idea is that there is a typical pattern of refinement we need to establish. This pattern consists of a large conjunction $\bigwedge C_j$ on the right side, and a parallel composition of large conjunctions on the left side (with possible restriction). To establish such a weak refinement, it is sufficient to establish the refinement for each conjunct C_j. However, concentrating on a specific component C_j, a lot of the details of the implementation on the left side can (hopefully) be disregarded, thus it will be sufficient to restrict the proof to subsets of the conjuncts in the parallel components of the left hand side. These subsets will generally depend on j.

This is formalized by the following ***sufficient proof condition***:

Theorem 5.1. *Assume index sets $I_1, \ldots I_k, I$, and modal transition systems $A_i^\ell, C_j (\ell \in \{1, \ldots, k\}, i \in I_\ell, j \in I)$. If there are subsets $I_{\ell,j} \subseteq I_\ell$ for each $\ell \in \{1, \ldots, k\}$ and $j \in I$, such that*

$$\forall j \in I.\; \Big(\bigwedge_{i\in I_{1,j}} A_i^1 \,|\, \ldots \,|\, \bigwedge_{i\in I_{k,j}} A_i^k\Big)\backslash L \;\trianglelefteq\; C_j \tag{1.7}$$

then

$$\Big(\bigwedge_{i\in I_1} A_i^1 \mid \dots \mid \bigwedge_{i\in I_k} A_i^k\Big)\backslash L \trianglelefteq \bigwedge_{j\in I} C_j \tag{1.8}$$

holds as well.

Proof. Starting from the assumption (1.7) for an arbitrary j, we can shift all conjunctions from the inside of the formula out by using distributivity of conjunction over parallel composition and restriction:

$$\begin{aligned} \bigwedge_{i_1\in I_{1,j},\dots,i_k\in I_{k,j}} (A_{i_1}^1 \mid \dots \mid A_{i_k}^k)\backslash L &\trianglelefteq \Big(\bigwedge_{i\in I_{1,j}} A_i^1 \mid \dots \mid \bigwedge_{i\in I_{k,j}} A_i^k\Big)\backslash L \\ &\trianglelefteq C_j \end{aligned} \tag{1.9}$$

Conjuncting (1.9) over all $j \in I$ gives us

$$\bigwedge_{i_1\in I_1',\dots,i_k\in I_k'} (A_{i_1}^1 \mid \dots \mid A_{i_k}^k)\backslash L \trianglelefteq \bigwedge_{j\in I} C_j$$

for subsets $I_\ell' \subseteq I_\ell$. As adding constraints refines a specification, the following is a refinement of the left hand side:

$$\bigwedge_{i_1\in I_1,\dots,i_k\in I_k} (A_{i_1}^1 \mid \dots \mid A_{i_k}^k)\backslash L$$

Using the distributivity of conjunction over parallel composition and restriction once more, this can further be refined to

$$\Big(\bigwedge_{i\in I_1} A_i^1 \mid \dots \mid \bigwedge_{i\in I_k} A_i^k\Big)\backslash L$$

Finally, the transitivity of $\trianglelefteq$ allows us to combine the last three lines in order to establish our claim. □

Of course, in general the power of this proof principle strongly depends on a good choice of the $I_{\ell,j}$, which was trivial in our example.

5.1 Application to the RPC Problem

With the same argumentation, to prove (1.5) it is sufficient to show

$$\forall z \in Z.\ \Big(R(z) \mid M(z)/H\Big)\backslash A[f] \trianglelefteq M(z)/H \tag{1.10}$$

6 Skolemization and Abstraction

So far we have reduced the overall verification problem of (1.4) to that of (1.6). At first sight this doesn't seem much of a reduction as (1.6) requires a refinement proof to be established for each natural number. Fortunately, these proofs are not really sensitive to the actual value of the natural number n. Letting k be an arbitrary natural number (or a Skolem constant) it suffices to prove:

$$\left(A_k \mid B_k\right)\backslash\{b\} \trianglelefteq C_k \tag{1.11}$$

in order to infer (1.6). Thus we are now left with the problem of establishing a *single* refinement. But still, though finite *state* the specifications A_k and B_k both have infinitely many *transitions* (as $a_{\neq k}$ is an inifinite label set).

However we can find an equivalence relation on the actions of the components which is of finite index, but still fine enough to establish the proof goal. Replacing a system with a new one gained by collapsing w.r.t. an equivalence relation is called *abstraction*.

In the following, $[s]^{\equiv}$ is the equivalence class of s under $\equiv$.

If the equivalence relation is understood from the context, we write $[s]$.

In general, an equivalence relation on states and transitions is needed, but for the examples here an equivalence relation on transitions suffices:

Definition 6.1. *Let P be a TMS over an alphabet* Act *with transition relations $\rightarrow_\Box, \rightarrow_\Diamond$. Each equivalence relation $\equiv$ on* Act *induces a* collapsed TMS $P^{\equiv}$ *over the alphabet* $\texttt{Act}_{\equiv} := \{[a] \mid a \in \texttt{Act}\}$ *and transition relations $\rightarrow'_\Box, \rightarrow'_\Diamond$ defined by*

$$\frac{p \xrightarrow{a}_\Box p'}{p \xrightarrow{[a]}{}'_\Box\, p'} \qquad \frac{p \xrightarrow{a}_\Diamond p'}{p \xrightarrow{[a]}{}'_\Diamond\, p'}$$

An equivalence relation $\equiv$ on Act *is* compatible *with P iff for all $a' \in [a]$ and all reachable states p, p' of P:*

$$p \xrightarrow{a}_\Box p' \;\; \textit{iff} \;\; p \xrightarrow{a'}_\Box p' \qquad \textit{and} \qquad p \xrightarrow{a}_\Diamond p' \;\; \textit{iff} \;\; p \xrightarrow{a'}_\Diamond p'$$

Compatible equivalence relations satisfy the following three properties:

Proposition 6.2. *Let P and Q be two TMS's and $\equiv$ an equivalance relation on their common alphabet compatible with P and Q. Then the following holds:*

1. *$P^{\equiv} \trianglelefteq Q^{\equiv}$ implies $P \trianglelefteq Q$,*
2. *if $[\tau] = \{\tau\}$ then $\equiv$ is compatible with $P \mid Q$,*

3. if $[\tau] = \{\tau\}$ and for $L \subseteq \mathtt{Act}$ and every $a \in \mathtt{Act}$ either $[a] \cap L = [a]$ or $[a] \cap L = \emptyset$[4], then $\equiv$ is compatible with $P \setminus L$.

Proof. 1. $P^{\equiv} \trianglelefteq Q^{\equiv}$ implies the existence of a weak refinement relation between the states of $P^{\equiv}$ and $Q^{\equiv}$. As no states are collapsed, we can use the same relation to establish $P \trianglelefteq Q$ exploiting its compatitiblity:

If Q requires an a-step, then $Q^{\equiv}$ requires an $[a]$-step by definition. As $P^{\equiv}$ is a weak refinement of $Q^{\equiv}$, it requires an $[a]$-step as well. Thus by definition P requires an a'-step for some $a' \in [a]$. Compatibility now guarantees an a'-step for every $a' \in [a]$, in particular for a itself.

The part for may-transitions follows analogously.

2. Assume $P \mid Q \xrightarrow{a}_{\Box} P' \mid Q'$. Then we must show that for all $a' \in [a]$ we have $P \mid Q \xrightarrow{a'}_{\Box} P' \mid Q'$ as well.

If $a = \tau$, then $[a] = \{a\}$, so $a' = a$. Thus the proposition is true.

If $a \neq \tau$, then w.l.o.g. $P \xrightarrow{a}_{\Box} P'$ and $Q = Q'$, and the compatibility of $\equiv$ with P guarantees $P \xrightarrow{a'}_{\Box} P'$, and therefore $P \mid Q \xrightarrow{a'}_{\Box} P' \mid Q'$.

The proof for $\xrightarrow{a}_{\Diamond}$ follows the same lines.

3. Assuming $P \setminus L \xrightarrow{a}_{\Box} P' \setminus L$, it suffices to show $P \setminus L \xrightarrow{a'}_{\Box} P' \setminus L$ for all $a' \in [a]$.

If $a = \tau$, then by the same argument as above $a' = a$, and the proposition holds.

If $a \neq \tau$, then $a \notin L$ and $P \xrightarrow{a}_{\Box} P'$. Thus the compatibility yields $P \xrightarrow{a'}_{\Box} P'$, and therefore $P \setminus L \xrightarrow{a'}_{\Box} P' \setminus L$, as the condition in 3. guarantees $a' \notin L$.

The part for $\xrightarrow{a}_{\Diamond}$ follows along the same lines. □

This Proposition allows us to reduce verification problems for infinite systems to problems for finite systems, as soon as an appropriate equivalence relation can be found.

For our example, let us consider the equivalence relation $\equiv$ defined by $x_k \equiv x_k$ and $x_i \equiv x_j$ whenever $i, j \neq k$, where x ranges over $\{a, b, c\}$. Further τ builds an equivalence class of its own.

Obviously, $\equiv$ is compatible with A_k, B_k and C_k. As further all conditions of Prop. 6.2 are met, $\equiv$ is also compatible with $\left(A_k^{\equiv} \mid B_k^{\equiv}\right)\setminus\{b\}$. Thus the verification of (1.4) can further be reduced to the refinement proof between the finite $\equiv$-abstracted versions of A_k, B_k and C_k

$$\left(A_k^{\equiv} \mid B_k^{\equiv}\right)\setminus\{b\} \trianglelefteq C_k^{\equiv} \tag{1.12}$$

which can easily be done by means of the automatic verification tool EPSILON.

[4] i.e. L is union of some equivalence classes

6.1 *Application to the RPC Problem*

Instead of proving (1.10) for all z, a proof for a prototypical z is sufficient here. Most of the abstraction is already carried out by using abstracted actions. Note however that the abstracted actions are in general ***not*** the required equivalence classes. For the RPC problem e.g. `write`(z) is an equivalence class of its own, and the set `write(id,.,.)` $\setminus$ `write`(z) is another equivalence classes. This specific partitioning of the atomic write actions reflects the fact that we must distinguish between a write of the correct value to the correct location and all other writes from the same process.

Looking at the diagrams of Sect. 4.1 easily reveals that the resulting transition systems are small and easily in the range of the EPSILON tool.

7 Specifications with Time

The above examples can be extended to deal with real time. For the specification we use Wang Yi's Timed CCS (see [Yi91]) together with modal specifications. For details on these so called ***Timed Modal Specifications*** see [CGL93]. This method can be used with any totally ordered time domain, while in the following we will assume the positive real numbers.

The passing of time is modelled by a delay action $\varepsilon(d)$, where d is a positive real number. The intuitive meaning of such a delay is that a time amount of d passes until the end of this action. Normal actions are enabled immediately, and can be taken at any time. As an example, the process $a_\Box x.\varepsilon(2).\overline{b_\Box} x$ can execute $a_\Box x$ at any time. Thereafter it must delay for at least two time units before it can engage in $b_\Box x$.

Further we assume ***maximal progress***, i.e. a communication must be performed as soon as possible. Putting $a_\Box x.\varepsilon(2).\overline{b_\Box} x$ in parallel with $\overline{a_\Box} x.\varepsilon(3).b_\Box x$ would force the communication via channel a to take place immediately, and the communication via channel b to happen after exactly three time units.

For our specification, the macro $a[l,u]$ is convenient, where a is an action and l, u are real numbers with $l < u$. The intuition is that a process $a[l,u].P$ ***may*** enable a after l time units and ***must*** enable a after u time units. In other words, communication via a may be possible after at least l time units, and will be possible at any time after u time units.[5] This macro is defined as $a[l,u].P = (\varepsilon(l).a_\Diamond + \varepsilon(u).a_\Box).P$.

In our examples, the lower bound is always zero. The graphical presentation we use for $a[0,u].P$ is:

[5]Note that u is not a ***time-out***, but a switching point between a may and a must reuirement!

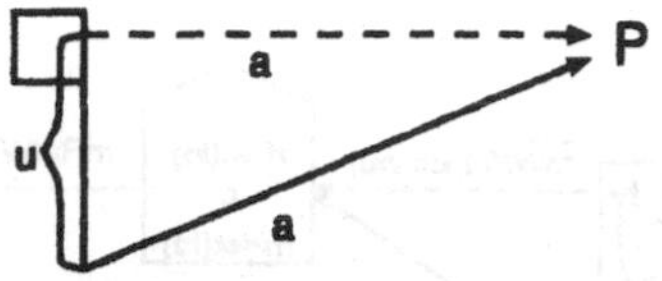

Let d be a fixed real number. Then we specify a timed process $A(d)$, which reads port a and subsequently outputs its input onto port b within d time units, by $a_\Box x.\overline{b}x[0,d]$. Note that this is a timed version of process A. The same construction gives timed versions $B(d)$ and $C(d)$ of B and C.

We are now going to establish that a 'pipeline' with two components with delay d should not be slower than one component with delay $2d$, i.e.

$$\left(A(d) \mid B(d)\right) \setminus \{b\} \trianglelefteq C(2d)$$

The same method as in the untimed case reduces the situation to

$$\left(A_k{}^{\equiv}(d) \mid B_k{}^{\equiv}(d)\right) \setminus \{b\} \trianglelefteq C_k{}^{\equiv}(2d)$$

for a Skolem constant k and the equivalence relation of the previous section. Now, given a specific value for d this proof can be carried out using the EPSILON tool, which treats real valued timer domains by means of the clock region automaton technique (see [AD94] for details). This technique relies on integer values for all explicit timer constants in the specification, which can be achieved by multiplication with an appropriate constant in most applications. As all timer constants are multiplied by the same constant, this does not affect the principle behaviour of the system. In our example, the obvious choice for this constant is $1/d$, leaving us with the following refinement problem

$$\left(A_k{}^{\equiv}(1) \mid B_k{}^{\equiv}(1)\right) \setminus \{b\} \trianglelefteq C_k{}^{\equiv}(2)$$

which can be solved using EPSILON.

Note that this proof indeed covers the statement for any d. Thus even in the presence of real time, the original verification problem is reduced to a very simple, automatically solvable problem.

7.1 Application to the RPC Problem

The following is a timed version of R_1, where passing through the calls and returns takes not more than δ seconds:

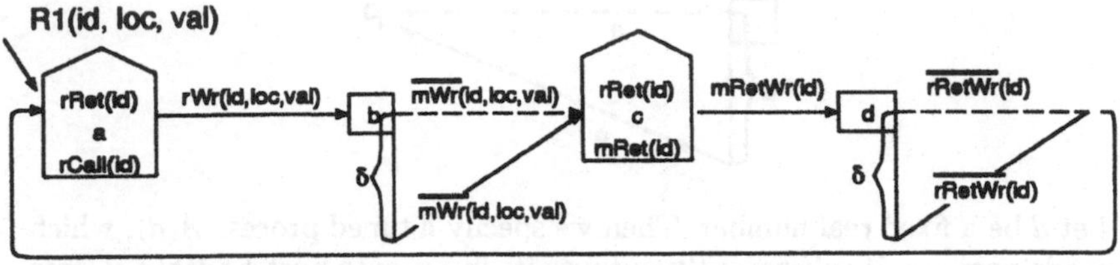

Note that actions without a timing constraint are enabled at any time. The timed version of R_2 is defined analogously (although unnecessary for the reliable memory). Call the timed RPC R^{δ}.

In the same way as the RPC we specify a demon which signals a failure if a call to the RPC does not return within $2\delta+\varepsilon$ seconds. The actions of the demon are the same as those of the RPC, only the prefix r is replaced by a d. Timeout is modelled by a τ-transition. The specification of the demon $D_1(z)$ is

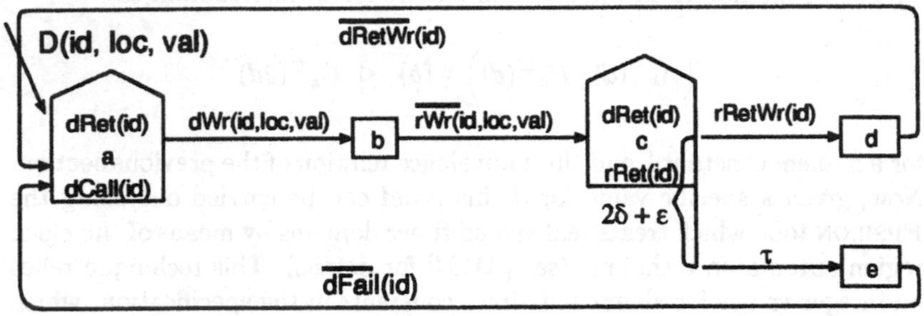

To define a timed reliable memory, we only need to alter property $P0$ by requiring the return to occur within ε time. This is done by the following:

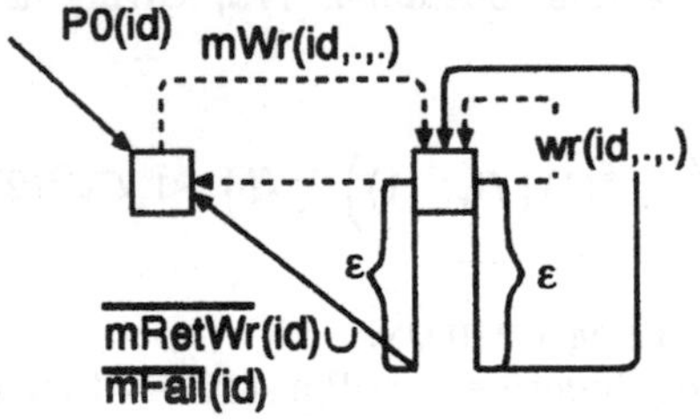

We call the resulting timed specification of the reliable memory M_R^{ε}. The timed verification problem then is

$$\left(D^{2\delta+\varepsilon} \mid R^{\delta} \mid M_R^{\varepsilon}/H\right)\backslash A[f] \trianglelefteq M_R/H$$

Note that the memory on the right hand side is the "untimed" M_R, where we interprete all actions to be enabled all the time. Further the set A

and the relabelling f have to be adjusted. This problem can once again be reduced by our method to a problem concerning transition systems of small size, as we only need to look at a prototypical z.

However, having two parameters δ and ε in the timing constraints, the standard multiplication trick is not sufficient to produce a parameterless situation. Luckily, this particular example is equivalent to a one parameter problem: computing $R^{\delta} \mid M_R^{\varepsilon}/H$ by hand one finds a transiton system, which can be regarded as parameterized in $2\delta + \varepsilon$ only. Now the previously used multiplication trick is applicable opening the problem to automatic verification by means of EPSILON.

8 Conclusion and Future Work

We have introduced a new constraint-oriented method for the (automated) verification of concurrent systems. Key concepts of our 'divide and conquer' method are ***projective views***, ***separation of proof obligations***, ***Skolemization*** and ***abstraction***, which together support a drastic reduction of the complexity of the relevant subproblems. Of course, our proof methodology does neither guarantee the possibility of a finite state reduction nor a straightforward method for finding the right amount of separation or the adequate abstraction. Still, there is a large class of problems and systems, where the method can be applied quite straightforwardly. Typical examples are systems with limited data dependence. Whereas involved data dependencies may exclude any possibility of 'horizontal' decomposition, our approach elegantly extends to real time systems, even over a dense time domain. In fact, the resulting finite state problems can be automatically verified using the EPSILON verification system. All this has been illustrated using a simple example of pipelined buffers. Our experience indicates that our method scales up to practically relevant problems, as demonstrated by the problem of the transparent RPC.

Beside further case studies and the search for good heuristics for proof obligation separation and abstraction, we are investigating the limits of tool support during the construction of constraint based specifications and the application of the three reduction steps. Whereas support by graphical interfaces and interactive editors is obvious and partly implemented in META-Frame, a management system for synthesis, analysis and verification currently developed at the university of Passau, the limits of consistency checking and tool supported search for adequate separation and abstraction are still an interesting open research topic.

As pointed out, one major problem are parameters in the timing constraints. We are currently investigating methods – similar to the approach presented for parametrized timed automata in [AHV93] – for checking bisimulation and (weak) refinement for ***parametrized modal transition systems***.

9 References

[ASW94] H. Andersen, C. Stirling, G. Winskel. *A Compositional Proof System for the Modal Mu-Calculus*. in: Proc. LICS 1994.

[AD94] R. Alur, D.L. Dill. *A Theory of Timed Automata*. in: Theoretical Computer Science Vol. 126, No. 2, April 1994, pp. 183-236.

[AHV93] R. Alur, T.A. Henzinger, M.Y. Vardi. *Parametric real-time reasoning*. Proc. 25th STOC, ACM Press 1993, pp. 592–601.

[BL93] M. Broy, L. Lamport. *Specification Problem*. Case study for the Dagstuhl Seminar 9439, 1994.

[Br86] R. Bryant. *Graph-Based Algorithms for Boolean Function Manipulation*. in: IEEE Transactions on Computation, 35 (8). 1986.

[BCMDH90] J. Burch, E. Clarke, K. McMillan, D. Dill, L. Hwang. *Symbolic Model Checking: 10^{20} States and Beyond*. in: Proc. LICS'90.

[BS90] J. Bradfield, C.Stirling. *Local Model Checking for Finite State Spaces*. LFCS Report Series ECS-LFCS-90-115, June 1990

[CES83] E. Clarke, E.A. Emerson, A.P. Sistla. *Automatic Verification of Finite State Concurrent Systems using Temporal Logic Specifications: A Practical Approach*. In Proc. 10th POPL'83

[CGL93] K. Čerāns, J.C. Godesken, K.G. Larsen. *Timed Modal Specification - Theory and Tools*. in: C. Courcoubetis (Ed.), Proc. 5th CAV, 1993. LNCS 697, Springer Berlin 1993, pp. 253–267.

[CGL92] E. Clarke, O. Grumber, D. Long. *Model Checking and Abstraction*. in: Proc. XIX POPL'92.

[CLM89] E. Clarke, D. Long, K. McMillan. *Compositional Model Checking*. in: Proc. LICS'89.

[CC77] P. Cousot, R. Cousot. *Abstract Interpretation: A Unified Lattice Model for Static Analysis of Programs by Construction or Approximation of Fixpoints*. in: Proc. POPL'77.

[EFT91] R. Enders, T. Filkorn, D. Taubner. *Generating BDDs for Symbolic Model Checking in CCS*. in: Proceedings CAV'91, LNCS 575, 1991, pp. 203–213

[EL86] E. Emerson, J. Lei. *Efficient model checking in fragments of the propositional mu-calculus*. In Proc. LICS'86, pp. 267–278.

[GW91] P. Godefroid, P. Wolper. *Using Partial Orders for the Efficient Verification of Deadlock Freedom and Safety Properties*. in: Proc. CAV'91, LNCS 575, pp. 332–342.

[GP93] P. Godefroid, D. Pirottin. *Refining Dependencies Improves Partial-Order Verification Methods.* in: Proceedings CAV'93, LNCS 697, 1991, pp. 438–449.

[GL93] S. Graf, C. Loiseaux. *Program Verification using Compositional Abstraction.* in: Proceedings FASE/TAPSOFT'93.

[GS90] S. Graf, B. Steffen. *Using Interface Specifications for Compositional Minimization of Finite State Systems.* in: Proc. CAV'90.

[Koz83] D. Kozen. *Results on the Propositional mu-Calculus.* TCS 27, 333-354, 1983

[HL89] H. Hüttel and K. Larsen. *The use of static constructs in a modal process logic.* Proceedings of Logic at Botik'89. LNCS 363, 1989.

[Lar90] K.G. Larsen. *Modal specifications.* In: Automatic Verification Methods for Finite State Systems LNCS 407, 1990.

[LT88] K. Larsen and B. Thomsen. *A modal process logic.* In: Proceedings LICS'88, 1988.

[Mil89] R. Milner. *Communication and Concurrency.* Prentice-Hall, 1989.

[Par81] D. Park. *Concurrency and automata on infinite sequences.* In P. Deussen (ed.), LNCS 104, pp. 167–183, 1981.

[Ste89] B. Steffen. *Characteristic Formulae.* In Proc. ICALP'89, LNCS 372, 1989

[Ste93] B. Steffen. *Generating data flow analysis algorithms from modal specifications.* in: Science of Computer Programming 21, (1993), 115 - 139.

[Val93] A. Valmari. *On-The-Fly Verification with Stubborn Sets.* in: C. Courcoubetis (Ed.), Proc. 5th CAV, 1993. LNCS 697, pp. 397–408.

[Yi91] W. Yi. *CCS + Time = an Interleaving Model for Real-Time Systems,* Proc.18th Int. Coll. on Automata, Languages and Programming (ICALP), Madrid, July 1991. LNCS 510, Springer New York 1991, pp. 217-228.

A User Guide to HyTech

Thomas A. Henzinger
Pei-Hsin Ho
Howard Wong-Toi

ABSTRACT HyTech is a tool for the automated analysis of embedded systems. This document, designed for the first-time user of HyTech, guides the reader through the underlying system model, and through the input language for describing and analyzing systems. The guide gives several examples of usage, and some hints for gaining maximal computational efficiency from the tool.
The version of HyTech described in this guide was released in August 1995, and is available through anonymous ftp from ftp.cs.cornell.edu in the directory ~pub/tah/HyTech, and through the World-Wide Web via HyTech's home page http://www.cs.cornell.edu/Info/People/tah/hytech.html.

1 Introduction

The control of physical systems with embedded hardware and software is a growing application area for computerized systems. Since many embedded controllers occur in safety-critical situations, it is important to have reliable design methodologies that ensure that the controllers operate correctly. HyTech aids in the design of embedded systems by not only checking systems requirements, but also performing parametric analysis. Given a parametric system description, HyTech returns the exact conditions on the parameters for which the system satisfies its safety and timing requirements.

For completeness, we begin with a brief presentation of the underlying theoretical framework of *linear hybrid automata* [ACHH93, ACH+95], which we use to describe system specifications and requirement specifications. These automata model the continuous activities of analog variables (such as temperature, time, and distance), as well as discrete events (such as interrupts and output signals). Communication is modeled through event synchronization and shared variables. HyTech's input consists of two

This research was supported in part by the ONR YIP award N00014-95-1-0520, by the NSF CAREER award CCR-9501708, by the NSF grants CCR-9200794 and CCR-9504469, by the AFOSR contract F49620-93-1-0056, and by the ARPA grant NAG2-892.

parts: a system description and analysis commands. The system-description language allows us to represent linear hybrid automata textually. The tool forms the parallel composition of a collection of automata, each describing a modular component of an embedded system. The analysis-command language allows us to write simple iterative programs for performing tasks such as reachability analysis and error-trace generation.

We illustrate the use of the tool on several examples taken from the literature, and provide hints for a verification engineer to gain the maximal possible efficiency from HyTech.

Outline Section 2 reviews linear hybrid automata, their semantics, parallel composition, and associated analysis techniques. A brief history of HyTech appears in Section 3. Sections 4 and 5 describe the HyTech input language, first the system-description part, and then the analysis-command part. Section 6 illustrates the use of the tool on several examples. Section 7 is a short guide to designing specification requirements using HyTech's command language. Section 8 provides information on installing and running HyTech. Section 9 contains hints for the efficient use of HyTech.

A full version of this user guide, including the complete grammar for the input language and additional examples, appears as [HHWT95b].

2 Linear Hybrid Automata

We model systems as the parallel composition of a collection of linear hybrid automata [ACHH93, ACH+95]. Informally, a linear hybrid automaton consists of a finite set X of real-valued variables and a labeled multigraph. The vertices represent control modes, each with its own constraints on the slopes of variables in X. The edges represent discrete events and are labeled with guarded assignments to X. The state of the automaton changes either through the instantaneous action associated with an event or, while time elapses, through the continuous activity associated with a control mode. We also explicitly model *urgent* events, which must take place as soon as they are enabled (unless another instantaneous action disables them).

We use the linear hybrid automata that model a simple railroad crossing [LS85, AHH93] as a running example. The system consists of three components: a train, a gate, and a controller. The train is initially some distance — at least 2000 feet — away from the track intersection with the gate fully raised. As the train approaches, it triggers a sensor — 1000 feet ahead of the intersection — signaling its upcoming entry to the controller. The controller then sends a lower command to the gate, after a delay of up to α seconds. When the gate receives a lower command, it lowers at a rate of 9 degrees per second. After the train has exited the intersection and is 100 feet away, it sends an exit signal to the controller. The controller then

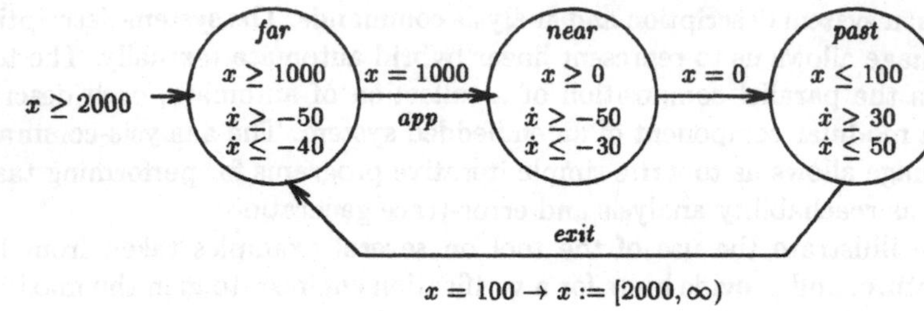

FIGURE 1. Train automaton

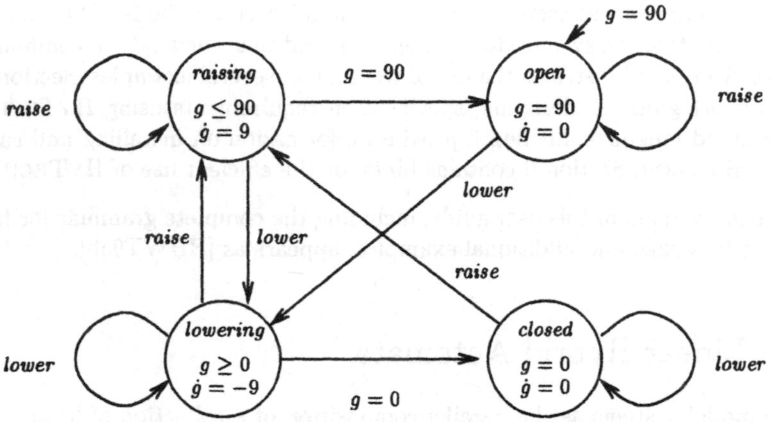

FIGURE 2. Gate automaton

commands the gate to be raised. The role of the controller is to ensure that the gate is always closed whenever the train is in the intersection, and that the gate is not closed unnecessarily long. The linear hybrid automata for the train, the gate, and the controller appear in Figures 1, 2 and 3.

2.1 Definition

We give an informal description of linear hybrid automata, and refer the reader to [AHH93, HHWT95a] for detailed definitions. A ***linear hybrid automaton*** consists of the following components.

Variables The automaton uses a finite ordered set $X = \{x_1, x_2, \ldots, x_n\}$ of real-valued *variables* to model continuous activities. For example, the position of the train is determined by the value of the variable x, which represents the distance of the train from the intersection. The variable g models the angle of the gate. When $g = 90$, the gate is completely open;

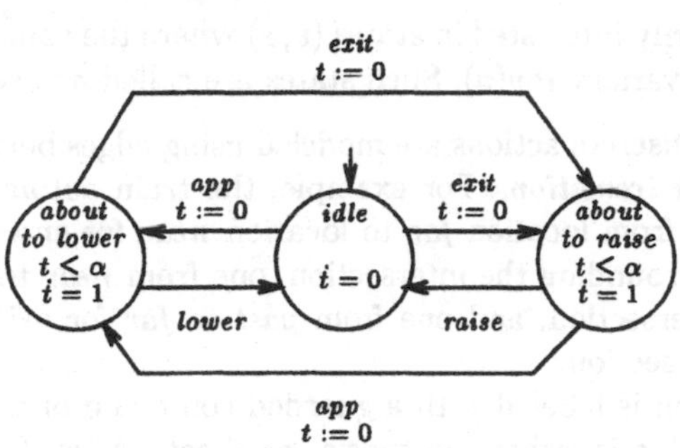

FIGURE 3. Controller automaton

when $g = 0$, it is completely closed.

A *valuation* is a point $(a_1, a_2, \ldots, a_n)$ in the n-dimensional real space $\mathbb{R}^n$, or equivalently, a function that maps each variable x_i to its value a_i. A *linear expression* over a set X of variables is a linear combination of variables in X with rational coefficients. A *linear inequality* is a non-strict[1] inequality between linear expressions. A *convex predicate* is a finite conjunction of linear inequalities, *e.g.* $x_1 \geq 3 \wedge 3x_2 \leq x_3 + 5/2$. A *predicate* is a finite disjunction of convex predicates, defining a set of valuations.

Locations Control modes are modeled using a finite set of vertices called *locations*. For example, the gate automaton has the locations *open*, *raising*, *lowering*, and *closed*. A *state* (v, s) of the automaton A consists of a location v and a valuation s. We use the term *region* to refer to a set of states.

Initial condition There is a designated initial location and an initial predicate ϕ_0 defining the set of initial values of the variables. For example, the gate is initially in location *open* with the value of g equal to 90. In the graphical representation, a small incoming arrow identifies the initial location, and is labeled with the predicate ϕ_0.

Invariant conditions Each location v is labeled with a convex predicate $inv(v)$ over X, the *invariant* of v. The automaton control may reside in location v only while its invariant is true, so the invariants can be used to enforce progress in the automaton. For example, in the gate automaton, $inv(open) = (g = 90)$, $inv(lowering) = (g \geq 0)$, $inv(raising) = (g \leq 90)$, and $inv(closed) = (g = 0)$. The invariant at location *lowering* implies that the gate can only be lowered until it is fully closed, at which point control moves out to location *closed*. In the graphical representation, the invariant *true* is omitted.

[1]The requirement that all inequalities be non-strict is not essential. Our current implementation inherits this restriction from the polyhedral manipulation library we use.

We are primarily interested in states (v, s) where the valuation s satisfies the location's invariant $inv(v)$. Such states are called *admissible*.

Transitions Discrete actions are modeled using edges between locations, which are called *transitions*. For example, the train automaton has three transitions; one from location *far* to location *near* for entering the region immediately surrounding the intersection, one from *near* to *past* for going through the intersection, and one from *past* to *far* for exiting the region around the intersection.

Each transition is labeled with a guarded command of the form $\phi \rightarrow \alpha$, where the guard ϕ is either the special predicate ASAP (which is always satisfied) or a convex predicate, and α is a set of assignments. Each assignment maps a variable into either a single linear expression over X, or a closed interval, whose endpoints are either finite (given as linear expressions over X), or infinite (given as $-\infty$ or ∞). In the train automaton, the transition between locations *past* and *far* is labeled with the guarded command $x = 100 \rightarrow x := [2000, \infty)$. In the graphical representation, we omit the guard *true* and empty assignment sets.

In order for a transition to take place from the state (v, s) its guard must be satisfied in s. We describe how the set of assignments causes a change in the valuation from s to some s'. The lower and upper bound expressions of each assignment interval are evaluated at the valuation s, and each reassigned variable is nondeterministically given a value that lies in each interval to which it is assigned. If a variable cannot be assigned any value within the prescribed intervals, the transition cannot take place. Any variables for which there is no assignment in α remain unchanged. We define the binary *transition-step* relation, $\xrightarrow{\sigma}$, over admissible states such that $(v, s) \xrightarrow{\sigma} (v', s')$ iff the state (v', s') can be reached from the state (v, s) by taking a transition.

Each transition is optionally given a synchronization label. The synchronization labels are used to define the parallel composition of hybrid automata. For example, in the gate automaton, the transition from *open* to *lowering* has the synchronization label *lower*, and this synchronizes (*i.e.* must be taken simultaneously) with the transition labeled *lower* in the controller automaton.

A transition is *urgent* if its guard is ASAP. The full version [HHWT95b] of this guide illustrates the use of urgent transitions in the modeling of a distributed control system. There, a sensor waits to send a reading to the controller as soon as the controller is ready to receive the data.

Rate conditions We denote the rate of change of the variable $x \in X$ by $\dot{x}$, and we let $\dot{X}$ be the set $\{\dot{x}_1, \dot{x}_2, \ldots, \dot{x}_n\}$. Each control location v is labeled with a convex predicate $act(v)$ over $\dot{X}$, called the *rate condition* of v. For a given location, the rate condition restricts the rates of change of the variables. In the gate automaton, the rate condition for locations *open* and *closed* is $\dot{g} = 0$, for location *raising*, it is $\dot{g} = 9$, and for *lowering*, it is

$\dot{y} = -9$. There is a technical restriction on the rate conditions allowed. All predicates that define bounded sets over $\dot{X}$ are permitted, and all examples in this guide meet this condition[2].

A location v is urgent if there is an urgent transition originating from v. No time is allowed to pass in such a location. We define the ***time-step*** relation, $\xrightarrow{\tau}$, such that $(v, s) \xrightarrow{\tau} (v', s')$ iff $v = v'$, and there exists a real $\delta \geq 0$ such that $\delta > 0$ implies v is not urgent, and there is a function $f: [0, \delta] \to \mathbb{R}^n$ such that (1) $f(0) = s$, (2) $f(\delta) = s'$, (3) for all $t \in [0, \delta]$, $f(t)$ satisfies $inv(v)$, and (4) for all time $t \in (0, \delta)$ $(df_1(t)/dt, df_2(t)/dt, \ldots, df_n(t)/dt)$ satisfies $act(v)$, where $f_i(t)$ denotes the value of variable x_i in the valuation $f(t)$.

2.2 *Parallel composition*

A hybrid system typically consists of several components which operate concurrently and communicate with each other. Each component is described as a separate linear hybrid automaton. The component automata coordinate through shared variables, and synchronization labels on the transitions are used to model message-type coordination. The linear hybrid automaton for the entire system is then obtained from the component automata using a product construction.

The control locations of the parallel composition of two automata A_1 and A_2 are pairs of locations, the first from A_1 and the second from A_2. The location (v_1, v_2) has the conjunction of v_1 and v_2's invariants as its invariant, and the conjunction of their rate conditions as its rate condition. A location is initial iff its components are initial in their respective automata. The initial convex predicate is the conjunction of the components' initial convex predicates. Transitions from the components are interleaved, unless they share the same synchronization label, in which case they are synchronized and executed simultaneously, if at all. In the train-gate controller example, the system is composed of the train, gate, and controller automata of Figures 1, 2 and 3. The controller communicates with the train by synchronizing on approach and exit events. It issues commands to the gate on the synchronized events *raise* and *lower*. The train's transition from location *near* to *far* is unlabeled, so it does not synchronize with any of the other components. In particular, this means the controller does not know the precise time at which the train enters the intersection.

We require a technical condition that the composition be well-formed: whenever two components synchronize on a label, if one transition has the guard ASAP then the other's guard must be either an ASAP guard or the

[2] The precise condition for the rate condition ψ to be allowed is that the set of vectors $\{\dot{y} \mid$ there exists a real $k \geq 0$ and $\dot{x}$ satisfying ψ such that $\dot{y} = k\dot{x}\}$ is bounded. In theory, the condition we require is not essential: it results from our current implementation's restriction to non-strict inequalities.

predicate *true* (in which case the synchronized transition has guard ASAP), or the predicate *false* (in which case the synchronized transition has guard *false*).

2.3 Reachability and safety verification

At any time instant, the state of a hybrid automaton specifies a location and the values of all variables. If the automaton has the location set V and n variables, the state space is defined as $V \times \mathbb{R}^n$. We define the binary successor relation $\rightarrow_A$ over states as $\xrightarrow{\tau} \cup \xrightarrow{\sigma}$. For a region W, we define $post(W)$ to be the set of all successor states of W, *i.e.* all states reachable from a state in W via a single transition or time step. The region *forward reachable* from W is defined as the set of all states reachable from W after a finite number of steps, *i.e.* the infinite union $post^*(W) = \bigcup_{i \geq 0} post^i(W)$. Similarly, we define $pre(W)$ to be the set of all predecessor states of W, and we let the region *backward reachable* from W be the infinite union $pre^*(W) = \bigcup_{i \geq 0} pre^i(W)$.

In practice, many problems to be analyzed can be posed in a natural way as reachability problems. Often, the system is composed with a special monitor process that "watches" the system and enters a violation state whenever the execution violates a given safety requirement. Indeed all timed safety requirements [Hen92], including bounded-time response requirements, can be verified in this way. See Section 7. A state (v, s) is *initial* if v is the initial location, and s satisfies the initial predicate. A system with initial states I is correct with respect to violation states Y iff $post^*(I) \cap Y = \emptyset$, or equivalently iff $pre^*(Y) \cap I$ is empty.

HYTECH computes the forward reachable region by finding the limit of the infinite sequence I, $post(I)$, $post^2(I)$, ... of regions. Analogously, the backward reachable region is found by iterating *pre*. These iteration schemes are semidecision procedures: there is no guarantee of termination. Nevertheless, we find that in practice, HYTECH's reachability procedures terminate on most examples we have attempted. In addition, it has been shown that for a large class of systems [HKPV95], a linear hybrid automaton can be automatically preprocessed into an equivalent automaton over which the iterations converge.

2.4 Parametric analysis

A major strength of HYTECH is its ability to perform parametric analysis. Often a system is described using parameters, and the system designer is interested in knowing which values of the parameters are required for correctness. Since the system is incorrect for parameter values for which there exists a state in the region $post^*(I) \cap Y$, we may obtain necessary and sufficient conditions for system correctness by performing reachability analysis followed by existential quantification [CH78].

Our study of the train-gate controller demonstrates this technique. The controller decides when to issue *lower* commands to the gate based on the amount of time since the train last passed the sensor located 1000 feet ahead of the intersection. We consider the problem of determining exactly how long the controller can wait before issuing commands, while maintaining the requirement that the gate be closed whenever the train is within 10 feet of the intersection. The parameter α corresponds to the latest possible moment the controller can wait. We then use HyTech to determine that the composed system includes violations whenever α is greater than or equal to 49/5. Thus we conclude that the system is correct for values of the parameter strictly less than 49/5.

3 A Brief History of HyTech

3.1 *Implementation*

There have been three generations of HyTech. The very earliest prototype [AHH93] was written entirely in the symbolic computation tool Mathematica. Regions were represented as symbolic formulas. The evaluation of time-step successors used existential quantifications that are easily encoded in this language. While Mathematica offers powerful symbolic manipulation, and allows rapid development and experimentation with algorithms and heuristics, its operations over predicates turned out to be computationally inefficient. In particular, quantifier-elimination operations for computing time-step successors were expensive. HyTech [HH95b] was rewritten to avoid this bottleneck in Mathematica. The second version of the verifier used a Mathematica main program that called efficient C++ routines from Halbwachs' polyhedral manipulation library [Hal93, HRP94] for computing time-step successors. While this verifier achieved a total speed-up of roughly one order of magnitude, it required inefficient conversions between Mathematica expressions and C++ data structures. It still relied on Mathematica for computing transition-step successors by substitution.

The third generation HyTech described here avoids Mathematica altogether and is built entirely in C++. It is roughly two to three orders of magnitude faster again than the second generation verifier. In addition, the input automata now allow nondeterministic assignments to variables, simultaneous assignments, more general rate conditions, and urgent events.

3.2 *A guide to* HyTech*-related papers*

The following papers explain the theory behind linear hybrid automata in more detail, provide examples of their use, and discuss HyTech and related tools.

Theory of hybrid automata Hybrid automata are based on timed automata [AD94] and were introduced in [ACHH93]. A related model appeared in the same volume [NOSY93]. Analysis methods included reachability and state-space minimization. The specification language Integrator Computation Tree Logic (ICTL) and a model-checking algorithm were introduced in [AHH93]. Approximations and abstract interpretation strategies for the algorithmic analysis of hybrid automata are discussed in the papers [HRP94, OSY94, HH95c]. The paper [ACH⁺95] provides an overview of the analysis techniques, including approximations. The analysis of nonlinear automata by translations to linear automata is described in [HH95a, HWT95a]. Decidability results appear in [Cer92, ACH93, KPSY93, AD94, MV94, PV94, BER94a, BER94b, BR95, MPS95, Hen95, HHK95, HKPV95]. In particular, [HKPV95] shows that the reachability problem is decidable, and HyTech's analysis terminates, on the class of *rectangular automata*, where all convex predicates are of the form $a \leq x \leq b$ ($a \leq \dot{x} \leq b$).

HYTECH The earliest version of HyTech is mentioned in [AHH93], and performs full model-checking of ICTL formulas. The second generation of HyTech is discussed in [HH95b]. The thesis [Ho95] describes the first two generations of HyTech in more detail, as well as summarizing much of the theory of hybrid automata. The current version of HyTech is described in [HHWT95a]. The full version of this guide appears in [HHWT95b].

Case studies Numerous examples have been analyzed using linear hybrid automata. We mention only the first appearances of examples in the hybrid automata literature. A gas burner is studied in [ACHH93], together with a simple water monitor. The trajectories of a billiard ball, and the temperature of a reactor core are modeled in [NOSY93]. Fischer's timing-based mutual exclusion protocol is considered in [AHH93]. The paper [HH95b] includes a parametric analysis. A simple train-gate controller and a scheduler appear in [AHH93]. A manufacturing robot system and Corbett's distributed control system are also discussed in [HH95b]. The paper [HWT95b] describes the verification (see also [HH95b]) and error analysis of an audio control protocol. The benchmark generic railroad crossing example and an active structure controller are considered in [HHWT95a]. A nonlinear temperature controller appears in [HH95a], and a predator-prey system in [HWT95a].

Related Tools The analysis of linear hybrid automata supported by HyTech is based on symbolic region manipulation techniques first presented for real-time systems [HNSY94]. For the restricted case of real-time systems, these techniques have also been implemented in the tools Kronos [NSY92, DOY94, ACH⁺95, DY95] and Uppaal [LPY95]. Polka [Hal93, HRP94] is a tool for analyzing hybrid systems that concentrates on abstract interpretation strategies.

```
define(raise_rate,9)
define(lower_rate,-9)

automaton gate
synclabs: raise, lower;
initially open & g=90;
loc up: while g<=90 wait {g'=raise_rate}  -- gate is being raised
        -- gate is fully raised
        when g=90 goto open;
        -- selfloops for input enabledness
        when True sync raise goto up;
        when True sync lower goto down ;
loc open: while True wait {g'=0}          -- wait for command
        when True sync raise goto open;
        when True sync lower goto down;
loc down: while g>=0 wait {g'=lower_rate} -- gate is being lowered
        -- gate is fully down
        when g=0 goto closed;
        when True sync lower goto down;
        when True sync raise goto up;
loc closed: while True wait {g'=0}        -- wait for command
        when True sync raise goto up;
        when True sync lower goto closed;
end -- gate
```

FIGURE 4. HyTech input for the gate automaton

4 Input Language: System Description

HyTech's input consists of a text file containing a system description and a list of iterative analysis commands. The language is case-sensitive.

The system description language is a straightforward textual representation of linear hybrid automata. The user describes a system as the composition of a collection of components. Each component is given as a linear hybrid automaton. The system analyzed is taken as the product of all components given.

HyTech first passes its input through the macro preprocessor **m4**, allowing clear definition of constants in the system[3]. For example, we may declare and use the constant *raise_rate* in the gate automaton of Figure 2, as shown in the sample HyTech input appearing in Figure 4. Whitespace (blank spaces, tabs, new lines) between tokens is ignored. The syntax is described in more detail below. The complete grammar appears in [HHWT95b].

Comments The rest of an input line after two adjacent dashes (--) is taken as a comment.

[3]For details of the Unix command **m4**, type **man m4**.

Variables All variables in the system are declared at the top of the description, in a single declaration. Variables may be of the following types: discrete, clock, stopwatch, parameter, analog. The type declarations allow more readable descriptions and enable simple static checking by the parser. A clock variable always has rate 1, and a discrete variable always has rate 0. The rate of a stopwatch must be either 0 or 1. Parameters have rate 0 in all locations, and may never be assigned values. Analog variables have no syntactic restrictions. Variables of type discrete, clock and parameter are said to be *fixed rate* variables, since their rate intervals are fixed by their type, namely 0, 1 and 0 respectively. Constraints on their rates are automatically added to the rate conditions for each location; indeed, it is illegal for the user to constrain explicitly the rate of a fixed rate variable. For example, the variables for the train-gate controller example are declared as

```
var  x,                   -- distance from intersection
     g: analog;           -- angle of gate
     t: stopwatch;        -- controller's timer
                          -- cutoff point for controller
     alpha: parameter;    -- to issue commands
```

Linear terms, expressions and constraints A linear term is either (a) a variable multiplied by a rational coefficient, or (b) a rational number. A linear expression is an additive combination of linear terms. A linear constraint is a non-strict inequality (<=, >=) or equality (=) between linear expressions. Note that rational coefficients must either (a) be an integer, (b) have an integer as numerator and a nonzero integer as denominator, or (c) be omitted, in which case it is understood to be 1. For example, `1/2x - 24/5y <= z + 5t -6 + y` is a syntactically legal linear constraint.

Automaton components Each automaton is given a name which may be used later in the specification. Its synchronization labels are declared. Its initial location and the initial condition on its variables must also be provided. For example, the header for the train automaton is as follows:

```
automaton train
synclabs : app,        -- approach signal
           exit;       -- signal that train is leaving
initially far & x>=2000;
```

Each automaton component includes a list of locations, described below, terminated by the keyword **end**.

Locations Each location is named and labeled with its invariant. Rate conditions may also be provided. The syntax `g' in [10,20]` is shorthand for `g' >= 10 & g' <= 20`. For example, `loc far: while x>=100 wait {x' in [-50,-40]}` is the header for the location *far* with invariant $x \geq 100$, and rate condition $-50 \leq \dot{x} \leq -40$.

Invariants may be conjunctions of linear constraints, such as `x>=1/2 & y<=2/3+x`, but must *not* be disjunctions[4]. Conjunctive rate conditions are separated by commas, as in `wait {x'=z', y' in [2,4]}`.

Each location is associated with a list of transitions originating from it.

Transitions Each transition lists a guard on enablement and the successor location. Both the synchronization label and the assignments are optional. Infinite bounds are expressed as either `-inf` or `inf`. For example, the following are legal transitions.

```
when True goto far;
when x=1 & y<=2 do {} goto far;
when x=0 do {x:=[1,2],g := (-inf,x+3]} sync exit goto far;
when asap sync exit do {y:=[5,inf)} goto far;
```

Again, notice that guards may be conjunctions of linear constraints, but not disjunctions (use multiple transitions). Also, the order of the synchronization information and the assignments is interchangeable, if they appear at all, but the guard must appear first and the successor location last. The ASAP guard on the last transition listed indicates it is an urgent transition which must take place as soon as possible. Recall that there is a syntactic restriction that non-trivial guards are not permitted on urgent transitions or any transitions in other components with the same synchronization label as an urgent transition.

Composition It is assumed that the system being described is the parallel composition of all listed components.

5 Input Language: Analysis Commands

The analysis section of the input consists of two parts: declaration of variables for regions, and a sequence of iterative command statements. Analysis commands provide a means of manipulating and outputting regions. Commands are built using objects of two basic types: *region expressions* for describing regions of interest, and *boolean expressions* used in the control of command statements. Regions may be stored in variables, provided the region variables are declared via a statement such as

```
var
    init_reg, final_reg: region;
```

which declares two region variables called *init_reg* and *final_reg*. HYTECH provides a number of operations for manipulating regions, including computing the reachable set, successor operations, existential quantification, convex hull, and basic boolean operations.

---

[4]In order to model a disjunctive invariant, split the location into several locations, one for each disjunct [AHH93].

```
var
    final_reg, init_reg : region;

init_reg :=    loc[train] = far & x>=2000 & loc[controller] = idle
            & loc[gate] = open & g=90;
final_reg :=     loc[gate] = up & x<=10 | loc[gate]=open & x<=10
            |  loc[gate] = down & x<=10;
print omit all locations
        hide non_parameters in
             reach forward from init_reg endreach & final_reg
        endhide;
```

FIGURE 5. Analysis commands for train-gate controller

For example, the specification commands in Figure 5 are for analyzing the train-gate controller. Their overall effect is to determine the critical bound on the parameter α. First, the two regions *final_reg* and *init_reg* are declared. The first two statements assign values to these regions using direct constraints on the states. Notice that disjunctions may be used. The third statement outputs the constraint on the parameter α under which the system is not correct. This printing command is given by the prefix `print omit all locations`, which tells HYTECH to output the region enclosed between the words `hide` and `endhide`, but only after hiding all information about locations. We choose to omit all location information since for any particular value of α the specific final location reached is irrelevant. HYTECH evaluates the region expression between the hide keywords by first performing reachability analysis from the initial region specified by *init_reg*, intersecting the reachable states with the final region (*final_reg*), and then existentially quantifying out all variables that are not declared as parameters. After 1.72 seconds computation on a Sparcstation 20, HYTECH produces the following output, showing that the system is correct whenever $\alpha < 49/5$.

```
5alpha >= 49
```

5.1 Region expressions

Region expressions are built from linear inequalities, constraints on locations, and region names, by existential quantification, *pre*, *post*, and convex hull operations, reachability, conjunction, and disjunction. Each region expression defines a region. The symbol ⟨*reg_exp*⟩ denotes an arbitrary region expression.

Linear inequalities The most basic region expression is a linear inequality. For example, `x <= 100` is a region expression, defining the set of all states where the variable x has value no greater than 100.

Location constraints `loc[`⟨*aut_name*⟩`] =` ⟨*loc_name*⟩.
The location name ⟨*loc_name*⟩ must be the name of a location in the

automaton ⟨*aut_name*⟩. For example, the region expression `loc[gate] = open` defines the set of all states where the location component corresponding to the gate is *open*.

Boolean combinations ⟨*reg_exp*⟩ `&` ⟨*reg_exp*⟩ , ⟨*reg_exp*⟩ `|` ⟨*reg_exp*⟩
The disjunction of region expressions, written using the operator `|`, is a region expression (representing the union of its operands), as is the conjunction of region expressions (representing the intersection of its operands), written with the operator `&`. The `&` operator has precedence, so that an expression without parentheses is considered to be a disjunction of conjunctions. In addition, the boolean constants `True` and `False` have the expected meaning.

Parentheses Expressions not in conjunctive normal form may be given using parentheses. For example, `x<=4 & (y<=5 | y>=5)` is equivalent to `x<=4`.

Region name A region expression may be any declared region variable. There is no automatic check that the region variable has been assigned a value. The value of the expression is the region most recently assigned to the variable.

Existential quantification `hide` ⟨*var_list*⟩ `in` ⟨*reg_exp*⟩ `endhide`
The `hide` expression evaluates to the region obtained by existentially quantifying a list of variables. For example, the command `print hide x in x<=1 & x=y endhide` outputs the region where $y \leq 1$. In general, quantified variables may be listed, separated by commas, as in `print hide x, z in x<=1 & y<=x+3 & z = y-x endhide`. Alternatively, the list ⟨*var_list*⟩ may be replaced by the keywords `all` (for all variables) or `non_parameters` (for all variables not declared as parameters).

Pre/Post `pre(`⟨*reg_exp*⟩`)`, `post(`⟨*reg_exp*⟩`)`
The `pre` and `post` expressions evaluate to the regions obtained by applying *pre* and *post* respectively to their arguments.

Convex hull `hull(`⟨*reg_exp*⟩`)`
The expression `hull(`⟨*reg_exp*⟩`)` returns the region where each location v is associated with the convex hull of all valuations s for which (v, s) is in the region defined by ⟨*reg_exp*⟩. For example,

```
loc1 := loc[P1]=loc_a & loc[P2]=loc_b_1;
loc2 := loc[P1]=loc_a & loc[P2]=loc_b_2;
approx := hull(loc1 & x=0 | loc1 & x=1 | loc2 & x=1);
```

assigns `approx` the region represented by `loc1&0<=x&x<=1 | loc2&x=1`.

Reachability `reach forward from` ⟨*reg_exp*⟩ `endreach`
`reach backward from` ⟨*reg_exp*⟩ `endreach`
There are two specialized expressions for returning the set of states reachable from any arbitrary region: one for forward reachability and one for

backward reachability. For example, the expression **reach forward from init_reg endreach** appearing in the analysis commands in Figure 5 evaluates to the region reachable from *init_reg* by iterating *post*. The backward reachability expression iterates *pre* until convergence.

5.2 Boolean expressions

Boolean expressions are built from region comparisons and region emptiness checks using boolean operators. Boolean expressions are used in conditional statements and while loops. The symbol ⟨*bool_exp*⟩ denotes an arbitrary boolean expression.

Comparison between regions ⟨*reg_exp*⟩ ⟨*relop*⟩ ⟨*reg_exp*⟩
The relational operator ⟨*relop*⟩ is one of the symbols **<**, **<=**, **=**, **>=**, and **>**, representing the binary set comparison operators $\subset$, $\subseteq$, $=$, $\supseteq$, and $\supset$ respectively. For example, the following are legal boolean expressions.

```
init_reg = final_reg
init_reg >= loc1 & x <= 5
```

Emptiness **empty(**⟨*reg_exp*⟩**)**
The unary predicate **empty** applied to a region expression evaluates to true iff its argument contains no states. For example, the following code could be used to determine whether the system satisfies its safety requirement.

```
reached := reach forward from init_reg endreach;
if empty(reached & final_reg)
   then prints "System verified";
   else prints "System contains violations";
endif;
```

Boolean combinations ⟨*bool_exp*⟩ **and** ⟨*bool_exp*⟩, ⟨*bool_exp*⟩ **or** ⟨*bool_exp*⟩
not ⟨*bool_exp*⟩
Boolean expressions may be combined to yield boolean expressions. The negation of a boolean expression is a boolean expression. For example, **not empty(reached)** is a boolean expression. The conjunction and disjunction of boolean expressions is a boolean expression, with the natural meaning, written using the keywords **and** and **or**. Note that region expressions use the symbols **&** and **|**. Negation has highest priority and conjunctions bind more tightly than disjunctions.

5.3 Command statements

There are commands to perform common tasks such as error-trace generation and parametric analysis. Command statements are built from primitives for printing and assigning regions. Command statements may also occur within conditional statements and while statements. Each command is terminated by a semicolon.

Printing There are four basic commands for outputting information. All output appears on `stdout`.

`print` ⟨*reg_exp*⟩ The basic print command outputs the states in the region defined by its region expression argument. For example, the command `print init_reg` (see Figure 5) would produce the output

```
Location: far.idle.open
g = 90 & x >= 2000
```

The valuations ***associated with*** a location v within a region W are the valuations s such that $(v, s) \in W$. The print command prints out a list of locations and predicates defining the states associated with them. Non-convex predicates are output as disjunctions of convex predicates. Locations for which there are no associated valuations in the region do not appear in the output. The string `far.idle.open` indicates that the valuations satisfying the convex predicate $g = 90 \wedge x \geq 2000$ are associated with the control location where the train component is far from the intersection, the controller component is in its idle location, and the gate component in its open location. Note that location information is printed with periods separating the locations for each component, and that components are listed in the order in which they are declared.

`print omit` ⟨*loc_list*⟩ `locations` ⟨*reg_exp*⟩ This command generalizes the basic print command by first eliminating information about the locations of all components listed after the `omit` keyword. For example, if *strange_reg* is first assigned to

```
init_reg | loc[gate]=closed & 1000<=x & loc[train]=far
```

then `print omit gate, controller locations strange_reg` produces the output

```
Location: far..
x >= 1000
```

indicating that the region given includes only locations in the product automaton for which the train component is in its far location, and that all valuations for which the value of x is greater than or equal to 1000 appear in some such location. The absence of a location name for the second and third component automata indicates that information for these components' locations has been existentially quantified.

As shorthand, the keyword `all` may appear in place of a list of automata names, in which case all location information is quantified out, as in Figure 5.

prints ⟨*string*⟩ This command prints strings, enclosed in double quotes, directly to **stdout**. For example, the statement **prints "Hi there"** outputs the string "**Hi there**" followed by a carriage return.

printsize ⟨*reg_name*⟩ This command prints information about the "size" of the region stored in the region variable given as an argument. Information output includes the number of product locations for which the associated predicate is nonempty and the total number of convex predicates used in representing the region.

Assignment ⟨*reg_name*⟩ := ⟨*reg_exp*⟩
Any region expression may be assigned to any region name. For example, we may initialize the final region with the statement

```
final_reg := x<=10 & (  loc[gate] = up
                      | loc[gate] = open
                      | loc[gate] = down);
```

which is equivalent to the assignment appearing in Figure 5.

Conditional The **if-then** and **if-then-else** statements have the expected meaning. For example, the following are legal conditional statements.

```
if init_reg<=final_reg then prints "Hi"; print strange_reg; endif;
if init_reg=final_reg then prints "Equal";
   else prints "Not equal"; endif;
```

The boolean expression comparing regions is first evaluated, and then the appropriate list of statements (if any) is executed.

Iteration The **while** statement has the expected meaning. For example,

```
reached := init_reg;
old := init_reg;
reached := post(old);
while not ( reached <= old ) do
   old := reached;
   reached := post(reached);
endwhile;
```

computes the set of reachable states from the initial states by iterating the ***post*** operation until a fixpoint is obtained.

Error trace generation **print trace to** ⟨*reg_exp*⟩ **using** ⟨*reg_name*⟩
HyTech provides a simple facility for generating error traces for faulty systems. One must first use the built-in reachability utility (see Subsection 5.1), which causes HyTech to store internal information that can be used to generate traces. Second, the command to generate traces is issued, specifying both the target region of the traces, and the name of the region variable previously used to store the result of the reachability analysis. This is best illustrated by an example. Suppose we are using forward reachability

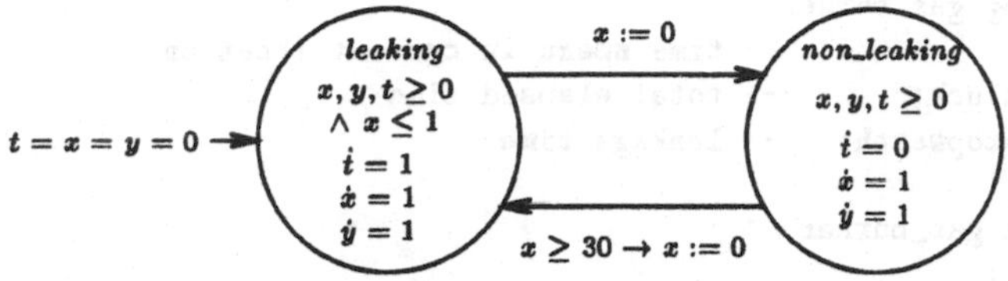

FIGURE 6. Automaton for the leaking gas burner

analysis to see whether any state in the violation region *final_reg* is reachable from the initial region *init_reg*. The following sequence of commands causes HyTech to generate an error trace, if one exists.

```
reached := reach forward from init_reg;
if empty(reached & final_reg)
  then prints "System verified";
  else prints "System contains violations";
       print trace to final_reg using reached;
endif;
```

The trace output consists of regions, *i.e.* sets of states, not individual states. Each region will be accessible from the previous via a time step allowing the continuous variables to evolve, followed by a transition step. The trace generated is minimal in length, and includes the synchronization labels, if any, for transitions between regions along the trace. Regardless of whether forward or backward reachability is used, the trace is always printed in an absolute forward direction.

Note: this command is rather fragile, and should be used with some care. The error trace generation command always assumes—without any automatic checks—that the region variable appearing after the keyword `using` (`reached` in the above example) has been assigned a reachable region using the built-in `reach` expression, and that no `reach` expression has since been evaluated.

6 Examples

Additional examples may be found in the directory `examples` of the software distribution. We discuss two of them here in more detail.

6.1 Gas burner

The "leaking gas burner" example has appeared in the early literature on formal methods applied to hybrid systems [CHR91, ACHH93]. We show how this simple system can be analyzed in HyTech. The gas burner is

```
-- leaking gas burner
var  x,                 -- time spent in current location
     y: clock;          -- total elapsed time
     t: stopwatch;      -- leakage time

automaton gas_burner
synclabs:;
initially leaking & t = 0 & x = 0 & y=0;
loc leaking: while x>=0 & y>=0 & t>=0 & x <=1 wait {t'=1}
   when True do {x:=0} goto not_leaking;
loc not_leaking: while  x>=0 & y>=0 & t>=0  wait {t'=0}
   when x>=30 do {x:=0} goto leaking;
end

var init_reg, final_reg, b_reachable: region;

init_reg := loc[gas_burner] = leaking & x=0 & t=0 & y=0;
final_reg :=  y>=60 & t >= 1/20 y;
b_reachable := reach backward from final_reg endreach;
if empty( b_reachable & init_reg)
  then prints "Non-leaking duration requirement satisfied";
  else prints "Non-leaking duration requirement not satisfied";
endif;
```

FIGURE 7. Input file for the analysis of the gas burner

in one of two modes; it is either leaking or not leaking. Leakages are detected and stopped within 1 second. Furthermore, once a leakage has been stopped, the burner is guaranteed not to leak again until at least 30 seconds later. The system is initially leaking.

The linear hybrid automaton of Figure 6 models the gas burner. The clock x records the time elapsed since last entering the current location, and is sufficient for modeling the behavior of the system. However, in order to analyze the system, we need to add the auxiliary variables t and y. The stopwatch t measures the cumulative leakage time. It increases at rate 1 in the location *leaking*, and at rate 0 in location *non_leaking*. The clock y measures the total elapsed time. Using these auxiliary variables, we prove that if at least 60 seconds have passed, then the burner has been leaking for less than one twentieth of the total elapsed time. The requirement holds unless there is a state, forward reachable from the initial states, in which $y \geq 60$ and $t \geq y/20$. We compute the region backward reachable from all states satisfying $y \geq 60 \wedge t \geq y/20$. Since this region does not include any initial states, the requirement is satisfied. In fact, forward reachability for this system does not terminate. In general, it is not easy to determine ahead of time whether forward or backward reachability analysis is preferable.

The complete input file for this example appears in Figure 7. HyTech outputs the string "Non-leaking duration requirement satisfied". The com-

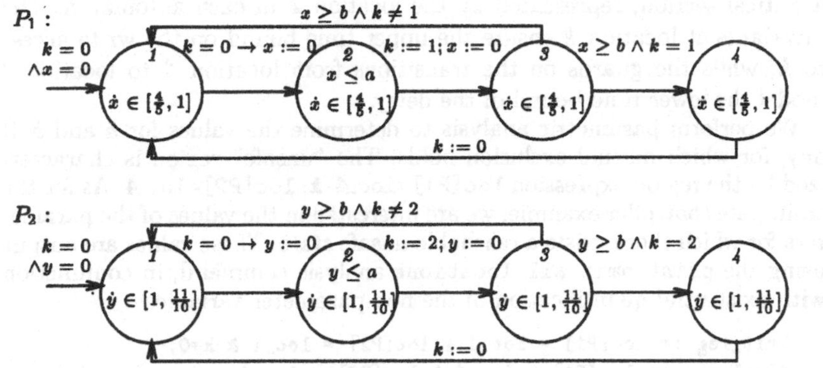

FIGURE 8. Automata for processes P_1 and P_2 in Fischer's mutual exclusion protocol

putation takes 0.62 seconds on a SparcStation 20, using a maximum of 0.73 MB of memory.

6.2 *Fischer's mutual exclusion protocol*

We demonstrate parametric analysis through a drifting clock version of the simple timing-based mutual-exclusion protocol due to Fischer [Lam87, AHH93]. The system consists of two processes, P_1 and P_2, each performing atomic read and write operations on a shared memory variable k. Each process P_i, for $i = 1, 2$, models the following algorithm:

repeat
  repeat
    await $k = 0$; $k := i$; **delay** b
  until $k = i$
  Critical section
  $k := 0$
forever

The instruction **delay** b delays a process for at least b time units as measured by its local clock. Each process uses its own local clock to measure the delay times. Process P_i is allowed to enter its critical section iff $k = i$. Furthermore, each process takes no more than a local time units to write a value into the variable k, *i.e.* the assignment $k := i$ occurs within a time units after the **await** statement completes. To complicate matters, the two processes use drifting clocks. Process P_1's clock is slow, and its rate may vary between 0.8 and 1, while that of P_2 is fast with rate between 1 and 1.1.

The automata for the two processes appear in Figure 8. Each process is modeled using the private clocks x and y, respectively. Each process has a critical section, represented by the location *4* in each automaton. The invariants at location *2* ensure the upper time bound on the write access to k, while the guards on the transitions from location *3* to location *4* model the lower time bound of the delay.

We perform parametric analysis to determine the values for a and b, if any, for which mutual exclusion holds. The "unsafe" region is characterized by the region expression `loc[P1]=loc_4 & loc[P2]=loc_4`. As for the train-gate controller example, we are interested in the values of the parameters for which there exists a reachable unsafe state. These values are output using the `print omit all locations` analysis command, in conjunction with existential quantification of the non-parameter variables:

```
init_reg := loc[P1] = loc_1 & loc[P2] = loc_1 & k=0;
final_reg := loc[P1] = loc_4 & loc[P2] = loc_4 ;
print omit all locations hide non_parameters in
  reach forward from init_reg endreach & final_reg endhide;
```

HyTech's computation takes 3.79 seconds using 1.1 MB of memory, producing the following output, which indicates that the system is correct whenever $a < 8b/11$.

```
11a >= 8b & a >= 0
```

7 Designing Requirement Specifications

It is not always obvious how to specify requirements of systems. This section provides some hints to the verification engineer by outlining how to check for many common classes of requirements. All forms of specifications below rely on the use of reachability analysis.

7.1 Simple safety

A safety requirement intuitively asserts that "nothing bad ever happens". Many specifications are expressed naturally as safety requirements. A system is said to be correct iff its reachable states all satisfy an invariant ϕ, defining a set of safe states: the "bad thing" to happen is to reach a state that does not satisfy the invariant[5]. For example, Fischer's mutual exclusion protocol should guarantee that processes P_1 and P_2 are never in their critical sections at the same time. Also, the train-gate controller is required to ensure that the gate is always down whenever the train is within 10 feet.

As discussed above (Subsection 2.3), safety requirements can be verified in HyTech using the region $\neg\phi$. One method is to perform forward reachability analysis from the system's initial states, and then check whether

[5]The reader familiar with temporal logics should observe that such requirements are expressed in the form $\forall\Box\phi$, meaning intuitively that ϕ is always true for all reachable states of the system.

the intersection with the violating states $\neg\phi$ is empty. Assuming the region *init_reg* has been assigned the set of initial states, and *viol* has been set to the region $\neg\phi$, the following HyTech input checks the safety requirement, and generates an error trace if any exist.

```
f_reachable := reach forward from init_reg endreach;
reached_viol := f_reachable & viol;
if empty(reached_viol)
  then prints "System verified";
  else prints "System not verified";
       prints "The violating states reached are";
       print reached_viol;
       print trace to viol using f_reachable;
endif;
```

Alternatively, the analogous backward reachability analysis can be used.

```
b_reachable := reach backward from viol endreach;
init_reach_viol := b_reachable & init_reg;
if empty(init_reach_viol)
  then prints "System verified";
  else prints "System not verified";
       print trace to viol using b_reachable;
endif;
```

Strict equalities When the invariant ϕ involves non-strict inequalities, it may be impossible to express the violating states $\neg\phi$ using only non-strict inequalities. This problem can be overcome in two different ways. First, if the invariant ϕ itself can be expressed using non-strict inequalities only, HyTech can check directly whether all reachable states satisfy the invariant using the containment operator.

```
if f_reachable <= phi
  then prints "System verified";
  else prints "System contains violations";
endif;
```

Alternatively, one may instead use the set closure $(\neg\phi)^c$ of $\neg\phi$ as the set of violating states, and then check that the only reachable states in $(\neg\phi)^c$ lie in ϕ, or equivalently, lie in the intersection of $(\neg\phi)^c$ and ϕ. For example, consider the task of verifying the gate is always down whenever the train is strictly less than 10 feet away. The invariant ϕ is given as $loc[gate] = down \vee x \geq 10$. Its negation $\neg\phi$ is $loc[gate] \neq down \wedge x < 10$, which is inexpressible using non-strict inequalities only. The following analysis can be used to verify this requirement.

```
cl_neg_phi :=  (loc[gate]=open | loc[gate]=closed | loc[gate]=up)
               & x<=10;
if f_reachable & cl_neg_phi <= x=10
  then prints "System verified";
  else prints "System not verified";
endif;
```

Despite being more complicated, this alternative is often faster than the first, since the <= operator can be expensive when applied to complex expressions.

7.2 Simple possibility

A simple possibility requirement asserts that "something good can always happen." If the notion of "something good" can be expressed as a region expression ϕ, then such requirements maintain that all states forward reachable from the initial states are backward reachable from a state in ϕ.[6] For example, we may wish to prove that for Fischer's mutual exclusion protocol, there is always a possibility that process P_1 will enter its critical section sometime in the future. The following HYTECH code checks this assertion.

```
b_reachable := reach backward from loc[P1] = cs endreach;
f_reachable := reach forward from init_reg endreach;
if f_reachable <= b_reachable
  then prints "Requirement satisfied";
  else prints "Requirement not satisfied";
endif;
```

7.3 Simple real-time and duration requirements

Many simple real-time requirements can be specified by introducing clocks and stopwatches to measure delays between events, or the length of time a particular condition holds. In the gas burner example, we assert that as long as a minute or more has passed, the burner has been leaking no more than 5% of the time. In this case, we introduce a new variable for each time duration of interest. We need to know the total elapsed time and the time spent in location *leaking*. These quantities are measured by the clock y and stopwatch t respectively. The duration requirement we are interested in then becomes the safety requirement where the violating states are given by the predicate $y \geq 60 \wedge t \geq y/20$.

7.4 Additional requirements

By no means do all requirement specifications fall into the categories discussed above. However, a simple technique can be used to reduce many requirements to safety requirements. The idea is to build a separate monitor automaton for the requirement being checked [VW86]. The monitor typically contains special states which are only reachable by violating executions. The monitor must act strictly as an observer of the original system, without changing its behavior. Reachability analysis may then be performed on the parallel composition of the system and the monitor, with the

[6]These requirements are expressed in temporal logics in the form $\forall\Box\exists\Diamond\phi$.

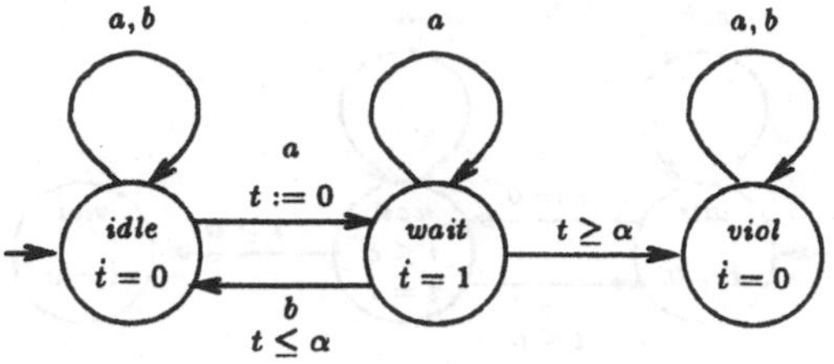

FIGURE 9. Generic bounded-response monitor automaton

system correct iff no violating state in the monitor is reached. To illustrate the technique, we use the category of bounded response requirements.

Bounded response A bounded-response requirement asserts that if something (a trigger event, *a* say) happens, then a response, *b* say, occurs strictly within a certain time limit α.[7] For example, one may assert that every approach of the train is followed by a *raise* command within 10 seconds. To verify these requirements, it is often easiest to introduce a new stopwatch variable, *t* say, and build a monitor process with three locations: *idle*, *wait* and *viol*. Figure 9 depicts a generic automaton for bounded response requirements. Control is initially in the *idle* location. When a trigger event occurs in a non-violating location, control may pass to the *wait* location and the clock *t* is reset. Response events cause control to return to the *idle* location. The unlabeled transition from the *wait* location to *viol* is only enabled when $t \geq \alpha$, *i.e.* time for the response event has passed by. This automaton will reach its violation location iff it is possible for α time units to pass after an *a* event without a *b* event occurring. Therefore, the violation location is not reachable iff every *a* event is followed by a *b* event occurring less than α time units later.

To assert that the response event may occur any time up to and including α time units after the trigger event, we may use the same monitor automaton as above, but checking that the violation location is only ever reached with the value of *t* being α.

Since bounded response requirements occur frequently, we demonstrate how strict bounded response requirements can be verified slightly more efficiently, *i.e.* the response event must occur before the response time — occurring when exactly α time units have passed is not acceptable. The monitor in Figure 10 is slightly more deterministic than that of Figure 9 and will generally lead to a less complex reachable region. Note that the selfloops on the violation location have been omitted. Although this affects the behavior of the system, it does so in a way that has no effect on its correctness, assuming we use forward reachability; once a violation has been

[7] This assertion is denoted $\forall\Box(a \Rightarrow \forall\Diamond_{<\alpha} b)$.

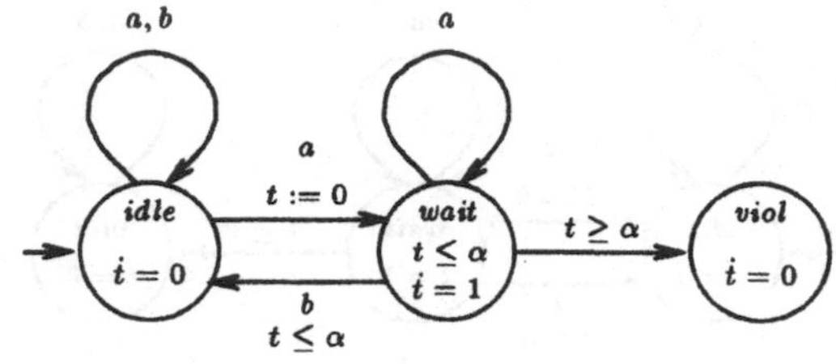

FIGURE 10. Bounded-response monitor automaton — strict bound

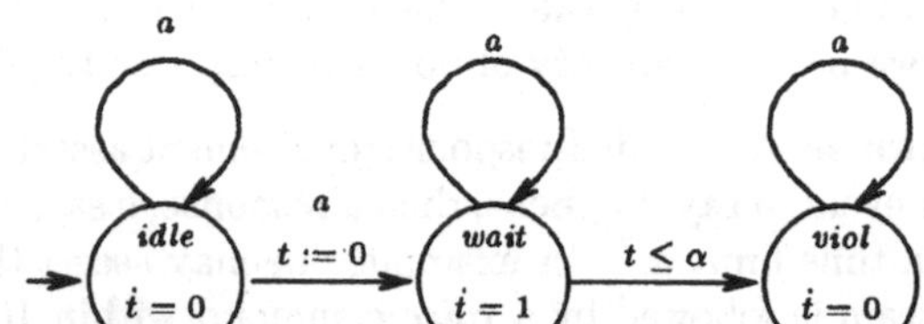

FIGURE 11. Monitor automaton for minimal event-separation time

detected, which additional states are reachable is irrelevant.

Minimal event separation Monitor processes can be built to verify that events occur with some minimal separation time. For example, Figure 11 shows the automaton for verifying that no two instances of the event a occur within α time units of each other.

8 Installing and Running HyTech

8.1 Installation

Currently the executable file is available for the Sun4 architecture only. We plan to have versions available for a variety of platforms, including DEC workstations and PC's. Most jobs we have run require less than 20MB, many less than 10MB. However, obviously, the more memory the better.

The version of HyTech described here was released in August 1995, and is available through anonymous ftp via ftp.cs.cornell.edu in the directory ~pub/tah/HyTech, and through the World-Wide Web via HyTech's home page http://www.cs.cornell.edu/Info/People/tah/hytech.html. Download the file `hytech.tar.Z`. It must be uncompressed to `hytech.tar`, and then expanded using the Unix `tar` command. The following sequence of commands will produce the directory `HyTech`.

```
uncompress hytech.tar.Z
tar -xf hytech.tar
```

The HyTech directory contains the subdirectories `src`, `bin`, `user_guide`, `examples`, and `papers`, containing the source code, executables, a more comprehensive version of this user guide, examples, and many papers on hybrid automata, respectively. The main directory also contains the files `README` and `license`. Please sign a copy of the license and follow the instructions given on the form. Licensed users will be assured of being informed about new releases of the software. We would also appreciate hearing about your experiences with HyTech and the applications you analyze with it.

8.2 *Executing* HyTech

You must have the files `hytech` and `hytech.exe` in your current directory. Assuming your input file is called `a.hy`, the basic command to run HyTech is `hytech a.hy`. The `.hy` suffix on the filename may be omitted. Output appears on `stdout`, so it is usually directed to a file via a command such as `hytech a.hy > a.log`. HyTech creates a temporary file by adding `-temp.hy` to the source filename, *e.g.* for the commands above, the file `a.hy-temp.hy` is temporarily created and then destroyed. Clearly, you should avoid using file names ending in `-temp.hy`.

Options Available options are displayed by executing HyTech with no input file. Options are given in the form -⟨*flag_type*⟩⟨*n*⟩, and must occur before the filename on the command line. The only options so far are for controlling the amount of output generated (`-p0`, `-p1`, and `-p2`, where the higher numbers indicate more verbose output), and the format of the output (`-f0` for conjunctions output along a single line, and `-f1` for conjuncts listed one per line).

Examples Numerous sample input files and their output logs can be found in the subdirectory `examples`. Examine these to familiarize yourself with the input description language. Some of them are discussed in the user guide and [HHWT95a].

Bugs, comments, suggestions Please report any bugs or installation and maintenance problems to hytech@cs.cornell.edu. We do not have the resources to provide commercial-level support, but we can probably help you. We also welcome comments and suggestions, since the experience of HyTech's users will help to improve future versions of the software.

9 Hints for the Efficient Use of HyTech

This section describes hints on how to make the most of HyTech's computational power. If HyTech does not terminate on your input file, and you cannot figure out why, trying these heuristics may well help. Sometimes a slightly modified description will make a tremendous difference. As a general principle, keep your model of the system as simple as possible at first. Once HyTech has successfully analyzed the system, slowly add more detail to your model.

Keep the system description small. Generally, the smaller the better, *i.e.* try to minimize the number of components, locations, and variables. For example, try to model only a small number of the system's components first. Share locations wherever possible, *e.g.* error locations can often be combined into one. Some locations may be eliminated if they are "intermediate" locations not involved in direct synchronization with other components, and time spent in these locations can be transferred to the immediately adjacent locations.

Encode discrete variables into locations. For a bounded discrete variable, it is generally more efficient to split each location into several locations, one for each value of the variable, than to declare the variable as a real-valued variable. However, the increased efficiency often carries the disadvantage of a less compact description.

Manually compose tightly coupled components. When taking the product of two automata, many product locations are irrelevant since they are unreachable. If two components are tightly coupled with synchronized events, the reachable product automaton can be substantially smaller than the complete product. It may be beneficial to input the reachable product of such automata, instead of their components, since this version of HyTech constructs complete products only.

Keep constants simple. Generally, the lower the lcm:gcd ratio of the constants in the system, the faster the reachability analysis. Indeed, lowering the ratio may be necessary for reachability to terminate. To achieve low lcm:gcd ratios, it is often possible to verify an abstracted system where lower bounds are rounded down to smaller constants, and upper bounds are rounded up.

Model urgent events explicitly. If an event is urgent, model this fact directly where possible by using the ASAP guard. This is more efficient than introducing an auxiliary clock.

Exploit "don't care" information. In many locations of an automaton, not all variable values are relevant. However, reachability analysis will record the exact values of such "don't care" variables. Thus to simplify the reachable region, it is helpful to make these variables completely unknown wherever they are irrelevant. This can be achieved by explicitly assigning them into the interval $(-\infty, \infty)$ on all transitions into the appropriate locations. A tempting option is to set them to a particular fixed value while control remains in a given location. However, this strategy is not as beneficial as assigning them into $(-\infty, \infty)$, since there is a nontrivial relationship between them and any other variables as time passes.

Use strong invariants. Sometimes it is helpful to restrict reachability analysis as much as possible through the use of strong invariants. For instance, enforcing implicit invariants can be advantageous, particularly when performing backward reachability analysis. In the gas burner example, backward reachability is required, since forward reachability does not terminate. It would be easy (and natural) to model the system without using the invariants $x \geq 0$, $y \geq 0$, and $t \geq 0$ for the clock and stopwatch variables. These invariants would play no role in forward analysis. However, backward analysis is nonterminating without these invariants, whereas adding them causes termination in seven iterations.

Use the reachability facility provided. It is optimized for its task and faster than writing your own while loops. It also enables error traces to be generated.

Try forward and backward analysis. It is often not easy to predict which direction will terminate faster.

10 References

[ACH93] R. Alur, C. Courcoubetis, and T.A. Henzinger. Computing accumulated delays in real-time systems. In C. Courcoubetis, editor, *CAV 93: Computer-aided Verification*, Lecture Notes in Computer Science 697, pages 181–193. Springer-Verlag, 1993.

[ACH+95] R. Alur, C. Courcoubetis, N. Halbwachs, T.A. Henzinger, P.-H. Ho, X. Nicollin, A. Olivero, J. Sifakis, and S. Yovine. The algorithmic analysis of hybrid systems. *Theoretical Computer Science*, 138:3–34, 1995.

[ACHH93] R. Alur, C. Courcoubetis, T.A. Henzinger, and P.-H. Ho. Hybrid automata: an algorithmic approach to the specification and verification of hybrid systems. In R.L. Grossman, A. Nerode, A.P. Ravn, and H. Rischel, editors, *Hybrid Systems*, Lecture Notes in Computer Science 736, pages 209–229. Springer-Verlag, 1993.

[AD94] R. Alur and D.L. Dill. A theory of timed automata. *Theoretical Computer Science*, 126:183–235, 1994.

[AHH93] R. Alur, T.A. Henzinger, and P.-H. Ho. Automatic symbolic verification of embedded systems. In *Proceedings of the 14th Annual Real-time Systems Symposium*, pages 2–11. IEEE Computer Society Press,

1993. Full version available as Technical Report TR-1492, Department of Computer Science, Cornell University, Ithaca, NY 14853, 1995.

[BER94a] A. Bouajjani, R. Echahed, and R. Robbana. Verification of context-free timed systems using linear hybrid observers. In D.L. Dill, editor, *CAV 94: Computer-aided Verification*, Lecture Notes in Computer Science, pages 118–131. Springer-Verlag, 1994.

[BER94b] A. Bouajjani, R. Echahed, and R. Robbana. Verifying invariance properties of timed systems with duration variables. In H. Langmaack, W.-P. de Roever, and J. Vytopil, editors, *FTRTFT 94: Formal Techniques in Real-time and Fault-tolerant Systems*, Lecture Notes in Computer Science 863, pages 193–210. Springer-Verlag, 1994.

[BR95] A. Bouajjani and R. Robbana. Verifying ω-regular properties for subclasses of linear hybrid systems. In P. Wolper, editor, *CAV 95: Computer-aided Verification*, Lecture Notes in Computer Science 939, pages 437–450. Springer-Verlag, 1995.

[Cer92] K. Cerāns. Decidability of bisimulation equivalence for parallel timer processes. In G. von Bochmann and D.K. Probst, editors, *CAV 92: Computer-aided Verification*, Lecture Notes in Computer Science 663, pages 302–315. Springer-Verlag, 1992.

[CH78] P. Cousot and N. Halbwachs. Automatic discovery of linear restraints among variables of a program. In *Proceedings of the Fifth Annual Symposium on Principles of Programming Languages*. ACM Press, 1978.

[CHR91] Z. Chaochen, C.A.R. Hoare, and A.P. Ravn. A calculus of durations. *Information Processing Letters*, 40(5):269–276, 1991.

[DOY94] C. Daws, A. Olivero, and S. Yovine. Verifying ET-LOTOS programs with KRONOS. In *Proceedings of Seventh International Conference on Formal Description Techniques*, 1994.

[DY95] C. Daws and S. Yovine. Two examples of verification of multirate timed automata with KRONOS. In *Proceedings of the 16th Annual Real-time Systems Symposium*. IEEE Computer Society Press, 1995.

[Hal93] N. Halbwachs. Delay analysis in synchronous programs. In C. Courcoubetis, editor, *CAV 93: Computer-aided Verification*, Lecture Notes in Computer Science 697, pages 333–346. Springer-Verlag, 1993.

[Hen92] T.A. Henzinger. Sooner is safer than later. *Information Processing Letters*, 43:135–141, 1992.

[Hen95] T.A. Henzinger. Hybrid automata with finite bisimulations. In Z. Fülöp and F. Gécseg, editors, *ICALP 95: Automata, Languages, and Programming*, Lecture Notes in Computer Science 944, pages 324–335. Springer-Verlag, 1995.

[HH95a] T.A. Henzinger and P.-H. Ho. Algorithmic analysis of nonlinear hybrid systems. In P. Wolper, editor, *CAV 95: Computer-aided Verification*, Lecture Notes in Computer Science 939, pages 225–238. Springer-Verlag, 1995.

[HH95b] T.A. Henzinger and P.-H. Ho. HyTech: The Cornell Hybrid Technology Tool. In A. Nerode, editor, *Proceedings of the 1994 Workshop on Hybrid Systems and Autonomous Control*, Lecture Notes in Computer Science. Springer-Verlag, 1995.

[HH95c] T.A. Henzinger and P.-H. Ho. A note on abstract-interpretation strategies for hybrid automata. In A. Nerode, editor, *Proceedings of the 1994 Workshop on Hybrid Systems and Autonomous Control*, Lecture Notes in Computer Science. Springer-Verlag, 1995.

[HHK95] M.R. Henzinger, T.A. Henzinger, and P.W. Kopke. Computing simulations on finite and infinite graphs. In *Proceedings of the 36th Annual Symposium on Foundations of Computer Science*. IEEE Computer Society Press, 1995.

[HHWT95a] T. A. Henzinger, P.-H. Ho, and H. Wong-Toi. HyTech: the next generation. In *Proceedings of the 16th Annual Real-time Systems Symposium*. IEEE Computer Society Press, 1995.

[HHWT95b] T. A. Henzinger, P.-H. Ho, and H. Wong-Toi. A user guide to HyTech. Technical Report TR-1532, Department of Computer Science, Cornell University, 1995.

[HKPV95] T.A. Henzinger, P.W. Kopke, A. Puri, and P. Varaiya. What's decidable about hybrid automata? In *Proceedings of the 27th Annual Symposium on Theory of Computing*, pages 373–382. ACM Press, 1995.

[HNSY94] T.A. Henzinger, X. Nicollin, J. Sifakis, and S. Yovine. Symbolic model checking for real-time systems. *Information and Computation*, 111(2):193–244, 1994.

[Ho95] Pei-Hsin Ho. *Automatic Analysis of Hybrid Systems*. PhD thesis, Department of Computer Science, Cornell University, 1995.

[HRP94] N. Halbwachs, P. Raymond, and Y.-E. Proy. Verification of linear hybrid systems by means of convex approximation. In B. LeCharlier, editor, *SAS 94: Static Analysis Symposium*, Lecture Notes in Computer Science 864, pages 223–237. Springer-Verlag, 1994.

[HWT95a] T. A. Henzinger and H. Wong-Toi. Phase portrait approximations of hybrid systems. Submitted, 1995.

[HWT95b] P.-H. Ho and H. Wong-Toi. Automated analysis of an audio control protocol. In P. Wolper, editor, *CAV 95: Computer-aided Verification*, Lecture Notes in Computer Science 939, pages 381–394. Springer-Verlag, 1995.

[KPSY93] Y. Kesten, A. Pnueli, J. Sifakis, and S. Yovine. Integration graphs: a class of decidable hybrid systems. In R.L. Grossman, A. Nerode, A.P. Ravn, and H. Rischel, editors, *Hybrid Systems*, Lecture Notes in Computer Science 736, pages 179–208. Springer-Verlag, 1993.

[Lam87] L. Lamport. A fast mutual exclusion algorithm. *ACM Transactions on Computer Systems*, 5(1):1–11, 1987.

[LPY95] K. G. Larsen, P. Pettersson, and W. Yi. Compositional and symbolic model-checking of real-time systems. In *Proceedings of the 16th Annual Real-time Systems Symposium*. IEEE Computer Society Press, 1995.

[LS85] N. Leveson and J. Stolzy. Analyzing safety and fault tolerance using timed petri nets. In *Proceedings of International Joint Conference on Theory and Practice of Software Development*, Lecture Notes in Computer Science 186, pages 339–355. Springer-Verlag, 1985.

[MPS95] O. Maler, A. Pnueli, and J. Sifakis. On the synthesis of discrete controllers for timed systems. In E.W. Mayr and C. Puech, editors, *STACS 95: Symposium on Theoretical Aspects of Computer Science*, Lecture Notes in Computer Science 900, pages 229–242. Springer-Verlag, 1995.

[MV94] J. McManis and P. Varaiya. Suspension automata: a decidable class of hybrid automata. In D.L. Dill, editor, *CAV 94: Computer-aided Verification*, Lecture Notes in Computer Science 818, pages 105–117. Springer-Verlag, 1994.

[NOSY93] X. Nicollin, A. Olivero, J. Sifakis, and S. Yovine. An approach to the description and analysis of hybrid systems. In R.L. Grossman, A. Nerode, A.P. Ravn, and H. Rischel, editors, *Hybrid Systems*, Lecture Notes in Computer Science 736, pages 149–178. Springer-Verlag, 1993.

[NSY92] X. Nicollin, J. Sifakis, and S. Yovine. Compiling real-time specifications into extended automata. *IEEE Transactions on Software Engineering*, SE-18(9):794–804, 1992.

[OSY94] A. Olivero, J. Sifakis, and S. Yovine. Using abstractions for the verification of linear hybrid systems. In D.L. Dill, editor, *CAV 94: Computer-aided Verification*, Lecture Notes in Computer Science 818, pages 81–94. Springer-Verlag, 1994.

[PV94] A. Puri and P. Varaiya. Decidability of hybrid systems with rectangular differential inclusions. In D.L. Dill, editor, *CAV 94: Computer-aided Verification*, Lecture Notes in Computer Science 818, pages 95–104. Springer-Verlag, 1994.

[VW86] M.Y. Vardi and P. Wolper. An automata-theoretic approach to automatic program verification. In *Proceedings of the First Annual Symposium on Logic in Computer Science*, pages 322–331. IEEE Computer Society Press, 1986.

Modal μ-Calculus, Model Checking and Gauß Elimination

Angelika Mader *†

ABSTRACT In this paper we present a novel approach for solving Boolean equation systems with nested minimal and maximal fixpoints. The method works by successively eliminating variables and reducing a Boolean equation system similar to Gauß elimination for linear equation systems. It does not require backtracking techniques. Within one framework we suggest a global and a local algorithm. In the context of model checking in the modal μ-calculus the local algorithm is related to the tableau methods, but has a better worst case complexity.

1 Introduction

The modal μ-calculus [Koz83, Sti92] is a powerful logic. It is particularly useful for expressing properties of parallel processes with finite (or even infinite) state spaces; it finds application in process algebra [Wal89] and in Petri nets [Bra92]. Proving whether a property expressed in the modal μ-calculus holds for particular states of a process is called model checking [CE81, CES86]. Various algorithms are available. The main approaches are model checkers based on the fixpoint approximation [EmL86, CDS92, And92, BCMDH92, LBCJM94] and tableau based model checkers [StW89, Cle90, Lar92, Mad92]. One important technique consists of the transformation of a property and a model to a (Boolean) equation system [AC88, And92, CDS92, Lar92, VeL92]. Then model checking is equivalent to the computation of a certain fixpoint. In fact, various correctness problems may be represented in this way.

In this paper we present a novel, algebraic approach for solving Boolean equation systems. It does not use approximation techniques and therefore does not require backtracking. The method works straightforward by successively eliminating variables and reducing the Boolean equation system,

*Institut für Informatik, Technische Universität München, Arcisstr.21, D-80333 München, Germany, email: mader@informatik.tu-muenchen.de.

†Supported by Siemens AG, Corporate Research and Development, and a grant from the Hochschulsonderprogramm II.

similar to Gauß elimination for linear equation systems. Homogeneous, hierarchical and alternating fixpoints are treated uniformly. Contrary to other techniques Gauß elimination leads to both a global and a local model checking algorithm within one framework.
The elimination of a variable is based on a simple observation: the equation $X = A(X)$ (with monotone A) has the least fixpoint A(false) and the greatest fixpoint A(true). The reduction of a Boolean equation system is done by syntactical substitution of variables by expressions.
The difference between the global version of Gauß elimination and the local one can be characterized as follows: The global version solves the whole equation system, whereas the local version only takes a subset of equations into account which is necessary to determine the variable of interest. The selection of a suitable subset of equations is demand-driven. Whereas the global version is more of theoretical interest (approximation techniques have better worst case complexity), the local version has advantages in the context of model checking. It is closely related to the tableau methods, and can be interpreted as a combination of top-down strategy of the tableau method and bottom-up evaluation which avoids redundancy caused by recomputation of subtableaux. Therefore its worst case complexity is only exponential, in contrast to double exponential worst case of tableau based algorithms.
Section 2 introduces Boolean equation systems and their solution. Gauß elimination for Boolean equation systems is presented in section 3. Section 4 contains a short introduction into the modal μ-calculus, and the transformation of the model checking problem into a equation solving problem. Comparison with other work is discussed in section 5. Examples are in section 6. Section 7 is the conclusion. The appendix contains correctness proofs.

2 Boolean Equation Systems

In this section we define Boolean equation systems and what we regard as solution of a Boolean equation system.

Definition 1 *Let $\mathcal{X} = \{X_1, \ldots, X_n\}$ be a set of Boolean variables, $<$ a linear order on $\mathcal{X}$, and $\{A_1, \ldots, A_n\}$ a set of negation free Boolean expressions containing variables from $\mathcal{X}$. Then the set of labeled equations $E_i : X_i \stackrel{\sigma_i}{=} A_i$, where $\sigma_i \in \{\mu, \nu\}$, is a Boolean equation system.*

In the following we assume that the order on the variables is according to their indices.
As the Boolean expressions are negation free and therefore monotone the equation system (the plain one without order and labels) has a set of fixpoints. In the context here we are interested in a distinguished fixpoint

which we call the solution of the Boolean equation system. Below we give the definition of the solution.
We introduce some notation first. The vector $(X_1,\ldots,X_n)$ of Boolean variables will be abbreviated by $\underline{X}$; analogously $\underline{\sigma}$, $\underline{A}$ and $\underline{E}$ denote the vectors of labels, expressions and equations respectively. A Boolean equation system can now be written as: $\underline{E}$: $\underline{X} \stackrel{\underline{\sigma}}{=} \underline{A}(\underline{X})$. Further abbreviations will be used. $\underline{Y}^{(i)}$ stands for the i-th rest $(Y_i,\ldots Y_n)$ of the Boolean vector $\underline{Y}$, and again analogously $\underline{\sigma}^{(i)}$, $\underline{A}^{(i)}$, and $\underline{E}^{(i)}$ denote the i-the rests of the related vectors. By $\underline{E}^{(i)}[Y_j/X_j]$ we mean the equation system $\underline{E}^{(i)}$ where all *unbound* occurrences of X_j are substituted by Y_j. $\underline{E}^{(i)}[\underline{Y}/\underline{X}]$ is an abbreviation for $\underline{E}^{(i)}[Y_1/X_1,\ldots,Y_n/X_n]$.
Let $<_\sigma$ on $\mathbf{B}$ for $\sigma \in \{\mu,\nu\}$ be such that $\mathsf{false} <_\mu \mathsf{true}$ and $\mathsf{true} <_\nu \mathsf{false}$.

Definition 2 *Let $\underline{Y},\underline{Y}' \in \mathbf{B}^n$, $\underline{\sigma} \in \{\mu,\nu\}^n$. The vectors $\underline{Y},\underline{Y}'$ are ordered lexicographically, $\underline{Y} <_{\underline{\sigma}} \underline{Y}'$, iff $\exists i, 1 \le i \le n : Y_i <_{\sigma_i} Y_i'$ and $\forall j, 1 \le j < i : Y_j = Y_j'$.*

Definition 3 *$\underline{Y}^{(i)} \in \mathbf{B}^{n-i+1}$ is the solution of the Boolean equation system $\underline{E}^{(i)}[Y/X]$, iff for $i = n$ $\underline{Y}^{(i)}$ is wrt. $<_{\sigma_n}$ the least fixpoint of $\underline{E}^{(i)}[Y/X]$, and for $i < n$ $\underline{Y}^{(i)}$ is wrt. $<_{\underline{\sigma}^{(i)}}$ the least one of those fixpoints of $\underline{E}^{(i)}[Y/X]$ which satisfy the following property: $\underline{Y}^{(i+1)}$ is solution of $\underline{E}^{(i+1)}[Y/X]$.*

There exist several algorithms to determine the set of fixpoints of a Boolean equation system; for examples see [Rud74]. However, even if the set of fixpoints is given, it is not trivial to select the one fixpoint which satisfies the definition of the solution above. This indicates that the existing equation solving methods do not help in our case. We will illustrate this by two small examples.
The first example shows that the solution is not the lexicographic least fixpoint. The equation system $X_2 \stackrel{\mu}{=} X_2$ has two fixpoints true and false. With respect to the order $<_\mu$ false is the least one. Now consider the equation system $X_1 \stackrel{\nu}{=} X_2, X_2 \stackrel{\mu}{=} X_2$, where $X_1 < X_2$. The lexicographic least fixpoint is $(\mathsf{true},\mathsf{true})$, whereas $(\mathsf{false},\mathsf{false})$ is the solution as indicated by the first equation system and as defined above.
In the following example two Boolean equation systems are given, both having the same set of fixpoints and the same labels on the equations, but different solutions. The equation system $X_1 \stackrel{\nu}{=} X_2, X_2 \stackrel{\mu}{=} X_2$, where $X_1 < X_2$, has the fixpoints $(\mathsf{true},\mathsf{true})$ and $(\mathsf{false},\mathsf{false})$. The solution is $(\mathsf{false},\mathsf{false})$ as in the previous example.
The equation system $X_1 \stackrel{\nu}{=} X_2, X_2 \stackrel{\mu}{=} X_1$, where $X_1 < X_2$, also has the fixpoints $(\mathsf{true},\mathsf{true})$ and $(\mathsf{false},\mathsf{false})$, but the solution here is $(\mathsf{true},\mathsf{true})$.

3 Gauß Elimination

In this section we present two algorithms which determine the solution of a Boolean equation system as in definition 3. In contrast to other methods we do not make use of approximation and backtracking techniques. Instead we stepwise reduce a Boolean equation system to a Boolean equation systemconsisting one equation and one variable less. The steps of eliminating a variable from an expression and of substituting variables by expressions remind very much to Gauß elimination for linear equation systems.
The following propositions are the basis for the Gauß elimination. Proofs are contained in the appendix.

Proposition 1 *For the solution Y of the equation system $X \stackrel{\sigma}{=} A(X)$ consisting of one single equation it holds:*

$$Y = \begin{cases} A(\mathsf{false}) & \text{if } \sigma = \mu \\ A(\mathsf{true}) & \text{if } \sigma = \nu. \end{cases}$$

Proposition 1 can be extended to expressions and equation systems. It allows a representation of the Boolean expression A_i with no occurrence of X_i. In the algorithm we will call this the Gauß division step.

Proposition 2 *$\underline{Y}$ is the solution of the Boolean equation system $\underline{E}$ of the form $\underline{X} \stackrel{\underline{\sigma}}{=} \underline{A}(\underline{X})$, iff $\underline{Y}$ also is the solution of the modified Boolean equation system $\underline{F}$, where the equations are of the following form:*

$$\begin{array}{lcl} X_1 & \stackrel{\sigma_1}{=} & A_1(X_1, \quad \ldots \quad, X_n) \\ \vdots & & \\ X_i & \stackrel{\sigma_i}{=} & A_i(X_1, \ldots, X_{i-1}, \mathsf{b}_i, X_{i+1}, \ldots, X_n) \\ \vdots & & \\ X_n & \stackrel{\sigma_n}{=} & A_n(X_1, \quad \ldots \quad, X_n) \end{array}$$

$$\text{where } \mathsf{b}_i = \begin{cases} \mathsf{true} & \text{if } \sigma_i = \nu \\ \mathsf{false} & \text{if } \sigma_i = \mu \end{cases} \quad \text{for } 1 \le i \le n.$$

The next proposition shows that an occurrence of a variable X_j in an expression A_i may be substituted by the expression A_j, if $i < j$. This is the basis for the Gauß elimination step.

Proposition 3 *The Boolean vector $\underline{Y}$ is the solution of the equation system $\underline{E}$, iff it is the solution of the equation system $\underline{G}$, where $\underline{G}$ is the modified equation system:*

$$\begin{array}{lcl} X_1 & \stackrel{\sigma_1}{=} & A_1(X_1, \quad \ldots \quad, X_n) \\ \vdots & & \\ X_i & \stackrel{\sigma_i}{=} & A_i(X_1, \ldots, X_{j-1}, A_j(X_1, \ldots, X_n), X_{j+1}, \ldots, X_n) \\ \vdots & & \\ X_n & \stackrel{\sigma_n}{=} & A_n(X_1, \quad \ldots \quad, X_n) \end{array}$$

$$where\ 1 \leq i < j \leq n.$$

Based on these two Gauß steps we now propose two algorithms to determine the solution of a Boolean equation system. One algorithm operates on the whole equation system; this is the global version of Gauß elimination. The basic idea is that a Boolean equation system can be reduced to a Boolean equation system with the same solution, but one equation less. The reduction is performed by an elimination step, where in the last equation, say $X_j \stackrel{\sigma_j}{=} A_j(X_1, \ldots, X_j)$, all occurrences of X_j on the right hand side are instantiated by $\mathsf{b}_j = \mathsf{true}$ or $\mathsf{b}_j = \mathsf{false}$ depending on σ_j, and a substitution step, where in all other equations each occurrence of X_j is substituted by the expression $A_j(X_1, \ldots, X_{j-1}, \mathsf{b}_j)$. The result is an equation system with no free occurrence of X_j. Now the same reduction can be applied to the equation system consisting of the first $j-1$ equations and so on. In the end we get a variable free expression for the variable X_1.

Assume $\underline{X} \stackrel{\underline{\sigma}}{=} \underline{A}(\underline{X})$ as input;
i := n;
while not (A_1 = true **or** A_1 = false)
do
Instantiate X_i in A_i to {true, false}; (Gauß-division)
Substitute A_i for X_i in $A_1, \ldots, A_{i-1}$; (Elimination step)
A_1:=Eval(A_1); ... ; A_{i-1}:=Eval(A_{i-1}) (Evaluation step)
i := i - 1;
od

FIGURE 1. Global Version of Gauß Elimination

In most contexts we are only interested in the first component of the solution, i.e. whether X_1 is true or false. Therefore the algorithm in figure 1 stops, if the solution of X_1 (A_1) is determined. If we are interested in the whole solution the Gauß division step and elimination step have to be applied n times giving an expression for every X_i where the variables $X_i, \ldots, X_n$ do not occur. A straight backward substitution leads to the whole solution.

If only the first variable is of interest, it suffices to consider only the subset of equations which is necessary to determine the solution for X_1. The relevant subset of equations is selected in a top-down manner. This observation leads to the local version of Gauß elimination given in figure 2. The idea is as follows. We start with the equation system $\underline{E}'$ consisting only of the equation $X_1 \stackrel{\sigma_1}{=} A_1(X_1, \ldots, X_j)$. As long as X_1 is not evaluated to true or false we select a free variable from A_1, insert its equation in $\underline{E}'$, apply the

Create E_1 and let E_1 be $\underline{E}'$;
Instantiate X_1 in A_1; (Gauß-division)
$A_1 := \text{Eval}(A_1)$; (Evaluation step)
while not (A_1 = true **or** A_1 = false)
  do
    Select X_j, where j is such that $E_j \notin \underline{E}'$;
    Create E_j, insert E_j in $\underline{E}'$
      and extend the order on $\underline{E}'$ to E_j;
    Apply Gauß-elimination on $\underline{E}'$
  od

FIGURE 2. Local Model Checking Algorithm

global version of Gauß elimination, and continue in the same way with the modified equation system $\underline{E}'$.

4 The Modal μ-Calculus and Model Checking

This section gives a brief introduction to the modal μ-calculus. For details see [Sti92].
The syntax of the modal μ-calculus is defined with respect to a set $\mathcal{Q}$ of atomic propositions including true and false, a denumerable set $\mathcal{Z}$ of propositional variables and a finite set $\mathcal{L}$ of action labels. The set μM of modal μ-calculus assertions is determined by the following grammar:

$$\Phi ::= Z \mid Q \mid \Phi \wedge \Phi \mid \Phi \vee \Phi \mid [a]\Phi \mid \langle a\rangle\Phi \mid \mu Z.\Phi \mid \nu Z.\Phi$$

M denotes the set of variable and fixpoint free assertions, i.e., the expressions of the **propositional modal logic**, Π_0 denotes the set of fixpoint free assertions, $M \subset \Pi_0$. In the following an expression of the form $\sigma Z.\Phi$, where $\sigma \in \{\mu, \nu\}$, is called a **fixpoint expression**. Formulae of the modal μ-calculus with the set $\mathcal{L}$ of action labels are interpreted relative to a **labeled transition system** $\mathcal{T} = (\mathcal{S}, \{\xrightarrow{a} \mid a \in \mathcal{L}\})$, where $\mathcal{S}$ is a finite set of states and $\xrightarrow{a} \subseteq \mathcal{S} \times \mathcal{S}$ for every $a \in \mathcal{L}$ is a binary relation on states. A **valuation function** $\mathcal{V}$ assigns to every propositional variable Z and atomic proposition Q a set of states $\mathcal{V}(Z) \subseteq \mathcal{S}$ and $\mathcal{V}(Q) \subseteq \mathcal{S}$. Let V[S'/Z] be the valuation such that V[S'/Z](Z) = S', and otherwise as V. The pair $\mathcal{T}$ and $\mathcal{V}$ is called a **model** of the μ-calculus. The semantics of each μ-calculus formula Φ is the set of states $\|\Phi\|^{\mathcal{T}}_{\mathcal{V}}$ defined inductively as follows:

$$\begin{aligned}
\|Z\|_{\mathcal{V}}^{\mathcal{T}} &= \mathcal{V}(Z)\\
\|Q\|_{\mathcal{V}}^{\mathcal{T}} &= \mathcal{V}(Q)\\
\|\Phi_1 \vee \Phi_2\|_{\mathcal{V}}^{\mathcal{T}} &= \|\Phi_1\|_{\mathcal{V}}^{\mathcal{T}} \cup \|\Phi_2\|_{\mathcal{V}}^{\mathcal{T}}\\
\|\Phi_1 \wedge \Phi_2\|_{\mathcal{V}}^{\mathcal{T}} &= \|\Phi_1\|_{\mathcal{V}}^{\mathcal{T}} \cap \|\Phi_2\|_{\mathcal{V}}^{\mathcal{T}}\\
\|[a]\Phi\|_{\mathcal{V}}^{\mathcal{T}} &= [\![a]\!]^{\mathcal{T}}\ \|\Phi\|_{\mathcal{V}}^{\mathcal{T}}, \text{where } [\![a]\!]^{\mathcal{T}}S' = \{s \mid \forall s' \in S.\ \text{if } s \xrightarrow{a} s' \text{then } s' \in S'\}\\
\|\langle a\rangle\Phi\|_{\mathcal{V}}^{\mathcal{T}} &= \langle\!\langle a\rangle\!\rangle^{\mathcal{T}}\ \|\Phi\|_{\mathcal{V}}^{\mathcal{T}},\ \text{where } \langle\!\langle a\rangle\!\rangle^{\mathcal{T}}S' = \{s \mid \exists s' \in S'.s \xrightarrow{a} s'\}\\
\|\mu Z.\Phi\|_{\mathcal{V}}^{\mathcal{T}} &= \bigcap\{S' \subseteq S \mid \|\Phi\|_{\mathcal{V}[S'/Z]}^{\mathcal{T}} \subseteq S'\}\\
\|\nu Z.\Phi\|_{\mathcal{V}}^{\mathcal{T}} &= \bigcup\{S' \subseteq S \mid S' \subseteq \|\Phi\|_{\mathcal{V}[S'/Z]}^{\mathcal{T}}\}
\end{aligned}$$

Given a model $\mathcal{M} = (\mathcal{T}, \mathcal{V})$ model checking is to examine the question whether a certain expression Φ holds for the initial state $s \in S$ of the transition system $\mathcal{T}$, i.e., whether $s \in \|\Phi\|_{\mathcal{V}}^{\mathcal{T}}$. We transform the model checking problem into the problem of solving a Boolean equation system. This was already done by several authors, e.g. see [AC88, And92, Lar92, ClS91, CDS92, VeL92]. In contrary to their approaches here arbitrary negation free expressions are considered as right hand sides of the equations (no restriction to simple expressions). Furthermore we create one Boolean equation system for the whole problem with a partial order defined on its variables and equations.

Roughly the transformation is performed by the following steps: a fixpoint expression can be represented by an equation system with an additional ordering on the equations. On the semantic part we interpret the equation system with respect to a model, i.e., a fixpoint equation of modal logic becomes a fixpoint equation over the powerset of a state space. An isomorphic representation of a powerset of states is a Boolean vector space. This allows us to derive a Boolean equation system from the original fixpoint expression and its model.

A modal μ-calculus formula can be represented as an ordered equation system. For example the fixpoint expression $\nu Z_1.[a]\mu Z_2.[b]((Z_1 \wedge Q) \vee Z_2)$ is equivalent to the equation system $\mathcal{E}$: $Z_1 \stackrel{\nu}{=} [a]Z_2$, $Z_2 \stackrel{\mu}{=} [b]((Z_1 \wedge Q) \vee Z_2)$, where the variables are ordered by $Z_1 < Z_2$. Note that in general here the order on the variables is a partial order in contrast to the variable ordering as in definition 1.

The transformation is as follows: Recall that M is the set of variable and fixpoint free expressions of the modal μ-calculus, i.e., the expressions of the propositional modal logic. The equivalence classes of M together with the implication ordering form a lattice $(M/\Leftrightarrow, \Rightarrow)$. The powerset of the state space $\mathcal{S} = \{s_1, \ldots, s_n\}$ with the inclusion order forms a complete lattice $(\mathcal{P}(\mathcal{S}), \subseteq)$. The evaluation function $\|\ \|_{\mathcal{V}}^{\mathcal{T}} : M \to \mathcal{P}(\mathcal{S})$ is monotone

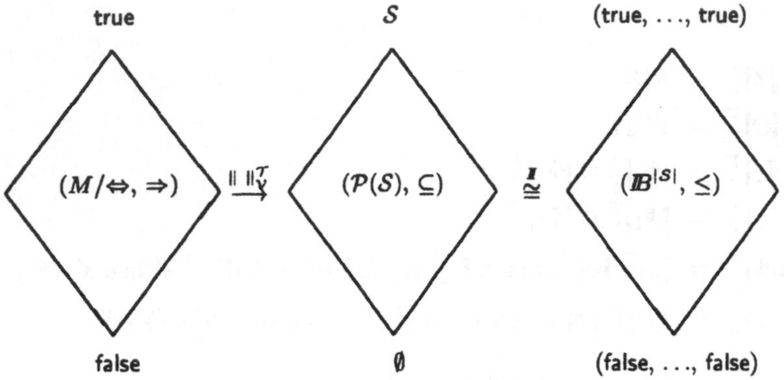

FIGURE 3. The lattices and the mappings

(and continuous). The extension of the evaluation function from M to fixpoint equations over M maps modal operators $[a], \langle a \rangle$ to set operators $[\![a]\!]^{\mathcal{T}}, \langle\!\langle a \rangle\!\rangle^{\mathcal{T}}$, modal variables to set variables and the logical operators $\wedge, \vee$ to the set operators $\cap, \cup$. Thus we get an equation system over the powerset of the state space. The labels $\{\nu, \mu\}$ and the partial order on the equations remain the same as in the original equation system. Defining **false** $\leq$ **true** the Boolean lattice $(\mathbb{B}^{|S|}, \leq^{|S|})$ with pointwise ordering is isomorphic to $(\mathcal{P}(S), \subseteq)$. The last step leads from a vector valued equation system in $\mathbf{B}^n$ to a Boolean equation system; every vector equation is split into n equations and the operators $[\![a]\!]^{\mathcal{T}}, \langle\!\langle a \rangle\!\rangle^{\mathcal{T}}$ are evaluated.
Altogether a μ-calculus equation $Z \stackrel{\sigma}{=} \Phi$ is mapped inductively to the (not ordered) set of n Boolean equations $\quad \mathbf{I}_Z(s_i) \stackrel{\sigma}{=} \mathbf{I}_\Phi(s_i) \quad$ for $1 \leq i \leq n$, where

$$
\begin{aligned}
\mathbf{I}_Q(s) &= \textsf{true}, \text{ if } s \in \|Q\|^{\mathcal{T}}_{\mathcal{V}} \\
\mathbf{I}_Q(s) &= \textsf{false}, \text{ if } s \notin \|Q\|^{\mathcal{T}}_{\mathcal{V}} \\
\mathbf{I}_Z(s) &= X_{Z,s} \\
\mathbf{I}_{\Phi_1 \wedge \Phi_2}(s) &= \mathbf{I}_{\Phi_1}(s) \wedge \mathbf{I}_{\Phi_2}(s) \\
\mathbf{I}_{\Phi_1 \vee \Phi_2}(s) &= \mathbf{I}_{\Phi_1}(s) \vee \mathbf{I}_{\Phi_2}(s) \\
\mathbf{I}_{[a]\Phi}(s) &= \bigwedge_{s \xrightarrow{a} s'} \mathbf{I}_\Phi(s') \\
\mathbf{I}_{\langle a \rangle\Phi}(s) &= \bigvee_{s \xrightarrow{a} s'} \mathbf{I}_\Phi(s')
\end{aligned}
$$

Note that the Boolean equations derived in this way do not contain negations or modal operators. A μ-calculus equation system of the size k deter-

mines a Boolean equation system of size $k * |S|$. There is a partial order on the Boolean equations inherited from the partial order on the μ-calculus equations. Two Boolean equations derived from one vector equation are not ordered. Thus the tree-like order on the set equations becomes an acyclic order on the Boolean equations.
We now show that the two algorithms proposed in the previous section can be applied to the Boolean equation systems derived from a modal μ-calculus equation system and a model. There are remaining two open questions: first, whether the partial order on the Boolean equations here matches the linear order on the Boolean equations and variables as in definition 1, and second, whether the solution of a Boolean equation system coincides with the semantics of the modal μ-calculus.

Proposition 4 *Given a μ-calculus expression and a transition system let $\underline{A}$ be the corresponding Boolean equation system. On its equations a partial order $<_\mathcal{E}$ is defined. For each two extensions of $<_\mathcal{E}$ to linear orders $<_l, <_{l'}$ it holds: $\underline{Y}$ is the solution of $\underline{A}$ with the order $<_l$, iff $\underline{Y}$ is the solution of $\underline{A}$ with the order $<_{l'}$.*

Proof: (Sketch) For unnested fixpoints an order of equations is not relevant for the solution (see [Bek84]). The order of the nested fixpoints is preserved by each extension of the partial order $<_\mathcal{E}$ to a linear order. □

Proposition 5 *Given a fixpoint expression Φ of the modal μ-calculus and a transition system $\mathcal{T}$ with the initial state s, let $\underline{A}$ be the corresponding Boolean equation system. For the solution $\underline{Y}$ of $\underline{A}$ holds: $Y_{\Phi,s} =$ true, iff Φ holds at s.*

Proof: It is easy to see that the algorithm of Emerson and Lei [EmL86] calculates the solution as in Definition 2. □

5 Comparison to Other Work and Complexity

The model checking problem encoded as equation system was already treated by several authors [AC88, And92, CDS92, Lar92]. The method presented here differs from these approaches. Roughly speaking, the difference is that they get the solution by approximating sets. This approach was introduced by Emerson and Lei [EmL86] and continued for example by Cleaveland, Dreimüller and Steffen [CDS92]. In [And92] Andersen gives an algorithm based on Boolean equations. However, by representing a Boolean equation system as a graph his basic algorithm applies only for unnested fixpoints. The extension of the global version of his algorithm to the full calculus is due to the fixpoint approximation technique of Emerson and Lei. Also Larsen's algorithm [Lar92] deals with unnested fixpoints.

The Gauß elimination for model checking in its local version is more closely related to the tableau method of Stirling and Walker [StW89] and Cleaveland [Cle90]. In a Boolean equation system a variable is introduced for each pair of a state and a fixpoint formula. Each node in a tableau is labeled by a sequent consisting of a pair of a state and a formula. Hence a Boolean equation can be seen like a reduced form of a subtableau containing only sequents with fixpoint formulae, which is the only relevant part for the structure of the tableau. The top-down construction of the tableau can also be found in the local version of the Gauß elimination. While constructing a tableau the decision which path should be extended is equivalent to the selection of a variable from the top equation and creating the related equation. The condition for a leaf in the tableau of being successful or not corresponds to the Gauß division step: a cycle with a minimal fixpoint is regarded as unsuccessful (false), a cycle with a maximal fixpoint is regarded as successful (true). The advantage of the Gauß elimination over the tableau method has its roots in the bottom-up evaluation. On one hand it spares the introduction of different constants for the same fixpoint expression, on the other hand there is no redundant evaluation of identical subexpressions (subtrees). Altogether the local version of the Gauß elimination for model checking can be regarded as a combination of the top-down strategy of the tableau allowing to explore only the relevant part of the state space, and a bottom-up strategy which avoids recomputation of identical subtrees. The maximal size of a tableau is bounded by $O(b^{(|\Phi|*|S|)^{f(\Phi)}})$, where b is the maximal branching degree of the transition system, $|S|$ the number of states, $|\Phi|$ the size of the formula and $f(\Phi)$ the number of fixpoint operators in Φ. For the Gauß elimination the number of derived equations is determined by the size of the state space and the number of fixpoint operators in Φ. Substituting Boolean expressions leads to expressions exponential in the number of equations. The maximal size of the Boolean equation system constructed by the Gauß elimination is bound by $O((b^{a(\Phi)} * |\Phi|)^2 * 2^{|S|*f(\Phi)})$, where additional to the abbreviations above $a(\Phi)$ is the maximal nesting depth of modal operators in the formula Φ. Hence it is a natural idea to use the local version of the Gauß elimination for an implementation of the tableau method.

6 Examples

The aim of this section is to demonstrate the possible advantage of the local version of Gauß elimination over a tableau based model checker.
The first both examples are academic ones, without a special meaning. They do not show the advantage of local model checking, because the whole state space has to be traversed. However, they show how our algorithm avoids recomputation of subexpressions, or subtrees resp., whereas

the tableau method does not.
In the third example we prove a fairness property for the mutual exclusion algorithm of Peterson.
A prototype of the local version of Gauß elimination was implemented in C++ using BDDs [Bry92] as data structure for Boolean expressions. In the examples here we compared our implementation with a tableau-based model checker as in [StW89] and with the tableau-based model checker incorporated in the Concurrency Workbench (CWB), which uses techniques for avoiding some recomputations. All implementations run on a SUN SPARC2.
We wish to determine whether $s1 \models_{\mathcal{M}} \nu X.[a]\langle b\rangle X$ (every a-successor has a b-successor and this recursively) holds in the transition system given in figure 4

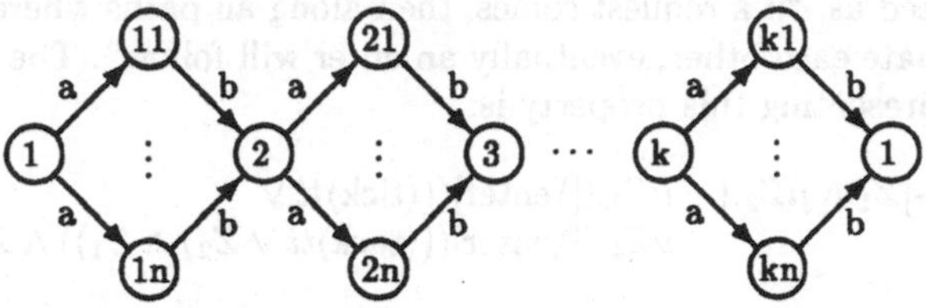

FIGURE 4. example: scalable transition system

The example consists of a scalable (n, k)-spindle where the final state is again identified with the start state. It has $kn + k$ states.
The local Gauß elimination creates k equations, each of the form: $X_i \stackrel{\nu}{=} \bigwedge_{j=1..n} X_{i+1 \ mod \ k}$ for $1 \leq i \leq k$ which can be reduced to $X_i \stackrel{\nu}{=} X_{i+1 \ mod \ k}$. It takes k elimination steps to determine the solution. The tableau based model checker as in [StW89] builds a tree with $1 + 2n + 2n^2 + \ldots + 2n^k$ sequents. For this property the number of equations is thus linear in the variable k of the (n, k)-spindle, whereas the size of the tableau is exponential in the variable k.
Does the following $s1 \models_{\mathcal{M}} \nu Z_1.\langle a\rangle\mu Z_2.\langle a\rangle\langle a\rangle Z_2 \vee \langle a\rangle\langle a\rangle Z_1$ hold in (all transitions labeled with a):
This property was proved by our new local model checker with the following results: It created 6 equations and took one second time for the whole procedure. The tableau based model checker was interrupted after having generated more than 22 million (!) tableau sequents.
The model checker of the Concurrency Workbench could cope well with both examples: it "quickly" returned the result. The techniques for avoiding recomputation came in useful. This was not the case in the following example.
We considered the two process mutual exclusion algorithm of Peterson,

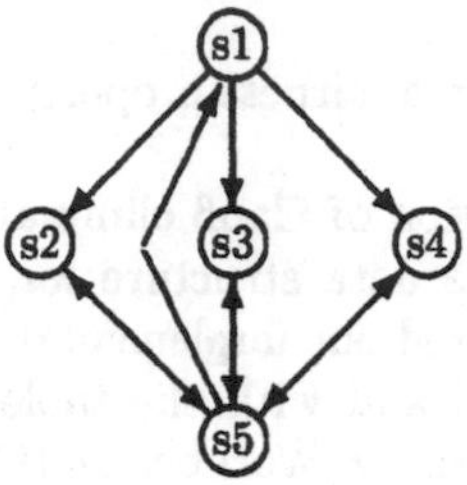

FIGURE 5. example: transition system

given in [Wal89]. The property we proved is: "As long as process 1 proceeds, after a request it eventually enters the critical section." In order to detect progress we added "tick" and "tack" dummy actions which alternate each other when process 1 performs some action. Then the property to prove can be formulated as: "if a request comes, then along all paths where ticks and tacks alternate each other, eventually an enter will follow". The μ-calculus formula representing this property is:

$$\nu Z_1.([-]Z_1 \wedge \mu Z_2.(\quad \nu Z_3.([\backslash\text{enter}]((\langle\text{tick}\rangle tt \vee \\ \nu Z_4.([\backslash\text{enter}]((\langle\text{tack}\rangle tt \vee Z_2) \wedge Z_4)) \wedge Z_3)))))$$

This modal μ-calculus formula is of alternation depth 2 and nesting depth 3. Unfortunately the full discussion of this example exceeds the aim of the paper.

This property, together with our extended Peterson-2 algorithm, was fed to the model checker, with the following result: The model checker came back with a positive result after slightly more than 10 minutes of CPU time. The CWB model checker on the other hand could not compute an answer for the same input within 24 hours elapsed time. During execution our model checker created 156 out of a possible 240 Boolean equations. This example is typical of the results we got from an extensive investigation into several mutual exclusion algorithms with different liveness properties.

7 Conclusion

We presented a novel, algebraic approach for solving Boolean equation systems. As main application model checking in the full modal μ-calculus was intended. In contrast to other approaches using equation systems our method is not based on approximation techniques and backtracking. The method works straightforward by successively eliminating variables and reducing the Boolean equation system, similar to Gauß elimination for linear equation systems. Homogeneous, hierarchical and alternating fixpoints are treated uniformly. Contrary to other techniques Gauß elimination leads to

both a global and a local model checking algorithm within one framework. The local version is closely related to the tableau methods, but has a better worst case complexity. An extension to model checking for infinite state spaces is in work.
There exists a prototype implementation of the Gauß elimination using BDDs for the representation of Boolean expressions. Several examples (e.g. fairness properties for mutex algorithms) showed that the local version of our algorithm beats existing tableau methods.

Acknowledgments
Frank Wallner implemented the local version of the algorithm. The examples were elaborated together with Dieter Barnard. I thank Javier Esparza, Astrid Kiehn, Bernhard Steffen, Bart Vergauwen and Frank Wallner for proof reading and helpful comments.

8 References

[And92] H. Andersen. Model Checking and Boolean Graphs. In *Proc. of ESOP'92*, LNCS 582, 1992.

[AC88] A. Arnold, P. Crubille. A Linear Algorithm to Solve Fixed-Point Equations on Transition Systems. *Information Processing Letters*, vol. 29, 57-66, 1988.

[BCMDH92] J.R. Burch and E.M. Clarke and K.L. McMillan and D.L. Dill and L.J. Hwang. Symbolic Model Checking: 10^{20} States and Beyond. *Information and Computation*, Vol. 98, pp. 142-170, 1992.

[Bek84] H. Bekic. Definable operations in general algebras, and the theory of automata and flow charts. In C.B.Jones, editor, *Hans Bekic: Programming Languages and Their Definition*, LNCS 177, 1984.

[Bra92] J. Bradfield. *Verifying Temporal Properties of Systems.* Birkhäuser,1992.

[BS91] J. Bradfield, C. Stirling. Verifying Temporal Properties of Processes. *Proc. of CONCUR'90*, LNCS 458, 1991.

[Bry92] R.E. Bryant. Symbolic Boolean Manipulation with Ordered Binary-Decision Diagrams. *ACM Computing Surveys*, Vol. 24, No. 3, September 1992.

[CE81] E. M. Clarke and E. A. Emerson. Design and synthesis of synchronization skeletons using branching time temporal logics. In LNCS 131, pp.52-71, 1981.

[CES86] E. M. Clarke, E. A. Emerson and A. P. Sistla. Automatic verification of finite-state concurrent systems using temporal logic specifications. In *ACM Trans. on Programming Languages and Systems 8* , pp. 244-263, 1986.

[Cle90] R. Cleaveland. Tableau-based model checking in the propositional mu-calculus. *Acta Informatica*, Vol. 27, pp. 725-747, 1990.

[ClS91] R. Cleaveland and B. Steffen. A Linear-Time Model Checking Algorithm for the Alternation-Free Modal Mu-Calculus. In *Proc. of CAV'91*, LNCS 575, 1992.

[CDS92] R. Cleaveland, M. Dreimüller and B. Steffen. Faster Model Checking for the Modal Mu-Calculus. In *Proc. of CAV'92*, LNCS 663, 1993.

[EmL86] E.A. Emerson and C.-L. Lei. Efficient model checking in fragments of the propositional mu-calculus. In *Proc. of LICS'86*, Computer Society Press, 1986.

[Koz83] D. Kozen. Results on the Propositional μ-Calculus. *TCS*, Vol. 27, 1983, pp. 333-354.

[Lar92] K. Larsen. Efficient Local Correctness Checking. In *Proc. of CAV'92*, LNCS 663, 1993.

[LBCJM94] D. E. Long, A. Browne, E. M. Clarke, S. Jha, W. R. Marrero. An improved algorithm for the evaluation of fixpoint expressions. In *Proc. of CAV'94*, LNCS 818, 1994.

[Mad92] A. Mader. Tableau Recycling. In *Proc. of CAV'92*, LNCS 663, 1993.

[Rud74] S. Rudeanu. *Boolean Functions and Equations*. North-Holland Publishing Company, 1974.

[Sti92] C. Stirling. Modal and Temporal Logics. In *Handbook of Logic in Computer Science*, Oxford University Press, 1992.

[StW89] C. Stirling and D. Walker. Local model checking in the modal mu-calculus. In *Proc. of TAPSOFT'89*, LNCS 351, 1989.

[Tar55] A. Tarski. A Lattice Theoretical Fixpoint Theorem and its Applications. In *Pacific Journal of Mathematics*, 5, 1955.

[VeL92] B. Vergauwen and J. Lewi A linear algorithm for solving fixed-point equations on transition systems. In *Proc. of CAAP'92*, LNCS 581, 1992.

[Wal89] D. Walker. *Automated Analysis of Mutual Exclusion Algorithms using CCS.* Technical Report ECS-LFCS-89-91, University of Edinburgh, 1991.

[Xin92] Liu Xinxin. *Specification and Decomposition in Concurrency.* PhD Thesis, Aalborg University Center, Denmark, 1992.

1 Appendix: Proofs

Proposition 1 *For the solution Y of the equation system* $X \stackrel{\sigma}{=} A(X)$ *consisting of one single equation it holds:*

$$Y = \begin{cases} A(\mathsf{false}) & \text{if } \sigma = \mu \\ A(\mathsf{true}) & \text{if } \sigma = \nu \end{cases}$$

Proof: The essential idea is, that there exist only three different monotone Boolean functions in one variable: the both constant functions *true* and *false* and the identity.
For $\sigma = \mu$ there are three cases:

1) $A(X) = \mathsf{true}$, i.e. the evaluation of the expression A is independent of the valuation of the free variable X. Then the solution is $Y = \mathsf{true}$.
2) $A(X) = \mathsf{false}$, i.e. the evaluation of the expression A is independent of the valuation of the free variable X. Then the solution is $Y = \mathsf{false}$.
3) In the remaining case because of monotonicity of $A(X)$ the following holds: $A(\mathsf{false}) = \mathsf{false}$ and $Y = \mathsf{false}$ is the solution.

Analogously it holds $Y = A(\mathsf{true})$ that is the solution of $X \stackrel{\nu}{=} A(X)$. □

Often the solution of $X \stackrel{\sigma}{=} A(X)$ will be denoted by the expression $\sigma X.A(X)$.

Proposition 2 $\underline{Y}$ *is the solution of the Boolean equation system* $\underline{E}$ *of the form* $\underline{X} \stackrel{\underline{\sigma}}{=} \underline{A}(\underline{X})$, *iff* $\underline{Y}$ *also is the solution of the modified Boolean equation system* $\underline{F}$, *where the equations are of the following form:*

$$\begin{array}{lcl} X_1 & \stackrel{\sigma_1}{=} & A_1(X_1, \quad \ldots \quad, X_n) \\ \vdots & & \\ X_i & \stackrel{\sigma_i}{=} & A_i(X_1, \ldots, X_{i-1}, \mathsf{b}_i, X_{i+1}, \ldots, X_n) \\ \vdots & & \\ X_n & \stackrel{\sigma_n}{=} & A_n(X_1, \quad \ldots \quad, X_n) \end{array}$$

$$\text{where } \mathsf{b}_i = \begin{cases} \mathsf{true} & \text{if } \sigma_i = \nu \\ \mathsf{false} & \text{if } \sigma_i = \mu \end{cases} \quad \text{for } 1 \le i \le n.$$

Proof: First we show, that for $1 \leq k \leq n$ every fixpoint of $\underline{F}^{(k)}$ is also a fixpoint of $\underline{E}^{(k)}$. Let $\underline{Z}^{(k)}$ be a fixpoint of $\underline{F}^{(k)}$. Then $\underline{Z}^{(k)}$ fulfills all equations $Z_j = A_j(Z_1, \ldots, Z_n)$ for $j \neq i$. For Z_i holds $Z_i = A_i(Z_1, \ldots, Z_{i-1}, \mathsf{b}_i, Z_{i+1}, \ldots, Z_n)$. The question now is whether $Z_i = A_i(Z_1, \ldots, Z_n)$.

(1) $Z_i = \mathsf{b}_i$. Then the equality holds obviously.

(2) $Z_i \neq \mathsf{b}_i$. Then, because of monotonicity of A_i, $A_i(Z_1, \ldots, Z_{i-1}, X_i, Z_{i+1}, \ldots, Z_n)$ is independent of X_i and the equality holds.

Now the proof is done by induction.
Let $\underline{Z}^{(j)}$ be the solution of $\underline{F}^{(j)}[\underline{Y}/\underline{X}]$, and $\underline{W}^{(j)}$ the solution of $\underline{E}^{(j)}[\underline{Y}/\underline{X}]$.
induction basis:

$i \neq n$ Then $\underline{F}^{(n)}[\underline{Y}/\underline{X}]$ and $\underline{E}^{(n)}[\underline{Y}/\underline{X}]$ are identical and obviously $\underline{Z}^{(n)} = \underline{W}^{(n)}$.

$i = n$ Then $\underline{Z}^{(n)} = \underline{W}^{(n)}$ because of proposition 1.

induction hypothesis: $\underline{E}^{(j+1)}[Y/X]$ and $\underline{F}^{(j+1)}[Y/X]$ have the same solution for all $\underline{Y}$.

induction step: We know

(1) $\underline{Z}^{(j)}$ is fixpoint of $\underline{E}^{(j)}[Y_1/X_1, \ldots, Y_{j-1}/X_{j-1}]$.

(2) $\underline{Z}^{(j+1)}$ is the solution of $\underline{F}^{(j)}[Y_1/X_1, \ldots, Y_{j-1}/X_{j-1}, Z_j/X_j]$.

(3) $\underline{Z}^{(j+1)}$ is the solution of $\underline{E}^{(j)}[Y_1/X_1, \ldots, Y_{j-1}/X_{j-1}, Z_j/X_j]$ (induction hypothesis).

From (1) and (3) and the definition of the solution follows, that
(*) $\underline{W}^{(j)} \leq_{\underline{\sigma}^{(j)}} \underline{Z}^{(j)}$.
If $\underline{W}^{(j)}$ is also a fixpoint of $\underline{F}^{(j)}[\underline{Y}/\underline{X}]$ then also $\underline{Z}^{(j)} \leq_{\underline{\sigma}^{(j)}} \underline{W}^{(j)}$, and the solutions must be identical (induction hypothesis and definition of the solution).
If $i \neq j$ then $\underline{W}^{(j)}$ fulfills the first equation of $\underline{F}^{(j)}[\underline{Y}/\underline{X}]$ and by induction hypothesis we know, that $\underline{W}^{(j+1)}$ is the solution of $\underline{F}^{(j+1)}[Y_1/X_1, \ldots, Y_{j-1}/X_{j-1}, W_j/X_j]$. Hence $\underline{W}^{(j)}$ is a fixpoint of $\underline{F}^{(j)}[\underline{Y}/\underline{X}]$.
If $i = j$ we have to show, that for $W_j' := A_j(Y_1, \ldots, Y_{j-1}, \mathsf{b}_j, W_{j+1}, \ldots, W_n)$ holds $W_j = W_j'$. Because of monotonicity we know: $W_j' \leq_{\sigma_j} W_j$. If $W_j = W_j'$ we are done, so assume $W_j' <_{\sigma_j} W_j$. But by (*) we know that $W_j \leq_{\sigma_j} Z_j$ and from $W_j' <_{\sigma_j} W_j$ we can conclude that $W_j = Z_j$. By induction hypothesis we know then, that $\underline{W}^{(j)} = \underline{Z}^{(j)}$. □

Proposition 3 *The Boolean vector $\underline{Y}$ is the solution of the equation system $\underline{E}$, iff it is the solution of the equation system $\underline{G}$, where $\underline{G}$ is the modified equation system:*

$$\begin{array}{lcl} X_1 & \stackrel{\sigma_1}{=} & A_1(X_1, \quad \ldots \quad, X_n) \\ \vdots & & \\ X_i & \stackrel{\sigma_i}{=} & A_i(X_1, \ldots, X_{j-1}, A_j(X_1, \ldots, X_n), X_{j+1}, \ldots, X_n) \\ \vdots & & \\ X_n & \stackrel{\sigma_n}{=} & A_n(X_1, \quad \ldots \quad, X_n) \end{array}$$

where $1 \leq i < j \leq n$.

Proof: For $1 \leq k \leq n$ let $\underline{Z}^{(k)}$ be the solution of $\underline{G}^{(k)}[\underline{Y}/\underline{X}]$, and $\underline{W}^{(k)}$ be the solution of $\underline{E}^{(k)}[\underline{Y}/\underline{X}]$.

(1) Every fixpoint of $\underline{E}^{(k)}[\underline{Y}/\underline{X}]$ is also a fixpoint of $\underline{G}^{(k)}[\underline{Y}/\underline{X}]$.

(2) Every fixpoint of $\underline{G}^{(k)}[\underline{Y}/\underline{X}]$ is also a fixpoint of $\underline{E}^{(k)}[\underline{Y}/\underline{X}]$. Note, that this property does not hold for $j < i$. In this case it does not hold in general, that $Y_j = A_j(Y_1, \ldots, Y_{k-1}, Z_k, \ldots, Z_n)$.

(3) Proof by induction:

induction basis: $\underline{G}^{(n)}[\underline{Y}/\underline{X}]$ and $\underline{E}^{(n)}[\underline{Y}/\underline{X}]$ have the same solution for all $\underline{Y}$.

induction hypothesis: $\underline{G}^{(k+1)}[\underline{Y}/\underline{X}]$ and $\underline{E}^{(k+1)}[\underline{Y}/\underline{X}]$ have the same solution for all $\underline{Y}$.

induction step: from (1), (2), the induction hypothesis and the definition of the solution follows, that $\underline{E}^{(k)}[\underline{Y}/\underline{X}]$ and $\underline{G}^{(k)}[\underline{Y}/\underline{X}]$ have the same solution for all $\underline{Y}$.

□

Mona: Monadic Second-Order Logic in Practice

**Jesper G. Henriksen*
Jakob Jensen*
Michael Jørgensen*
Nils Klarlund†
Robert Paige‡
Theis Rauhe*
Anders Sandholm***

ABSTRACT [1] The purpose of this article is to introduce Monadic Second-order Logic as a practical means of specifying regularity. The logic is a highly succinct alternative to the use of regular expressions. We have built a tool MONA, which acts as a decision procedure and as a translator to finite-state automata. The tool is based on new algorithms for minimizing finite-state automata that use binary decision diagrams (BDDs) to represent transition functions in compressed form. A byproduct of this work is an algorithm that matches the time but improves the space of Sieling and Wegener's algorithm to reduce OBDDs in linear time.

The potential applications are numerous. We discuss text processing, Boolean circuits, and distributed systems. Our main example is an automatic proof of properties for the "Dining Philosophers with Encyclopedia" example by Kurshan and MacMillan. We establish these properties for the parameterized case *without* the use of induction.

Our results show that, contrary to common beliefs, high computational complexity may be a desired feature of a specification formalism.

*BRICS, Centre of the Danish National Research Foundation for Basic Research in Computer Science, Department of Computer Science, University of Aarhus.

†The corresponding author is Nils Klarlund, who is with BRICS, Department of Computer Science, University of Aarhus, Ny Munkegade, DK-8000 Aarhus C. E-mail: klarlund@daimi.aau.dk.

‡Department of Computer Science, CIMS, New York University, 251 Mercer St. New York, New York, USA; research partially supported by ONR grant N00014-93-1-0924, AFOSR grant AFOSR-91-0308, and NSF grant MIP-9300210.

[1]This article is a heavily revised version of [JJK94].

1 Introduction

In computer science, ***regularity*** amounts to the concept that a class of structures is recognized by a finite-state device. Often phenomena are so complicated that their regularity either

- may be overlooked, as in the case of parameterized verification of distributed finite-state systems with a regular communication topology; or

- may not be exploited, as in the case when a search pattern in a text editor is known to be regular, but in practice inexpressible as a regular expression.

In this paper we argue that the ***Monadic Second-Order Logic*** or ***M2L*** can help in practice to identify and to use regularity. In M2L, one can directly mention positions and subsets of positions in the string. This feature distinguishes the logic from regular expressions or automata. Together with quantification and Boolean connectives, an extraordinary succinct formalism arises.

Although it has been known for thirty-five years that M2L defines regular languages (see [Tho90]), the translator from formulas to automata that we describe in this article appears to be one of the first implementations.

The reason such projects have not been pursued may be the staggering theoretical lower-bound: any decision procedure is bound to sometimes require as much time as a stack of exponentials that has height proportional to the length of the formula.

It is often believed that the lower the computational complexity of a formalism is, the more useful it may be in practice. We want to counter such beliefs in this article — at least for logics on finite strings.

1.1 Why use logic?

Some simple finite-state languages easily described in English call for convoluted regular expressions. For example, the language L_{2a2b} of all strings over $\Sigma = \{a, b, c\}$ containing at least two occurrences of a *and* at least two occurrences of b seems to require a voluminous expression, such as

$$\begin{array}{ll} & \Sigma^* a\Sigma^* a\Sigma^* b\Sigma^* b\Sigma^* \\ \cup & \Sigma^* a\Sigma^* b\Sigma^* a\Sigma^* b\Sigma^* \\ \cup & \Sigma^* a\Sigma^* b\Sigma^* b\Sigma^* a\Sigma^* \\ \cup & \Sigma^* b\Sigma^* b\Sigma^* a\Sigma^* a\Sigma^* \\ \cup & \Sigma^* b\Sigma^* a\Sigma^* b\Sigma^* a\Sigma^* \\ \cup & \Sigma^* b\Sigma^* a\Sigma^* a\Sigma^* b\Sigma^*. \end{array}$$

If we added $\cap$ to the operators for forming regular expressions, then the language L_{2a2b} could be expressed more concisely as $(\Sigma^* a\Sigma^* a\Sigma^*)\cap(\Sigma^* b\Sigma^* b\Sigma^*)$.

Even with this extended set of operators, it is often more convenient to express regular languages in terms of positions and corresponding letters. For example, to express the set $L_{\mathbf{aafterb}}$ of strings in which every b is followed by an a, we would like a formal language allowing us to write something like

> "for every position p, if there is a b in p then for some position q after p, there is an a in q."

The extended regular languages do not seem to allow an expression that very closely reflects this description — although upon some reflection a small regular expression can be found. But in M2L we can express $L_{\mathbf{aafterb}}$ by a formula

$$\forall p : 'b'(p) \Rightarrow \exists q : p < q \land 'a'(q)$$

(Here the predicate $'b'(p)$ means "there is a b in position p".) In general, we believe that many errors can be avoided if logic is used when the description in English does not lend itself to a direct translation into regular expressions or automata. However, the logic can easily be combined with other methods of specifying regularity since almost any such formalism can be translated with only a linear blow-up into M2L.

Often regularity is identified by means of ***projections***. For example, if L_{trans} is regular on a cross-product alphabet $\Sigma \times \Sigma$ (e.g. describing a parameterized transition relation, see Section 5) and L_{start} is a regular language on Σ describing a set of start strings, then the set of strings that can be reached by a transition from a start string is $\pi_2(L_{trans} \cap \pi_1^{-1}(L_{start}))$, where π_1 and π_2 are the projections from $(\Sigma \times \Sigma)^*$ to the first and second component. Such language-theoretic operations can be very elegantly expressed in M2L.

1.2 Our results

In this article, we discuss applications of M2L to text processesing and the description of parameterized Boolean circuits. Our principal application is a new proof technique for establishing properties about parameterized, distributed finite-state systems with regular communication topology. We illustrate our method by showing safety and liveness properties for a nontrivial version of the Dining Philosophers' problem as proposed in [KM89] by Kurshan and MacMillan.

We present MONA, which is our tool that translates formulas in M2L to finite-state machines. We show how BDDs can be used to overcome an otherwise inherent problem of exponential explosion. Our minimization algorithm works very fast in practice thanks to a simple generalization of the unary apply operation of BDDs.

1.3 Comparisons to other work

Parameterized circuits are described using BDDs in [GF93]. This method relies on formulating inductive steps as finite-state devices and does not provide a single specification language. The work in [RS93] is closer in spirit to our method in that languages of finite strings are used although not as part of a logical framework. In [BSV93], another approach is given based on iterating abstractions. The parameterized Dining Philosopher's problem is solved in [KM89] by a finite-state induction principle.

A tool for M2L on finite, binary trees has been developed at the University of Kiel [Ste93]. Apparently, this tool has only been used for very simple examples.

In [CR94], a programming language for finite domains based on a fixed point logic is described and used for verification of non-parameterized finite systems.

1.4 Contents

In Section 2, we explain the syntax and semantics of M2L on strings. We recall the correspondence to automata theory in Section 3. We give several applications of M2L and the tool in Section 4: text patterns, parameterized circuits, and equivalence testing. Our main example of parameterized verification is discussed in Section 5. We give an overview of our implementation in Section 6.

2 The Monadic Second-order Logic on Strings

Let Σ be an alphabet and let w be a string over Σ. The semantics of the logic determines whether a closed M2L formula ϕ holds on w. The language $L(\phi)$ denoted by ϕ is the set of strings that make ϕ hold. Assume now that w has length n and consists of letters $a_0 a_1 ... a_{n-1}$. The ***positions*** in w are then $0,...,n-1$. We can now describe the three syntactic categories of M2L on strings.

A ***position term*** t is either

- the constant 0 (which denotes the position 0);
- the constant \$ (which denotes the last position, i.e. $n-1$);
- a position variable p (which denotes a position i);
- of the form $t \oplus i$ (which denotes the position $j + i \bmod n$, where j is the interpretation of t); or
- of the form $t \ominus i$ (which denotes the position $j - i \bmod n$, where j is the interpretation of t);

(Position terms are only interpreted for non-empty strings).
A ***position set term*** T is either

- the constant $\emptyset$ (which denotes the empty set);
- the constant **all** (which denotes the set $\{0, ..., n-1\}$);
- a position set variable P (which denotes a subset of positions);
- of the form $T_1 \cup T_2$, $T_1 \cap T_2$, or $\complement T_1$ (which are interpreted in the natural way);
- of the form $T+i$ (which denotes the set of positions in T shifted right by an amount of i); or
- of the form $T-i$ (which denotes the set of positions in T shifted left by an amount of i);

A ***formula*** ϕ is either of the form

- $'a'(t)$ (which holds if letter a_i in $w = a_0 a_1 \cdots$ is a, where i is the interpretation of t);
- $t_1 = t_2$, $t_1 < t_2$ or $t_1 \leq t_2$ (which are interpreted in the natural way);
- $T_1 = T_2$, $T_1 \subseteq T_2$, or $t \in T$ (which are interpreted in the natural way);
- $\neg\phi_1$, $\phi_1 \wedge \phi_2$, $\phi_1 \vee \phi_2$, $\phi_1 \Rightarrow \phi_2$, or $\phi_1 \Leftrightarrow \phi_2$ (where ϕ_1 and ϕ_2 are formulas, and which are interpreted in the natural way);
- $\exists p : \phi$ (which is true, if there is a position i such that ϕ holds when i is substituted for p);
- $\forall p : \phi$ (which is true, if for all positions i, ϕ holds when i is substituted for p);
- $\exists P : \phi$ (which is true, if there is a subset of positions I such that ϕ holds when I is substituted for P); or
- $\forall P : \phi$ (which is true, if for all subsets of positions I, ϕ holds when I is substituted for P);

3 From M2L to Automata

In this section, we recall the method for translating a formula in M2L to an equivalent finite-state automaton (see [Tho90] for more details). Note that any formula ϕ can be interpreted, given a string w and a ***value assignment*** $\mathcal{I}$ that fixes values of the free variables. If ϕ then holds, we write $w, \mathcal{I} \models \phi$. The key idea is that a value assignment and the string may be described together as a word over an extended alphabet consisting of Σ and extra binary tracks, one for each variable. By structural induction, we then define for each formula an automaton that exactly recognizes the words in the extended alphabet corresponding to pairs consisting of a string and an assignment that satisfy the formula.

Example

Assume that the free variables are $\mathcal{P} = \{P_1, P_2\}$ and that $\Sigma = \{a, b\}$. Let us consider the string $w = abaa$ and value assignment

$$\mathcal{I} = [P_1 \mapsto \{0,2\}, P_2 \mapsto \emptyset].$$

The set $\mathcal{I}(P_1) = \{0,2\}$ can be represented by the bit pattern 1010, since the numbered sequence

$$\underset{0}{1}\;\underset{1}{0}\;\underset{2}{1}\;\underset{3}{0}$$

defines that 0 is in the set (the bit in position 0 is 1), 1 is not in the set (the bit in position 1 is 0), etc. Similarly, the bit pattern 0000 describes $\mathcal{I}(P_2) = \emptyset$.

If these patterns are laid down as extra "tracks" along w, we obtain an *extended word* α, which may be depicted as:

a	b	a	a
1	0	1	0
0	0	0	0

Technically, we define $\alpha = \alpha_0 \cdots \alpha_3$ as the word $(a,1,0)(b,0,0)(a,1,0)$ $(a,0,0)$ over the alphabet $\Sigma \times \mathbb{B} \times \mathbb{B}$ of *extended letters*, where $\mathbb{B} = \{0,1\}$ is the set of truth values.

This correspondence can be generalized to any w and any value assignment for a set of variables $\mathcal{P}$ (which can all be assumed to be second-order).

By structural induction on formulas, we construct automata $A^{\phi,\mathcal{P}}$ over alphabet $\Sigma \times \mathbb{B}^k$—where $\mathcal{P} = \{P_1, \cdots, P_k\}$ is any set of variables containing the free variables in ϕ—satisfying the *fundamental correspondence*:

$$w, \mathcal{I} \models \phi \text{ iff } (w, \mathcal{I}) \in L(A^{\phi,\mathcal{P}})$$

Thus $A^{\phi,\mathcal{P}}$ accepts exactly the pairs $(w, \mathcal{I})$ that make ϕ true.

Example

Let ϕ be the formula $P_i = P_j + 1$. Thus when ϕ holds, P_i is represented by the same bit pattern as that of P_j but shifted right by one position. This can be expressed by the automaton $A^{\phi,\mathcal{P}}$:

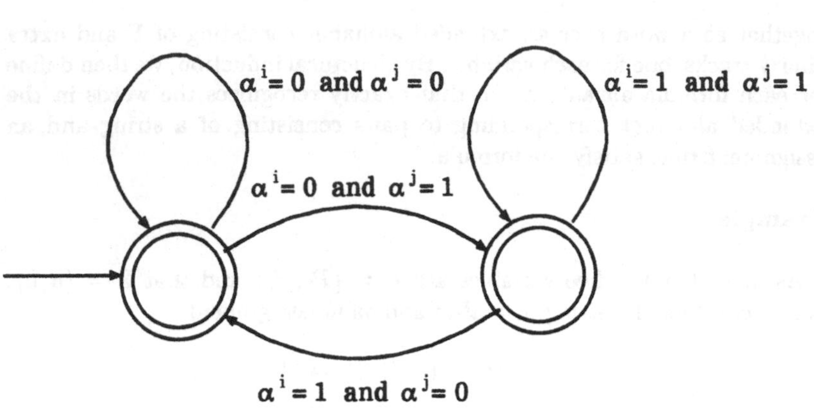

In this drawing, α^i refers to the ith extra track. Thus, the automaton checks that the ith track holds the same bit as the jth track the instant before.

4 Applications

4.1 *Text patterns*

The language L_{2a2b} of strings containing at least two occurrences of a and two occurrences of b can be described in M2L by the formula

$$(\exists p_1, p_2 : 'a'(p_1) \land 'a'(p_2) \land p_1 \neq p_2) \land$$
$$(\exists p_1, p_2 : 'b'(p_1) \land 'b'(p_2) \land p_1 \neq p_2)$$

Our translator yields the minimal automaton, which contains nine states, in a fraction of a second.

The language $L_{a\text{after}b}$ given by the formula

$$\forall p : 'b'(p) \Rightarrow \exists q : p < q \land 'a'(q)$$

is translated to the minimal automaton, which has two states, in .3 seconds.

A far more complicated language to express is $L_{<1\text{apart}}$ consisting of every string over $\{a, b\}$ such that for any prefix the number of a's and b's are at most one apart. When using regular expressions or M2L, one needs to struggle a bit, but in M2L there is a strategy for describing the functioning of the finite-state machine that comes to mind.

We observe that a position p may be used to designate a prefix; for example, 0 denotes the prefix consisting of the first letter and \$ (the last position) denotes the whole input string. We may now recognize a string in $L_{<1\text{apart}}$ by identifying three sets of positions: the set P_0 corresponding to prefixes with an equal number of a's and b's, the set P_{+1} corresponding

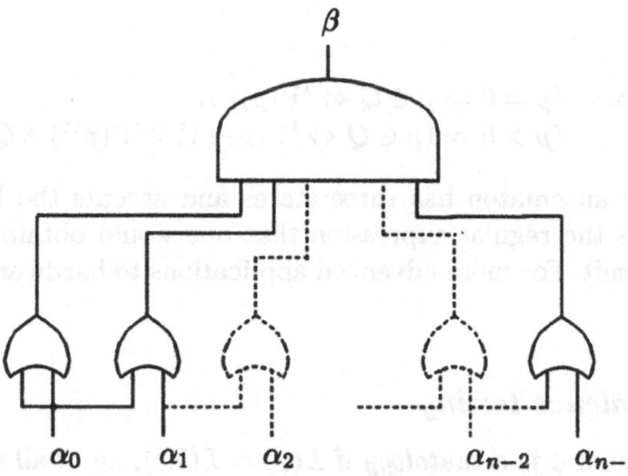

FIGURE 1. A parameterized circuit.

to prefixes where the number of a's is one greater than the number of b's, and the set P_{-1} corresponding to prefixes where the number of a's is one less than the number of b's:

$$
\begin{aligned}
\exists P_0, P_{+1}, P_{-1} : P_0 \cup P_{+1} \cup P_{-1} &= \mathbf{all} \\
&\wedge\ 0 \notin P_0 \\
&\wedge\ 0 \in P_{+1} \Leftrightarrow {}'a'(0) \\
&\wedge\ 0 \in P_{-1} \Leftrightarrow {}'b'(0) \\
&\wedge\ \forall p : (p > 0 \Rightarrow \\
&\qquad p \in P_0 \Leftrightarrow ({}'a'(p) \wedge p \ominus 1 \in P_{-1}) \\
&\qquad\qquad \vee ({}'b'(p) \wedge p \ominus 1 \in P_{+1}) \\
&\qquad \wedge\ p \in P_{+1} \Leftrightarrow {}'a'(p) \wedge p \ominus 1 \in P_0 \\
&\qquad \wedge\ p \in P_{-1} \Leftrightarrow {}'b'(p) \wedge p \ominus 1 \in P_0)
\end{aligned}
$$

The resulting four-state automaton is calculated in a fraction of a second.

4.2 Parameterized circuits

Assume that we are given a drawing as in Figure 1 denoting a parameterized Boolean function.

How do we describe the language $L_{ex} \subseteq \mathbb{B}^*$ of input bit patterns that make the output true? From the drawing, no immediate description as a regular expression or finite-state automaton is apparent. In M2L, however, it is easy to model the outputs of the n or-gates as a second-order variable Q, which allows the language to be described from a direct interpretation of the drawing. Note that the or-gate at position $p > 0$ is true if either there is a 1 at $p - 1$ or p, or in other words: $p \in Q \Leftrightarrow {}'1'(p \ominus 1) \vee {}'1'(p)$. Since the output is 1 if and only if all or-gates are 1, i.e. if $Q = \mathbf{all}$, the language L_{ex} is given by the formula

$$\exists Q : (\forall p : \quad (p = 0 \Rightarrow p \in Q \Leftrightarrow \text{'1'}(p)) \wedge \\ (p > 0 \Rightarrow (p \in Q \Leftrightarrow \text{'1'}(p \ominus 1) \vee \text{'1'}(p))) \wedge Q = \mathbf{all})$$

The resulting automaton has three states and accepts the language $(1 \cup 10)^*$, which is the regular expression that one would obtain by reasoning about the circuit. For more advanced applications to hardware verification, see [BK95].

4.3 Equivalence testing

A closed formula ϕ is a *tautology* if $L(\phi) = L(\Sigma^*)$, i.e. if all strings over Σ satisfy ϕ. The equivalence of formulas ϕ and ψ then amounts to whether $\phi \Leftrightarrow \psi$ is a tautology.
Example. That a set P contains exactly the even positions in a non-empty input string may be expressed in M2L by the following two rather different approaches: either by the formula *even1*$(P) \equiv$

$$0 \in P \ \wedge \ \forall p : ((p \in P \ \wedge \ p < \$ \Rightarrow p \oplus 1 \notin P) \\ \wedge \ (p \notin P \ \wedge \ p < \$ \Rightarrow p \oplus 1 \in P)),$$

or as a formula *even2*$(P) \equiv$

$$P \cup (P + 1) = \mathbf{all} \ \wedge \ P \cap (P + 1) = \emptyset \ \wedge \ P \neq \emptyset$$

To show the equivalence of the two formulas, we check the truth value of the bi-implication:

$$\forall P : \mathit{even1}(P) \Leftrightarrow \mathit{even2}(P)$$

The translation of this formula does indeed produce an automaton accepting Σ^*, and thus verifies our claim.

5 Dining Philosophers with Encyclopedia

A distributed system is *parameterized* when the number n of processes is not fixed a priori. For such systems the state space is unbounded, and thus traditional finite-state verification methods cannot be used. Instead, one often fixes n to be, say two or three. This yields a finite state space amenable to state exploration methods. However, the validity of a property for $n = 2, 3$ does not necessarily imply that the property holds for all n.

A central problem in verification is automatically to validate parameterized systems. One way to attack the problem is to formulate induction principles such that the base case and the inductive steps can be formulated as finite-state problems. Kurshan and MacMillan [KM89] used such

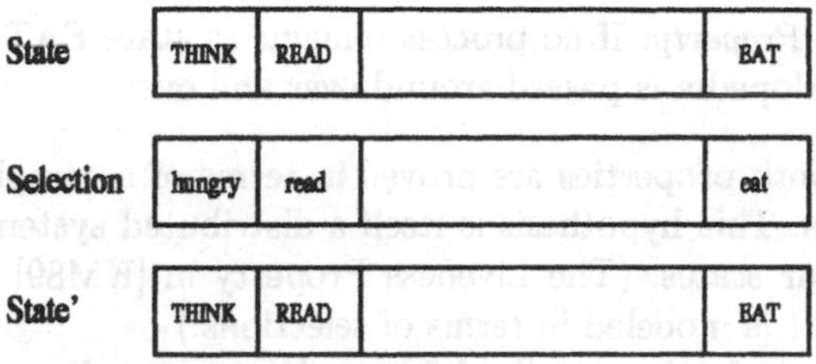

FIGURE 2. Dining Philosophers with Encyclopedia

a method to verify safety and liveness properties of a non-trivial version of the Dining Philosophers example.

In this system, symmetry is broken by an encyclopedia that circulates among the philosophers. Thus each philosopher is in one of three states: EAT, THINK, or READ. The global state can be described as a string *State* of length n over the alphabet $\Sigma_{\text{State}} = \{\text{EAT}, \text{THINK}, \text{READ}\}$, see Figure 2.

The system makes a transition according to external events that constitute a ***selection*** . Each process is presented with an event in the alphabet $\Sigma_{\text{Selection}} = \{\text{eat}, \text{think}, \text{read}, \text{hungry}\}$. Thus the selection can be viewed as a string *Selection* over $\Sigma_{\text{Selection}}$, see Figure 2. As shown, all processes make a synchronous transition to a new global *State'* on a selection according to a transition relation trans(*State*, *State'*, *Selection*), which is shown in Figure 3[2] together with an auxiliary predicate blocking(*Selection*) used in its definition. Thus the new state of each process is dependent on its old state and on the selection events presented to itself and its neighbors. The transition relation is so complicated that it is hard to grasp the functioning of the system.

Fortunately, the parameterized transition relation can be translated into basic M2L on strings. For example, we encode *State* using two second-order variables P and Q with the convention that

$$\begin{aligned}
\text{EAT}_p(State) &\equiv p \in P \ \wedge\ p \in Q \\
\text{READ}_p(State) &\equiv p \notin P \ \wedge\ p \in Q \\
\text{THINK}_p(State) &\equiv p \notin P \ \wedge\ p \notin Q
\end{aligned}$$

Similarly, *State'* and *Selection* can also each be encoded using two second-order variables. Thus, the predicate trans(*State*, *State'*, *Selection*) becomes a formula with six free second-order variables.

For this distributed system there are two important properties to verify:

- ***Safety Property***: The encyclopedia is neither lost nor replicated. Thus there is always exactly one process in state READ.

[2] We use '#' in the beginning of a line to indicate that this line is a comment.

- *Liveness Property*: If no process remains in state EAT forever, then the encyclopedia is passed around over and over.

In [KM89] both properties are proved in terms of a complicated induction hypothesis. This hypothesis is itself a distributed system, where each process has four states. (The Liveness Property in [KM89] is technically different since it is modeled in terms of selections.)

Our strategy is fundamentally different. We cannot directly verify liveness properties. But we can easily verify properties about the transition relation in the parameterized case and *without* induction as follows.

Let ϕ be an M2L formula about the global state. For example, we might consider the property that if a philosopher eats, then his neighbors do not:

$$\phi_{\mathrm{mutex}}(\mathit{State}) \equiv \forall p : \mathrm{EAT}_p(\mathit{State}) \Rightarrow \neg\mathrm{EAT}_{p\ominus 1}(\mathit{State}) \;\wedge\; \neg\mathrm{EAT}_{p\oplus 1}(\mathit{State})$$

A property given as a formula ϕ can be verified using the *invariance principle*:

$$\begin{aligned}&\forall \mathit{State}, \mathit{State}', \mathit{Selection} :\\ &\qquad \phi(\mathit{State}) \wedge \mathrm{trans}(\mathit{State}, \mathit{State}', \mathit{Selection}) \Rightarrow \phi(\mathit{State}'),\end{aligned}$$

which is also a formula in M2L. In this way, we have verified for the parameterized case that both ϕ_{mutex} and the Safety Property that exactly one philosopher reads, i.e. $\exists! p : \mathrm{READ}_p(\mathit{State})$, are invariant. MONA verifies such a formula in approximately 3 seconds on a Sparc 20.

Note that this method does not rely on a state space exploration (which is impossible since the state space is unbounded). Instead, it is based on the Invariance Principle: to show that a property holds for all reachable states, it is sufficient to show that it holds for the initial state and is preserved under any transition.

5.1 Establishing the liveness property

The Liveness Property can be expressed in Temporal Logic as

$$\Box(\mathrm{READ}_{p\ominus 1} \;\Rightarrow\; \Diamond\mathrm{READ}_p), \tag{1.1}$$

that is, it always holds that if philosopher $p \ominus 1$ reads, then eventually philosopher p reads. We must prove this property under the assumption that no philosopher eats forever:

$$\Box(\mathrm{EAT}_p \;\Rightarrow\; \Diamond\neg\mathrm{EAT}_p). \tag{1.2}$$

So assume that $\mathrm{READ}_{p\ominus 1}$ holds. We must prove that $\Diamond\mathrm{READ}_p$ holds. There are two cases as follows.

$\mathbf{blocking}(\mathit{Selection}) \equiv$
$\mathbf{eat}_{p\oplus 1}(\mathit{Selection}) \lor \mathbf{hungry}_{p\ominus 1}(\mathit{Selection})$
$\lor\ \mathbf{eat}_{p\ominus 1}(\mathit{Selection})$

$\mathbf{trans}(\mathit{State}, \mathit{State}', \mathit{Selection}) \equiv$
$\forall p :$

$\#\mathrm{THINK} \to \mathrm{THINK} :$
$(\mathrm{THINK}_p(\mathit{State}) \land \mathrm{THINK}_p(\mathit{State}') \Rightarrow$
$\mathbf{think}_p(\mathit{Selection}) \land \neg(\mathbf{read}_{p\ominus 1}(\mathit{Selection}))$
$\lor$
$\mathbf{hungry}_p(\mathit{Selection}) \land \mathbf{blocking}(\mathit{Selection}))$

$\land$
$\#\mathrm{THINK} \to \mathrm{EAT} :$
$(\mathrm{THINK}_p(\mathit{State}) \land \mathrm{EAT}_p(\mathit{State}') \Rightarrow$
$\mathbf{hungry}_p(\mathit{Selection}) \land \neg(\mathbf{blocking}(\mathit{Selection})))$

$\land$
$\#\mathrm{THINK} \to \mathrm{READ} :$
$(\mathrm{THINK}_p(\mathit{State}) \land \mathrm{READ}_p(\mathit{State}') \Rightarrow$
$\mathbf{think}_p(\mathit{Selection}) \land \mathbf{read}_{p\ominus 1}(\mathit{Selection}))$

$\land$
$\#\mathrm{EAT} \to \mathrm{THINK} :$
$(\mathrm{EAT}_p(\mathit{State}) \land \mathrm{THINK}_p(\mathit{State}') \Rightarrow$
$\mathbf{think}_p(\mathit{Selection}) \land \neg(\mathbf{read}_{p\ominus 1}(\mathit{Selection})))$

$\land$
$\#\mathrm{EAT} \to \mathrm{EAT} :$
$(\mathrm{EAT}_p(\mathit{State}) \land \mathrm{EAT}_p(\mathit{State}') \Rightarrow$
$\mathbf{eat}_p(\mathit{Selection}))$

$\land$
$\#\mathrm{EAT} \to \mathrm{READ} :$
$(\mathrm{EAT}_p(\mathit{State}) \land \mathrm{READ}_p(\mathit{State}') \Rightarrow$
$\mathbf{think}_p(\mathit{Selection}) \land \mathbf{read}_{p\ominus 1}(\mathit{Selection}))$

$\land$
$\#\mathrm{READ} \to \mathrm{THINK} :$
$(\mathrm{READ}_p(\mathit{State}) \land \mathrm{READ}_p(\mathit{State}') \Rightarrow$
$\mathbf{read}_p(\mathit{Selection}) \land \mathbf{think}_{p\oplus 1}(\mathit{Selection}))$

$\land$
$\#\mathrm{READ} \to \mathrm{EAT} :$
$(\mathrm{READ}_p(\mathit{State}) \land \mathrm{EAT}_p(\mathit{State}') \Rightarrow$
$\mathbf{false})$

$\land$
$\#\mathrm{READ} \to \mathrm{READ} :$
$(\mathrm{READ}_p(\mathit{State}) \land \mathrm{READ}_p(\mathit{State}') \Rightarrow$
$\mathbf{read}_p(\mathit{Selection}) \land \neg(\mathbf{think}_{p\oplus 1}(\mathit{Selection})))$

FIGURE 3. The transition relation

- Case EAT_p holds. By asssumption (1.2), there is an instant when $\text{EAT}_p \wedge \neg \bigcirc \text{EAT}_p$ holds. Thus if

$$\text{READ}_{p\ominus 1} \wedge \text{EAT}_p \wedge \neg \bigcirc \text{EAT}_p \Rightarrow \bigcirc \text{READ}_p \qquad (1.3)$$

is a valid property of the transition system, $\Diamond\text{EAT}_p$ holds. In fact, we verified using MONA that (1.3) indeed holds.

- Case $\neg\text{EAT}_p$ holds. If EAT_p becomes true, then use the previous case. Otherwise, $\neg\text{EAT}_p$ continues to hold. Now, by the assumption (1.2) at some point $\neg\text{EAT}_{p\oplus 1}$ will hold. We then use the property

$$\text{READ}_{p\ominus 1} \wedge \neg\text{EAT}_p \wedge \neg\bigcirc\text{EAT}_{p\oplus 1} \Rightarrow \bigcirc\text{READ}_p \vee \bigcirc\text{EAT}_p, \quad (1.4)$$

which we have also verified using MONA, to show that eventually READ_p holds (or eventually EAT_p holds, which contradicts the assumption that $\neg\text{EAT}_p$ continues to hold).

6 Implementation.

MONA is our implementation of the decision procedure, which translates formulas of M2L to finite-state automata as outlined in Section 3. Our tool is implemented in Standard ML of New Jersey. A previous version of MONA was written in C with explicit garbage collection and based on representing transition functions in a conjunctive normal form. Our present tool runs up to 50 times faster due to improved algorithms.

6.1 Representation of automata

Since the size of the extended alphabet grows exponentially with the number of variables, a straightforward implementation based on explicitly representing the alphabet would only work for very simple examples. Instead, we represent the transition relation using Binary Decision Diagrams (BDDs) [Bry92, Bry86]. In this way, the alphabet is never explicitly represented. For the external alphabet of ASCII-characters, we choose an encoding based on seven extra tracks holding the binary representation. Thus, character classes such as `[a-zA-Z]` become represented as very simple BDDs.

A deterministic automaton A is represented as follows. The state space is $Q = \{0, 1, \ldots, n-1\}$, where n is size of the state space; $\mathbb{B}^k$ is the extended alphabet; $i_0 \in Q$ is the initial state; $\delta : Q \times \mathbb{B}^k \to Q$ is the transition function; and $F \subseteq Q$ is the set of accepting states. We use a bit vector of size n to represent F and an array containing n pointers to roots of multi-terminal BDDs representing δ. A leaf of a BDD holds the integer designating the next state. An internal node v is called a *decision node* and

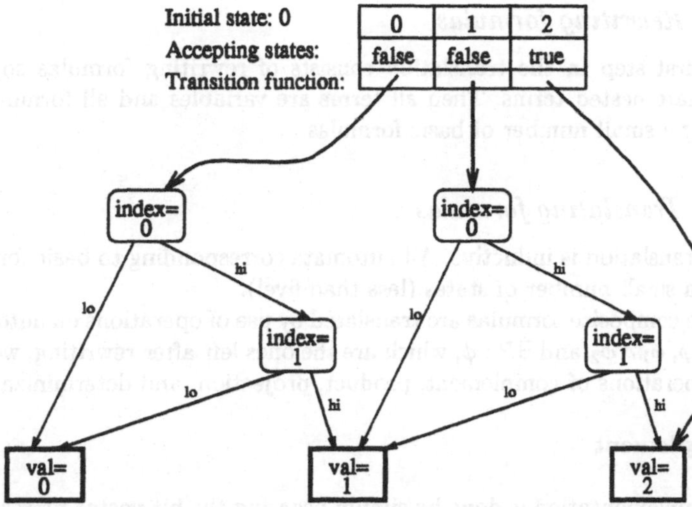

FIGURE 4. BDD automaton representation

contains an *index* denoted *v.index*, where $0 \leq v.index < k$, and high and low successors *v.hi* and *v.lo*. If b is a sequence of k bits, i.e. $b \in \mathbb{B}^k$, then $\delta(q, b)$ is found by looking up the qth entry in the array and following the decision nodes according to b until a leaf is reached (node v is followed by selecting the high successor if the *v.index*th component of b is 1 and the low successor if it is 0).

For example, the following finite automaton accepting all strings over $\mathbb{B}^2$ with at least two occurrences of the letter "11"

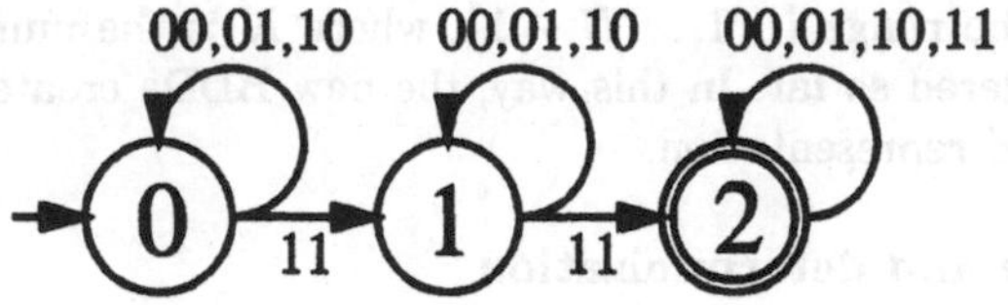

could be represented as in Figure 4.

The use of BDDs makes the representation very succinct in comparison to our earlier attempt to handle automata with large alphabets [JJK94]. In most cases, we avoid the exponential blow-up associated with an explicit representation of the alphabet. We shall see that all operations on automata needed can be performed by means of simple BDD operations.

Another possibility would have been to use a two-dimensional array of ordinary BDDs. But that would complicate the operations on automata, because many more BDD operations would be needed.

6.2 *Rewriting formulas*

The first step in the translation consists of rewriting formulas so as to eliminate nested terms. Then all terms are variables and all formulas are among a small number of basic formulas.

6.3 *Translating formulas*

The translation is inductive. All automata corresponding to basic formulas have a small number of states (less than five!).

The composite formulas are translated by use of operations on automata. For $\neg\phi$, $\phi_1 \wedge \phi_2$ and $\exists P : \phi$, which are the ones left after rewriting, we need the operations of complement, product, projection, and determinization.

Complement

Complementation is done by simply negating the bit vector representing the set of final states.

Product

The product automaton A of two automata A_1 and A_2 is

$$(Q_1 \times Q_2, \mathbb{B}^k, (i_1, i_2), \delta, F_1 \times F_2),$$

where $\delta((q_1, q_2), b) = (\delta_1(q_1, b), \delta_2(q_2, b))$. We are careful, however, to consider only those states of A that are reachable from (i_1, i_2).

When considering a new state (q_1, q_2), we need to construct the BDD representing the corresponding part of the transition function δ. We use the binary apply operation on the BDDs corresponding to q_1 and q_2. For each pair of states (q', q'') encountered in a pair of leaves, we associate a unique integer in the range $\{0, 1, \ldots N-1\}$, where N is the number of different pairs considered so far. In this way, the new BDDs created conform with the standard representation.

Projection and determinization

Projection is the conversion of an automaton over $\mathbb{B}^{k+1}$ to a nondeterministic automaton over $\mathbb{B}^k$ necessary for translating a formula of the form $\exists P : \phi$. On any letter $b \in \mathbb{B}^k$, there are two transitions possible in the nondeterministic automaton corresponding to whether the P-track is 0 or 1. Therefore this automaton is not hard to construct using the projection (restriction) operation of BDDs.

Determinization is done according to the subset construction. The use of the apply operation is similar to that of the product construction except that leaves hold subsets of states.

6.4 Minimizing

Minimization seems essential in order to obtain an effective decision procedure. For example, if a tautology occurs during calculations, then it is obviously a good idea to represent it using a one-state automaton instead of an automaton with e.g. 10,000 states.

The difficulty in obtaining an efficient minimization algorithm stems from the requirement to keep our shared BDDs in reduced form. Recall that a reduced BDD has no duplicate terminals or nonterminals. Such a BDD is just a specialized form of directed acyclic graph that has been compressed by combining structurally isomorphic nodes (see Aho, Hopcroft, and Ullman [AHU74] or Section 3.4 of Cai and Paige [CP94]). In addition, a reduced BDD has no redundant tests [Bry92]. Such a BDD is obtained by repeatedly pruning every internal vertex v that has both outedges leading to the same vertex w, and redirecting all of v's incoming edges to w.

Suppose that the shared BDD had all duplicate terminals and nonterminals eliminated, but did not have any of its redundant tests eliminated. Then it would be easy to treat the deterministic finite automaton combined with its BDD machinery as a single automaton whose states were the union of the BDD nodes and the original automaton states, and whose alphabet were zero and one. If this derived automaton had n states, then it could be minimized in $O(n \log n)$ steps using Hopcroft's algorithm [Hop71]. Unfortunately, such an automaton would be too big.

For our purposes, the space savings due to redundant test removal is of crucial importance. But the important 'skip' states that arise from redundant test removal complicates minimization. Our algorithm combines techniques based on [AHU74] with new methods adapted for use with the shared BDD representation of the transition function. For a finite automaton with n states and a transition function represented by m BDD nodes, the algorithm presented here achieves worst-case running time $O(\max(n, m)n)$.

Terminology

A ***partition*** $\mathcal{P}$ of a finite set U is a set of disjoint nonempty subsets of U such that the union of these sets is all of U. The elements of $\mathcal{P}$ are called its ***blocks***. A ***refinement*** $\mathcal{Q}$ of $\mathcal{P}$ is a partition of U such that any block of $\mathcal{Q}$ is a subset of a block of $\mathcal{P}$. If $q \in U$, then $[q]_{\mathcal{P}}$ denotes the block of partition $\mathcal{P}$ containing the element q, and when no confusion arises, we drop the subscript.

Let $A = (Q, \mathbb{B}^k, i_0, \delta, F)$ denote a deterministic finite automaton, and let $\mathcal{P}$ be a partition of Q, and $\mathcal{Q}$ a refinement of $\mathcal{P}$. A block B of $\mathcal{Q}$ ***respects*** the partition $\mathcal{P}$ if for all $q, q' \in B$ and for all $b \in \mathbb{B}^k$, $[\delta(q, b)]_{\mathcal{P}} = [\delta(q', b)]_{\mathcal{P}}$. Thus, δ cannot distinguish between the elements in B relative to the partition $\mathcal{P}$. A partition $\mathcal{Q}$ ***respects*** $\mathcal{P}$ if every block of $\mathcal{Q}$ respects

$\mathcal{P}$. A partition is ***stable*** if it respects itself. The ***coarsest, stable partition*** $\mathcal{Q}$ ***respecting*** $\mathcal{P}$ is a unique partition such that any other stable partition respecting $\mathcal{P}$ is a refinement of $\mathcal{Q}$.

The refinement algorithm

The minimal automaton A' recognizing $L(A)$ is isomorphic to the automaton defined by the coarsest stable partition $\mathcal{Q}^A$ of Q respecting the partition $\{F, Q \setminus F\}$. The states of A' are $\mathcal{Q}^A$, the transition function δ' is defined by $\delta'([p], b) = [\delta(p, b)]$, the initial state is $[i_0]$, and the set of final states is $F' = \{[f] | f \in F\}$.

Now we are ready to sketch our minimizing algorithm, which works by gradually refining a current partition.

- First split Q into an initial partition $\mathcal{Q} = \{F, Q \setminus F\}$. Note that $\mathcal{Q}^A$ is a refinement of this partition.
- Now let $\mathcal{P}$ be the current partition. We construct the new current partition $\mathcal{Q}$ so that it respects $\mathcal{P}$ while $\mathcal{Q}^A$ remains a refinement of $\mathcal{Q}$.

  For each state q in Q consider the functions $f_q : \mathbb{B}^k \to \mathcal{P}$ defined by $f_q(b) = [\delta(q, b)]_{\mathcal{P}}$ for all q and b. Now let the equivalence relation $\equiv$ be defined as $q \equiv q' \Leftrightarrow (f_q = f_{q'} \wedge [q]_{\mathcal{P}} = [q']_{\mathcal{P}})$. The new partition $\mathcal{Q}$ then consists of the equivalence classes of $\equiv$. By definition of the f_q's, $\mathcal{Q}$ respects $\mathcal{P}$ and is the coarsest such partition implying the invariant.

  We repeat this process until $\mathcal{P} = \mathcal{Q}$.

It can be shown that the final partition $\mathcal{Q}$ is obtained in at most n iterations and equals $\mathcal{Q}^A$. The preceding algorithm is an abstraction of the initial naive algorithm presented in Section 4.13 of [AHU74].

The difficult step in the above algorithm is the splitting according to the functions f_q. However, we can here elegantly take advantage of the shared BDD representation. The idea is to construct a BDD representing the functions f_q for each state. We represent a partition of the states Q, by associating with each state $q \in Q$ a *block id* identifying its block. The BDD for f_q is calculated by performing a unary apply on the collection of shared BDDs, where the value calculated in a leaf is the block id. By a suitable generalization of the standard algorithm, it is possible to carry out these calculations while visiting each node at most once (assuming that hashing takes constant time). Thus the split operation requires time $O(\max(n, m))$. Since we use shared BDDs, we may use the results of the apply operations directly as new block ids.

The splitting step without hashing

An alternative implementation of the splitting step is possible that achieves the same worst case time bound $O(\max(n, m))$ without hashing. It is instructive to first consider the case in which the shared BDDs are reduced only by eliminating redundant nodes but not by eliminating redundant tests. In this case the BDD may be regarded as an acyclic deterministic automaton D whose states are the BDD nodes, and whose alphabet is zero and one. Consider a partition $\mathcal{P}'$ of the BDD nodes defined by equivalence classes of the following relation. Two BDD leaves are equivalent iff their next states belong to the same block of partition $\mathcal{P}$. All decision nodes of the BDD are equivalent. The coarsest stable partition $\mathcal{Q}'$ that respects $\mathcal{P}'$ for automaton D can be solved in $O(m)$ worst case time by Revuz [Rev92] and Cai and Paige [CP94], Sec. 3.4. Finding the equivalence classes of states in Q that point to BDD roots belonging to the same block of $\mathcal{Q}'$ (i.e., finding the coarsest partition $\mathcal{Q}$ that respects $\mathcal{P}$) solves the splitting step in the original automaton in time $O(n)$.

In the case of fully reduced BDDs, the splitting step is somewhat harder, and a closer look at the BDD structure is needed. For each decision node v, $v.index$ represents a position in a string of length k such that $v.index < (v.lo).index \wedge v.index < (v.hi).index$. For each BDD leaf v we have $v.index = k$, and let $v.lo = v.hi$ be an automaton state belonging to Q. For each BDD node v we define function $f_v : \mathbb{B}^k \to \mathcal{P}$ much like the way functions f_q were defined earlier on automaton states. For each nonleaf v, f_v is defined by the rule $f_v(b) = f_{v.lo}(b)$ if $b_{v.index} = 0$; $f_v(b) = f_{v.hi}(b)$ if $b_{v.index} = 1$. For each leaf v, f_v is a constant function that maps every argument into an element (i.e., a block) of partition $\mathcal{P}$.

If $q \in Q$ is an automaton state that points to a BDD root v, then, clearly, $f_q = f_v$. It is also not hard to see that for any two nonleaf BDD nodes v and v', $f_v = f_{v'}$ iff either of the following two conditions hold:

1. $v.index = v'.index \wedge f_{v.hi} = f_{v'.hi} \wedge f_{v.lo} = f_{v'.lo}$, or
2. $f_{v.hi} = f_{v.lo} = f_v \wedge v.hi = v'$.

This leads to the more concrete equivalence relation $\equiv$ on BDD nodes defined as $v \equiv v'$ iff $f_v = f_{v'}$ iff either,

1. $v.index = v'.index = k \wedge [v.lo]_{\mathcal{P}} = [v'.lo]_{\mathcal{P}}$, or
2. $v.index = v'.index < k \wedge v.hi \equiv v'.hi \wedge v.lo \equiv v'.lo$, or
3. $v.index < k \wedge v.lo \equiv v.hi \equiv v'$.

Note that two BDD nodes of different index can be equivalent only by condition (3). Note also, that we can strengthen condition (2) with the additional constraint $v.hi \not\equiv v.lo$ without modifying the equivalence relation. These two observations allow us to construct the equivalence classes inductively using a bottom-up algorithm that processes all BDD nodes of the same index in descending order, proceeding from leaves to roots. The steps are sketched just below.

1. In a linear time pass through all of the BDD nodes, place each node in a bucket according to its index. An array of $k+1$ buckets can be used for this purpose.
2. Next, distribute the BDD leaves (contained in the bucket associated with index k) into blocks whose nodes all have lo successors that belong to the same block of $\mathcal{P}$. This takes time proportional to the number of leaves.
3. For $j = k-1, ..., 0$ examine each node v with $v.index = j$. Both nodes $v.lo$ and $v.hi$ have already been examined, and have been placed into blocks. Hence, a streamlined form of multiset sequence discrimination [CP94] can be used to place v either in an old block (according to condition (3)) or a new block (according to condition (2)) for nodes whose children belong pair-wise to the same old block.

The preceding algorithm computes the equivalence classes as the final set of blocks in $O(m)$ time. As before, we can use these equivalence classes to find the coarsest partition $\mathcal{Q}$ that respects $\mathcal{P}$, which solves the splitting step in the original automaton, in time $O(n)$. Thus, the total worst-case time to solve the splitting step is $O(\max(n, m))$ (without hashing).

In an efficient implementation of finite-state automaton minimization, when the splitting algorithm above is is performed repeatedly, we only need to perform the first step of that algorithm (i.e., sorting BDD nodes according to index) once. Thus, the full DFA minimization algorithm runs in worst case time $O(\max(n, m)n)$ without hashing.

BDD reduction without hashing

Sieling and Wegener[SW93] were the first to compress an arbitrary BDD into fully reduced form in linear time. Their result depended on a radix sort, which is closely related to the multiset discrimination technique that we use. However, their algorithm needs to maintain integer representations of BDD nodes, and it utilizes two arrays of size m. We can show how our algorithm just described can be modified to fully reduce an arbitrary BDD in worst case time linear in the number of BDD nodes (without hashing), but with expected auxiliary space k times smaller than Sieling and Wegener's algorithm.

Let $\mathcal{Q}'$ be the partition of BDD nodes produced by the algorithm. The states of the reduced BDD are the blocks in $\mathcal{Q}'$. For each block $B \in \mathcal{Q}'$,

B.index is the largest index of any BDD node contained in B. Let v' be any node belonging to B of maximum index. If v' is a BDD leaf, then B is a leaf in the reduced BDD (i.e., $B.index = k$), and $B.lo = B.hi = v'.lo$. Otherwise, $B.lo = [v'.lo]_{Q'}$ and $B.hi = [v'.hi]_{Q'}$. The *hi* and *lo* successor blocks can be determined during the multiset sequence discrimination pass when a new block is first created. The index of the first node placed in a newly created block is the index for that block.

What distinguishes our algorithm from that of Sieling and Wegener is that our buckets in steps (2) and (3) are associated with actual BDD nodes (inside the main BDD data structure). Their buckets are associated with components of two auxiliary arrays of size m each. If we replaced each equivalence class by a single witness (as they do) each iteration of step (3), then our auxiliary space would be bounded by the maximum number of BDD nodes that have the same index. If BDD nodes were uniformly distributed among indexes, then this number is m/k, which would give us a k-fold advantage in auxiliary space over their algorithm. We expect a minor constant factor advantage in time as well, because our BDD nodes are represented by their locations instead of by computed integer values, and because we avoid array access in favor of less expensive list and pointer processing.

Work is in progress for exploring the "processing the smaller half" idea found in e.g. [PT87]. We should mention, however, that the current implementation of the minimization algorithm in practice seems to run faster than the procedures for constructing product and subset automata.

6.5 MONA *features*

MONA is enriched by facilities similar to those of programming languages.

Predicates

The user may declare predicates that can later be instantiated. For example, if the predicate P is declared by $P(X,x) = (0 = x \wedge x \in X)$, then P can be instantiated as the formula $P(\complement Y, p \oplus 1)$ with the obvious meaning.

Libraries

MONA supports creation of user-defined libraries of predicates.

Separate translation

MONA automatically stores the automaton for a translated predicate. If there are n free variables, then there may be up to $n!$ different automata corresponding to different orderings of variables in the BDD representation.

6.6 *To be done*

In the current implementation, variables are ordered in their BDDs according to the level of syntactic nesting in the formula; i.e. innermost variables receive the highest index. This strategy is obviously often far from optimal and we are working on implementing heuristics to improve variable ordering. Another orthogonal optimization strategy is to reorder the product constructions by heuristics. In both cases, however, it is not hard to see that finding optimal orderings is NP-complete.

Acknowledgements

We are thankful to Vladimiro Sassone for comments on an earlier version, and to Andreas Potthoff for his advice based on the M2L implementation at the University of Kiel.

7 References

[AHU74] A. Aho, J. Hopcroft, and J. Ullman. *Design and Analysis of Computer Algorithms*. Addison-Wesley, 1974.

[BK95] D. Basin and N. Klarlund. Hardware verification using monadic second-order logic. Technical Report RS-96-7, BRICS, 1995. To appear in CAV '95 Proceedings.

[Bry86] R.E. Bryant. Graph-based algorithms for boolean function manipulation. *IEEE Transactions on Computers*, C-35(8):677–691, Aug 1986.

[Bry92] R. E. Bryant. Symbolic Boolean manipulation with ordered binary-decision diagrams. *ACM Computing surveys*, 24(3):293–318, September 1992.

[BSV93] F. Balarin and A.L. Sangiovanni-Vincentelli. An iterative approach to language containment. In *Computer Aided Verification, CAV '93, LNCS 697*, pages 29–40, 1993.

[CP94] J. Cai and R. Paige. Using multiset discrimination to solve language processing problems without hashing. *to appear Theoretical Computer Science*, 1994. also, U. of Copenhagen Tech. Report, DIKU-TR Num. D-209, 94/16, URL ftp://ftp.diku.dk/diku/semantics/papers/D-209.ps.Z.

[CR94] M-M Corsini and A. Rauzy. Symbolic model checking and constraint logic programming: a cross-fertilisation. In *5th. Europ. Symp. on Programming, LNCS 788*, pages 180–194, 1994.

[GF93] A. Gupta and A.L. Fisher. Parametric circuit representation using inductive boolean functions. In *Computer Aided Verification, CAV '93, LNCS 697*, pages 15–28, 1993.

[Hop71] J. Hopcroft. An $n \log n$ algorithm for minimizing states in a finite automaton. In Z. Kohavi and Paz A., editors, *Theory of machines and computations*, pages 189–196. Academic Press, 1971.

[JJK94] J. Jensen, M. Jørgensen, and N. Klarlund. Monadic second-order logic for parameterized verification. Technical report, BRICS Report Series RS-94-10, Department of Computer Science, University of Aarhus, 1994.

[KM89] B. Kurshan and K. McMillan. A structural induction theorem for processes. In *Proc. Eigth Symp. Princ. of Distributed Computing*, pages 239–247, 1989.

[PT87] R. Paige and R. Tarjan. Three efficient algorithms based on partition refinement. *SIAM Journal of Computing*, 16(6), 1987.

[Rev92] D. Revuz. Minimisation of acyclic deterministic automata in linear time. *Theoretical Computer Science*, 92(1):181–189, 1992.

[RS93] J-K. Rho and F. Somenzi. Automatic generation of network invariants for the verification of iterative sequential systems. In *Computer Aided Verification, CAV '93, LNCS 697*, pages 123–137, 1993.

[Ste93] M. Steinmann. Übersetzung von logischen Ausdrücken in Baumautomaten: Entwicklung eines Verfahrens und seine Implementierung. Unpublished, 1993.

[SW93] D. Sieling and I. Wegener. Reduction of OBDDs in linear time. *IPL*, 48:139–144, 1993.

[Tho90] W. Thomas. Automata on infinite objects. In J. van Leeuwen, editor, *Handbook of Theoretical Computer Science*, volume B, pages 133–191. MIT Press/Elsevier, 1990.

Efficient Simplification of Bisimulation Formulas

Uffe H. Engberg*
Kim S. Larsen†‡

ABSTRACT The problem of checking or optimally simplifying bisimulation formulas is likely to be computationally very hard. We take a different view at the problem: we set out to define a very fast algorithm, and then see what we can obtain. Sometimes our algorithm can simplify a formula perfectly, sometimes it cannot. However, the algorithm is extremely fast and can, therefore, be added to formula-based bisimulation model checkers at practically no cost. When the formula can be simplified by our algorithm, this can have a dramatic positive effect on the better, but also more time consuming, theorem provers which will finish the job.

1 Introduction

The need for validity checking or optimal simplification of first order bisimulation formulas has arisen from recent work on symbolic bisimulation checking of *value-passing calculi* [4, 9, 15]. The NP-completeness of checking satisfiability of propositional formulas [3] implies that validity checking of that class of formulas is co-NP complete. Additionally, checking of quantified formulas is P-space hard [7], so there is not much hope for a fast algorithm for deciding exactly when a bisimulation formula is valid.

Instead, we set out to solve the problem of what you can get for free, i.e., to what extent is it possible to decide validity simply while reading the formula? As it turns out, there is almost nothing that can be done in linear time. The most simple tasks of storing and retrieving information about variables will cost $O(n \log n)$. So, we allowed ourselves this extra log-factor and changed the question to what you can get *almost* for free. As we shall demonstrate in this paper, the algorithm we have designed is very fast. Not alone does it run in $O(n \log n)$; the constant is also very small. On average, we read through the formulas at a rate of about 75 Kbytes per second. Of course, this is only interesting if the algorithm outputs

*BRICS (Basic Research in Computer Science, a Centre of the Danish National Research Foundation), Department of Computer Science, University of Aarhus, Denmark.
†Department of Mathematics and Computer Science, Odense University, Denmark.
‡The initial part of this work was done while this author was at University of Aarhus.

useful answers reasonably frequently, i.e., in the absence of an obvious notion of optimal simplification (to a minimal equivalent formula), if the algorithm can reasonably frequently guarantee that the formula is valid, rule out that the formula could be valid, or maybe simplify a huge formula to a much smaller equivalent one. It is not easy to measure how often the algorithm produces a useful answer, but through examples, we show that there are families of process expressions which give rise to formulas, where our algorithm is successful.

2 Applications

The algorithm makes a single pass over the formula making no assumptions about the variable names. Notice that this also implies that if formulas are passed on to our algorithm from another program, they do not have to be saved at any point, but can be passed on to our program via pipelining.

As already mentioned, in addition to validity checking, we can also simplify formulas. This greatly increases the usefulness of this work. Even if our algorithm fails to prove the validity of a formula, it will quite often simplify the formula so drastically that the validity of the formula (or the opposite) can easily be asserted by the user. Another possibility is to check the simplified formula for validity using other tools. Tools that would succeed more often, but the complexity of which would make it impossible to work on the original formula. The main advantage of simplifying formulas is that the algorithm can be built into the program generating the bisimulation formulas and simplify the formula on the fly. Also, intermediate simplifications can be used to prune the generation of other subformulas. This can be of vital importance since the formulas can become exponentially large.

Our algorithms work just as well on formulas with free variables as on closed formulas. This means that by simplifying a formula with free variables, we actually characterize the conditions, in terms of the free variables, under which two processes are bisimilar.

Though this work is motivated by the need for checking bisimulation formulas, the method is sound for first order formulas in general, so there may be other interesting applications. Depending on the concrete application, extra facilities can be built in at no extra cost (with regards to asymptotic time complexity). For example, when our algorithm has deduced that some variables must be equivalent, in the rest of the formula, all occurrences of these variables can be replaced by one representative.

3 Bisimulation Formulas

In this section, we rather briefly describe the context in which bisimulation

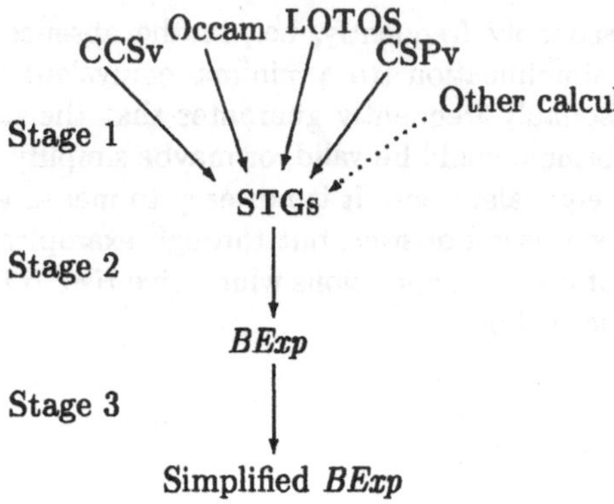

FIGURE 1. Verification stages.

formulas arise and how they are constructed. This section can be skipped if one believes that such formulas characterizing bisimilarity of two processes can be generated.

In [4, 9], bisimulation formulas are used in a three stage process (cf. figure 1) of verifying bisimilarity of value-passing programs ([15] obtain similar formulas, albeit with a different approach).

However, because we mainly want to convey the intuition of how bisimulation formulas are obtained we chose a simple presentation avoiding the notions of symbolic bisimulation and symbolic operational semantics in [9].

Stage 1

In the first stage, symbolic transition graphs (a generalization of the standard notion of labelled transition graphs) are generated from terms of some value-passing language, say the full CCS calculus [14], CCSv, with terms

$$t ::= \mathbf{0} \mid \tau.t \mid a!e.t \mid a?x.t \mid \textbf{if } c \textbf{ then } t \mid t+t \mid t|t \mid t\setminus b \mid A(\bar{e})$$

where a and b range over channel names, x range over a set, V, of variables, e range over a given set of expressions (including V) over some value domain D with elements d, c is a condition ranging over boolean expressions, and A range over names with associated declaration of the form $A(\bar{x}) \Leftarrow t$. As usual the set of programs or processes, *Proc*, are the closed terms (no free variables, where $?x$ acts as binder).

Following [14], $\mathbf{0}$ is the process having no actions, whereas the prefixed process $\tau.p$ can make an internal action and then act as p. Similarly, there are input (output) prefixes $a?x.$ ($a!x.$) for receiving (sending) values on channel a. The expression **if** c **then** p can do the actions of p, provided the condition c evaluates to true, T. The process $p + p'$ acts as either p or p'. In $p \mid q$, the parallel subprocesses p and q are (continuously) acting in

$$\begin{array}{ll}
\tau.p \xrightarrow{\tau} p, \quad a!d.p \xrightarrow{a!d} p, \quad a?x.p \xrightarrow{a?x} p & \\
\textbf{if T then } p \xrightarrow{\alpha} p' & \text{if } p \xrightarrow{\alpha} p' \\
p+q \xrightarrow{\alpha} p' & \text{if } p \xrightarrow{\alpha} p' \\
p \mid q \xrightarrow{\alpha} p' \mid q & \text{if } p \xrightarrow{\alpha} p' \\
p \mid q \xrightarrow{\tau} p'[d/x] \mid q' & \text{if } p \xrightarrow{a?x} p',\ q \xrightarrow{a!d} q' \\
p \setminus b \xrightarrow{\alpha} p' \setminus b & \text{if } p \xrightarrow{\alpha} p',\ b \notin \alpha \\
A(\bar{d}) \xrightarrow{\alpha} p' & \text{if } t[\bar{d}/\bar{x}] \xrightarrow{\alpha} p' \text{ and } A(\bar{x}) \Leftarrow t
\end{array}$$

FIGURE 2. Operational interpretation of CCSv.

parallel through either an internal communication of a value or a separate action of one of the subprocesses. $p \setminus b$ can do those external actions of p not involving communication on b. Finally, $A(\bar{e})$ acts as the process obtained by instantiating the associated term with the parameters of A.

Formally processes are equipped with action relations,

$$\xrightarrow{\tau}, \xrightarrow{a!d} \subseteq Proc \times Proc, \quad \xrightarrow{a?} \subseteq Proc \times (D \to Proc), \quad \text{where}$$

$p \xrightarrow{a?} \lambda d.p'[d/x]$ if $p \xrightarrow{a?x} p'$ and the remaining are defined as the least relations satisfying the rules of figure 2 (symmetric rules left out) where α range over actions of the form τ, $a!d$ or $a?x$, and $b \notin \alpha$ means $b \neq a$.

Bisimilarity of processes is defined by means of bisimulations. A relation, $\mathcal{R}$, on processes is a bisimulation, if it is symmetric and $(p,q) \in \mathcal{R}$ implies

1. $p \xrightarrow{\tau} p' \Rightarrow \exists q'\colon\ q \xrightarrow{\tau} q'$ and $(p',q') \in \mathcal{R}$
2. $p \xrightarrow{a!d} p' \Rightarrow \exists q'\colon\ q \xrightarrow{a!d} q'$ and $(p',q') \in \mathcal{R}$
3. $p \xrightarrow{a?} p' \Rightarrow \exists q'\colon\ q \xrightarrow{a?} q',\ \forall d \in D\colon\ (p'd, q'd) \in \mathcal{R}$

Then p and q are bisimilar, $p \sim q$, iff $p \mathcal{R} q$ for some bisimulation $\mathcal{R}$.

This is in fact what is usually called *late* bisimulation equivalence for value-passing processes. The *early* version (used in [14]) is obtained by merely moving the universal quantification completely to left of the right hand side of the implication in clause 3—the effect being that a (possibly new) q' can be found for each d.

Stage 1 and 2 of the verification process (and the associated theory) can equally well be carried through for early bisimulation. The simplification in stage 3, which is the main concern of the article, is essentially independent of the bisimulation equivalence in question. Henceforth we shall tacitly stick to late bisimulation equivalence.

We shall now generalize the notion of bisimilarity to open terms, i.e., parametrized programs, in such a way that it allows us to formally characterize the conditions, in terms of the parameters, under which the (parametrized) programs are bisimilar.

$$\begin{array}{ll}
\tau.t \xmapsto{\mathsf{T},\tau} t, \quad a!e.t \xmapsto{\mathsf{T},a!e} t, \quad a?x.t \xmapsto{\mathsf{T},a?\#} t & \\
\textbf{if } c \textbf{ then } t \xmapsto{c\wedge c',\alpha} p' & \text{if } t \xmapsto{c',\alpha} t' \\
t + u \xmapsto{c,\alpha} t' & \text{if } t \xmapsto{c,\alpha} t' \\
t \mid u \xmapsto{c,\alpha} t' \mid u & \text{if } t \xmapsto{c,\alpha} t' \\
t \mid u \xmapsto{c\wedge c',\tau} t'[e/\#] \mid u' & \text{if } t \xmapsto{c,a?\#} t',\ u \xmapsto{c',a!e} u' \\
t \setminus b \xmapsto{c,\alpha} t' \setminus b & \text{if } t \xmapsto{c,\alpha} t',\ b \notin \alpha \\
A(\bar{e}) \xmapsto{c,\alpha} t' & \text{if } t[\bar{e}/\bar{x}] \xmapsto{c,\alpha} t' \text{ and } A(\bar{x}) \Leftarrow t
\end{array}$$

FIGURE 3. Generating symbolic transition graphs from CCSv.

An *environment*, is a function from V to D, typically denoted ρ. It is then standard how to define when ρ *satisfies* a formula c, written $\rho \models c$. Given an environment ρ and a term t, we use t_ρ to denote the closed term obtained by substituting $\rho(x)$ for each free variable x in t. $\sim$ is then generalized by

$$t \sim^c u \text{ iff } \forall\rho \models c\colon\ t_\rho \sim u_\rho.$$

A boolean expression, c, is *most general* for terms t and u if it satisfies $t \sim^c u$ and if $t \sim^{c'} u$, then c' implies c.

Now for *symbolic transition graphs*. A symbolic transition graph is merely a labelled directed graph satisfying certain well-formedness conditions. Nodes are labelled with variables and the edges ($\mapsto$) labelled with (symbolic) actions of the form τ, $a!e$ or $a?x$, each guarded with some boolean condition. Intuitively, a graph is well-formed if the (free) variables of the expressions labelling any edge leading from node n to node m only mention variables of n and a variable, x, of m not in n is due to the edge being labelled with an input action $a?x$ binding x.

The advantage of symbolic transition graphs is their independence of a particular process language. Various calculi can be translated into them as we shall see now for CCSv.

It is relatively simple to *generate a symbolic transition graph* from a CCSv term. Edges are (modulo symbolic actions) inferred similarly to the action relations in figure 2, except that conditions met are collected (taking the conjunction) and used as guarding condition. For example, consider the rules of figure 3 (where # is a special place holder variable not in V) and let $t \xmapsto{c,a?x} t''$ if $t \xmapsto{c,a?\#} t'$, $t'' = t'[x/\#]$ and x is the first variable not free in t'. A (not particularly sophisticated) translation is then obtained by letting nodes being terms labelled with their free variables and edges given according to the rules. To get finite graphs more often, one can apply modifications of standard techniques used to avoid state explosion in tools for process languages without value-passing.

Below, two processes are shown together with their associated graphs.

$$
\begin{array}{lll}
m_\rho \xrightarrow{\tau} n_\rho & \text{if } \rho \models c \text{ and } m \xmapsto{c,\tau} n \\
m_\rho \xrightarrow{a!\rho(e)} n_\rho & \text{if } \rho \models c \text{ and } m \xmapsto{c,a!e} n \\
m_\rho \xrightarrow{a?} \lambda d.n_{\rho[x\mapsto d]} & \text{if } \rho \models c \text{ and } m \xmapsto{c,a?x} n
\end{array}
$$

FIGURE 4. Operational interpretation of symbolic transition graphs.

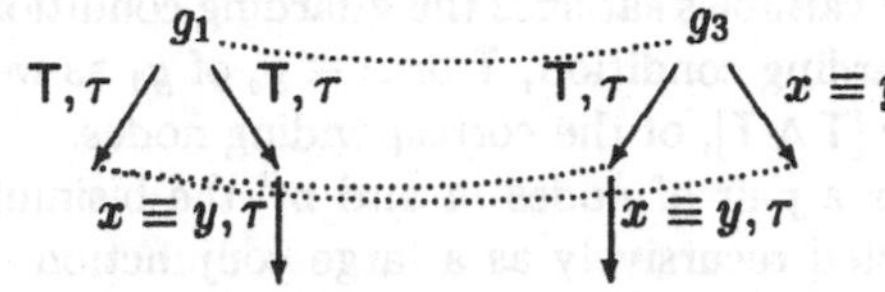

FIGURE 5. Generating symbolic bisimulation formulas.

$A_1(x,y) \stackrel{\text{def}}{=} \tau.0 + \tau.\textbf{if } x \equiv y \textbf{ then } \tau.0$ $\quad A_3(x,y) \stackrel{\text{def}}{=} \tau.(\textbf{if } x \equiv y \textbf{ then } \tau.0) + \textbf{if } x \equiv y \textbf{ then } \tau.0$

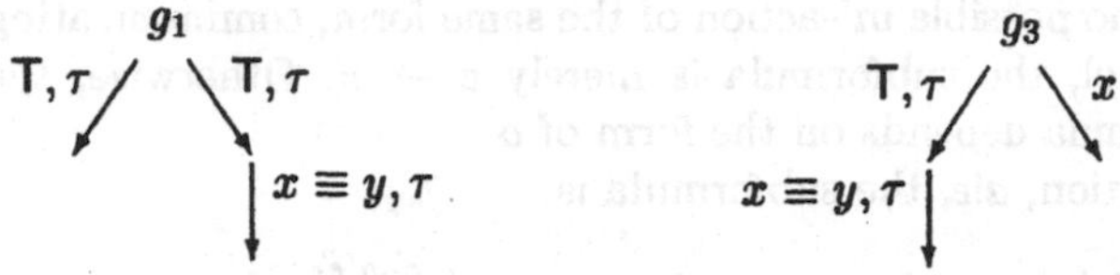

To shorten the presentation, all nodes except for root nodes, have been omitted from the graphs and in the conditions, conjunctions with T have been removed. The initial conditions of the graph g_1 associated with A_1 are T, whereas the last condition is $x \equiv y$ (or rather $x \equiv y \wedge \mathsf{T}$), i.e., x and y should have equivalent values.

The symbolic transition graphs can now be given an operational interpretation which closely relates the interpretation of translated CCSv terms with the original interpretation of the terms. Given an environment ρ and a node n the associated state is denoted n_ρ. The transition relations are then given by the rules of figure 4, where $\rho[x \mapsto d]$ denotes an environment identical to ρ except that it yields d for x. Notice that $\lambda d.n_{\rho[x\mapsto d]}$ applied to a $d' \in D$ gives the state $n_{\rho[x\mapsto d']}$.

Two graphs are ***bisimilar*** [4, 9, 10] iff the two terms they are translated from, are bisimilar in the traditional sense.

Stage 2

In the next stage, an algorithm is used for finding a first order boolean expression *mgb*, called the ***most general boolean***; a bisimulation formula characterizing the conditions for which two finite symbolic transition graphs are bisimilar.

Intuitively, two processes are bisimilar if, whenever one process can do an action, the other has a matching action such that the resulting two processes are again bisimilar. This is reflected in the bisimulation formula. For example, the fact that g_3 must match (see figure 5) an action corresponding to the left edge of g_1, is captured in the mgb_{g_1,g_3} subformula

$$\mathsf{T} \to \vee \begin{array}{l} \mathsf{T} \wedge [\mathsf{T} \wedge (x \equiv y \to \mathsf{F})] \\ x \equiv y \wedge [\mathsf{T} \wedge \mathsf{T}] \end{array}$$

If an instantiation of variables satisfies the guarding condition T of g_1, then it must satisfy a guarding condition, T or $x \equiv y$, of g_3 as well as the *mgb*, $[\mathsf{T} \wedge (a \equiv y \to \mathsf{F})]$ or $[\mathsf{T} \wedge \mathsf{T}]$, of the corresponding nodes.

More precisely, for a pair of nodes m and m' the bisimulation formula $mgb_{m,m'}$ is constructed recursively as a large conjunction of subformulas each capturing the possibility of matching an m-action with m'-actions (and vice versa) and recursively being able to do so.

If there are no actions to match, the subformula is simply T. Otherwise, for each action $m \xmapsto{c,\alpha} n$, the subformula expresses that the guarding condition c imply the possibility of finding a matching m'-action.

Hence, if there are no possible m'-action of the same form, communicating on the same channel, the subformula is merely $c \to \mathsf{F}$. Otherwise, the constructed subformula depends on the form of α.

If α is an output action, $a!e$, the subformula is

$$c \to \bigvee_i [c'_i \wedge e = e'_i \wedge mgb_{n,n'_i}], \text{ where } m' \xmapsto{c'_i, a!e'_i} n'_i$$

meaning that whenever a process environment satisfies c there is at least one m-action which in the same environment and on the same channel can send the same value.

Similarly, for input, universal quantification is used to express that for all values received, the processes are bisimilar, i.e., for α of the form $a?x$

$$c \to \bigvee_i [c'_i \wedge \forall x, x'_i\colon\ x = x'_i \to mgb_{n,n'_i}]$$

For internal actions, the subformula is just $c \to \bigvee_i [c'_i \wedge mgb_{n,n'_i}]$.

The construction clearly stops if there are no cycles in the graphs. But if there are, it will go on forever. However, as we proceed down in the subformulas, more and more constraints are accumulated through the conditions. Hence, intuitively, if the accumulated constraints imply the *mgb* we are about to construct, the recursion can in principle be stopped with subformula T. It turns out that for the examples considered here, this is in fact the case whenever previously visited pairs of nodes are met again.

Stage 3

In the final stage, validity of the bisimulation formula is checked. If it is valid, the original programs are bisimilar under all instantiations. Otherwise, the formula expresses the weakest conditions on the instantiations for which they are bisimilar. Later, in section 9, we shall see that mgb_{g_1,g_3} is in fact valid.

4 Logic Notions

We now fix the set of bisimulation formulas and introduce a few general notions from formal logic.

Formally, the class of formulas, which we will work with in the rest of this paper, is defined by the syntax

$$E ::= P \mid E \wedge E \mid E \vee E \mid P \rightarrow E \mid \forall x\colon E \quad \text{and} \quad P ::= \mathsf{T} \mid \mathsf{F} \mid x \equiv y$$

As usual, formulas are closed if they have no free variables. Notice that bisimulation formulas only have universal quantification. The binary predicate symbol $\equiv$ is assumed be interpreted as an equivalence relation $\equiv_D$ over a nonempty domain D. An environment satisfies a set of formulas Γ, if it satisfies each formula of Γ. Γ *semantically entails* E, written $\Gamma \models E$, if E is satisfied by any environment satisfying Γ. E is *valid*, $\models E$, if $\emptyset \models E$.

The class of bisimulation formulas is a subset of the class of all quantified formulas and checking validity of bisimulation formulas is not P-space hard. An easy reduction shows that checking satisfiability with respect to an environment is NP complete, so presumably checking validity of bisimulation formulas is co-NP complete.

We now state some general properties of entailment relevant for the development of the algorithm. For simplicity, we write Γ as $E_1, \ldots, E_n$ when $\Gamma = \{E_1, \ldots, E_n\}$. Similarly, we write Γ, Δ for $\Gamma \cup \Delta$.

Theorem 1 (Entailment)

a) If $\Gamma \models E$ then $\Gamma, \Delta \models E$ (Ext)

b) If $E \in \Gamma$ then $\Gamma \models E$ (Rep)

c) If $\Gamma \models E$ and $\Gamma, E \models E'$ then $\Gamma \models E'$ (Cut)

d) If $\Gamma \models E$ and $E \models E'$ then $\Gamma \models E'$ (Trans)

e) $\Gamma \models E$ and $\Gamma \models E'$ iff $\Gamma \models E \wedge E'$ (Conj)

f) $\Gamma, E \models E'$ iff $\Gamma \models E \rightarrow E'$ (Imp)

Proof Standard, see [16], for example. □

In general, there is not any similar disjunction theorem allowing both introduction and elimination to the right. However, from the entailment theorems and a few tautologies, we get proposition 2. As a consequence of $\equiv_D$ being an equivalence relation we also have proposition 3.

Proposition 2 If $\Gamma \models E$ or $\Gamma \models E'$, then $\Gamma \models E \vee E'$.

Proposition 3 a) $\models x \equiv x$ b) $x \equiv y \models y \equiv x$ c) $x \equiv y, y \equiv z \models x \equiv z$

5 The Abstract Algorithm

We now set out to design an algorithm for checking validity of formulas with an equivalence predicate. We keep it as abstract as possible to allow for a large degree of freedom in the choice of data structures in the actual implementation.

Intuitively, the idea of the algorithm is to collect in a relation R (over variables) information about variables known to be equivalent when checking subformulas. For instance, checking the validity of a formula like $x \equiv y \rightarrow E$ is reduced to checking E under the assumption that x and y are equivalent, i.e., (x, y) is added to R and E then checked. To exploit that $\equiv$ is an equivalence relation, the symmetric and transitive closure, is taken before proceeding to E. However, when checking E of the formula $\forall x : E$ the situation is quite the opposite. Since a new scope is entered, all previous collected information in R concerning x, must be removed before E is checked.

Formally, for R denote the symmetric and transitive closure by $R^{\oplus}$, the reflexive closure, $R \cup \{(x, x) \mid x \in V\}$, by R^0 and the removal of x, $\{(y, z) \in R \mid y \neq x, z \neq x\}$, by $R \setminus x$. Notice, $R \setminus x \subseteq R$, and if R is symmetrically and transitively closed, then so is $R \setminus x$.

In order to connect with the logic, we associate with R the set of formulas $R_{\equiv} \stackrel{\text{def}}{=} \{x \equiv y \mid (x, y) \in R\}$. The notions of closures and removal extend to $R_{\equiv}$ in the natural way: $R_{\equiv} \setminus x$ is $(R \setminus x)_{\equiv}$ etc.

The algorithm is conveniently described using Kleene's three-valued logic [11], the three truth-values being **t** for "true", **f** for "false" and **u** for "undefined"/ "unknown". The Kleene truth tables for conjunction, $\wedge_K$, disjunction, $\vee_K$, and implication, $\rightarrow_K$, are:

$\wedge_K$	**t**	**f**	**u**
t	**t**	**f**	**u**
f	**f**	**f**	**f**
u	**u**	**f**	**u**

$\vee_K$	**t**	**f**	**u**
t	**t**	**t**	**t**
f	**t**	**f**	**u**
u	**t**	**u**	**u**

$\rightarrow_K$	**t**	**f**	**u**
t	**t**	**f**	**u**
f	**t**	**t**	**t**
u	**t**	**u**	**u**

The abstract algorithm is expressed in terms of a function, $\Vdash$, which given a bisimulation formula E and a symmetrically and transitively closed relation R, returns **t** only if $R \models E$, and **f** only if $R \not\models E$. From now on, R is assumed to be symmetrically and transitively closed. Writing $\Vdash$ infix, the definition is given in figure 6.

Notice that $\Vdash$ is well-defined because we take the symmetric and transitive closure of $(R \cup \{(x, y)\})$.

$$
\begin{array}{l}
R \models E \textbf{ is case } E \textbf{ of} \\
\qquad\qquad \mathsf{T} \quad : \mathbf{t} \\
\qquad\qquad \mathsf{F} \quad : \mathbf{f} \\
\qquad\quad x \equiv y \quad : \textbf{if } x\, R^0\, y \textbf{ then t else u} \\
\qquad\quad E' \wedge E'' : R \models E' \wedge_K R \models E'' \\
\qquad\quad E' \vee E'' : R \models E' \vee_K R \models E'' \\
\qquad\quad E' \to E'' : R \models E' \to_K R' \models E'', \\
\qquad\qquad\qquad \text{where } R' = \begin{cases} (R \cup \{(x,y)\})^{\oplus}, & \text{if } E' \text{ is } x \equiv y \\ R, & \text{if } E' \text{ is } \mathsf{T} \text{ or } \mathsf{F} \end{cases} \\
\qquad\quad \forall x\colon E' \;: R \setminus x \models E'
\end{array}
$$

FIGURE 6. The abstract algorithm.

Given a formula E, the initial call to this function will be $\emptyset \models E$, where $\emptyset$ is the empty relation.

Proving correctness is a matter of proving soundness of $\models$ relative to $\models$. First, we need a small result linking $R_{\equiv}$ to universal quantification.

Lemma 4 If $R_{\equiv} \setminus x \models E$, then $R_{\equiv} \models \forall x\colon E$.

Proof Assume that $R_{\equiv} \setminus x \models E$ and let an environment ρ satisfying $R_{\equiv}$ be given. Because $R_{\equiv} \setminus x \subseteq R_{\equiv}$, ρ must satisfy $R_{\equiv} \setminus x$ as well. Now x does not occur in any formula of $R_{\equiv} \setminus x$ so all environments differing from ρ only on the value of x, will then also satisfy $R_{\equiv} \setminus x$. By the assumption each such environment also satisfies E wherefore the original environment ρ satisfies $\forall x\colon E$. □

Writing $\models E$ for $\emptyset \models E$, we can now state the correctness of the algorithm.

Theorem 5 (Correctness)

a) If $\models E = \mathbf{t}$, then $\models E$.

b) If $\models E = \mathbf{f}$, then $\not\models E$.

Proof Part a) of the theorem follows from the stronger statement

$$\text{if } R \models E = \mathbf{t} \text{ then, } R_{\equiv} \models E$$

which we prove by induction on the structure of E. Assume $R \models E = \mathbf{t}$. We consider the forms of E:

T, F: In general, $\Gamma \models \mathsf{T}$, so also $R_{\equiv} \models \mathsf{T}$. The case of F is trivial, since $R \models \mathsf{F} \neq \mathbf{t}$.

$x \equiv y$: By definition of $\_^0$, it follows that $R \models x \equiv y = \mathbf{t}$ iff either $x\, R\, y$ or $x = y$.

Now, $x\, R\, y$ is equivalent to $x \equiv y \in R_{\equiv}$. By (Rep), we get $R_{\equiv} \models x \equiv y$. In the case $x = y$, the situation is really that E is $x \equiv x$. By (Ext) and a) of proposition 3, we directly obtain $R_{\equiv} \models x \equiv x$.

$E' \wedge E''$: By definition, $R \models E' \wedge E'' = \mathbf{t}$ implies $R \models E' = \mathbf{t}$ and $R \models E'' = \mathbf{t}$. By induction, we obtain that $R_{\equiv} \models E'$ and $R_{\equiv} \models E''$. Using (Conj), we obtain that $R_{\equiv} \models E' \wedge E''$.

$E' \vee E''$: Similar, using proposition 2 instead of (Conj).

$E' \to E''$: By the definition of $\to_K$, we must have $R \models E' = \mathbf{f}$ or $R' \models E'' = \mathbf{t}$. The forms of E':

T: Then $R' = R$ and because $R \models \mathsf{T} = \mathbf{t}$, it follows that $R \models E'' = \mathbf{t}$. As above we deduce $R_{\equiv} \models E''$. Using (Ext), we get $R_{\equiv}, \mathsf{T} \models E''$ and therefore $R_{\equiv} \models \mathsf{T} \to E''$ follows by (Imp).

F: In general $\Gamma, \mathsf{F} \models E$, so in particular $R_{\equiv}, \mathsf{F} \models E''$. By (Impl), $R_{\equiv} \models \mathsf{F} \to E''$.

$x \equiv y$: We have $R \models x \equiv y = \mathbf{t}$ or $R \models x \equiv y = \mathbf{u}$. In either case, we must have $R' \models E'' = \mathbf{t}$, where $R' = (R \cup \{(x,y)\})^{\oplus}$. By induction, we get $R'_{\equiv} \models E''$, which is the same as $(R_{\equiv}, x \equiv y)^{\oplus} \models E''$. Now any $z \equiv w$ in $(R_{\equiv}, x \equiv y)^{\oplus}$ can be deduced from $R_{\equiv}, x \equiv y$ so by repeated use of (Cut), each of these $z \equiv w$ can be removed from the hypothesis and we finally get $R_{\equiv}, x \equiv y \models E''$. Thus, by (Impl), $R_{\equiv} \models x \equiv y \to E''$.

$\forall x$: E': By the induction hypothesis we get that $R_{\equiv} \setminus x \models E'$. The result follows from lemma 4.

Part b) follows similarly from the stronger statement that if $R \models E = \mathbf{f}$, then $R_{\equiv} \models \neg E$. □

6 The Concrete Algorithm

In this section, we discuss the implementation of the abstract algorithm outlined in section 5. The function $\models$, which is defined there, closely follows the structure of a formula E. The concrete implementation in this section will follow this structure in exactly the same way. So, the primary task is to find a representation of the relation R such that operations on this relation (union, closure, checking for equivalence, etc.) can be performed efficiently.

The primary operations are to make two variables equivalent and to test whether two variables are already equivalent. This is an instance of the so-called disjoint set problem, which is usually solved using rooted trees [6]. To obtain the best possible performance, path compression (McIllroy and Morris) and union by rank [17] (or similar schemes) are normally used to obtain an amortized complexity of $O(A^{-1}(n))$ per find operation [17, 19], where A^{-1} is the inverse of the (unary) Ackermann function [1].

However, when processing formulas like $(x \equiv y \to E) \wedge E'$, we need to first form the union of the equivalence classes of x and y, then process the expression E, and then deunion (undo) the last union before processing E'. Path compressions are impossible to undo without ruining the complexity,

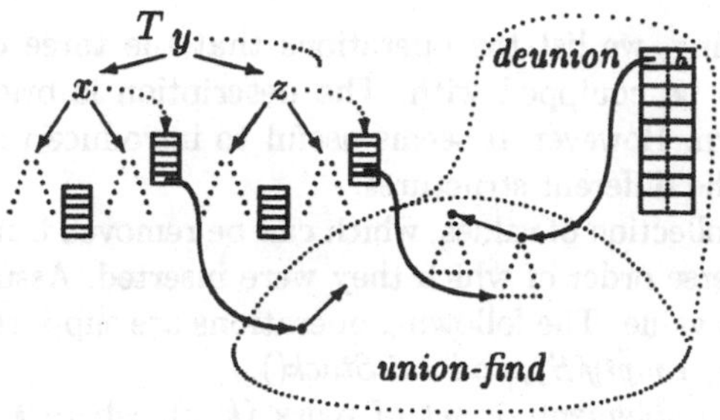

FIGURE 7. The combined structure.

so we only use union by rank, and obtain a complexity of $O(\log n)$ per find [18]. In order to undo the unions, each union operation is registered on a stack. In this way, deunions can be done in constant time (unions are still constant time). These three operations, find, union, and deunion, can also be implemented such that the amortized complexity for the find operation becomes $O(\log n/(\log\log n))$. That proposal is from [12]. See [20] for the analysis. However, the size of the overhead is so large that for formulas that we consider (up to approximately 5 Mbytes), this method is slower. For further details on disjoint set implementations, see [13]. We call the structure we use a ***union-find-deunion*** (UFD) ***structure.***

For formulas without universal quantification, this would be all we would need. However, formulas like $(\forall x:\ E)\wedge E'$ require that the variable x is freed from previous unions while processing E. Afterwards, for the processing of E', all the old information on x must be restored. Having to keep track of several versions of variables means that the variables cannot be used directly in the *UFD* structure. Instead, we do the following: at any point during the processing of a formula, each variable, x, has an associated stack of pointers corresponding to the number of active versions of x. In greater detail, when a quantifier construction $\forall x:$ is encountered, a pointer is pushed onto x's stack. The pointer points to a new item in the *UFD* structure not related to anything, which was previously there. In this way, the old environment can be restored by simply popping the stack.

In order to access the stacks associated with variable names as fast as possible, variable names (along with the pointer to the stacks) are organized in a red-black tree [2, 8], which is one of the efficient implementations of dictionaries with a complexity of $O(\log n)$ per operation, where n is the number of elements in the tree.

To summarize, we use a red-black tree that has variable names as keys and stacks of pointers as values. All these pointers point into a common *UFD* structure. In addition, the *UFD* structure has its own stack of undo information. We refer to the structure consisting of all these other data structures as the *combined* structure. See figure 7.

In the following, we list the operations that the three data structures are assumed to be equipped with. The description is brief as all this is quite well known. However, it seems useful to introduce the names of the operations on the different structures.

A stack is a collection of values, which can be removed from the structure only in the reverse order of which they were inserted. Assume that S is a stack and v is a value. The following operations are supported: *Push*(S,v), *Pop*(S), *Top*(S), *Empty*(S), and *InitStack*$()$.

A dictionary implements a set of pairs (k,v), where k is a key value from a totally ordered domain and v is any value. We assume that each key value appears at most once in the dictionary. If T is a dictionary, then the following operations are supported: *Insert*(T,k,v), *Delete*(T,k), *Member*(T,k), *LookUp*(T,k), and *InitTree*$()$.

A *UFD* structure is a collection of elements some of which may be equivalent with other elements. The following operations are supported: *Union*(U,p,q), *Find*(U,p), *Deunion*(U), and *InitUFD*$()$. Obviously, the implementation is basically the well-known union-find structure using a stack to save information about the unions.

A Kleene boolean is an implementation of Kleenes three-valued logic. The three Kleene truth-values *TRUE*, *FALSE*, and *UNKNOWN* correspond to **t**, **f**, and **u**, respectively. The operations *Kand*, *Kor*, and *Kimp* implement the operations $\wedge_K$, $\vee_K$, and $\rightarrow_K$ as described in the tables of section 5. Furthermore, *Ktu* turns an ordinary boolean into the Kleene boolean *TRUE* if it is true and otherwise into *UNKNOWN*.

The Algorithm

In this section, we present the concrete algorithm, which implements the abstract algorithm from section 5. Basically, this is all about representing the relation R using advanced data structures. We assume that the formula E has a representation in the form of a syntax tree. There are well-developed standard techniques to define and manipulate syntax trees. For clarity, we leave out these details.

Also, to present the crucial parts of the algorithm as clearly as possible, we treat $E_1 \wedge E_2$ and $E_1 \vee E_2$ independently. In reality, as we want to process the formula using pipelining, we should process E_1 first and not until after that has been done can we decide whether a conjunction or a disjunction is been processed. Another reasonable assumption would be to require that the program generating the formula does this using a prefix notation like $\wedge(E_1, E_2)$ and $\vee(E_1, E_2)$.

For simplicity, we assume that the formulas are closed, i.e., they do not have any free variables. This is no serious simplification since free variables can be treated as if they were bound at the outermost level.

The concrete implementation, figure 8, follows the structure of the formula in the same way as $\models$, except that the call for the left-hand operand

```
function check(E: formula) → Kleene boolean;
  var
    r: Kleene boolean;
    p,q: pointers; (* into the UFD structure *)
  case E of
    T:            r := TRUE;
    F:            r := FALSE;
    x ≡ y:        r := Ktu(Find(U,Top(LookUp(T,x))) =
                         Find(U,Top(LookUp(T,y))));
    E1 ∧ E2:      r := Kand(check(E1),check(E2));
    E1 ∨ E2:      r := Kor(check(E1), check(E2));
    T → E1:       r := check(E1);
    F → E1:       r := TRUE;
    (x ≡ y) →E1:  p := Find(U,Top(LookUp(T,x)));
                  q := Find(U,Top(LookUp(T,y)));
                  if p ≠ q then Union(U,p,q);
                  r := Kimp(Ktu(p ≠ q),check(E1));
                  if p ≠ q then Deunion(U);
    ∀x: E1:       if ¬Member(T,x) then Insert(T,x,InitStack());
                  new(p); Push(LookUp(T,x),p);
                  r := check(E1);
                  Pop(LookUp(T,x)); free(p);
                  if Empty(LookUp(T,x)) then Delete(T,x);
  end;
  return r;
end;
```

FIGURE 8. The concrete algorithm.

of implication is unfolded and incorporated directly into the case analysis.

Before use, T is declared as a red-black tree and properly initialized using InitTree(). Similarly, U is declared as a *UFD* structure and initialized by a call to InitUFD().

Correctness

Proposition 6 The combined structure immediately after a call to the function check is exactly as it were immediately before the call to check.

Proof By induction in the number of calls to the function check. The base case is when this number is one, which means that check is not called recursively. Thus, we must be in one of the cases T, F, or $x \equiv y$. The result follows since the combined structure is not altered in any of these cases.

For the induction step, the result follows trivially from the induction hypothesis in the case where E is $E' \wedge E''$, $E' \vee E''$, $\mathsf{T} \to E'$, or $\mathsf{F} \to E'$, since the combined structure is not changed.

Assume that E is $(x \equiv y) \rightarrow E'$. By the induction hypothesis, the call check(E') leaves the structure unchanged. The claim follows as Deunion(U) will undo the last union not yet undone. This must be Union(U,p,q), as the combined structure after the call to check(E') is exactly as it were before the call.

Assume that E is $\forall x : E'$. By the induction hypothesis, the call check(E') leaves the structure unchanged. Since LookUp(T,x) is a stack, the statement Pop(LookUp(T,x)) will undo the effect of Push(LookUp(T,x),p). Furthermore, if the stack LookUp(T,x) is empty, then this stack must have been inserted into T by this current invocation of check, so the empty stack should be deleted. □

Proposition 7 Let F be a bisimulation formula, and let E be a subexpression of F with x and y bound in the context of E. Immediately before the call check(E), the combined structure is an exact representation of R in the corresponding call $R \models E$, i.e.,

$$x\ R^0\ y \Leftrightarrow \text{Find(U,Top(LookUp(T,x)))} = \text{Find(U,Top(LookUp(T,y)))}$$

Proof By induction in the structure of E. The base case is when $E = F$, in which case both R (and thus also R^0) and the combined structure are empty. For the induction step, we consider all possible forms that E could have.

If E is T, F, $x \equiv y$, $E' \wedge E''$, $E' \vee E''$, $\mathsf{T} \rightarrow E'$, or $\mathsf{F} \rightarrow E'$, then the combined structure remains unchanged and the same R is used in the recursive application of $\models$.

Assume that E is $(x \equiv y) \rightarrow E'$. Then $\models$ is called with the relation formed by adding (x, y) to R and taking the symmetric and transitive closure. In the combined structure, if x and y do not already belong to the same equivalence class, then the equivalence classes of x and y are joined. Notice that given the representation of the combined structure and the way it is used, it is automatically closed reflexively, symmetrically, and transitively.

Assume that E is $\forall x : E'$. Then $\models$ is called with the relation formed from R by deleting all pairs that include x. In the combined structure, a new pointer into the *UFD* structure is created and placed on the top of x's variable stack, thus effectively hiding any pairs involving x; except that the pair (x, x) will belong to the structure ensuring reflexitivity. □

Lemma 8 The function, check, correctly implements $\models$.

Proof From proposition 6, it follows that a function semantically equivalent to the function check can be written by letting the combined structure be a value-passing parameter to check. As the two algorithms are structurally equivalent modulo unfolding, it is sufficient to consider the use of the combined structure and R. From proposition 7, it follows that the combined structure is an exact representation of R^0. □

Theorem 9 Let E be a bisimulation formula, and let n be the size of E. Then the time-complexity of check(E) is $O(n \log n)$.

Proof The algorithm is recursive in the structure of E, and clearly, there are a constant number of statements per symbol in E. These statements either perform constant-time operations, or they operate on one of the data structures. As these are initially empty, and as they share the property that n operations are carried out in time $O(n \log n)$, the result follows. □

7 Extensions of the Algorithm

In this section, we consider various extensions of the algorithm. For each extension, we sketch the modifications of the abstract algorithm from section 5, and we discuss the correctness issues briefly.

Many more extension than the ones presented here are possible. However, we have decided only to present extensions according to the criteria:

a) the asymptotic complexity should not change.

b) the increase in the actual complexity should be very low (lees than a factor of 10).

c) it should still be a one pass algorithm.

It is not hard to deal with constants and through the obvious transformation suggested by the equivalence

$$(E \wedge E') \rightarrow E'' \quad \dashv\models \quad E \rightarrow (E' \rightarrow E''),$$

the algorithm can easily cover implication subformulas with conjunctions of predicates to the left. It is straight forward to cope with multiple equivalence relations by letting the function $\models$ work with multiple relations over variables.

The function $\models$ is only able to return **t** (**f**) if the formula is valid (unsatisfiable). However, the algorithm, $\models_c$, obtained from $\models$ by returning the result of $(R \cup \{(x, y)\})^{\oplus} \models_c E'$ in case of formulas of the form $(x \equiv y) \rightarrow E'$, is able to deal with *contingent* formulas as well.

Theorem 10 a) If $\models_c E = \mathbf{t}$ then $\models E$. b) If $\models_c E = \mathbf{f}$ then $\not\models E$.

Proof The proof of a) is almost exactly as the corresponding proof of theorem 5. Part b) is proved by showing that if $R \models_c E = \mathbf{f}$ then E it is not satisfied by environments identifying all variables. □

$\models_c$ is clearly as good as $\models$. It is also strictly better because $\models x \equiv y \rightarrow \mathsf{F} = \mathbf{u}$ and $\models_c x \equiv y \rightarrow \mathsf{F} = \mathbf{f}$.

8 Simplifications

In this section, we discuss changes to the algorithm with the purpose of outputting a simplified formula equivalent to the original formula. The algorithm should contain the validity checking algorithm as a special case, i.e., if the validity checking algorithm deems a formula valid, then this new algorithm should simplify the formula to T. Also, we would like the algorithm to fulfill the criteria of the previous section.

Like the $\models$ function, the new function, $\models_r$, takes as arguments a relation, R, over variables and a first order formula, but now it returns a first order formula instead of a truth-value of three-valued logic. We use the same case analysis, but turn the Kleene truth tables into simplification tables, essentially by replacing **u** by the argument formula. Compare with the Kleene truth tables in section 5. However, this is not quite sufficient. In the $\forall x\colon E'$ case of $\models$, $\forall x$ is eliminated completely. This cannot be done here when E' does not simplify to T or F, so a simplification table for $\forall$ is also needed.

$\wedge_r$	T	F	E'
T	T	F	E'
F	F	F	F
E	E	F	$E \wedge E'$

$\rightarrow_r$	T	F	E'
T	T	F	E'
F	T	T	T
E	T	$E \rightarrow$ F	$E \rightarrow E'$

$\vee_r$	T	F	E'
T	T	T	T
F	T	F	E'
E	T	E	$E \vee E'$

$\forall_r\, x\colon$	
T	T
F	F
E'	$\forall x\colon E'$

We are now ready to define $\models_r$.

$$
\begin{array}{rll}
R \models_r E \textbf{ is case } E \textbf{ of} & x \equiv y & : \textbf{if } x\, R^0\, y \textbf{ then } \mathsf{T} \textbf{ else } x \equiv y \\
& E' \wedge E'' & : R \models_r E' \wedge_r R \models_r E'' \\
& E' \vee E'' & : R \models_r E' \vee_r R \models_r E'' \\
& E' \rightarrow E'' & : R \models_r E' \rightarrow_r \mathbf{Upd}(R, E') \models_r E'' \\
& \forall x\colon E' & : \forall_r\, x\colon\, R \setminus x \models_r E' \\
& E & : E
\end{array}
$$

The final case deals with T and F and for convenience, we have introduced an explicit update function:

$$
\mathbf{Upd}(R, E) = \begin{cases} (R \cup \{(x, y)\})^{\oplus}, & \text{if } E \text{ is } x \equiv y \\ R, & \text{otherwise} \end{cases}
$$

The simplified formula is logically equivalent with the original as stated in the following correctness theorem.

Theorem 11 E if and only if $\models_r E$.

Proof This follows from the statement below which is proved by induction. We omit the details.

$$R_{\equiv} \rightarrow E \text{ iff } R_{\equiv} \rightarrow (R \models_r E)$$

□

The next proposition expresses that $\models_r$ is at least as good as $\models$.

Proposition 12 If $\models E = \mathbf{t}$ ($\mathbf{f}$), then $\models_r E = \mathsf{T}$ (F).

The next section contains examples of simplifications using this algorithm.

A straightforward improvement of the simplification algorithm can be obtained from the semantic equivalence

$$E' \wedge E'' \quad \dashv\models \quad E' \wedge (E' \rightarrow E''). \tag{.1}$$

Exploiting the simplification of E', the conjunction case is changed to:

$$\textbf{let } E'_r = R \models_r E' \textbf{ in } E'_r \wedge_r \mathbf{Upd}(R, E'_r) \models_r E''.$$

In this way, the algorithm can simplify $(F \vee x \equiv y) \wedge (x \equiv y \rightarrow F)$, for example, to F.

Along the same lines, the algorithm can be improved further by using:

$$E \vee E' \quad \dashv\models \quad (\neg E) \rightarrow E'.$$

Writing $x \not\equiv y$ for the common occurring formula $x \equiv y \rightarrow \mathsf{F}$, we get as a special case:

$$x \not\equiv y \vee E \dashv\models x \equiv y \rightarrow E. \tag{.2}$$

As the algorithm is formulated now, there is a priori nothing that prevents the algorithm from working with more predicates such as $x \not\equiv y$ and $x \leq y$. In fact, the simplification algorithm is still sound since the new predicates are not simplified and do not give rise to updates of R through $\mathbf{Upd}(\_,\_)$. However, we can use R to simplify the new predicates in some cases, e.g., for $x \not\equiv y$, we can add the case

$$\textbf{if } x\ R^0\ y \textbf{ then } \mathsf{F} \textbf{ else } x \not\equiv y.$$

Now, we turn our attention to another type of simplification. The idea is that universal quantifications can be pushed inwards over conjunctions and that quantified predicates in some cases then can be simplified.

We use this observation to maintain a set, X, of variables corresponding to universal quantified variables met solely by simplification of conjunctions, and define a function $\models_{re}$, which, compared to $\models_r$, takes X as an extra argument.

$$
\begin{array}{lll}
R \models_{re}^{X} E \textbf{ is case } E \textbf{ of } & x \equiv y & : \textbf{if } x\, R^0\, y \textbf{ then } \mathsf{T} \\
 & & \quad \textbf{elseif } x \in X \textbf{ or } y \in X \textbf{ then } \mathsf{F} \\
 & & \quad \textbf{else } x \equiv y \\
 & E' \wedge E'' & : R \models_{re}^{X} E' \wedge_r R \models_{re}^{X} E'' \\
 & E' \vee E'' & : R \models_{re}^{\emptyset} E' \vee_r R \models_{re}^{\emptyset} E'' \\
 & E' \rightarrow E'' & : R \models_{re}^{\emptyset} E' \rightarrow_r \textbf{Upd}(R, E') \models_{re}^{\emptyset} E'' \\
 & \forall x\colon E' & : \forall_r\, x\colon R \setminus x \models_{re}^{X \cup \{x\}} E' \\
 & E & : E
\end{array}
$$

The soundness of $\models_{re}$ follows from

$$
\begin{array}{rcl}
\forall x\colon E \wedge E' & \dashv\models & (\forall x\colon E) \wedge (\forall x\colon E') \\
\forall x\colon x \equiv y & \dashv\models & \mathsf{F}.
\end{array}
$$

Actually, the soundness of the latter requires the quotient set of the domain by the equivalence, $D/\!\equiv_D$, to have a size of at least two. However, for empty or singleton quotient sets,

do not seem very useful, so the restriction should not be significant in practice.

Notice that with the exception of the extension concerning contingent formulas, all extensions can all be combined.

9 Examples

In the first half of this section, we focus on qualitative aspects of the simplification algorithm by means of five examples used to illustrate different simplification ideas. In the second half, we deal with some quantitative aspects of the simplification algorithm and the Kleene algorithm through time measures of concrete implementations applied to increasingly larger input.

Consider the following symbolic transition graphs:

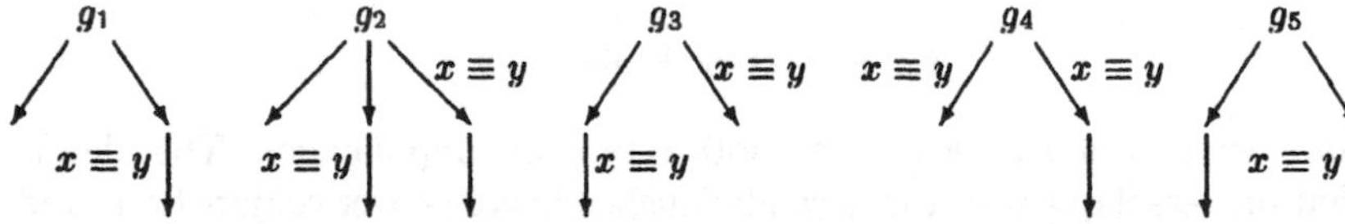

All actions are internal, so τ has been omitted from the graphs together with the trivial guarding conditions T. Before proceeding, we invite the reader to try to see which graphs are bisimilar.

Now, applying $\models_r$ to the bisimulation formula mgb_{g_i,g_j} ($\leftrightarrow mgb_{g_j,g_i}$), we get the table of simplified formulas

$i \backslash j$	1	2	3	4
2	T			
3	$x \not\equiv y \vee x \equiv y$	$x \not\equiv y \vee x \equiv y$		
4	$x \equiv y \wedge E$	$x \equiv y \wedge E$	E	
5	$x \equiv y \wedge x \not\equiv y$	$(x \equiv y \vee x \equiv y) \wedge x \not\equiv y$	$x \equiv y \wedge x \not\equiv y$	$x \equiv y \wedge E \wedge x \not\equiv y$

where $E = ((x \equiv y \wedge x \not\equiv y) \vee (x \equiv y \wedge x \equiv y))$, and for sake of readability, $x \equiv y \rightarrow \mathsf{F}$ is written $x \not\equiv y$.

If, in stead, we apply $\models_r$ with the modifications corresponding to (.1), many of the formulas are simplified considerably, some even completely as shown in the following table.

$i \backslash j$	1	2	3	4
2	T			
3	$x \not\equiv y \vee x \equiv y$	$x \not\equiv y \vee x \equiv y$		
4	$x \equiv y$	$x \equiv y$	$x \equiv y$	
5	F	$(x \equiv y \vee x \equiv y) \wedge x \not\equiv y$	F	F

If we are interested in knowing whether the graphs are bisimilar under all instantiations of x and y, we can check validity of the universal closure of the formulas, i.e., simplify the universally closed formulas to T or F if possible. The result of applying $\models_{re}$ (with the modifications mentioned above) yields the table below. We have omitted the quantifiers in the formulas different from T and F.

$i \backslash j$	1	2	3	4
2	T			
3	$x \not\equiv y \vee x \equiv y$	$x \not\equiv y \vee x \equiv y$		
4	F	F	F	
5	F	$(x \equiv y \vee x \equiv y) \wedge x \not\equiv y$	F	F

Adding to $\models_{re}$ an extra case for $\not\equiv$, the formula in entry $(i, j) = (5, 2)$ would also simplify to F, and if the modification suggested from (.2), i.e., transforming $x \not\equiv y \vee E$ to $x \equiv y \rightarrow E$, is incorporated into the algorithms as well, then the last two entries would also simplify completely, but this time to T.

Turning to the quantitative aspects of the concrete algorithms, we consider processes defined for $i \geq 0$ by

$$p_{i+2} \xrightarrow{\mathsf{T},a?x_0} q_{i+1}, \quad q_{i+1} \xrightarrow{\mathsf{T},a?x_1} r_1^i, \quad r_k^{i+1} \xrightarrow{c_k,a?x_{k+1}} r_{k+1}^i \text{ and } r_k^0 \xrightarrow{c_k,b!x_k} \mathbf{0},$$

where c_k is the equality $x_{k-1} = x_k$. Initially two values are unconditionally received on a and then, iteratively, values are received on a provided the two most recently received values are equal. Finally, after i iterations and under the same proviso, the last value is send on b. Similarly, we define primed versions which only differ in that c'_k is the equality $x'_0 = x'_k$. That is, the last value received on a is compared with very first.

In order to give the reader examples of how concrete bisimulation formulas look like, we now describe the most general boolean, $mgb_{r^i_k, r'^i_k}$, characterizing those instantiations (environments) of r^i_k and r'^i_k for which they are bisimilar.

$$mgb_{r^{i+1}_k, r'^{i+1}_k} = \bigwedge \begin{array}{l} c_k \rightarrow (c'_k \wedge \forall x_{k+1}\colon \forall x'_{k+1}\colon x_{k+1} = x'_{k+1} \rightarrow mgb_{r^i_{k+1}, r'^i_{k+1}}) \\ c'_k \rightarrow (c_k \wedge \forall x'_{k+1}\colon \forall x_{k+1}\colon x'_{k+1} = x_{k+1} \rightarrow mgb_{r^i_{k+1}, r'^i_{k+1}}) \end{array}$$

$$mgb_{r^0_k, r'^0_k} = \bigwedge \begin{array}{l} c_k \rightarrow (c'_k \wedge x_k = x'_k \wedge \mathsf{T}) \\ c'_k \rightarrow (c_k \wedge x'_k = x_k \wedge \mathsf{T}) \end{array}$$

The most general booleans for the p's and q's are similar to the first formula above, except that the conditions here are T.

For $2 \leq i \leq 13$, we have measured the average time of five runs of a C implementation of $\models_c$ ($\models_r$) processing $mgb_{p_{i+2}, p'_{i+2}}$ on a SPARC station ELC. To give a few examples, $mgb_{p_{13+2}, p'_{13+2}}$ of size 5.754 Mb was simplified to t (T) in 77284 (78912) milliseconds. Similarly, $mgb_{p_{13+2}, p'_{13+3}}$, which is 4.477 Mb large, was simplified to f in 62958 milliseconds. On average, $\models_c$ and $\models_r$ process input at a rate of about 75 Kbytes per second.

10 References

[1] W. Ackermann. Zum Hilbertschen Aufbau der reellen Zahlen. *Math. Annalen*, 99:118–133, 1928.

[2] R. Bayer. Symmetric Binary B-Trees. *Acta Inform.*, 1:290–306, 1972.

[3] S.A. Cook. The Complexity of Theorem-Proving Procedures. In *ACM STOC*, pages 151–158, 1971.

[4] U.H. Engberg. Simple Symbolic Bisimulations. In preparation.

[5] U.H. Engberg and K.S. Larsen. Efficient Reduction of Bismulation Formulas. Preprint 47, Dept. of Math. and Computer Science, Odense University, 1993.

[6] B.A. Galler and M.J. Fischer. An improved equivalence algorithm. *Comm. ACM*, 7:301–303, 1964.

[7] M.R. Garey and D.S. Johnson. *Computers and Intractability.* W. H. Freeman, 1979.

[8] L.J.Guibas and R.Sedgewick. A Dichromatic Framework for Balanced Trees. *IEEE FOCS*, 8–21, 1978.

[9] M. Hennessy and H. Lin. Symbolic Bismulations. Tech. Rep. 1/92, University of Sussex, 1992. Appear in *Theoretical Computer Science* 138 (1995) 353–389.

[10] M. Hennessy and H. Lin. Proof systems for message-passing process algebras. *CONCUR '93*, pages 202–216, August 1993.

[11] G.J. Klir and T.A. Folger. *Fuzzy Sets, Uncertainty, and Information.* Prentice-Hall, 1988.

[12] H. Mannila and E. Ukkonen. The set union problem with backtracking. *LNCS 226*, 236–243, 1986.

[13] K. Mehlhorn and A. Tsakalidis. Data Structures. In Jan van Leeuwen, editor, *Handbook of Theoretical Computer Science*, chapter 6, pages 301–341. Elsevier Science Publishers, 1990.

[14] R. Milner. *Communication and Concurrency.* Prentice-Hall, 1989.

[15] Z. Schreiber. Verification of Value-Passing Systems. In *First North American Process Algebra Workshop*, pages 9.1–9.20. Tech. Rep. 92-15, Johns Hopkins University, 1992.

[16] D. Scott. Notes on the formalization of logic. Technical report, Subfaculty of Phil., Oxford, 1981.

[17] R.E. Tarjan. Efficiency of a good but not linear set union algorithm. *JACM*, 22:215–225, 1975.

[18] R.E. Tarjan. *Data Structures and Network Algorithms.* Soc. for Industrial and Applied Math., 1983.

[19] R.E.Tarjan and J.v.Leeuwen. Worst-Case Analysis of Set Union Algorithms. *JACM*, 31:245–281, 1984.

[20] J. Westbrook and R.E. Tarjan. Amortized analysis of algorithms for set union with backtracking. *SIAM J. Comput.*, 18(1):1–11, 1989.

Hierarchical Compression for Model-Checking CSP or How to Check 10^{20} Dining Philosophers for Deadlock

A.W. Roscoe*†, P.H.B. Gardiner†, M.H. Goldsmith†, J.R. Hulance†, D.M. Jackson† J.B. Scattergood*†

1 Introduction

FDR (Failures-Divergence Refinement) [6] is a model-checking tool for CSP [10]. Except for the recent addition of determinism checking [20, 22] (primarily for checking security properties) its method of verifying specifications is to test for the refinement of a process representing the specification by the target process. The presently released version (FDR 1) uses only *explicit* model-checking techniques: it fully expands the state-space of its processes and visits each state in turn. Though it is very efficient in doing this and can deal with processes with approximately 10^7 states in about 4 hours on a typical workstation, the exponential growth of state-space with the number of parallel processes in a network represents a significant limit on its utility. A new version of the tool (FDR 2) is at an advanced stage of development at the time of writing (February 1995) which will offer various enhancements over FDR 1. In particular, it has the ability to build up a system gradually, at each stage compressing the subsystems to find an equivalent process with (hopefully) many less states. By doing this it can check systems which are sometimes exponentially larger than FDR 1 can – such as a network of 10^{20} (or even 10^{1000}) dining philosophers.

This is one of the ways (and the only one which is expected to be released in the immediate future) in which we anticipate adding direct *implicit* model-checking capabilities to FDR. By these means we can certainly rival the sizes of systems analysed by BDD's (see [2], for example) though, like the latter, our implicit methods will certainly be sensitive to what example they are applied to and how skillfully they are used. Hopefully the

*Oxford University Computing Laboratory, Wolfson Building, Parks Road, Oxford
†Formal Systems (Europe) Ltd,3 Alfred Street, Oxford

examples later in this paper will illustrate this.

The idea of compressing systems as they are constructed is not new, and indeed it has been used in a much more restricted sense in FDR for several years (applying bisimulation at the boundary between its low and high-level processes). The novelty of this paper consists in several of the specific compressions described and in their use in the context of FDR which differs from most other model-checking tools in (i) being based on CSP and (ii) being a refinement checker which compares two CSP processes rather than having the specification written in a different language such as μ-calculus or temporal logic.

The ideas presented in this paper are closely related to those of [8] (whose *interface specifications* – restrictions based on contexts – translate very naturally and usefully to the context of CSP), and also of [3] since we will make considerable use of optimisations resulting from restrictions to the sub-alphabet of interest (which in the important case of deadlock turns out to be the empty set). Most of the literature relates to compressions with respect to strong equivalences such as observational equivalence and bisimulation. The most similar work to our own, because it relates to the weaker, CSP style, equivalences is that of Valmari, for example [12, 25].

The main ideas behind FDR were introduced in a paper in the Hoare *Festschrift* [19] as, indeed, was part of the theory behind this compression.

In this paper we will introduce the main compression techniques used by FDR2 and give some early indications of their efficiency and usefulness.

2 Two views of CSP

The theory of CSP has classically been based on mathematical models remote from the language itself. These models have been based on observable behaviours of processes such as traces, failures and divergences, rather than attempting to capture a full operational picture of how the process progresses.

On the other hand CSP can be given an operational semantics in terms of labelled transition systems. This operational semantics can be related to the mathematical models based on behaviour by defining *abstraction* functions that 'observe' what behaviours the transition system can produce. Suppose Φ is the abstraction function to one of these models. An abstract operator *op* and the corresponding concrete/operational version **op** are congruent if, for all operational processes **P**, we have $\Phi(\mathbf{op}(\mathbf{P})) = op(\Phi(\mathbf{P}))$. The operational and denotational semantics of a language are congruent if all constructs in the language have this property, which implies that the behaviours predicted for any term by the denotational semantics are always the same as those that can be observed of its operational semantics. That the standard semantics of CSP are congruent to a natural operational semantics is shown in, for example, [18].

Given that each of our models represents a process by the set of its possible behaviours, it is natural to represent refinement as the reduction of these options: the reverse containment of the set of behaviours. If P refines Q we write $Q \sqsubseteq P$, sometimes subscripting $\sqsubseteq$ to indicate which model the refinement it is respect to.

In this paper we will consider three different models – which are the three that FDR supports. These are

- The *traces* model: a process is represented by the set of finite sequences of communications it can perform. $traces(P)$ is the set of P's (finite) traces.

- The *stable failures* model: a process is represented by its set of traces as above and also by its stable failures (s, X) pairs where s is a finite trace of the process and X is a set of events it can refuse after s which (operationally) means coming into a state where it can do no internal action and no action from the set X. *failures*(P) is the set of P's stable failures in this sense. (This model is relatively new; it is introduced in [11]. The concepts behind it will, however, be familiar to anyone well-versed in CSP. It differs from those of [12] in that it entirely ignores divergence.)

- The *failures/divergences* model [1]: a process P *diverges* when it performs an infinite unbroken sequence of internal actions. The set *divergences*(P) is those traces *after* or *during* which the process can diverge (this set is always suffix closed). In this model a process is represented by *divergences*(P) and a modified set of failures in which after any divergence the set of failures is extended so that we do not care how the process behaves

  $$failures_{\perp}(P) = failures(P) \cup \{(s, X) \mid s \in divergences(P)\}$$

  This is done both because one can argue that a divergent process looks from the outside rather like a deadlocked one (i.e., refusing everything) and because the technical problems of modelling what happens past divergence are not worth the effort.

We will also only deal with the case where the overall alphabet of possible actions is finite, since this makes the model a little more straightforward, and is an obvious prerequisite to model-checking.

All three of these models have the obvious congruence theorem with the standard operational semantics of CSP. In fact FDR works chiefly in the operational world: it computes how a process behaves by applying the rules of the operational semantics to expand it into a transition system. The congruence theorem are thus vital in supporting all its work: it can only claim to prove things about the abstractly-defined semantics of a process because we happen to know that this equals the set of behaviours of the operational process FDR works with.

The congruence theorems are also fundamental in supporting the hierarchical compression which is the main topic of this paper. For we know that, if $C[\cdot]$ is any CSP context, then the value in one of our semantic models of $C[P]$ depends only on the value (in the same model) of P, not on the precise way it is implemented. Therefore, if P is represented as a member of a transition system, and we intend to compute the value of $C[P]$ by expanding it as a transition system also, it may greatly be to our advantage to find another representation of P with fewer states. If, for example, we are combining processes P and Q in parallel and each has 1000 states, but can be compressed to 100, the compressed composition can have no more than 10,000 states while the uncompressed one may have up to 1,000,000.

3 Generalised Transition Systems

A labelled transition system is usually deemed to be a set of (effectively) structureless nodes which have visible or τ transitions to other nodes. ¿From the point of view of compression in the stable failures and failures/divergences models, it is useful to enrich nodes by a set of minimal acceptance sets and a divergence labelling. We will therefore assume that there are functions that map the nodes of a ***generalised labelled transition system*** (GLTS) as follows:

- ***minaccs***(P) is a (possibly empty) set of incomparable (under subset) subsets of Σ (the set of all events). $X \in$ ***minaccs***(P) if and only if P can stably accept the set X, refusing all other events, and can similarly accept no smaller set. Since one of these nodes is representing more than one 'state' the process can get into, it can have more than one minimal acceptance. It can also have τ actions in addition to minimal acceptances (with the implicit understanding that the τs are not possible when a minimal acceptance is). However if there is no τ action then there must be at least one minimal acceptance, and in any case all minimal acceptances are subsets of the visible transitions the state can perform.

  minaccs(P) represents the stable acceptances P can make ***itself***. If it has τ actions then these might bring it into a state where the process can have other acceptances (and the environment has no way of seeing that the τ has happened), but since these are not performed by the node P but by a successor, these minimal acceptances are not included among those of the node P.

- *div*(*P*) is either true or false. If it is true it means that *P* can diverge – possibly as the result of an infinite sequence of implicit τ-actions within *P*. It is as though *P* has a τ-action to itself. This allows us to represent divergence in transition systems from which all explicit τ's have been removed.

A node *P* in a GLTS can have multiple actions with the same label, just as in a standard transition system.

A GLTS combines the features of a standard labelled transition system and those of the normal form transition systems used in FDR 1 to represent specification processes [19]. These have the two sorts of labelling discussed above, but are (apart from the nondeterminism coded in the labellings) deterministic in that there are no τ actions and each node has at most one successor under each $a \in \Sigma$.

The structures of a GLTS allow us to compress the behaviour of all the nodes reachable from a single *P* under τ actions into one node:

- The new node's visible actions are just the visible transitions (with the same result state) possible for any *Q* such that $P \xrightarrow{\tau} {}^*Q$.

- Its minimal acceptances are the smallest sets of visible actions accepted by any stable *Q* such that $P \xrightarrow{\tau} {}^*Q$.

- It is labelled divergent if, and only if, there is an infinite τ-path (invariably containing a loop in a finite graph) from *P*.

- The new node has no τ actions.

It is this that makes them useful for our purposes. Two things should be pointed out immediately

1. While the above transformation is valid for all the standard CSP equivalences, it is not for most stronger equivalences such as refusal testing and observational/bisimulation equivalence. To deal with one of these either a richer structure of node, or less compression, would be needed.

2. It is no good simply carrying out the above transformation on each node in a transition system. It *will* result in a τ-free GLTS, but one which probably has as many (and more complex) nodes than the old one. Just because $P \xrightarrow{\tau} {}^*Q$ and *Q*'s behaviour has been included in the compressed version of *P*, this does not mean we can avoid including a compressed version of *Q* as well: there may well be a visible transition that leads directly to *Q*. One of the main strategies discussed below – diamond elimination – is designed to analyse which of these *Q*'s can, in fact, be avoided.

FDR2 is designed to be highly flexible about what sort of transition systems it can work on. We will assume, however, that it is always working with GLTS ones which essentially generalise them all. The operational semantics of CSP have to be extended to deal with the labellings on nodes: it is straightforward to construct the rules that allow us to infer the labelling on a combination of nodes (under some CSP construct) from the labellings on the individual ones.

Our concept of a GLTS has been discussed before in [19], and is similar to an "acceptance graph" from [4], though the latter is to all intents the same as the normal form graphs used in FDR1 and discussed in [19, 6].

4 Methods of compression

FDR2 uses at least five different methods of taking one GLTS and attempting to compress it into a smaller one.

1. Strong, node-labelled, bisimulation: the standard notion enriched (as discussed in [19] and the same as Π-bisimulations in [4]) by the minimal acceptance and divergence labelling of the nodes. This is computed by iteration starting from the equivalence induced by equal labelling. This was used in FDR1 for the final stage of normalising specifications.

2. τ-loop elimination: since a process may choose automatically to follow a τ-action, it follows that all the processes on a τ-loop (or, more properly, a strongly connected component under τ-reachability) are equivalent.

3. Diamond elimination: this carries out the node-compression discussed in the last section systematically, so as to include as few nodes as possible in the output graph.

4. Normalisation: discussed extensively elsewhere, this can give significant gains, but it suffers from the disadvantage that by going through powerspace nodes it can be expensive and lead to expansion.

5. Factoring by semantic equivalence: the compositional models of CSP we are using all represent much weaker congruences than bisimulation. Therefore if we can afford to compute the semantic equivalence relation over states it will give better compression than bisimulation to factor by this equivalence relation.

There is no need here to describe either bisimulation, normalisation, or the algorithms used to compute them. Efficient ways of computing the strongly connected components of a directed graph (for τ-loop elimination) can be found in many textbooks on algorithm design (e.g., [16]). Therefore we shall concentrate on the other two methods discussed above, and appropriate ways of combining the five.

Before doing this we will show how to factor a GLTS by an equivalence relation on its nodes (something needed both for τ-loop elimination and for factoring by a semantic equivalence). If $\mathcal{T} = (T, \rightarrow, r)$ is a GLTS (r being its root) and $\cong$ is an equivalence relation over it, then the nodes of $\mathcal{T}/\cong$ are the equivalence classes $\overline{n}$ for $n \in T$, with root $\overline{r}$. The actions are as follows:

- If $a \neq \tau$, then $\overline{m} \xrightarrow{a} \overline{n}$ if and only if there are $m' \in \overline{m}$ and $n' \in \overline{n}$ such that $m' \xrightarrow{a} n'$.
- If $\overline{m} \neq \overline{n}$, then $\overline{m} \xrightarrow{\tau} \overline{n}$ if and only if there are $m' \in \overline{m}$ and $n' \in \overline{n}$ such that $m' \xrightarrow{\tau} n'$.
- If $\overline{m} = \overline{n}$, then $\overline{m} \stackrel{\tau}{\not\longrightarrow} \overline{n}$ but (if we are concerned about divergence) the new node is marked divergent if and only if there is an infinite τ-path amongst the members of $\overline{m}$, or one of the $m' \in \overline{m}$ is already marked divergent.

The minimal acceptance marking of $\overline{m}$ is just the union of those of its members, with non-minimal sets removed.

4.1 Computing semantic equivalence

Two nodes that are identified by strong node-labelled bisimulation are always semantically equivalent in each of our models. The models do, however, represent much weaker equivalences and there may well be advantages in factoring the transition system by the appropriate one. The only disadvantage is that the computation of these weaker equivalences is more expensive: it requires an expensive form of normalisation, so

- there may be systems where it is impractical, or too expensive, to compute semantic equivalence, and
- when computing semantic equivalence, it will probably be to our advantage to reduce the number of states using other compression techniques first – see a later section.

To compute the semantic equivalence relation we require the *entire normal form* of the input GLTS $\mathcal{T}$. This is the normal form that includes a node equivalent to each node of the original system, with a function from the original system which exhibits this equivalence (the map need neither be injective – because it will identify nodes with the same semantic value – nor surjective – because the normal form sometimes contains nodes that are not equivalent to any single node of the original transition system).

Calculating the entire normal form is more time-consuming that ordinary normalisation. The latter begins its normalisation search with a single set (the τ-closure $\tau^*(r)$ of $\mathcal{T}$'s root),but for the entire normal form it has to be seeded with $\{\tau^*(n) \mid n \in T\}$ – usually[1] as many sets as there are nodes in T. As with ordinary normalisation, there are two phases: the first (pre-normalisation) computing the subsets of T that are reachable under any trace (of visible actions) from any of the seed nodes, with a unique-branching transition structure over it. Because of this unique branching structure, the second phase, which is simply a strong node-labelled bisimulation over it, guarantees to compute a normal form where all the nodes have distinct semantic values. We distinguish between the three semantic models as follows:

- For the traces model, neither minimal acceptance nor divergence labelling is used for the bisimulation.
- For the stable failures model, only minimal acceptance labelling is used.
- For the failures/divergences model, both sorts of labelling are used and in the pre-normalisation phase there is no need to search beyond a divergent node.

The map from T to the normal form is then just the composition of that which takes n to the pre-normal form node $\tau^*(n)$ and the final bisimulation.

The equivalence relation is then simply that induced by the map: two nodes are equivalent if and only if they are mapped to the same node in the normal form. The compressed transition system is that produced by factoring out this equivalence using the rules discussed earlier. To prove that the compressed form is equivalent to the original (in the sense that, in the chosen model, every node m is equivalent to $\overline{m}$ in the new one) one can use the following lemma and induction, based on the fact that each equivalence class of nodes under semantic equivalence is trivially τ-convex as required by the lemma.

LEMMA 1
Suppose $\mathcal{T}$ be any GLTS and let M be any set of nodes in $\mathcal{T}$ with the following two properties

- All members of M are equivalent in one of our three models $\mathcal{C}$.
- M is convex under τ (i.e., if $m, m' \in M$ and m'' are such that $m \xrightarrow{\tau} {}^*m'' \xrightarrow{\tau} {}^*m'$ then $m'' \in M$.

Then let $\mathcal{T}'$ be the GLTS $\mathcal{T}/\equiv$, where $\equiv$ is the equivalence relation which identifies all members of M but no other distinct nodes in $\mathcal{T}$. m is semanti-

[1]If and only if there are no τ-loops.

cally equivalent in the chosen model to $\overline{m}$ (the corresponding node in $\mathcal{T}'$).

PROOF
It is elementary to show that each behaviour (trace or failure or divergence) is one of $\overline{m}$ (this does not depend on the nature of $\equiv$).

Any behaviour of a node $\overline{m}$ of $\mathcal{T}'$ corresponds to a sequence σ of actions

$$\overline{m} = \overline{m_0} \xrightarrow{x_1} \overline{m_1} \xrightarrow{x_2} \overline{m_2} \ldots$$

either going on for ever (with all but finitely many x_i τ's), or terminating and perhaps depending on either a minimal acceptance or divergence marking in the final state. Without loss of generality we can assume that the m_r are chosen so that there is, for each r, m'_{r+1} such that $m_r \xrightarrow{x_r} m'_{r+1}$ and that (if appropriate) the final m_r possesses the divergence or minimal acceptance which the sequence demonstrates. Set $m'_0 = m$, the node which we wish to demonstrate has the same behaviour exemplified by σ.

For any relevant s, define $\sigma \uparrow s$ to be the final part of σ starting at $\overline{m_s}$:

$$\overline{m_s} \xrightarrow{x_{s+1}} \overline{m_{s+1}} \xrightarrow{x_{s+2}} \overline{m_{s+2}} \ldots$$

If M, the only non-trivial equivalence class appears more than once in the final (τ-only) segment of an infinite demonstration of a divergence, then all intermediate classes must be the same (by the τ-convexity of M). But this is impossible since an equivalence class never has a τ action to itself (by the construction of $\mathcal{T}/\equiv$).

Hence, σ can only use this non-trivial class finitely often. If it appears no times then the behaviour we have in $\mathcal{T}'$ is trivially one in $\mathcal{T}$. Otherwise it must appear some last time in σ, as $\overline{m_r}$, say. What we will prove, by induction for s from r down to 0, is that the node m'_s (and hence $m = m'_0$) possesses the same behaviour demonstrated by the sequence $\sigma \uparrow s$ in $\mathcal{T}'$.

If the special node M in T' becomes marked by a divergence or minimal acceptance (where relevant to $\mathcal{C}$) through the factoring then it is trivial that some member of the equivalence class has that behaviour and hence (in the relevant models) *all* the members of M do (though perhaps after some τ actions) since they are equivalent in $\mathcal{C}$. It follows that if $\overline{m_r}$ is the final state in σ, then our inductive claim holds.

Suppose $s \leq r$ is not final in σ and that the inductive claim has been established for all i with $s < i \leq r$. Then the node m_s is easily seen to possess in $\mathcal{T}$ the behaviour of $\sigma \uparrow s$. If the equivalence class of m_s is not M then $m_s = m'_s$ and there is nothing else to prove. If it is M then since m_s and m'_s are equivalent in $\mathcal{C}$ and m'_s has the behaviour, it follows that m'_s does also. This completes the proof of the lemma.

4.2 Diamond elimination

This procedure assumes that the relation of τ-reachability is a partial order on nodes. If the input transition system is known to be divergence free then this is true, otherwise τ-loop elimination is required first (since this procedure guarantees to achieve the desired state).

Under this assumption, diamond reduction can be described as follows, where the input state-machine is S (in which nodes can be marked with information such as minimal acceptances), and we are creating a new state-machine T from all nodes explored in the search:

- Begin a search through the nodes of S starting from its root N_0. At any time there will be a set of unexplored nodes of S; the search is complete when this is empty.
- To explore node N, collect the following information:
  - The set $\tau^*(N)$ of all nodes reachable from N under a (possibly empty) sequence of τ actions.
  - Where relevant (based on the equivalence being used), divergence and minimal acceptance information for N: it is divergent if any member of $\tau^*(N)$ is either marked as divergent or has a τ to itself. The minimal acceptances are the union of those of the members of $\tau^*(N)$, with non-minimal sets removed. This information is used to mark N in T.
  - The set $V(N)$ of initial visible actions: the union of the set of all non-τ actions possible for any member of $\tau^*(N)$.
  - For each $a \in V(N)$, the set $N_a = N$ *after* a of all nodes reachable under a from any member of $\tau^*(N)$.
  - For each $a \in V(N)$, the set $min(N_a)$ which is the set of all τ-minimal elements of N_a.
- A transition (labelled a) is added to T from N to each N' in $min(N_a)$, for all $a \in V(N)$. Any nodes not already explored are added to the search.

This creates a transition system where there are no τ-actions but where there can be ambiguous branching under visible actions, and where nodes might be labelled as divergent. The reason why this compresses is that we do not include in the search nodes where there is another node similarly reachable but demonstrably at least as nondeterministic: for if $M \in \tau^*(N)$ then N is always at least as nondeterministic as M. The hope is that the completed search will tend to include only those nodes that are τ-minimal: not reachable under τ from any other. Notice that the behaviours of the nodes not included from N_a are nevertheless taken account of, since their divergences and minimal acceptances are included when some node of $min(N_a)$ is explored.

It seems counter-intuitive that we should work hard *not* to unwind τ's rather than doing so eagerly. The reason why we cannot simply unwind τ's as far as possible (i.e., collecting the τ-maximal points reachable under a given action) is that there will probably be visible actions possible from the unstable nodes we are trying to bypass. It is impossible to guarantee that these actions can be ignored.

The reason we have called this compression ***diamond elimination*** is because what it does is to (attempt to) remove nodes based on the diamond-shaped transition arrangement where we have four nodes P, P', Q, Q' and $P \xrightarrow{\tau} P'$, $Q \xrightarrow{\tau} Q'$, $P \xrightarrow{a} Q$ and $P' \xrightarrow{a} Q'$. Starting ¿from P, diamond elimination will seek to remove the nodes P' and Q'. The only way in which this might fail is if some further node in the search forces one or both to be considered.

The lemma that shows why diamond reduction works is the following.

LEMMA 2
Suppose N is any node in $\mathcal{S}$, $s \in \Sigma^*$ and $N_0 \overset{s}{\Longrightarrow} N$ (i.e., there is a sequence of nodes $M_0 = N_0, M_1, ..., M_k = N$ and actions $x_1, ..., x_k$ such that $M_i \xrightarrow{x_i} M_{m+1}$ for all i and $s = \langle x_i \mid i = 1, .., n, x_i \neq \tau \rangle$). Then there is a node N' in $\mathcal{T}$ such that $N_0 \overset{s}{\Longrightarrow} N'$ in $\mathcal{T}$ and $N \in \tau^*(N')$.

PROOF
This is by induction on the length if s. If s is empty the result is obvious (as $N_0 \in T$ always), so assume it holds of s' and $s = s'\langle a \rangle$, with $N_0 \overset{s}{\Longrightarrow} N$. Then by definition of $\overset{s}{\Longrightarrow}$, there exist nodes N_1 and N_2 of S such that $N_0 \overset{s'}{\Longrightarrow} N_1$, $N_1 \xrightarrow{a} N_2$ and $N \in \tau^*(N_2)$.

By induction there thus exists N_1' in T such that $N_0 \overset{s'}{\Longrightarrow} N_1'$ in $\mathcal{T}$ and $N_1 \in \tau^*(N_1')$. Since $N_1' \in T$ it has been explored in constructing $\mathcal{T}$. Clearly $a \in V(N_1')$ and $N_2 \in (N_1')_a$. Therefore there exists a member N' of $min((N_1')_a)$ (a subset of the nodes of T) such that $N_2 \in \tau^*(N')$. Then, by construction of $\mathcal{T}$ and since $N \in \tau^*(N_2)$ we have $N_0 \overset{s}{\Longrightarrow} N'$ and $N \in \tau^*(N')$ as required, completing the induction.

This lemma shows that every behaviour displayed by a node of $\mathcal{S}$ is (thanks to the way we mark each node of $\mathcal{T}$ with the minimal acceptances and divergence of its τ-closure) displayed by a node of $\mathcal{T}$.

Lemma 2 shows that the following two types of node are certain to be included in $\mathcal{T}$:

- The initial node N_0.
- S_0, the set of all τ-minimal nodes (ones not reachable under τ from any other).

Let us call $S_0 \cup \{N_0\}$ the *core* of S. The obvious criteria for judging whether to try diamond reduction at all, and of how successful it has been once tried, will be based on the core. For since the only nodes we can hope to get rid of are the complement of the core, we might decide not to bother if there are not enough of these as a proportion of the whole. And after carrying out the reduction, we can give a success rating in terms of the percentage of non-core nodes eliminated.

Experimentation over a wide range of example CSP processes has demonstrated that diamond elimination is a highly effective compression technique, with success ratings usually at or close to 100% on most natural systems. To illustrate how diamond elimination works, consider one of the most hackneyed CSP networks: N one-place buffer processes chained together.

$$COPY \gg COPY \gg \ldots COPY \gg COPY$$

Here, $COPY = \mathit{left}?x \longrightarrow \mathit{right}!x \longrightarrow COPY$. If the underlying type has k members then $COPY$ has $k+1$ states and the network has $(k+1)^N$. Since all of the internal communications (the movement of data from one $COPY$ to the next) become τ actions, this is an excellent target for diamond elimination. And in fact we get 100% success: the only nodes retained are those that are not τ-reachable from any other. These are the ones in which all of the data is as far to the left as it can be: there are no empty $COPY$'s to the left of a full one. If $k = 1$ this means there are now $N+1$ nodes rather than 2^N, and if $k = 2$ it gives $2^{N+1} - 1$ rather than 3^N.

4.3 Combining techniques

The objective of compression is to reduce the number of states in the target system as much as possible, with the secondary objectives of keeping the number of transitions and the complexity of any minimal acceptance marking as low as possible.

There are essentially two possibilities for the best compression of a given system: either its normal form or the result of applying some combination of the other techniques. For whatever equivalence-preserving transformation is performed on a transition system, the normal form (from its root node) must be invariant; and all of the other techniques leave any normal form system unchanged. In many cases (such as the chain of $COPY$s above) the two will be the same size (for the diamond elimination immediately finds a system equivalent to the normal form, as does equivalence factoring), but there are certainly cases where each is better.

The relative speeds (and memory use) of the various techniques vary substantially from example to example, but broadly speaking the relative efficiencies are (in decreasing order) τ-loop elimination (except in rare complex cases), bisimulation, diamond elimination, normalisation and equivalence factoring. The last two can, of course, be done together since the entire normal form contains the usual normal form within it. Diamond elimination is an extremely useful strategy to carry out before either sort of normalisation, both because it reduces the size of the system on which the normal form is computed (and the number of seed nodes for the entire normal form) and because it eliminates the need for searching through chains of τ actions which forms a large part of the normalisation process.

One should note that all our compression techniques guarantee to do no worse than leave the number of states unchanged, with the exception of normalisation which in the worst case can expand the number of states exponentially[19, 13]. Cases of expanding normal forms are very rare in practical systems. Only very recently, after nearly four years, have we encountered a class of practically important processes whose normalisation behaviour is pathological. These are the "spy" processes used to seek errors in security protocols [21].

At the time of writing all of the compression techniques discussed have been implemented and many experiments performed using them. Ultimately we expect that FDR2's compression processing will be automated according to a strategy based on a combination of these techniques, with the additional possibility of user intervention.

5 Compression in context

FDR2 will take a complex CSP description and build it up in stages, compressing the resulting process each time. Ultimately we expect these decisions to be at least partly automated, but in early versions the compression directives will be included in the syntax of the target process.

One of the most interesting and challenging things when incorporating these ideas is preserving the debugging functionality of the system. The debugging process becomes hierarchical: at the top level we will find erroneous behaviours of compressed parts of the system; we will then have to debug the pre-compressed forms for the appropriate behaviour, and so on down. On very large systems (such as that discussed in the next section) it will not be practical to complete this process for all parts of the system. Therefore we expect the debugging facility initially to work out subsystem behaviours down as far as the highest level compressed processes, and only to investigate more deeply when directed by the user (through the X Windows debugging facility of FDR).

The way a system is composed together can have an enormous influence on the effectiveness of hierarchical compression. The following principles should generally be followed:

1. Put together processes which communicate with each other together early. For example, in the dining philosophers, you should build up the system out of consecutive fork/philosopher pairs rather than putting the philosophers all together, the forks all together and then putting these two processes together at the highest level.

2. Hide all events at as low a level as is possible. The laws of CSP allow the movement of hiding inside and outside a parallel operator as long

as its synchronisations are not interfered with. In general therefore, any event that is to be hidden should be hidden the first time (in building up the process) that it no longer has to be synchronised at a higher level. The reason for this is that the compression techniques all tend to work much more effectively on systems with many τ actions.

3. Hide all events that are irrelevant (in the sense discussed below) to the specification you are trying to prove.

Hiding can introduce divergence, and thereby invalidate many failures/divergences model specifications. However in the traces model it does not alter the sequence of unhidden events, and in the stable failures model does not alter refusals which contain every hidden event. Therefore if only trying to prove a property in one of these models – or if it has already been established by whatever method that one's substantive system is divergence free – the improved compression we get by hiding extra events makes it worthwhile doing so.

We will give two examples of this, one based on the *COPY* chain example we saw above and one on the dining philosophers. The first is probably typical of the gains we can make with compression and hiding; the second is atypically good.

5.1 Hiding and safety properties

If the underlying datatype T of the *COPY* processes is large, then chaining N of them together will lead to unmanageably large state-spaces whatever sort of compression is applied to the entire system. For it really does have a lot of distinct states: one for each possible contents the resulting N-place buffer might have. Of course there are analytic techniques that can be applied to this simple example that pin down its behaviour, but we will ignore these and illustrate a general technique that can be used to prove simple safety properties of complex networks. Suppose x is one member of the type T; an obviously desirable (and true) property of the *COPY* chain is that the number of x's input on channel *left* is always greater than or equal to the number output on *right*, but no greater than the latter plus N. Since the truth or falsity of this property is unaffected by the system's communications in the rest of its alphabet $\{left.y, right.y \mid y \in \Sigma \setminus \{x\}\}$ we can hide this set and build the network up a process at a time from left to right. At the intermediate stages you have to leave the right-hand communications unhidden (because these still have to be synchronised with processes yet to be built in) but nevertheless, in the traces model, the state space of the intermediate stages grows more slowly with n than without the hiding. In fact, with n *COPY* processes the hidden version compresses to exactly 2^n states whatever the size of T (assuming that this is at least 2).

This is a substantial reduction, but is perhaps not as good as one might ideally hope for. By hiding all inputs other than the chosen one, we are ignoring what the contents of the systems are apart from x, but because we are still going to compose the process with one which will take all of our outputs, these have to remain visible, and the number of states mainly reflects the number of different ways the outputs of objects other than x can be affected by the order of inputting and outputting x. The point is that we do not know (in the method) that the outputs other than x are ultimately going to be irrelevant to the specification, for we are not making any assumptions about the process we will be connected to.

Since the size of system we can compress is always likely to be one or two orders of magnitude smaller than the number of explicit states in the final refinement check, it would actually be advantageous to build this system not in one direction as indicated above, but from both ends and finally compose the two halves together. (The partially-composed system of n right-hand processes also has 2^N states.) Nothing useful would (in this example) be achieved by building up further pieces in the middle, since we only get the simplifying benefit of the hiding from the two ends of the system.

If the (albeit slower) exponential growth of states even after hiding and compressing the actual system is unacceptable, there is one further option: find a network with either less states, or better compression behaviour, that the actual one refines, but which can still be shown to satisfy the specification. In the example above this is easy: simply replace $COPY$ with

$$C_x = (\mu\, p.\mathit{left}.x \longrightarrow \mathit{right}.x \longrightarrow p) \parallel CHAOS(\Sigma \setminus \{\mathit{left}.x, \mathit{right}.x\})$$

the process which acts like a reliable one-place buffer for the value x, but can input and output as it chooses one other members of T. It is easy to show that $COPY$ refines this, and a chain of n C_x's compresses to $n+1$ states (even without hiding irrelevant external communications).

In a sense the C_x processes capture the essential reason why the chain of $COPY$'s satisfy the x-counting specification. By being clever we have managed to automate the proof for much larger networks than following the 'dumb' approach, but of course it is not ideal that we have had to be clever in this way.

The methods discussed in this section could be used to prove properties about the reliability of communications between a given pair of nodes in a complex environment, and similar cases where the full complexity of the operation of a system is irrelevant to why a particular property is true.

5.2 Hiding and deadlock

In the stable failures model, a system can deadlock if and only if $P \setminus \Sigma$ can. In other words, we can hide absolutely all events – and move this hiding as far into the process as possible using the principles already discussed.

Consider the case of the N dining philosophers (in a version, for simplicity, without a Butler process). A natural way of building this system up hierarchically is as progressively longer chains of the form

$$PHIL_0 \| FORK_0 \| PHIL_1 \| \ldots \| FORK_{m-1} \| PHIL_m$$

In analysing the whole system for deadlock, we can hide all those events of a subsystem that do not synchronise with any process outside the subsystem. Thus in this case we can hide all events other than the interactions between $PHIL_0$ and $FORK_{N-1}$, and between $PHIL_m$ and $FORK_m$. The failures normal form of the subsystem will have very few states (exactly 4). Thus we can compute the failures normal form of the whole hidden system, adding a small fixed number of philosopher/fork combinations at a time, in time proportional to N, even though an explicit model-checker would find exponentially many states.

We can, in fact, do even better than this. Imagine doing the following:

- First, build a single philosopher/fork combination hiding all events not in its external interface, and compress it. This will (with standard definitions) have 4 states.
- Next, put 10 copies of this process together in parallel, after suitable renaming to make them into consecutive pairs in a chain of philosophers and forks (the result will have approximately 4000 states) and compress it to its 4 states.
- Now rename this process in 10 different ways so that it looks like 10 adjacent groups of philosophers, compute the results and compress it.
- And repeat this process as often as you like...clearly it will take time linear in the number of times you do it.

By this method we can produce a model of 10^N philosophers and forks in a row in time proportional to N. To make them into a ring, all you would have to do would be to add another row of one or more philosophers and forks in parallel, synchronising the two at both ends. Depending on how it was built (such as whether all the philosophers are allowed to act with a single handedness) you would either find deadlock or prove it absent from a system with doubly exponential number of states.

On the prototype version of FDR2, we have been able to use this technique to demonstrate the deadlock of 10^{1000} philosophers in 15 minutes, and then to use the debugging tool described earlier to tell you the state of any individual one of them (though the depth of the parse tree even of the efficiently constructed system makes this tedious). Viewed through the eyes of explicit model-checking, this system has perhaps $7^{10^{1000}}$ states. Clearly this simply demonstrates the pointlessness of pure state-counting.

This example is, of course, extraordinarily well-suited to our methods. What makes it work are firstly the fact that the networks we build up have a constant-sized external interface (which could only happen in networks that were, like this one, chains or nearly so) and have a behaviour that compresses to a bounded size as the network grows.

On the whole we do not have to prove deadlock freedom of quite such absurdly large systems. We expect that our methods will also bring great improvements to the deadlock checking of more usual size ones that are not necessarily as perfectly suited to them as the example above.

6 Related Work

A wide range of automated systems have been proposed for the analysis of state-transition systems [5, 7, 14, 17] and it is instructive to examine where FDR, as an industrial product, falls in the range of possibilities identified by academic research. The more flexible tools, like the Concurrency Workbench of [5], permit a wide range of semantic operations to be carried out in those formalisms which exhibit less consensus about the central semantic models. Choosing an alternative approach, systems constructed to decide specific questions about suitably constructed finite-state representations can achieve much greater performance [9, 23].

In designing FDR we make a compromise between these extremes: the CSP language provides a flexible and powerful basis for describing problems, yet by concentrating on the standard CSP semantics we are able to achieve acceptable performance levels. Milner's scheduling problem (used as a benchmark in [5]) can be reduced to CSP normal form in around 3s for seven clients and around 45s for ten. (The admittedly somewhat outdated figure for bisimulation minimization using the Concurrency Workbench is 2000s for seven clients, and the ten client problem was too large to be considered.) Furthermore, the flexibility of CSP as a specification language removes much of the need for special-case algorithms to detect deadlock or termination (such as those proposed as additions to Winston in [15]).

Perhaps the most comparable approach is that taken by the SMV system [14], which decides whether CTL logical specifications are satisfied by systems expressed as state-variable assignments. The BDD representation used by SMV can encode very large problems efficiently, although as with any implicit scheme its effectiveness can vary with the manner in which a system is described: in this regard we hope that identifying candidate components for compression or abstraction may prove easier in practice than arranging that state variables respect a regular logical form. Unlike SMV, a key feature of FDR is its use of a process algebra for both specification and design, encouraging step-wise refinement and the combination of automatic verification with conventional proof. The underlying semantic model, and the extrinsic nature of FDR2 compression can, of course, be applied to any notation or representation which can be interpreted within the FDR framework. FDR2 is designed to facilitate such extension.

7 Conclusions

We have given details of how FDR2's compression works, and some simple examples of how it can expand the size of problem we can automatically check. At the time of writing we have not had time to carry out many evaluations of this new functionality on realistic-sized examples, but we have no reason to doubt that compression will allow comparable improvements in these.

It is problematic that the successful use of compression apparently takes somewhat more skill than explicit model-checking. Only by studying its use in large-scale case studies can we expect to assess the best ways to deal with this – by automated tactics and transformation, or by design-rule guidance to the user. In any case much work will be required before we can claim to understand fully the capabilities and power of the extended tool.

Acknowledgements

As well as our owing him a tremendous debt for his development of CSP, on which all this work is based, it was a remark by Tony Hoare that led the first author to realise how our methods could check the exponential systems of dining philosophers described in this paper.

We would like to thank the referees for some helpful remarks, in particular for pointing out the need for Lemma 1.

The work of Roscoe and Scattergood was supported in part by a grant from the US Office of Naval Research.

8 References

[1] S.D. Brookes and A.W. Roscoe, ***An improved failures model for communicating processes***, in Proceedings of the Pittsburgh seminar on concurrency, Springer LNCS 197 (1985), 281-305.

[2] J.R. Burch, E.M. Clarke, D.L. Dill and L.J. Hwang, ***Symbolic model checking:*** 10^{20} ***states and beyond***, Proc. 5th IEEE Annual Symposium on Logic in Computer Science, IEEE Press (1990).

[3] E.M. Clarke, D.E. Long and K.L.MacMillan, ***Compositional Model Checker***, Proceedings of LICS 1989.

[4] R. Cleaveland and M.C.B. Hennessy, *Testing Equivalence as a Bisimulation Equivalence*, FAC **5** (1993) pp1–20.

[5] R. Cleaveland, J. Parrow and B. Steffen, *The Concurrency Workbench: A semantics-based verification tool for finite state systems*, ACM TOPLAS Vol.15, N.1, 1993, pp.36-72.

[6] Formal Systems (Europe) Ltd., *Failures Divergence Refinement* User Manual and Tutorial, version 1.4 1994.

[7] J.-C. Fernandez *An implementation of an efficient algorithm for bisimulation equivalence.*, Science of Computer Programming 13: 219–236, 1989/1990.

[8] S.Graf and B. Steffen, *Compositional Minimisation of Finite-State Systems*, Proceedings of CAV1990 (LNCS 531).

[9] J.F. Groote and F. Vaandrager, *An efficient algorithm for branching bisimulation and stuttering equivalence*, Proc. 17th ICALP, Springer-Verlag LNCS 443, 1990.

[10] C.A.R. Hoare, *Communicating Sequential Processes*, Prentice-Hall 1985.

[11] L. Jategoankar, A Meyer and A.W. Roscoe, *Separating failures from divergence*, in preparation.

[12] R. Kaivola and A Valmari *The weakest compositional semantic equivalence preserving nexttime-less linear temporal logic* in Proc CONCUR '92 (LNCS 630).

[13] P.C. Kanellakis and S.A. Smolka, *CCS expressions, Finite state processes and three problems of equivalence*, Information and Computation **86**, 43-68 (1990).

[14] K.L. McMillan, Symbolic Model Checking, Kluwer, 1993.

[15] Malhotra, J., Smolka, S.A., Giacalone, A. and Shapiro, R., *Winston: A Tool for Hierarchical Design and Simulation of Concurrent Systems.*, In *Proceedings of the Workshop on Specification and Verification of Concurrent Systems*, University of Stirling, Scotland, 1988.

[16] K. Melhorn *Graph Algorithms and NP Completeness*, EATCS Monographs on Theoretical Computer Science, Springer-Verlag 1984.

[17] J. Richier, C. Rodriguez, J. Sifakis and J. Voiron, *Verification in XESAR of the Sliding Window Protocol*, Proc. of the 7th IFIP Symposium on Protocol Specification, Testing, and Verification, North-Holland, Amsterdam, 1987.

[18] A.W. Roscoe, *Unbounded Nondeterminism in CSP*, in 'Two Papers on CSP', PRG Monograph PRG-67. Also Journal of Logic and Computation **3**, 2 pp131-172 (1993).

[19] A.W. Roscoe, *Model-checking CSP*, in A Classical Mind: Essays in Honour of C.A.R.. Hoare, A.W. Roscoe (ed.) Prentice-Hall 1994.

[20] A.W. Roscoe, CSP and determinism in security modelling to ap pear in the proceedings of 1995 IEEE Symposium on Security and Privacy.

[21] A.W. Roscoe, *Modelling and verifying key-exchange protocols using CSP and FDR*, to appear in the proceedings of CSFW8 (1995), IEEE Press.

[22] A.W. Roscoe, J.C.P. Woodcock and L. Wulf, *Non-interference t hrough determinism*, Proc. ESORICS 94, Springer LNCS 875, pp 33-53.

[23] V. Roy and R. de Simone, *Auto/Autograph*, In Proc. Computer-Aided Verification '90, American Mathematical Society, Providence, 1991.

[24] J.B. Scattergood, *A basis for CSP tools*, To appear as Oxford University Computing Laboratory technical monograph, 1993.

[25] A. Valmari and M. Tienari *An improved failures equivalence for finite-state systems with a reduction algorithm*, in Protocol Specification, Testing and Verification XI, North-Holland 1991.

A Front-End Generator for Verification Tools

Rance Cleaveland[*†]
Eric Madelaine[*‡]
Steve Sims[*†]

ABSTRACT This paper describes the Process Algebra Compiler (PAC), a front-end generator for process-algebra-based verification tools. Given descriptions of a process algebra's concrete and abstract syntax and semantics as structural operational rules, the PAC produces syntactic routines and functions for computing the semantics of programs in the algebra. Using this tool greatly simplifies the task of adapting verification tools to the analysis of systems described in different languages; it may therefore be used to achieve source-level compatibility between different verification tools. Although the initial verification tools targeted by the PAC are MAUTO and the Concurrency Workbench, the structure of the PAC caters for the support of other tools as well.

1 Introduction

The past ten years have seen the development of a variety of automatic verification tools for finite-state systems expressed in process algebra; examples include MAUTO [6], the Concurrency Workbench [10], TAV [14], and Aldébaran [11]. In general, these tools support a specific language, such as CCS [19], Meije [1], or Basic Lotos [5], for describing systems and provide users different methods, such as equivalence checking, preorder checking, model checking, random simulation, and abstraction mechanisms, for analyzing their behavior. The utility of these tools has been demonstrated via several case studies [7, 18]. However, the impact on system design practice of such tools has been limited by the fact that the languages they support, while possessing nice theoretical properties, are not widely used by system

[*]This work is partially funded by NSF-INRIA collaboration # CCR-9247478, ESPRIT Basic Research Action CONCUR2, NSF/DARPA grant CCR-9014775, ONR Young Investigator Award N00014-92-J-1582, and NSF Young Investigator Award CCR-9257963.

[†]Department of Computer Science, North Carolina State University, Raleigh, NC 27695-8206, USA

[‡]INRIA, B.P. 93, 06902 Sophia Antipolis Cedex, France

engineers. In addition, as each tool in general supports a different language, it is difficult to compare the tools and to investigate approaches to using them in collaboration with one another.

This paper presents the Process Algebra Compiler (PAC), a system that substantially simplifies the task of changing the language supported by verification tools. The PAC is a "front-end generator"; given a description of the syntax and semantics of a language, it produces routines for parsing and unparsing programs in the language and for computing user-defined semantic relations. By providing users with high-level notations for defining languages and managing the difficult and technically tedious development of syntactic and semantic functions, the PAC provides the research community with a useful tool for expanding the repertoire of languages their tools can support.

The remainder of the paper is organized along the following lines. The next section sharpens the motivation for the PAC by presenting two verification tools, MAUTO and the Concurrency Workbench (CWB), and the common semantic framework underlying the (different) languages each supports. The section following presents an overview of the architecture of the PAC and describes the specification language used for defining algebras and their semantics, while Section 4 discusses issues in generating semantic functions from their PAC specifications. Section 5 then gives experimental results obtained from PAC-produced front ends for the Concurrency Workbench; somewhat surprisingly, the PAC-generated code significantly outperforms existing hand-produced code built for this tool. The final section contains our conclusions and directions for future work.

2 Verification Tools and Structural Operational Semantics

This section presents an overview of two verification tools, MAUTO and the Concurrency Workbench. Although similar in intent, the tools differ markedly in terms of the analyses they support; however, at the moment there is no way for a user to use the tools collaboratively. On the other hand, the languages supported by the two tools have a semantics that is given in a very similar style, which we also discuss at the end of this section. These observations provided the impetus for the development of the PAC.

2.1 Verification tools

Both MAUTO and the Concurrency Workbench provide utilities for verifying finite-state systems expressed in process algebra. The specific process algebras supported differ, however, as do the supported analyses. The following provides more detail about the systems.

MAUTO.

MAUTO is a system for analyzing networks of finite-state systems. MAUTO builds automata from programs in the Meije process algebra and is capable of reducing and comparing them with respect to various bisimulation-based equivalences. It also provides a novel facility that enables users to define *abstract* transition relations on a given automaton and obtain a new system, usually smaller and more tractable, that highlights specific behaviors of the original system. Much attention has also been devoted to issues of efficiency. In particular, the building of automata from terms is mixed with the reduction of the automata using congruence properties of the semantic equivalences, thereby ensuring that automata are kept as small as possible. Facilities are also provided for explaining the results of analysis and for drawing the resulting automata in a graphical editor [21].

The Concurrency Workbench.

The Concurrency Workbench (CWB) is an extensible tool for verifying systems written in the process algebra CCS . In contrast with other process algebra tools, the CWB supports the computation of numerous different semantic equivalences and preorders; it does so in a modular fashion in that generic equivalence- and preorder-checking routines are combined with suitable process transformations (see, e.g., [8]) in order to compute different relations. The CWB also includes a flexible *model-checking* facility for determining when a process satisfies a formula in a very expressive temporal logic, the propositional mu-calculus. Recently the CWB has been extended to deal with a discrete-time version of CCS (TCCS), and with the synchronous algebra SCCS.

2.2 Structural Operational Semantics

MAUTO and the CWB are similar in that they analyze systems by converting them into finite automata and then invoking routines on these automata. However, the languages and forms of analysis they support, and the approaches they take to construct automata from systems, differ markedly. In the last case in particular, MAUTO adopts a "bottom-up" approach, with automata recursively constructed for subsystems and then assembled into a single machine for the entire system. The CWB, on the other hand, uses an "on-the-fly" approach, with transitions of components calculated and then combined appropriately into transitions for the over-all system.

One characteristic shared by MAUTO and the CWB, however, is that the languages they support have operational semantics given in the Structural Operational Semantic (SOS) [20] style; this fact motivates our inclusion in the PAC of capabilities for generating routines from SOS descriptions. A SOS for a language consists of rules for inferring the execution behavior of programs written in the language. Rules have the following general form.

$$\frac{premises}{conclusion}(side\ condition)$$

The intuitive reading of the rule is that if one is able to establish the premises, which typically involve statements about the execution behavior of subprograms of the one mentioned in the conclusion, and the side condition holds, then one may infer the conclusion. As an example, the following describes the synchronizations allowed by the parallel composition operation in CCS.

$$\frac{p \xrightarrow{a} p' \quad q \xrightarrow{b} q'}{p|q \xrightarrow{\tau} p'|q'}(a, b\ inverses)$$

The rule states that if p can engage in an action a and evolve to p' and q can engage in b and evolve to q', and a and b are inverses (i.e. constitute an input/output pair on the same communication channel), then $p|q$ can execute an internal action, τ, corresponding to the synchronized execution of a and b.

The SOS style has evolved in many ways since the Plotkin's seminal paper [20] and has been applied to many areas of language semantics. The SOS style is very flexible, as numerous languages with widely varying features have been given semantics using this framework. Recent work has focused on the metatheory of SOS [4, 17, 12, 2, 22]; in particular, researchers have shown that when SOS rules conform to different syntactic formats, the resulting languages have nice properties; in particular, certain operational equivalences are guaranteed to be congruences.

3 Using the PAC

This section provides an overview of the PAC architecture and indicates how users specify process algebras for processing by the PAC.

3.1 *PAC Overview*

Figure 1 sketches the organization of the PAC. The system takes as input files containing the syntactic and semantic description of a process algebra as well as libraries containing the definitions of any necessary auxiliary functions. It then produces two (sets of) files:

- A YACC/LEX[1] specification of the language's syntax.

[1] Using YACC/LEX provides an easy way of guaranteeing the compatibility of parsers generated for a given algebra by different back ends. Other parser-generators may also be used at the discretion of the back-end writer.

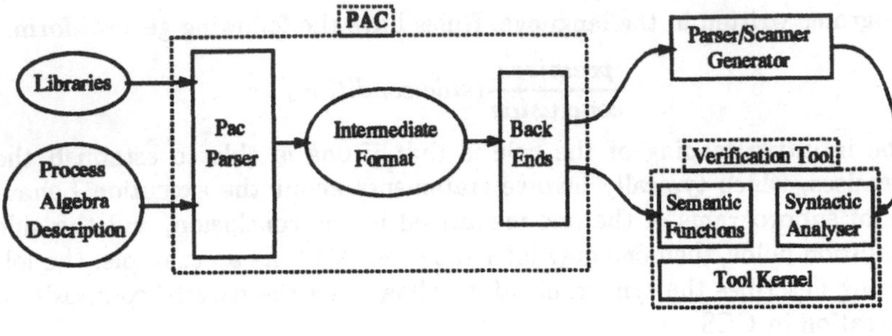

FIGURE 1. Architecture of the PAC

- Semantic routines to analyze programs written in the language.

To specialize a target verification tool to the given language, the PAC user must run YACC/LEX on the first set of files to produce a parser and then insert the parser and the semantic routines into the verification engine. Provided that the target tool separates the syntactic analysis of programs from their verification, the language-independent part of the verification tool (its *kernel*) need not change at all. It should be noted that the PAC is in fact a "compiler": it takes a PAC specification of a language as input and produces source code which is compiled along with the kernel of the target verification tool. There is no PAC run-time system that becomes part of the target verification tool. The PAC can also be viewed as a "compiler compiler" since the generated code is a "compiler" which accepts a process algebra program as input and produces a labeled transition system as output.

The PAC itself is organized into several components centered around an internal representation of the syntax and semantics of the language being processed. This internal structure is produced by the PAC parser from files provided by the user. From it, *back ends* produce the required routines for the target systems. As target verification tools are typically written in different languages (MAUTO in Lisp, the Concurrency Workbench in SML, Aldébaran in C, for example), there will in general be several back ends in the PAC. The initially targeted systems are MAUTO and the Workbench; accordingly, the existing prototype includes back ends that generate Lisp and SML, respectively.

The PAC parser.

The PAC parser tries to factor out as much of the back-end-independent work as possible from the processing of user-supplied algebra descriptions; in particular, it checks the PAC input for syntactic correctness and performs certain consistency checks. If user files satisfy these criteria, the parser then produces an intermediate representation of the input which contains:

- A representation of the abstract syntax of the process algebra.
- A structured description of the concrete syntax from which specifications for scanners, parsers, and unparsers may be generated.
- A representation of the sets of SOS rules used for defining the semantics of the operators in the algebra.

Back ends.

The back ends build the actual routines to be included in the verification tools. They accept as input the intermediate format generated by the PAC parser and generate as output a YACC/LEX specification together with routines that compute the semantics of a system from its abstract syntax. The routines typically differ from one verification tool to another; typical examples include those for computing the single-step transitions of a process, generating the composition of several automata by a given composition operator, computing sufficient syntactic conditions for a process to be finite-state [17], and calculating whether or not a process is divergent.

Implementation.

The PAC is implemented in Standard ML (SML). The system, which currently consists of roughly 15,000 lines of code, is batch-oriented; it processes inputs and either generates output files or reports error messages.

3.2 PAC Process Algebra Specifications

A PAC process algebra specification consists of two components. The `ALGEBRA` module contains descriptions of the concrete and abstract syntax of actions, processes and semantic relations. The `RULE_SET` modules contain SOS rules defining the relations used to define the semantics of processes. Users may also provide *library* files containing code that directly implements auxiliary structures (such as sets or environments) and operations (such as set membership or lookup functions) used in defining the semantics and for which users do not wish to provide SOS definitions. Back ends directly insert this code into the files they generate; consequently this code must be written in a language compatible with that of the target tool. The remainder of this section discusses each of these modules using as an example the CWB-6.0 version of Milner's CCS .

`ALGEBRA` *Modules*

`ALGEBRA` modules consist of several sections.

- In the `sorts` section, users define the syntactic categories for their language.
- The `cons` section defines the term constructors (i.e. the abstract syntax) to be used to build elements in the different syntactic categories.
- The `funs` sections introduces the names and "types" of functions that may be applied to elements of sorts. The implementations of these functions must be supplied by the PAC user.
- The `rels` section defines the names and "types" of the semantic relations to be defined by SOS rules and for which the PAC will generate an implementation. The `inputs` section then indicates what type the generated functions computing these relations should have (i.e. which positions in the relation should be "inputs" and which should be "outputs").
- The `pragmas` section contains back-end-specific directives, such as locations of library files and names to be assigned to functions generated by back ends.
- The `SYNTAX` and `RULE_SYNTAX` sections contain descriptions of the concrete syntax of both the process algebra and of the relations used to define the algebra's semantics.

To illustrate what appears in these sections, consider the (elided) version of an `ALGEBRA` module for CCS in Figure 2. The `sorts` section declares the kinds of objects that appear in the definition of the algebra, including `act` (actions), `agent` (CCS processes), `'a eqn` (equations), and `'a frame` (frames, or mappings from identifiers to values). Note that sorts may be polymorphic: in the case of `'a frame`, for instance, the `'a` may be instantiated with any well-formed sort. The PAC also includes three built-in sorts: `string` for character strings, `bool` for booleans, and `'a list` for polymorphic lists.

The next section of the example introduces the constructors used in CCS and their sorts. For example, `Tau` is introduced as a constructor taking no arguments and producing a value of sort `act`; that is, `Tau` is an action constant. `Input` and `Output` take an identifier (intuitively, a channel name) as an argument and produce an action. In the CWB version of CCS, users may bind identifiers to sets of actions and then use these identifiers in place of sets in the restriction operator. To cater for this possibility, the algebra introduces a sort `restriction` and two constructors, `Res_set` and `Res_var`, permitting sets of identifiers (i.e. a label set, in CCS terms) or a single identifier (a variable name bound to a set) to be viewed as "restrictions". `Eqn` is used to construct equations from identifiers and values, while the remaining constructors are used to build agents. Note that the `Fix` operator

```
ALGEBRA CCS
sorts
    id, act, id_set, restriction, ('a eqn), agent,
    ('a frame), ('a env), ...
cons
    Tau         : act
    Input       : id -> act
    Output      : id -> act
    Res_set     : id_set -> restriction
    Res_var     : id -> restriction
    Eqn         : id * 'a -> ('a eqn)
    Nil         : agent
    Bottom      : agent
    Ag_var      : id    -> agent
    Prefix      : act * agent -> agent
    Plus        : agent * agent -> agent
    Restriction : agent * restriction -> agent
    Fix         : agent * (agent frame) -> agent
    ...
funs
    id_parse    : string -> id
    id_eq       : id * id -> bool
    inverses    : act * act -> bool
    mk_id_set   : (id list) -> id_set
    member      : id * id_set -> bool
    mk_frame    : (('a eqn) list) -> ('a frame)
    mk_frame_inv: ('a frame) -> (('a eqn) list)
    empty       : 'a env
    push_frame  : ('a frame) * ('a env) -> ('a env)
    ...
rels
    transition  : (agent env) * (id_set env) *
                  agent * act * agent -> bool
    diverges    : (agent env) * (id_set env) * agent -> bool
inputs
    transition is [1,2,3]
    diverges is [1,2,3]
pragmas
    CWB "parser entries:  act, agent, id_set"
    ...
SYNTAX
    ...
RULE_SYNTAX
    ...
end
```

FIGURE 2. An **ALGEBRA** module for CCS

takes an agent and an agent frame as arguments; intuitively, the frame contains bindings for the free variables that may appear in the agent.

The **funs** section introduces operations that may be applied to elements of given sorts. These operations differ from constructors in that the PAC will generate implementations for the latter but not for the former; users must provide routines for these. This feature permits users to re-use existing code and to program efficient implementations of low-level data structures as appropriate.[2] Thus, to generate a CWB front end on the basis of the example algebra module a user would neet to provide implementations in Standard ML (the language in which the CWB is written) for operations such as **id_parse**, **mk_id_set** and **mk_frame**.

The **rels** component of the example introduces two semantic relations: **transition** and **diverges**. In this version of CCS, the transitions and potential for divergence of an agent depend on two environments: one to resolve free agent variables, and one to resolve free variables used in restrictions. Thus each relation includes an **agent environment** and an **id_set environment** argument.

For each relation the **inputs** section indicates the form the PAC-generated function for computing this relation should take. In the case of **transition**, for example, the input specification indicates that the generated function should have three inputs corresponding to the first three positions of the relation (here, two environment arguments and an agent). Given such a triple, the function will return the set of all action-agent pairs which, when combined with the triple, yield a quintuple in the relation. In the case of **diverges**, all places are mentioned in the input list; in this case, the PAC will generate a function taking three arguments and returning a boolean.

The **pragmas** section includes miscellaneous directives for specific back ends. In the above example, the given pragma indicates that the parser produced by the PAC back end for the CWB should have entries for agents, actions and identifier sets. These are needed since the CWB supports commands requiring users to provide information from these sorts. Other pragmas might be used to rename sorts appropriately (some tools might require a type **proc** rather than **agent**, for example) or supply names of library files.

Samples of the syntax sections of the CCS algebra specification appear in Figure 3. The **SYNTAX** component contains information needed to generate the parsers and unparsers to be used by the target tool; this currently

[2]PAC back ends also generate implementations of sorts having constructors declared for them; it relies on users to specify implementations of sorts for which no constructors have been specified. For example, **act** would have a PAC-supplied implementation, since three constructors have **act** as their return sort. The sort **'a frame**, on the other hand, does not have constructors defined for it; consequently, a user must supply code defining the data structure to be used to represent frames.

```
SYNTAX

tokens
   "nil"     => NIL
   "where"   => WHERE
   "and"     => AND
   "end"     => END
   ...

priorities
   ...

nonterminals
   agent of agent
   ag_eqn_list of (agent eqn) list
   ...

grammar
   agent : NIL                              (Nil())
         | agent WHERE agent_frame END (Fix(agent, agent_frame))
         ...
   agent_frame : ag_eqn_list                (mk_frame(ag_eqn_list))

lists
   ag_eqn_list is non_empty_list EMPTY_STR AND EMPTY_STR
                    of ag_eqn
   ...

RULE_SYNTAX
   ...

grammar
   relation :
      agent_env COMMA id_set_env COLON
      agent DASHDASH act ARROW agent
      (transition (agent_env, id_set_env, agent1, act, agent2))
...
```

FIGURE 3. A SYNTAX and RULE_SYNTAX section for CCS

takes the form of a YACC-like grammar whose semantic actions consists of "sort-correct" expressions built using the constructors and functions declared previously. In the example, the syntax of the fixpoint agent operator is defined to be a **where** e_1 **and** ... **and** e_n **end**, where each e_i is an equation. Note that PAC grammars extend YACC grammars by permitting list specifications; the nonterminal `ag_eqn_list`, for example, yields lists of `ag_eqn` (agent equations) whose beginning and ending delimiters are the empty string and whose separator is the token AND (**and** in concrete syntax). The **RULE_SYNTAX** section enriches this syntactic specification with information needed to parse the SOS rules that define the semantics of processes; in particular, it includes definitions of the concrete syntax of relations. This example defines the syntax of the `transition` relation to be *ae*, *se* : *p* --*a*--> *q*. The PAC fits this information into a general "rule template" in order to produce a grammar which is processed and then used to parse the user-supplied rules.

RULE_SET *Modules*

The second part of a PAC process algebra specification consists of the SOS rules needed to define the semantics of processes. In general, a user must supply a collection of rules for each relation introduced in the **ALGEBRA** module. Each rule in turn consists of four components: a name, a list of *premises*, a *side condition*, and a *conclusion*. In general, premises and conclusions involve relations, while side conditions can be any expression generated using the following grammar,

$$be ::= \texttt{true} \mid \texttt{not}\ be \mid be\ \texttt{and}\ be \mid be\ \texttt{or}\ be \mid P(t_1, ..., t_n)$$

where P is a predicate: any boolean-sorted function declared in the `funs` section or any relation in the `rels` section all of whose positions are input positions. The t_i should be terms in the appropriate sort, based on the definition of P. A fragment of the rules for the `transition` relation for CCS appears in Figure 4. Note that premises appear above, and conclusions below, a line of hyphens, with the side condition appearing in parentheses after the hyphens. All expressions in the rules are written using the concrete syntax declared in the **ALGEBRA** module; this enables the rules to look very close to what appears in the literature. In addition, functions defined in the **ALGEBRA** module may be used in the rules; for example, `parallel_3` contains a reference to the `inverses` predicate, which intuitively should hold when the given actions represent an input and output on the same channel (note that `t` is the concrete syntax that has been defined for the CCS internal action). Rule sets can refer to relations defined in other rule sets, although no such reference is made in this example.

```
RULE_SET transition

vars
    a, b                        : act
    p, p', p1, p1', p2, p2'     : agent
    s                           : id_set
    ae                          : (agent env)
    se                          : (id_set env)
    ...

rules

prefix

              --------------------------(true)
               ae, se: a.p -- a --> p

parallel_1
               ae, se: p1 -- a --> p1'
          ------------------------------------(true)
          ae, se: p1 | p2 -- a --> p1' | p2

parallel_2
               ae, se: p2 -- a --> p2'
          ------------------------------------(true)
          ae, se: p1 | p2 -- a --> p1 | p2'

parallel_3

ae, se: p1 -- a --> p1', ae, se: p2 -- b --> p2'
-------------------------------------------------(inverses(a,b))
        ae, se: p1 | p2 -- t --> p1' | p2'
...

end
```

FIGURE 4. A **RULE_SET** module for the CCS **transition relation**

4 PAC Back Ends

The PAC currently includes back ends dedicated to the CWB and to MAUTO. The former generates code in SML, the language in which the CWB is written, while the latter, which is still under construction, produces LeLisp, the programming language in which MAUTO is implemented. In each case, the produced code contains a parser, some unparsing functions, and a number of semantic functions encoding the SOS rules of the algebra. The parsers (generated using respectively LeLisp-Yacc and SML-Yacc) are fully compatible, meaning that PAC-generated front ends for MAUTO and the CWB handle the same syntax. As Section 2 indicated, however, the analysis functions of the target tools are different, as are the semantic functions. The following discusses what semantic functions the different back ends must produce and how they are generated from SOS specifications.

4.1 *The CWB Back End*

In addition to various parsing and unparsing routines, the CWB requires that its front end include implementations of types `act` and `agent` and functions `transition`, `diverges` and `sort`. The functions each take an agent and return a set of action-agent pairs, a boolean, and a set of actions, respectively. This section describes how the CWB back end generates code from the SOS definitions of semantic relations. Generally speaking, given a rule set for a particular semantic relation, the technique constructs a function whose inputs correspond to the places in the relation declared as inputs in the `inputs` section of the `ALGEBRA` module. On a given input, the generated routine produces a set of tuples as outputs; the idea is that each output tuple, when combined with the input tuple, yields an element in the relation. As an example, in the case of the `transition` relation defined in Section 3.2, positions 1, 2 and 3 of `transition` are declared as inputs; the procedure that is produced will therefore accept an $\langle$`agent env, id_set env, agent`$\rangle$ triple as input and produce a set of $\langle$`action, agent`$\rangle$ pairs as output with the property that if the input is $\langle ae, se, p\rangle$, then pair $\langle a, q\rangle$ is in the set of outputs if and only if $\langle ae, se, p, a, q\rangle$ is in relation `transition`.

In order for the procedure described below to work, the rules used to define semantic relations must obey certain syntactic restrictions. Recall from Sections 2.2 and 3.2 that SOS rules have the following general form:

$$\frac{\mathit{premises}}{\mathit{conclusion}}(\mathit{side\ condition})$$

where *conclusion* is an element of the relation being defined, *premises* is a list of elements of the relation being defined or of other relations declared in the `rels` section, and *side condition* is a boolean expression that may involve predicate expressions of the form $P(t_1, \ldots, t_n)$, with the t_i being terms that may involve variables. For the code produced by the CWB back end to compile, each rule must satisfy the following constraints.

1. All variables appearing in the input positions of the premises must appear in the input positions of the conclusion.
2. All variables appearing in the output positions of the conclusion or in the side condition must appear either in the input positions of the conclusion or in the output positions of a premise.
3. All variables appearing in the input positions of the conclusion or the output positions of a premise are distinct.

These constraints place restrictions on the "flow of data" through a rule: information flows from the inputs of the conclusion to the premises, and the outputs of premises flow (together with inputs of the conclusion) to the side condition and the outputs of the conclusion. Note also that patterns of arbitrary depth can appear in the input or output positions of the conclusion or premises. It should be noted that this rule format subsumes the positive GSOS format of [4] while being incomparable to the tyft/tyxt pattern of [12] and the path scheme of [2]. However, restriction 1 can be relaxed without too much difficulty to allow variables appearing in the output positions of premises to appear in the input positions of other premises; with this generalization, our format would subsume pure and well-founded tyft/tyxt and path. Other formats allow negative premises [4, 22] and are incomparable to ours.

The basic strategy used by the code generated from rules involves pattern matching: given a tuple of inputs, a generated function in essence determines which rules have conclusions whose input positions match the input tuple. Using the premises of these rules, appropriate (recursive) calls are issued, and the results which satisfy the side condition are combined into a set of result tuples using the form of the conclusion. To illustrate this idea, consider the rules given for CCS in Section 3.2, and suppose that the generated semantic function is given an input of the form $\langle \mathtt{ae}, \mathtt{se}, p|q \rangle$. In this case, three rules are applicable— `parallel_1`, `parallel_2` and `parallel_3`. Each of the rules mentions the transitions of p or q in the premises; consequently, the generated code would include recursive calls to calculate the transitions for $\langle \mathtt{ae}, \mathtt{se}, p \rangle$ and $\langle \mathtt{ae}, \mathtt{se}, q \rangle$. On the basis of the first rule, transitions of p would be combined appropriately with q, while the second rule would transform transitions of q by combining them with p. The final rule combines transitions of the form $\langle a, p' \rangle$ and $\langle b, q' \rangle$ into $\langle \tau, p'|q' \rangle$ *provided that* the predicate $\mathtt{inverses}(a, b)$ is satisfied. The results of these combinations are collected into one set and returned.

To improve the performance of the generated code, the CWB back end also employs several optimizations. For example, in order to minimize matching overhead, rules with the same input pattern in their conclusions are grouped and processed simultaneously. Also, the generated routines cache results of recursive calls in a hash table; before issuing a recursive call, this table is consulted to determine if the call has been made before. To demonstrate the savings from this technique, consider how the CWB would compile the agent $p|q$ into a labeled transition system. First, a call is made to the generated CCS transition function with $\langle ae, se, p|q\rangle$ as input (ae and se are the current agent and set environments). After making the recursive calls to compute the transitions of p and q, the generated `transition` function saves the results of these calls in a table. From *par_rule1*, it follows that $p|q$ has a transition $\langle a, p'|q\rangle$ for every transition $\langle a, p'\rangle$ of p. The next step in compiling the labeled transition system for $p|q$ will include computing the transitions of each $p'|q$; but, in this case instead of making recursive calls to recompute the transitions of q, `transition` would simply look this up in the transitions table. This strategy leads to significant time savings when computing the finite-state representation of a system; somewhat surprisingly, it can also lead to substantial space savings as well, since sharing becomes possible in the computation of output tuples.

4.2 The MAUTO Back End

MAUTO uses a "compositional" (bottom-up) approach to building automata; language constructs are interpreted as automaton transformations, and thus it is not in general possible to use directly the transition function described in the previous section. Instead, the same SOS rules that yield the *transition* function for the CWB are interpreted as specifying these automata transformers. Thus, the semantic functions generated by the PAC for MAUTO encode *transition system transducers* in the sense of Larsen and Xinxin [15]. Computing the automaton for $p|q$, for example, involves computing separately the finite automata describing the full behaviors of p and q, eventually reducing each of them according to any congruence at hand, then combining them using the transducer for parallel composition. In practice, the rule format required by this interpretation is more restrictive than the one in the preceding section: it ensures that the transducer generated for any context expression is finitely represented, and that the combination of finite automata always yields a finite global automaton. The structure of the functions produced for MAUTO is also very different from the structure of those produced for the CWB. In general, there are two functions for each operator, one describing the recursive structure of the bottom-up traversal, and one describing how to combine the transitions of a tuple of argument automata.

A static analysis of the structure of the SOS rules of the transition relation allows us to classify the process operators in the algebra. This is used to produce optimized automata-constructing routines, to ensure the finiteness of the produced transducers, and to guarantee *a priori* the termination of automata construction. The classification is a generalization of the notions defined in [17], and distinguishes between:

- *Combinators*, which are typically operators used for parallel composition. The format ensures that they do not generate infinite transition systems from finite arguments.
- *Switches*, which have only one process argument active at a time, and will eventually select one of them (sum, sequence). They are used for defining static conditions for finiteness of recursive definitions.
- *Sieves*, which have exactly one process argument and act as action transformers, keeping their structure unchanged (hiding, restriction, relabeling). Identifying sieves enables various run-time optimizations to be employed that avoid some intermediate automaton constructions.

We have produced code using these ideas that has proved to be very efficient and flexible, and easy to integrate with other compositional approaches.

5 Results

The current prototype of the PAC includes an algebra description parser and a back end for the CWB, with the development of the MAUTO back end in progress. In this section we describe our experience with using the PAC to generate front ends for the CWB. The experiments take two forms. In the first, we compare the efficiency of a PAC-generated front end for CCS with existing hand-coded front ends for CCS, while in the second we investigate the performance of front ends produced by the PAC for other languages. Our initial results suggest that the PAC does indeed ease the task of changing the language supported by the CWB and that the generated interfaces perform well. Our tests used a version of the Concurrency Workbench under development at North Carolina State University and were run on a Sun Sparc 5 with 128 megabytes of RAM. The functionality of this version of the CWB is similar to the Edinburgh CWB [10], but the NCSU version includes more efficient graph-construction and equivalence-checking routines.

Table .1 compares the performance of a PAC-generated front end with two hand-coded front ends for CCS. The first of these is the front end included with Version 6.0 of the CWB, while the second is a hand-tuned version of the first one developed at NCSU. The numbers describe the amount of processor time in seconds (time needed for system activities and for garbage collection have been omitted) needed by the NCSU CWB to build finite-state automata from different CCS sample programs using the transitions function supplied by the given interface. The example programs we used to test the interfaces included:

Example	*Number of states*	*Interface* CWB 6.0	NCSU CWB	PAC-generated
ABP	57	0.12	0.13	0.14
Jobshop	77	0.14	0.14	0.12
Dekker-2	127	0.38	0.35	0.39
802-2	331	1.67	1.33	1.83
Semaphore-2	468	2.66	2.44	2.25
Mail-system	1616	9.12	8.68	7.59
ABP | Jobshop	4389	18.82	13.76	10.73
Dekker-2 | Semaphore-2	59436	522.82	288.19	101.88
ABP | Mail-system	92112	*	*	340.90
Dekker-2 | Mail-system	205232	*	*	779.03

TABLE .1. Program time in seconds required by the different interfaces to construct automata for various CCS examples. A * indicates insufficient memory to construct the graph.

- Two communications protocols: an implementation of the Alternating Bit Protocol (ABP) and an implementation of part of the data link control layer of IEEE 802.2 (802-2).
- Two solutions of the two-process critical-section problem: an implementation of Dekker's algorithm (Dekker-2) and an implementation using semaphores (Semaphore-2).
- Milner's Jobshop example [19] (Jobshop).
- A specification of the Edinburgh mail system (Mail-system).

In addition, we tried some examples consisting of the parallel composition of these examples in order to assess the performance of the front ends on systems with large state spaces. In the table these examples have the form $System_1 | System_2$. As the table indicates, the PAC-generated CCS interface actually performs substantially better than existing CCS interfaces while using less memory; the main reason for this lies in the caching of recursive calls outlined in Section 4.1.

We have also used the PAC to generate CWB front ends for several other languages as well. Examples have included a simple language of regular expressions and a version of CCS in which actions take priority [9]; the latter is noteworthy in that its semantic account requires the use of auxiliary semantic relations. In general, the amount of effort required has been much less than what would be required to generate interfaces by hand, although more experience with the tool is necessary to substantiate this claim. However, the fact that the notations the tool provides for expressing semantic and syntactic specifications of languages are more abstract than those pro-

	Interface			
	CWB 6.0	NCSU CWB	PAC-generated CCS	PAC-generated Basic Lotos
States/sec	119.66	211.10	532.31	65.47

TABLE .2. Average number of states generated per second for four different interfaces.

vided by standard programming languages lead us to believe that the PAC will greatly simplify the production of front ends for verification tools.

Our most involved example has been the generation of a CWB front end for Basic Lotos, which is more complex, both syntactically and semantically, than the others we have tried. We have analyzed a number of Basic Lotos examples with the generated interface. Since no Basic Lotos interface existed previously for the CWB it is harder to evaluate the efficiency of the generated code than it was in the case of CCS. One crude measure, however involves comparing the states generated per unit time from LOTOS programs against a similar figure for the CCS front ends described previously. The states-per-second measures for the CCS front ends were computed from the first eight examples in the table above (the ones that all interfaces were able to handle), while the figure for the Basic Lotos interface was calculated based on timing results from the compilation of 8 examples ranging in size from 20 states to 45,000 states. The results are shown in Table .2, which shows that the front end generated for Basic Lotos is roughly 8 times slower than the one generated for CCS. This difference is not necessarily due to the inadequacy of the code-generating scheme used by the PAC, but rather arises from the fact that Basic Lotos is syntactically and semantically more complex than CCS.

6 Conclusions

In this paper we have presented the Process Algebra Compiler, a tool for generating front ends for verification tools. The PAC allows users to specify the syntax and semantics of a language they wish their verification tool to support; the system then produces the syntactic and semantic routines needed to specialize the given tool for the language. Experimental results indicate that PAC-generated routines exhibit performance that can in fact improve on that of hand-coded routines.

Regarding future work, our most immediate goal is to complete the MAUTO back end so that it and the CWB may become source-level compatible. Back ends for other verification tools could also be built and our experiences in building the CWB and MAUTO back ends would certainly ease this task. We anticipate that this will be possible for most tools based on transition system semantics, although some reorganization of the target tools may be necessary.

We would also like to investigate the addition of features in the PAC specification language. In particular, the lexical specifications supported by the PAC can be made more flexible, and providing some facility for modularity in the algebra section would be desirable. We have experimented with the latter; defining concrete syntax in a modular way, however, appears to be very difficult. We have also experimented with a less flexible, but much easier to use, format for expressing concrete syntax and plan to study this issue more. We have also worked on and would like to investigate further routines in the PAC for analyzing a rule set and reporting to the user whether it satisfies rule formats, such as those mentioned in Section 2.2.

We also would like to explore the possibility of using the PAC for activities other than generating front ends for verification tools. Given the widespread use of SOS rules for defining the semantics of languages, it might be possible to use the PAC to automatically generate interpreters and compilers. We are also examining the feasibility of using the PAC as an implementation engine for generating on-the-fly verification routines, as these may often be formulated using SOS-style rules [3]. Obviously, these uses are greatly different from the PAC's initial purpose, and it remains to be seen if they are indeed practical.

Related Work.

Other verification tools have also aimed at providing some parametricity with respect to the language analyzed. The ECRINS system [16] permitted users to specify the SOS semantics of their algebra, and to prove algebraic laws of their operators. MAUTO allows users to extend the syntax of the language it supports, although semantic routines must be altered by hand. As a compiler for syntactic and semantic specifications, the PAC is closely related to the CENTAUR system, and in particular to its semantic component TYPOL [13]. TYPOL provides a general framework for defining languages, interpreters, and compilers, using SOS rules. The more restrictive PAC rule format allows for the generation of simpler and more efficient code.

7 References

[1] D. Austry and G. Boudol. Algèbre de processus et synchronisation. *Theoretical Computer Science*, 30:91–131, 1984.

[2] J.C.M. Baeten and C. Verhoef. A congruence theorem for structured operational semantics with predicates. Technical Report 93/05, Eindhoven University of Technology, 1994.

[3] G. Bhat, R. Cleaveland, and O. Grumberg. Efficient on-the-fly model checking for CTL*. In *Tenth Annual Symposium on Logic in Computer*

Science (LICS '95), San Diego, July 1995. IEEE Computer Society Press.

[4] B. Bloom, S. Istrail, and A. Meyer. Bisimulation can't be traced. In *Fifteenth Annual ACM Symposium on Principles of Programming Languages (PoPL '88)*, pages 229–239, San Diego, January 1988. IEEE Computer Society Press.

[5] T. Bolognesi and E. Brinksma. Introduction to the ISO specification language LOTOS. In P.H.J.van Eijk, C.A.Vissers, and M.Diaz, editors, *The Formal Description Technique LOTOS*, pages 23–76. North-Holland, 1989.

[6] G. Boudol, V. Roy, R. de Simone, and D. Vergamini. Process calculi, from theory to practice: Verification tools. Rapport de Recherche RR1098, INRIA, October 1989.

[7] R. Cleaveland. Analyzing concurrent systems using the Concurrency Workbench. In P.E. Lauer, editor, *Functional Programming, Concurrency, Simulation and Automated Reasoning*, volume 693 of *Lecture Notes in Computer Science*, pages 129–144. Springer-Verlag, 1993.

[8] R. Cleaveland and M.C.B. Hennessy. Testing equivalence as a bisimulation equivalence. In *Proceedings of the Workshop on Automatic Verification Methods for Finite-State Systems*, pages 11–23. Springer-Verlag, 1989.

[9] R. Cleaveland and M.C.B. Hennessy. Priorities in process algebra. *Information and Computation*, 87(1/2):58–77, July/August 1990.

[10] R. Cleaveland, J. Parrow, and B. Steffen. The Concurrency Workbench: A semantics-based tool for the verification of finite-state systems. *ACM Transactions on Programming Languages and Systems*, 15(1):36–72, January 1993.

[11] J.C. Fernandez. Aldébaran: A tool for verification of communicating processes. Technical Report Spectre-c 14, LGI-IMAG, Grenoble, 1989.

[12] J.F. Groote and F. Vaandrager. Structured operational semantics and bisimulation as a congruence. *Information and Computation*, 2(100):202–260, 1992.

[13] G. Kahn. Natural semantics. Technical Report RR601, INRIA, 1987.

[14] K.G. Larsen, J.C. Godskesen, and M. Zeeberg. TAV, tools for automatic verification, user manual. Technical Report R 89-19, Dep^t of Mathematics and Computer Science, Ålborg university, 1989.

[15] K.G. Larsen and L. Xinxin. Compositionality through an operational semantics of contexts. In M.S. Paterson, editor, *Automata, Languages and Programming (ICALP '90)*, volume 443 of *Lecture Notes in Computer Science*, pages 526–539, Warwick, England, July 1990. Springer-Verlag.

[16] E. Madelaine, R. de Simone, and D. Vergamini. *ECRINS*, user manual, 1988. Technical Documentation.

[17] E. Madelaine and D. Vergamini. Finiteness conditions and structural construction of automata for all process algebras. In R. Kurshan, editor, *proceedings of Workshop on Computer Aided Verification*, New-Brunswick, June 1990. AMS-DIMACS.

[18] E. Madelaine and D. Vergamini. Specification and verification of a sliding window protocol in LOTOS. In K. R. Parker and G. A. Rose, editors, *Formal Description Techniques, IV*, volume C-2 of *IFIP Transactions*, Sydney, December 1991. North-Holland.

[19] R. Milner. *Communication and Concurrency*. Prentice Hall, 1989.

[20] G. Plotkin. A structural approach to operational semantics. Technical Report DAIMI FN-19, University of Aarhus, September 1981.

[21] V. Roy and R. de Simone. Auto and autograph. In R. Kurshan, editor, *proceedings of Workshop on Computer Aided Verification*, New-Brunswick, June 1990. AMS-DIMACS.

[22] C. Verhoef. A congruence theorem for structured operational semantics with predicates and negative premises. In B. Jonsson and J. Parrow, editors, *Proceedings CONCUR 94*, Uppsala, Sweden, volume 836 of *Lectures Notes in Computer Science*, pages 433–448. Springer-Verlag, 1994.

Analytic and Locally Approximate Solutions to Properties of Probabilistic Processes

C. Tofts*†

ABSTRACT Recent extensions to process algebra can be used to describe performance or error rate properties of systems. We examine how properties of systems expressed in these algebras can be elicited. Particular attention is given to the ability to describe the behaviour of system components parametrically. We present how analytic formulae for performance properties can be derived from probabilistic process algebraic descriptions; demonstrating how local approximate solutions can be derived for the properties when their exact solutions would be too computationally expensive to evaluate. As an example we derive the performance of an Alternating Bit Protocol with respect to its error and retry rates.

1 Introduction

Process algebra [Mil80, Mil83, BK84, Hoa85, BBK86, Mil90] is a methodology for formally calculating the behaviour of a system in terms of the behaviours of its components. Recent extensions have added: timing properties [RR86, Tof89, MT90, Yi90, CAM90]; probabilistic properties [GSST90, Tof90, SS90, Tof94]; priority properties [BBK86, Cam89, Tof90, SS90, Tof94] and combinations of the above [Tof90, Han92, Tof94]. Process algebras with these extensions can be exploited to formally analyse the performance (in terms of either success or failure) of the design of systems [VW92,Tof93]. The analysis of a design can be greatly facilitated if an analytic solution to the performance of the system can be generated from an abstract description of the performance of its components. A possibly more important question is how tolerant to error (in the precise value of component parameters) are system level predictions.

Within the process algebra community the standard approach to a ver-

*This work is supported by an EPSRC Advanced Fellowship.

†Department of Computer Science, The University, Manchester, M13 9PL, email: cmnt@cs.man.ac.uk

ification problem, is to describe and compose the system components and then verify by comparing the constructed system's behaviour with another (presumably correct) process [Chr90,JS90], or observing its compliance with a logical predicate [Han94,HJ94]. Whilst in many cases, where for instance design criterion are known in advance, this can be an appropriate methodology, it is however limited for the analysis of choices in system design. Often the requirement is to predict the effect of the component choice on system performance in the context of a service/cost trade-off, rather than compliance with a particular *ab initio* service requirement. Of great importance is the ability to 'track' the effect of a single component upon system performance. To achieve this we need two things, firstly a syntactic presentation of system components, secondly an abstract method of calculating the component's contribution to the system's performance.

Within a system subject to failure system requirements are often expressed in terms like; *the probability of error is less than 0.05.* It is hard to see how to interpret such a requirement in terms of the behaviour at a particular state. Indeed such requirements would often be re-expressed as *the probability of failure at* **any state** *is less than 0.05.* Whilst this condition is certainly sufficient to ensure the conformance of a system to the requirement, is it reasonable? Consider the following WSCCS [Tof90,Tof94] process:

$$P_1 \stackrel{def}{=} 9.\surd : P_1 + 1.\surd : P_2$$
$$P_2 \stackrel{def}{=} 1.error : P_1 + 9.\surd : P_1$$

The process P_1 certainly does not obey the condition that the probability of error in all states is less than 0.05 as this probability is 0.1 in state P_2. However, the process will only spend 10% of its time in state P_2 hence the probability of error is only 0.01, which does indeed meet our performance requirement. In order to calculate the error probability of this system we need to know the probability of the system being in any particular state. These probabilities can only be evaluated with respect to the complete system, and hence any logic suitable to express these properties will need to express probabilities of being in a particular state, and thus will not be an abstraction on any underlying transition description.

A frequently used method to formally derive the compliance of a probabilisitic system with some requirements is to express those requirements in the form of a 'standard' process [Chr90,JS90,Tof90], then demonstrating an equality between the intended implementation and the standard. If we attempt to describe our requirement on errors in this fashion we might write the following process:

$$Q \stackrel{def}{=} 95.\surd : Q + 5.error : Q$$

The above being a process which certainly does not produce errors at a greater rate than 0.05. There's appears to be no sensible formal relation between the process Q and our previous example P_1. Again the reason for this incompatibility is that we compare processes on a state by state basis.

A possibly more realistic question would be the following. Given the process:

$$R_1 \stackrel{def}{=} p.\surd : R_1 + 1.\surd : R_2$$
$$R_2 \stackrel{def}{=} 1.error : P_1 + q.\surd : P_1$$

what values of the expressions p and q will ensure that the process does not produce error actions at a greater rate than 0.05?

In many cases systemic requirements are expressed in terms of average performance. That is to say the average time before an error is seen will be greater than some amount, or alternatively the average time to see a 'good' outcome will be less than some amount. In order that such performance parameters can be derived we need to know not only the probability of reaching a particular state, but also how long it will take system to do so.

In Section 2 we present an extension to WSCCS to permit reasoning over weight expressions containing variables, and demonstrate how a Markov chain [Kei,Kle75,GS82] can be derived from a WSCCS process. In Section 3 we discuss how the properties of terminating processes can be derived. In Section 4 we discuss the solving for properties of finite processes. In particular, we examine how approximate analytic solutions can be derived when computing an exact analytic solution to the problem will be infeasible. The form of approximation we shall obtain will be in the form of a polynomial expansion of small perturbations about particular values for systemic parameters, and hence they are approximations valid only in a particular locality. We can obtain solutions over an arbitrary range of system parameters by exploiting a series of local approximations for our performance problem.

2 WSCCS

Our language WSCCS is an extension of Milner's SCCS [Mil83] a language for describing synchronous concurrent systems. To define our language we presuppose a free abelian group *Act* over a set of atomic action symbols with identity $\surd$, the inverse of a being $\overline{a}$, and action product denoted by #. As in SCCS, the complementary actions a (conventionally input) and $\overline{a}$ (output) form the basis of communication. Within our group we define that $\overline{a} = a^{-1}$.

2.1 *Expressions*

We define a set of expressions.

Definition 2.1 *A* relative frequency expression (RFE) *is formed from the following syntax, with x ranging over a set of variable names VRF, and c ranging over a fixed field (such as $\mathcal{N}$ or $\mathcal{R}$):*

$$e ::= x|c|e+e|e*e$$

Further we assume that the following equations hold for relative frequency expressions:

$$\begin{array}{lcl} e+f & = & f+e \\ (e+f)+g & = & e+(f+g) \\ e*f & = & f*e \\ (e*f)*g & = & e*(f*g) \\ e*(f+g) & = & e*f+e*g \end{array}$$

alternatively, we have commutative and associative addition and multiplication, with multiplication distributing over addition. We shall assume that two expressions are equivalent if they can be shown so by the above equations.

In the sequel we shall omit the $*$ in expressions, denoting expression multiplication by juxtaposition. It should be noted that unlike other calculi with expressions [Mil90, Hen91] the value of our expressions can have **no effect** on the structure of the transition graph of our system. Hence we should not expect that adding this extra structure to our probabilistic process algebra will cause any new technical difficulties.

2.2 Weights

We also take a set of weights $\mathcal{W}$, denoted by w_i, which are of the form $e\omega^k$. In the weight the relative frequency expression e denotes the relative frequency with which a process guarded by this weight will be chosen. The priority with which this choice should be taken is denoted by the strictly positive natural k. We take the following multiplication and addition rules (assuming $k \geq k'$) over weights.

$$e\omega^k + f\omega^{k'} = e\omega^k = f\omega^{k'} + e\omega^k \qquad e\omega^k + f\omega^k = (e+f)\omega^k = e\omega^k + f\omega^k$$
$$e\omega^k * f\omega^{k'} = (ef)\omega^{k+k'} = f\omega^{k'} * e\omega^k$$

As abbreviations we use e for the weight $e\omega^0$, and ω^k for the weight $1\omega^k$.

2.3 The Calculus

The collection of WSCCS expressions ranged over by E is defined by the following BNF expression, where $a \in Act$, $X \in Var$, $w_i \in \mathcal{W}$, S ranging over renaming functions, those $S : Act \longrightarrow Act$ such that $S(\surd) = \surd$ and $\overline{S(a)} = S(\overline{a})$, action sets $A \subseteq Act$, with $\surd \in A$, and arbitrary *finite* indexing sets I:

$$E ::= X \mid a.E \mid \sum\{w_i E_i | i \in I\} \mid E \times E \mid E\lceil A \mid \Theta(E) \mid E[S] \mid \mu_i \tilde{x}\tilde{E}.$$

We let Pr denote the set of closed expressions, and add **0** to our syntax, which is defined by $\mathbf{0} \stackrel{def}{=} \sum\{w_i E_i | i \in \emptyset\}$.

The informal interpretation of our operators is as follows:

- **0** a process which cannot proceed;
- X the process bound to the variable X;
- $a : E$ a process which can perform the action a whereby becoming the process described by E;
- $\sum\{w_i.E_i | i \in I\}$ the *weighted* choice between the processes E_i, the weight of the outcome E_i being determined by w_i. We think in terms of repeated experiments on this process and we expect to see over a large number of experiments the process E_i being chosen with a relative frequency of $\frac{w_i}{\sum_{i \in I} w_i}$.
- $E \times F$ the synchronous parallel composition of the two processes E and F. At each step each process must perform an action, the composition performing the composition (in *Act*) of the individual actions;
- $E\lceil A$ represents a process where we only permit actions in the set A. This operator is used to enforce communication and bound the scope of actions;
- $\Theta(E)$ represents taking the prioritised parts of the process E only.
- $E[S]$ represents the process E relabelled by the function S;
- $\mu_i \tilde{x}\tilde{E}$ represents the solution x_i taken from solutions to the mutually recursive equations $\tilde{x} = \tilde{E}$.

Often we shall omit the dot when applying prefix operators; also we drop trailing **0**, and will use a binary plus instead of the two (or more) element indexed sum, thus writing $\sum\{1_1.a : \mathbf{0},\ \ 2_2 : b.\mathbf{0} | i \in \{1,2\}\}$ as $1.a\ +\ 2.b$. Finally we allow ourselves to specify processes definitionally, by providing recursive definitions of processes. For example, we write $A \stackrel{def}{=} a.A$ rather than $\mu x.ax$. The weight n is an abbreviation for the weight $n\omega^0$, and the weight w^k is an abbreviation for the weight $1\omega^k$.

The semantics, congruences and equational theory of this (minor) extension of WSCCS are essentially identical to that of [Tof95] up to arithmetic on weight expressions.

The congruences of WSCCS[Tof90,Tof94] are important as they permit us to algebraically manipulate our processes. However, in many instances these equivalences are too fine, consider the following pair of processes:

$$2.(2.P + 4.Q) \qquad\qquad 4.P + 8.Q$$

in many instances we should like to be able to consider these processes as equivalent. Hence, we would like a notion of equivalence that permits us to disregard the structure of the choices and just look at the total chance of reaching any particular state. Whilst this notion of equivalence is useful it is known *not* to produce a congruence [SST89] for the complete language. However, such problems do not arise if we restrict our process syntax to only allow a single depth of summation, in which case our abstract relationship $\stackrel{a}{\sim}$, defined below, coincides with the original probability preserving congruence [Tof94].

Definition 2.2 *We define an abstract notion of evolution as follows;*

$$P \stackrel{a[w]}{\longrightarrow} P' \text{ iff } P \stackrel{w_1}{\longmapsto} \dots \stackrel{w_n}{\longmapsto}\stackrel{a}{\longrightarrow} P' \text{ with } w = \prod w_i.$$

As an example, $5.(3.(2.a : Q + 4.b : P) + 1.c : R) + 7.d : S \stackrel{a[30]}{\longrightarrow} Q$.

In order to define an equivalence which uses such transitions we need a notion of accumulation.

Definition 2.3 *Let S be a set of processes then:*

$$P \stackrel{a[w]}{\longrightarrow} S \text{ iff } w = \sum\{w_i | P \stackrel{a[w_i]}{\longrightarrow} Q \text{ for some } Q \in S\};$$ [1]

We can now define an equivalence that ignores the choice structure but not the choice values.

Definition 2.4 *We say an equivalence relation $R \subseteq Pr \times Pr$ is an* abstract bisimulation *if $(P, Q) \in R$ implies that:*

> *there are $e, f \in RFE$ such that for all $S \in Pr/R$ and for all $w, v \in \mathcal{W}$, $P \stackrel{a[w]}{\longrightarrow} S$ iff $Q \stackrel{a[v]}{\longrightarrow} S$ and $ew = fv$.*

Two processes are abstract bisimulation equivalent, *written $P \stackrel{a}{\sim} Q$ if there exists an abstract bisimulation R between them.*

In particular this description of a WSCCS process gives us (essentially) a **probability transition graph**[Paz71].

Definition 2.5 *A probabilistic transition graph is a quintuple (V, T, s_0, A, RFE) where V is a set of states, T a set of transitions $\subseteq V \times (a \times p) \times V$, $s_0 \in V$ is an initial state, A ranged over by a an alphabet, and RFE ranged over by p the set of relative frequency expressions.*

---

[1] Remembering this is a multi-relation so some of the Q and w_i may be the same process and value. We take all occurences of processes in S and add together all the weight arrows leading to them.

3 Terminating Systems

As an example consider the following simple game. Two identical (possibly) biased coins are tossed repeatedly. If the coins both show heads then the game is won, if the coins both show tails then the game is lost, otherwise the coins are tossed again. What is the probability of winning the game? And how many tosses will be needed on average to see an outcome?

$$\begin{aligned}
Coin &\stackrel{def}{=} p.\overline{head} : Coin + q.\overline{tail} : Coin \\
GR &\stackrel{def}{=} 1.head^2\#\overline{win} : 0 \\
&\quad\; 1.head\#tail : GR \\
&\quad\; 1.tail^2\#\overline{lose} : 0 \\
Game &\stackrel{def}{=} (Coin \times Coin \times GR)\lceil\{win, lose\}
\end{aligned}$$

The probability of winning a game can be computed by solving the following equation[2]:

$$P(win) = \frac{2pq}{(p+q)^2}P(win) + \frac{p^2}{(p+q)^2}.1$$

and the average number of coin tosses equired to reach an outcome:

$$\begin{aligned}
E(Game) &= \frac{2pq}{(p+q)^2}(E(Game)+1) + \frac{p^2}{(p+q)^2}(E(0)+1) \\
&\quad + \frac{q^2}{(p+q)^2}(E(0)+1) \\
E(0) &= 0
\end{aligned}$$

In the above we can rearrange the first equation to obtain the following:

$$E(Game) = \frac{2pq}{(p+q)^2}E(Game) + \frac{p^2}{(p+q)^2}E(0) + \frac{q^2}{(p+q)^2}E(0) + 1$$

Definition 3.1 *The total output of a state* $T(s) = \sum\{p | s \stackrel{a[p]}{\rightarrow} s'\}$.

Definition 3.2 *Let* $Win \subseteq A$ *be a set of winning actions, and* $P(s_0, Win)$ *be the probability of observing an action in the set* Win *starting from state* s_0*, and the average number of ticks before an action in* Win *is observed* $D(s_0, win)$.

$P(Win, s_0)$ is the solution of the following set of simultaneous equations, for all $s \in V$

$$\begin{aligned}
P(s, Win) &\stackrel{def}{=} \sum\{\tfrac{p_i}{T(s)}P(s', Win) | s \stackrel{a[p_i]}{\rightarrow} s', a \notin Win\} \\
&\quad + \sum\{\tfrac{p_j}{T(s)} | s \stackrel{a}{\longrightarrow} a[p_j], a \in Win\}
\end{aligned}$$

Similarly we can define $D(Win, s_0)$ to be the a solution of the following set of simulataneous equations:

[2] In general we obtain a set of simultaneous eqautions, one for each state.

$$
\begin{aligned}
D(s, Win) &\stackrel{def}{=} \infty \text{ if } s \stackrel{a[p]}{\not\rightarrow} \\
D(s, Win) &\stackrel{def}{=} \sum\{\tfrac{p_i}{T(s)} D(s', Win) | s \stackrel{a[p_i]}{\rightarrow} s', a \notin Win\} \\
&\quad +1
\end{aligned}
$$

Hence given a probabilistic transition graph with n states we can produce a set of n simultaneous equations which describe the probabilities and averages we are interested in. Generating the equations from the graph is straightforward and the equations can subsequently be solved by any symbolic mathematics package.

4 Finite State Non-terminating Systems

Consider the following process:

$$
\begin{aligned}
W1 &\stackrel{def}{=} 6.sunny : W1 + 4.cloudy : W2 \\
W2 &\stackrel{def}{=} 5.cloudy : W2 + 5.sunny : W1
\end{aligned}
$$

If we assume that the environment (of the process) is unbiased with respect to the *sunny* and *cloudy* actions then the above system can be represented by the following Markov [Kei, Paz71, Kle75, GS82] transition matrix:

$$
\begin{pmatrix} 0.6 & 0.5 \\ 0.4 & 0.5 \end{pmatrix}
$$

A question that is asked about the above system is with what probability is the action *sunny* seen. This question can be answered by knowing with what probability the system is likely to be in state $W1$ or $W2$ at an arbitrary time. In Markov chain theory this is known as the **stable distribution**[Kei,GS82] of the chain. For a chain whose transition matrix is $\underline{\underline{A}}$ then a stable distribution $\underline{v}$ is one which satisfies the following equation:

$$
\underline{\underline{A}}\underline{v} = \underline{v}
$$

and $|\underline{v}|$ is equal to 1.

In the case of the transition system above the stable distribution [Kei, Kle75,GS82] is given by the vector:

$$
\begin{pmatrix} 5/9 \\ 4/9 \end{pmatrix}
$$

and hence the probability of observing a *sunny* action is:

$$
\begin{aligned}
P(sunny) &= \tfrac{5}{9}\tfrac{6}{10} + \tfrac{4}{9}\tfrac{5}{10} \\
&= \tfrac{5}{9}
\end{aligned}
$$

Whilst in principle it is possible to convert a probability graph into its associated Markov chain and then solve for the stable distribution (by exploiting eigen theory) this is a highly inefficeint method of solving the problem. Given an n state probability transition graph the associated Markov chain matrix will be of size n^2. To represent the transition system as a matrix is clearly highly inefficient, and would prevent the consideration of systems composed of many components as their state space tends to grow exponentially in the number of components. An alternative manner of presenting the system is as follows. Remembering the original equation:

$$\underline{\underline{A}}\underline{\pi} = \underline{\pi}$$

by defining $r_i(\underline{\underline{A}})$ as the ith row of the matrix $\underline{\underline{A}}$ this is equivalent to solving the set of equations:

$$r_i(\underline{\underline{A}}).\underline{\pi} = \underline{\pi}_i$$

Whilst this would appear to still require $O(n^2)$ memory to represent the problem this is generally not the case. The probabilistic transition graphs that result,in practice, from process algebraic descriptions tend to be very sparse. On the whole very few of the states of a system are reachable from any particular state, in fact there is generally a (small) bound (k) on the number of permitted transitions from any particular state and therefore in this representation an amount $O(kn)$ of memory will be necessary to represent the solution.

We can define the necessary set of simultaneous[3] equations directly in terms of the original graph as follows:

$$\underline{\pi}_s \quad = \quad \{\sum \frac{p_j \underline{\pi}_j}{T(s_j)} | s_j \overset{a[p_j]}{\rightarrow} s\}$$

together with the condition that $\sum\{\underline{\pi}_s\} = 1$. the solution vector $\underline{\pi}$ being a stable distribution[4] for the transition system.

In this case the unstructured sparseness of the equation set makes the use of standard symbolic mathematical equation packages very inefficient. A sparse equation solver was written to directly solve sets of equations generated by the above. By solving equations in inverse order of their fan out a considerable speed up can be achieved. The system generates a back substitution list which can be evaluated using a symbolic mathematics package.

To calculate the mean occurence of an action, the probability of that action occuring at a particular state is multiplied by the probability of

---

[3]The set of equations derived for Markov transition matrix will *not* be independent [GS82] and hence an extra condition is neede to ensure a unique solution. This condition is derived from the definition that a probability distribution must sum to 1

[4]Care should be excersised when using stable distributions as their uniqueness is only guaranteed under restricted circumstances [Kei,GS82]

being in that state. For an exmaple of this form of calculation performed by our toolset see Example 1.1 in the Appendix.

Unfortunately, the solution of symbolic simultaneous equations requires NP-space in the number of equation to represent the solutions. In practice it appears that symbolic solutions are unfeasible for systems of more than about 30 states.

An alternative definition [GS82] of the stable distribution of a markov system is presented in the following fashion:

$$\underline{\pi_{i+1}} = \underline{\underline{A}}\underline{\pi_i}$$

with $\underline{\pi} = lim_{i \leadsto \infty} \underline{\pi}_i$ if there is a unique stable distribution.

Using the above definition we can define an iterative calculation over the probability transition graph in the following fashion:

$$\underline{\pi_{i+1}}_s = \{\sum \frac{p_j \underline{\pi_i}_j}{T(s_j)} | s_j \stackrel{a[p_j]}{\rightarrow} s\}$$

If an attempt is made to calculate an exact solution to the above iteration procedure then the same representation problem is encountered. However, it is possible to exploit the above method to provide an approximate solution (in the sense of a Taylor's expansion) to the stable vector problem. By truncating the $\underline{\pi_i}$ to a particular accuracy after each iteration of the calculation. If the terms (in a variable x say) are maintained to order k then, standard numerical solution of eigensystems theory [Wil65] shows that the solution will have an absolute error of $O(x^k)$.

Hence the following procedure can be exploited to give an approximate solution to the distribution problem, choose any non-zero length 1 $\underline{\pi_0}$[5]:

1. Compute $\underline{\pi_{i+1}}$ from $\underline{\pi_i}$;
2. truncate $\underline{\pi_{i+1}}$ to required accuracy k;
3. repeat from 1 until stability is achieved.

In practice one can compute a central approximation and then compute the further terms by increasing the approximation level steadily until the desired level is reached. An example of this solution method applied to the performance of the Alternating Bit Protocol can be found in the Appendix 1.2.

5 Conclusions

Whilst it is possible to verify the behaviour of a system by checking the process that describes it against another process[Mil80, Mil90, Chr90, JS90,

[5]In practice we use the vector $\underline{\pi_0}_i = \frac{1}{n}$ when the system has n states.

Tof90, SS90] or a predicate[Mil90, Han94, HJ94] this is often not the best approach. In many cases the intention of the design analysis is to determine how well a system can function which is why simulation[BDMN79, Bir79, Kre86, BFS87] is often resorted to. It is important in such circumstances to be able to identify the contribution of the underlying components to the overall system performance. The verify strategy works well when system requirements are known in advance but in many cases the design problem is one of: what is the best way of using these components to solve a particular problem? In this case the components are fixed, and we need to be able to derive the resulting systemic behaviour.

It might seem that we are not exploiting the algebraic properties of the process algebraic description in deriving our systemic properties. This is not the case. When the transition system for any process is computed within our tool we exploit the algebraic equivalences to try to produce as small a transition graph as possible. This does not necessarily produce a minimal system, but will exploit as much of the syntactic identity as made available in the description of the system provided. In practice this is only of value when the system contains repeated components, such as the two identical coins in our original example, where the number of states required to represent both coins can be reduced from 4 to 3 immediately. Over a large system these gains can significantly reduce the size of the states space, if we had six coins then we reduce the state space from 64 to 7.

Whilst it is true that for the majority of problems a symbolic approach to process representation will not admit a computationally feasible analytic solution, this approach still has major advantages. As we describe performance aspects of the system's components symbolically and construct its probability transition graph in terms of these symbols (a computationally costly operation, even if all of the transition probabilities are constants) it is subsequently possible to instantiate the graph with particular values of interest for the component's performance. Hence, with little extra computation cost, we can study the behaviour of our system under a wide range of conditions.

The generation of local approximations to the solutions of systems is of great importance. It has long been known that the behaviour of complex systems can critically dependent on the precise values of their parameters. In any real implementation of a system the true values of its components performances are liable to vary slightly from the exact values in our models. Local approximations allow us to assess the effect that these small variations may have on the systems true behaviour. For instance if performance could be heavily compromised by a small variance in one components performance it may be a good idea to redesign the system to be more tolerant or replace that component.

A sublanguage of WSCCS and the algorithms in this paper have been implemented as a set of SML functions (Probabilistic Algebra Tools set) which can be obtained from cmnt@cs.man.ac.uk. In terms of scale the exact solution generator can cope with systems of about 30 states, and will execute upon systems of this scale in 2 hours on a SPARCstation 2. The approximation method can cope with systems of 1000's of states and can take 24 hours to execute on such systems. Automatic scanning functions have been written to generate the piecewise approximations. For problems where there are no free weight parameters (all of the system constants are purely numerical) the tool set can successfully solve problems with 10000s of states.

6 References

[BBK86] J. Baeten, J. Bergstra and J. Klop, Syntax and defining equations for an interrupt mechanism in process algebra, Fundamenta Informatica IX, pp 127-168, 1986.

[BDMN79] G. Birtwistle, O-J Dahl, B. Myhrhaug and K. Nygaard, Simula Begin, 2nd Edition, Studentliteratur, Lund, Sweden, 1979.

[BFS87] P. Bratley, B. Fox and L. Schrage, A guide to simulation, second edition, 1987.

[Bir79] G. Birtwistle, DEMOS — discrete event modelling on Simula. Macmillen, 1979.

[BK84] J.A. Bergstra, J.W. Klop, The algebra of recursively defined processes and the algebra of regular processes, in Proc 11th ICALP, Springer LNCS 172, pp 82-85, 1984.

[CAM90] L. Chen, S. Anderson and F. Moller, A Timed Calculus of Communicating Systems, LFCS-report number 127

[Cam89] J. Camilleri. Introducing a Priority Operator to CCS, Computer Laboratory Technical Report, Cambridge University, 1989.

[Chr90] I. Christoff, Testing Equivalences and Fully Abstract Models for Probabilistic Processes, Proceedings Concur '90, LNCS 458, 1990.

[CPS93] Cleaveland, R., J. Parrow and B. Steffen, The Concurrency Workbench: A Semantics-Based Tool for the Verification of Finite-State Systems, ACM Transactions on Programming Languages and Systems, 15(1):36–72, 1993.

[DLSB82] V.A. Dyck, J.D. Lawson, J.D. Smith and R.J. Beach, Computing: An Introduction to Structured Problem Solving Using Pascal: Reston, Reston, 1982.

[GS82] G.R. Grimmet and D.R. Stirzaker, Probability and Random Processes, Oxford Science Publications, 1982.

[GSST90] R. van Glabbek, S. A. Smolka, B. Steffen and C.Tofts, Reactive, Generative and Stratified Models of Probabilistic Processes, proceedings LICS 1990.

[Han94] M.R. Hansen, Model checking discrete duration calculus, FACS 6A:826-845, 1994.

[Hen91] M. Hennessy, A proof system for CCS with value passing, FACS 3: 346-366.

[HJ94] H. Hansson and B. Jonsson, A Logic for Reasoning about Time and Reliability, FACS (6):512-535, 1994.

[Hoa85] C. A. R. Hoare, Communicating Sequential Processes, Prentice-Hall 1985.

[HR90] M. Hennessey and T. Regan, A Temporal Process Algebra, Technical Report, Department of Cognitive Science, Sussex University, 1990.

[Jon90] C. C. M. Jones, Probabilistic Non-determinism, PhD Thesis University of Edinburgh 1990.

[Kei] J. Keilson, Markov Chain Models - Rarity and exponentiality, Applied Mathematical Sciences 28, Springer Verlag.

[Kin69] J.F.C. Kingman, Markov Population Processes, Journal of Applied Probability, 6:1-18, 1969.

[Kle75] L. Kleinrock, Queueing Systems, Volumes I and II, John Wiley, 1975.

[Kre86] W. Kreutzer, System Simulation, Addison Wesley, 1986.

[JS90] C. Jou and S. Smolka, Equivalences, Congruences and Complete Axiomatizations for Probabilistic Processes, Proceedings Concur '90, LNCS 458, 1990.

[LS89] K. G. Larsen and A. Skou. Bisimulation through probabilistic testing. proceedings POPL 1989.

[Mil80] R. Milner, Calculus of Communicating System, LNCS92, 1980.

[Mil83] R. Milner, Calculi for Synchrony and Asynchrony, Theoretical Computer Science 25(3), pp 267-310, 1983.

[Mil90] R. Milner, Communication and Concurrency, Prentice Hall, 1990.

[MT90] F. Moller and C. Tofts, A Temporal Calculus of Communicating Systems, Proceedings Concur '90, LNCS 458, 1990.

[OW78] G. F. Oster and E. O. Wilson, Caste and Ecology in Social Insects, Princeton University Press, 1978.

[Paz71] A. Paz, Introduction to probabilistic automata, Academic Press, 1971.

[Plo81] G. D. Plotkin, A structured approach to operational semantics. Technical report Daimi Fn-19, Computer Science Department, Aarhus University. 1981.

[RR86] G. Reed and W. Roscoe, A Timed Model for CSP, Proceedings ICALP '86, LNCS 226, 1986.

[SS90] S. Smolka and B. Steffen, Priority as Extremal Probability, Proceedings Concur '90, LNCS 458, 1990.

[SST89] S. Smolka, B. Steffen and C. Tofts, unpublished notes. Working title, Probability + Restriction ⇒ priority.

[THF92] C. Tofts, M.J.Hatcher, N. Franks, Autosynchronisation in Leptothorax Acervorum; Theory, Testability and Experiment, Journal of Theoretical Biology 157: 71-82.

[TF92] C. Tofts, N. Franks, Doing the Right Thing: Ants, Bees and Naked Mole Rats, Trends in Evolution and Ecology 7: 346-349.

[Tof89] C. Tofts, Timing Concurrent Processes, LFCS-report number 103, 1989.

[Tof90] C. Tofts, A Synchronous Calculus of Relative Frequency, CONCUR '90, Springer Verlag, LNCS 458.

[Tof93] C. Tofts, Exact Solutions to Finite State Simulation Problems, Research Report, Department of Computer Science, University of Calgary, 1993.

[Tof94] C. Tofts, Using Process Algebra to Describe Social Insect Behaviour, Transactions on Simulation, 1993.

[Tof94] C. Tofts, Processes with Probabilities, Priorities and Time, FACS 6(5): 536-564, 1994.

[Yi90] Yi W., Real-Time Behaviour of Asynchronous Agents, Proceedings Concur '90 LNCS 458, pp 502-520, 1990.

[VW92] S. F. M. van Vlijmen, A. van Waveren, An Algebraic Specification of a Model Factory, Research report, University of Amsterdam Programming research Group, 1992.

[Wil65] J. Wilkinson, The Numerical Eigenvalue Problem, Oxford University press 1965.

1 PRobabilistic Algebra Toolset (PRAT)

The basic process definition mechanism is to present a file in Edinburgh concurrency workbench [CPS93] like syntax. The system then generates an extended probabilistic transition graph (it takes account of priorities) and provides a set of analysis functions which can be applied to the system.

1.1 Weights

Weights are defined by the following syntax, where n is an integer and *string* an ascii character string:

$$e ::= n|string|e - e^{6}$$
$$w ::= e@n$$

So the following are weights: `5, 1-p, 5@2, 1-p@3`. the last two being weights at priority level 2 and 3 repsectively. Note that we do not allow symbolic priorities, as this would actually affect the computational structure.

1.2 Actions

Actions are defined as products of powers of strings;

$$A ::= string[\hat{}n]|A\#A$$

again we do not allow symbolic action powers.

So the following are actions: `a, a^-1,a#b^-2, c^4#a#b^3`.

To form a permission free group we provide a binding operator for sets of actions:

```
bs Set a,b,c
```

binds the name `Set` to the actions `a,b,c`.

1.3 Processes

We define the following constructions on processes which we present by example; it should be noted that we only allow one depth of operator application, this permits automatic absorbtion of equivalent state in parallel compositions:

[6] It should be noted that the current parser works LR so that $1-p-q$ is actually $1-p+q$

Sequential	`bs Coin p.head:C1 + 1-p.tail:C2`
Parallel	`bpa Sys S1|S2`
Permission	`bperm S1 Sys/Set`
Priority	`bpi Sn S`
Pri(Perm(Par))	`btr Sys S1|S2|S3/Set`
Perm(Par)	`bpc Sys S1|S2/Set`
Comment	`*this is a comment`

As the sytem constructs processes it prints out the number of states it has allocated so far as an indication of the work left to do.

1.4 Analysis

The following functions are presented to allow the maintenance, exploration and analysis of systems:

- `cle()` clear the current process environment.
- `rf(filename)` read a process definition from `filename`.
- `dupo(filename)` duplicate all output to the file.
- `co()` close duplicate output file.
- `sim(Pname)` simulate the process state called `Pname`. The simulator presents a menu of actions. Typing the number of the action causes the system to continue from the labelled state. Hitting return takes option 0 and hitting q exits the simulator.
- `fd(Pname)` find deadlocks in the process `Pname`. If a deadlock is found then the shortest transition to that state is printed.
- `ll(Pname)` find livelocks in the process `Pname`.
- `do_prob(Pname,Win,Lose)` generate a set of equations describing the probability of seeing the `Win` action, ignoring other actions but terminating on the `Lose` action. Action syntax as above.
- `do_mean(Pname,Win,Lose)` generate a set of equations describing the mean number of ticks to see a `Win` or `Lose` action, ignore all other actions.
- `ibv(vn,real)` bind the weight variable `vn` to the real value `real`.
- `sc(Pname)` generate a set of back substitutions for the stable distribution of process `Pname`.
- `solmn(Pname,action,file)` produce an expression for the mean number of `action` in process `Pname` output the results to `file`. This is separate from the above to allow reuse of the stable solution information.

- **genfun(Pname,Action,vn,low,hi,step,inR,gR,aL)** generate a piecewise approximation to the mean number of actions **Action** the parameters are as follows:

Pname the process;

Action the action;

vn the variable name to range over;

low lower limit of solution generation;

hi upper limit of solution generation;

step step between solutions;

inR initial number of iterations at approx level 0, to generate coarse approximation;

gR number of iterations at final approx level;

aL required accuracy of the final answer.

- **genml(evrn,aprx,file)** generate an SML function to evaluate the piecewise approximation generated by above function, the error variable is given by **evrn** and **file** is the name of a file to copy the result to.

The system supplies two iterative solution packages, one for numeric solutions the other for local approximations, we describe their use below:

	Numerical	Analytical
Initialise	**start_iterate(Pname)**	**SI(Pname)**
Iterate	**itn(n)**	**APN(n)**
Print Sol	**pt()**	**CAP()**
Mean	**ma(action)**	**AM(action)**
Mean (Cyclic)	**mcyc(action,n)**	**APC(acs,n)**

In the above the **n** in the cyclic means is the number of states in the cycle. Often good approximations to nearly cyclic systems can be obtained cheaply by exploiting this function. A further function **sal(n)** is supplied to set the approximation level in the second set of functions.

As a first example we provide a system with an exact analytic solution.

Example 1.1 *Consider two processes competing for the same resource. Each process issues a request with probability* $1/p$ *after the last time it had the resource, and then will release the resource with probability* $1/q$ *at each instant.*

```
*Simple competition example

bs U1 p.t:U1G + 1-p.t:U1
```

```
bs U1G 1@1.get^-1:U1Got + 1.baulk:U1G
bs U1Got q.put^-1:U1 + 1-q.t:U1Got

bs Res 1.get:RG + 1.t:Res
bs RG 1.put:Res + 1.t:RG

basi C baulk

btr Sys U1|U1|Res/C
```

Having solved the equations the above system generates we obtain the average number of baulk actions seen at each tick is given by the following eqaution:

$$(8.\,p^{2} - 4.\,p^{3} - 4.44089\;10^{-15}\,p\,q + 4.\,p^{2}\,q - 8.\,p^{3}\,q + 4.\,p^{4}\,q + 1.\,(2. - 2.\,p)^{2}\,p^{2}\,q^{2})\;/$$

$$(8.\,p^{2} - 4.\,p^{3} + 8.\,p\,q + 4.44089\;10^{-15}\,p^{2}\,q - 8.\,p^{3}\,q + 4.\,p^{4}\,q + 4.\,q^{2} - 4.\,p^{2}\,q^{2} - 4.\,p^{3}\,q^{2} + 4.\,p^{4}\,q^{2})$$

As a result of using a real representation for numerical values in the toolset there are rounding errors[7] *in the above and if these are corrected we can obtain the following formula:*

$$\frac{p^2(4-2p+2q-4pq+4p^2q+(1-p)^2q^2)}{4p^2-2p^3+4p^3q-4p^3q+2p^4q+2q^2-2p^2q^2-2p^3q^2+2p^4q^2}$$

As a second example we demonstrate a performance analysis of the alternating bit protocol.

Example 1.2 *In [Mil90] Milner presents an implementation of the Alternating Bit Protocol in CCS, and demonstrates that the protocol is correct. Perforce this implementation ignores the temporal and probabilistic properties of the system and its components.*

Our alternating bit protocol realisation is depicted in Figure 1.

---

[7] Caused by the use of real numbers in the analysis system, easily identifiable as the terms are insignificant. The exponential growth of terms exhibited by products of processes forced the use of (truncated) real aritmetic in the tool, rather than the prefered (exact) integer arithmetic

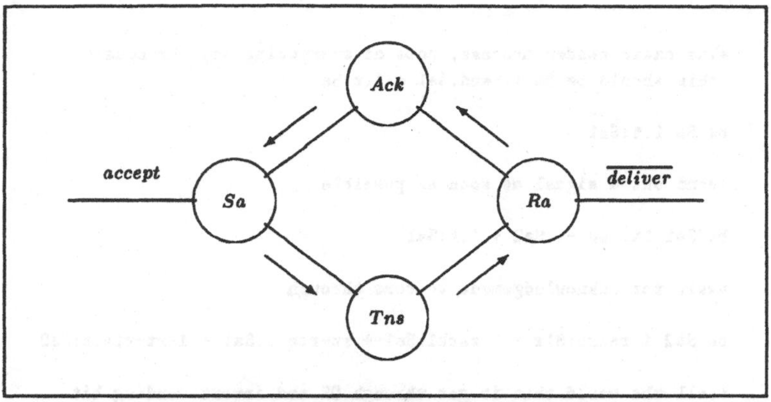

FIGURE 1. Alternating Bit Protocol

The process Sa will work in the following manner. After accepting a message, it sends it with bit b along the channel Tns and waits. Subsequently there are three possibilities:

- *it times out and retransmits the message;*
- *it gets an acknowledgement b from the Ack line (signifying a correct transmission), so that it can now accept another message;*
- *it gets an acknowledgement ¬b from the Ack line (signifying a superfluous extra acknowledgement of earlier message) which it ignores.*

The replier Ra works in a dual manner. After a message is delivered it sends an acknowledgement with bit b along the Ack line. Subsequently there are again three possibilities:

- *it times out, and retransmits the acknowledgement;*
- *it gets a new message with bit ¬b from the Tns line, which it delivers and acknowledges with bit ¬b;*
- *it gets a repetition of the old message with bit b which it ignores.*

We assume that messages are lost by the medium with probability err on each transmission. The sender and replier processes will retry with probability rt at for each tick whilst they are waiting for an acknowledgement or the message bit to change. In order that we can apply our peturbation theory to the variables err and rt, we assume perturbations of ere and rte upon their basic values.

```
*Probabilistic alternating bit protocol
*
*Chris Tofts 9/8/94 after CWB versions
*
```

```
*The basic sender process, note do everything asynchronously
*this should be Sa 1.send:Sa1 + 1.t:Sa

bs Sa 1.t:Sa1

*send out a signal as soon as possible

bs Sa1 1@1.s0^-1:Sa2 + 1.t:Sa1

*wait for acknowledgement to come through

bs Sa2 1.rack0:S1s + 1.rack1:Sa1 + rt-rte.t:Sa1 + 1-rt-rte.t:Sa2

*tell the world that it got through OK and invert sending bit

bs S1s 1.succ:S1

*the dual of the above system for sending with bit set to 1
*this should be bs S1 1.send:S11+ 1.t:S1

bs S1 1.t:S11
bs S11 1@1.s1^-1:S12 + 1.t:S11
bs S12 1.rack1:Sas + 1.rack0:S11 + rt-rte.t:S11 + 1-rt-rte.t:S12
bs Sas 1.succ:Sa

*the receiver for all of our endeavours....

bs Ra  1.r0:Rar1+1.r1:Ra2 + rt-rte.t:Ra2 + 1-rt-rte.t:Ra
bs Rar1 1.receive:Ra1

*try to send the data as quickly as possible

bs Ra1 1@1.sack0^-1:R1 + 1.t:Ra1 + 1.r0:R11 + 1.r1:Ra12
bs Ra2 1@1.sack1^-1:Ra + 1.t:Ra2 + 1.r1:R12 + 1.r0:Rar1
bs R1 1.r1:Ra12 + 1.r0:R11 + rt-rte.t:R11 + 1-rt-rte.t:R1
bs Ra12 1.receive:R12
bs R11 1@1.sack0^-1:R1 + 1.t:R11 + 1.r0:R11 + 1.r1:Ra12
bs R12 1@1.sack1^-1:Ra + 1.t:R12 + 1.r1:R12 + 1.r0:Rar1

*the lower channel for sending data on
*we send out data as soon as possible after the transmission
*time if it is not lost to error...

bs Ml1 1.s0:Ml1a0 + 1.s1:Ml110 + 1.t:Ml1

*decide if the data was transmitted OK, or was subject to error

bs Ml1a0 1-err-ere.t:Ml1a + err-ere.t:Ml1
bs Ml1a 1@1.r0^-1:Ml1 + 1.t:Ml1a
bs Ml110 1-err-ere.t:Ml11 + err-ere.t:Ml1
bs Ml11 1@1.r1^-1:Ml1 + 1.t:Ml11
```

```
*this is the transmitting medium for the return of the data

bs M12 1.sack0:M12a1 + 1.sack1:M1211 + 1.t:M12
bs M12a1 1-err-ere.t:M12a + err-ere.t:M12
bs M12a 1@1.rack0^-1:M12 + 1.t:M12a
bs M1211 1-err-ere.t:M121 + err-ere.t:M12
bs M121 1@1.rack1^-1:M12 + 1.t:M121

*That's all the sequential bits done so we can now have a go at putting
*it all together...

basi Allow send, receive, succ

*this is the complete system

btr ABP Ra|M11|M12|Sa/Allow
```

The PRAT tool can output a local approximation function to compute the average number of succ *actions observed per tick. For a value of* $rt = 0.5$ *and* $rte = 0.0$ *and* err *in the range* 0.05 *to* 0.35, *we obtain the following piecewise approximation for the average* succ *rate in the form of an SML function:*

```
fun ABP(vl)
=if 0.05<=vl andalso vl<=0.15
 then let val ere = (0.05+0.15)/2.0 - vl in
(26.2801394665775-285.522119242462 * ere * ere * ere
-94.9741260228557 * ere * ere + 26.6274947013716 * ere )/
(270.683502505543+1.32871491587139E~12 * ere * ere * ere -
7.47846229387505E~13 * ere -3.12638803734444E~13 * ere * ere )
end
else if 0.15<=vl andalso vl<=0.25
 then let val ere = (0.15+0.25)/2.0 - vl in
(11.7544078755176-83.86909484614 * ere * ere * ere
-16.6668138922172 * ere * ere +19.7005844688574 * ere )/
(139.000000000001-3.19744231092045E~13 * ere * ere * ere
- 4.01456645704457E~13 * ere -3.92574861507455E~13 * ere * ere )
end
else if 0.25<=vl andalso vl<=0.35
 then let val ere = (0.25+0.35)/2.0 - vl in
(9.68600554074613-41.7301838198085 * ere * ere * ere
+1.29897621781181 * ere * ere +20.937477181878 * ere )/
(139.0-1.59872115546023E~14* ere * ere * ere-
3.5438318946035E~13 * ere -2.46025422256935E~13 * ere * ere )
end
else 0.0;
```

As an example for a value of $err = 0.2$ *we obtain the result* 0.0845640854353778, *which equates (by inversion) to an average transmission time of* 11.8253510914415.

The total time to construct the process graph and the above approximations was about 1/2 hour on a SPARCstation 2.

Model Checking of Non-Finite State Processes by Finite Approximations

N. De Francesco*
A. Fantechi*†
S. Gnesi†
P. Inverardi‡

ABSTRACT In this paper we present a verification methodology, using an action-based logic, able to check properties for full CCS terms, allowing also verification on infinite state systems. Obviously, for some properties we are only able to give a semidecision procedure. The idea is to use (a sequence of) finite state transition systems which approximate the, possibly infinite state, transition system corresponding to a term. To this end we define a particular notion of approximation, which is stronger than simulation, suitable to define and prove liveness and safety properties of the process terms.

1 Introduction

Many verification environments are presently available which can be used to automatically verify properties of reactive systems specified by means of process algebras, with respect to behavioural relations and logical properties. Most of these environments [7, 12, 14, 21] are based on the hypothesis that the system can be modelled as a finite state Labelled Transition Systems (LTS) and that the logic properties are regular properties. That is, no means are provided to deal with non-finite state LTS's. Usually, in these environments, to avoid the nontermination of the generation phase a term must satisfy some finiteness syntactic conditions: in the case of CCS, for example, terms where a process variable x occurs in a parallel composition belonging to the definition of x are not handled [24].

We are interested here to deal with non finite-state systems; approaches

*Dipartimento di Ingegneria dell'Informazione, Univ. di Pisa, Italy, e-mail: nico@iet.unipi.it, fantechi@iet.unipi.it

†Istituto di Elaborazione dell'Informazione, C.N.R. Pisa, Italy, e-mail: gnesi@iei.pi.cnr.it

‡Dip. di Matematica Applicata, Univ. dell'Aquila, Italy, e-mail:inverard@iei.pi.cnr.it

have been proposed to this aim, which are not based on LTS's [1, 4, 16, 17, 18]; we consider instead LTS based verification. The idea is to use, for proving a logical property, a sequence of finite state LTSs approximating the, possibly infinite state, LTS corresponding to a term by the standard CCS semantics.

In this paper we present a verification methodology to check properties expressed in ACTL, an action based logic [11], on full CCS terms (with no syntactic restriction), thus allowing complete generality of the class of reactive systems to be specified. We are able to carry on the verification even though the "usual" LTS generation fails. Obviously, for some of the properties, we are able to give only a semidecision procedure. This procedure is based on a notion of approximation and on the study of the ACTL properties *preserved* by the approximation. In this way, we can infer the satisfaction of a property by the whole system from the satisfaction of the property by a chain of approximations. In particular, we define an approximation chain, denoted as $\{N_i\}$, which is very expressive with respect to liveness properties.

In order to reason on the properties that we are able to prove with approximation chains, we start giving a syntactic characterization of different kinds of properties. Moreover, we define a criterion to compare the suitability of approximation chains to prove properties. Following this notion, we formalize the fact that a chain is "better" than another one, if its set of provable properties is greater. Our work differs from the abstract interpretation approaches for model checking of transition systems [2, 6, 8] since we do not build an abstract (with respect to values) model on which the properties are proved, but a suitable chain of finite labelled transition systems based on the operational semantics: when dealing with infinite systems, this allows us to choose the approximation level case by case. Although the main goal of the presented approach is to verify (classes) of non-finite state systems, it can also be seen as a way to accomplish "on the fly" model checking, similarly to the "on the fly" equivalence verification proposed in [13].

2 Background

2.1 CCS

We summarize the most relevant definitions regarding CCS, and refer to [23] for more details. The CCS syntax is the following:
$p ::= \mu.p \mid nil \mid p+p \mid p|p \mid p\backslash A \mid x \mid p[f]$

Terms generated by p (*Terms*) are called *process terms* (called also *processes* or *terms*); x ranges over a set $\{X, Y, ..\}$, of process variables. A process variable is defined by a process definition $x \stackrel{def}{=} p$, (p is called the expan-

Act $\dfrac{}{\mu.p \xrightarrow{\mu} p}$	**Con** $\dfrac{p \xrightarrow{\mu} p',\ x \stackrel{def}{=} p}{x \xrightarrow{\mu} p'}$
Sum $\dfrac{p \xrightarrow{\mu} p'}{p+q \xrightarrow{\mu} p' \text{ and } q+p \xrightarrow{\mu} p'}$	**Par** $\dfrac{p \xrightarrow{\mu} p'}{p\vert q \xrightarrow{\mu} p'\vert q \text{ and } q\vert p \xrightarrow{\mu} q\vert p'}$
Com $\dfrac{p \xrightarrow{\alpha} p',\ q \xrightarrow{\overline{\alpha}} q'}{p\vert q \xrightarrow{\tau} p'\vert q'}$	**Res** $\dfrac{p \xrightarrow{\mu} p',\ \mu, \overline{\mu} \notin A}{p\backslash A \xrightarrow{\mu} p'\backslash A}$
Rel $\dfrac{p \xrightarrow{\mu} p'}{p[f] \xrightarrow{f(\mu)} p'[f]}$	

FIGURE 1. The SOS rules

sion of x). As usual, there is a set of visible actions $Vis = \{a, \overline{a}, b, \overline{b}, ...\}$ over which α ranges, while μ, ν range over $Act = Vis \cup \{\tau\}$, where τ denotes the so-called *internal action*. We denote by $\overline{\alpha}$ the action complement: if $\alpha = a$, then $\overline{\alpha} = \overline{a}$, while if $\alpha = \overline{a}$, then $\overline{\alpha} = a$. By *nil* we denote the empty process. The operators to build process terms are prefixing ($\mu.p$), summation ($p + p$), parallel composition ($p|p$), restriction ($p\backslash A$) and relabelling ($p[f]$), where $A \subseteq Vis$ and $f : Vis \to Vis$. Given a term p, an occurrence of a process variable x is ***guarded in*** p if it is within some sub-term of the form $\mu.q$. We assume that (i) Vis is finite; (ii) for each definition $x \stackrel{def}{=} p$, each occurrence of each process variable is guarded in p; (iii) all terms are closed, i.e. all variables occurring in a term are defined.

An operational semantics OP is a set of inference rules defining a relation $D \subseteq Terms \times Act \times Terms$. The relation is the least relation satisfying the rules. If $(p, \mu, q) \in D$, we write $p \xrightarrow{\mu}_{OP} q$. The rules defining the semantics of CCS [23], from now on referred to as SOS, are recalled in Figure 1.

A ***labelled transition system*** (or simply ***transition system***) TS is a quadruple (S, T, D, s_0), where S is a set of states, T is a set of transition labels, $s_0 \in S$ is the initial state, and $D \subseteq S \times T \times S$. A transition system is finite if D is finite.

A finite computation of a transition system is a sequence $\mu_1\mu_2..\mu_n$ of labels such that:
$s_0 \xrightarrow{\mu_1}_{OP} .. \xrightarrow{\mu_n}_{OP} s_n$.

Given a term p (and a set of process variable definitions), and an operational semantics OP, $OP(p)$ is the transition system $(Terms, Act, D, p)$, where D is the relation defined by OP. For example, $SOS(p)$ is the transition system defined by the SOS semantics for the term p.

Let $TS_1 = (S_1, T_1, D_1, s_{0_1})$ and $TS_2 = (S_2, T_2, D_2, s_{0_2})$ be transition systems and let $s_1 \in S_1$ and $s_2 \in S_2$. s_1 and s_2 are ***strongly equivalent*** (or simply *equivalent*) ($s_1 \sim s_2$) if there exists a *strong bisimulation* that relates s_1 and s_2. $\mathcal{B} \subseteq S_1 \times S_2$ is a strong bisimulation if $\forall (s_1, s_2) \in \mathcal{B}$ (where $\mu \in T_1 \cup T_2$),

- $s_1 \xrightarrow{\mu}_1 s_1'$ implies $\exists s_2' : s_2 \xrightarrow{\mu}_2 s_2'$ and $(s_1', s_2') \in \mathcal{B}$; $s_2 \xrightarrow{\mu}_2 s_2'$ implies $s_1 \xrightarrow{\mu}_1 s_1'$ and $(s_1', s_2') \in \mathcal{B}$

s_2 *simulates* s_1 if there exists a *strong simulation* that relates s_1 and s_2. $\mathcal{R} \subseteq S_1 \times S_2$ is a strong simulation if $\forall (s_1, s_2) \in \mathcal{R}$ (where $\mu \in T_1 \cup T_2$): $s_1 \xrightarrow{\mu}_1 s_1'$ implies $\exists s_2' : s_2 \xrightarrow{\mu}_2 s_2'$ and $(s_1', s_2') \in \mathcal{R}$.

TS_1 and TS_2 are said to be *equivalent* ($TS_1 \sim TS_2$) if a strong bisimulation exists for s_{0_1} and s_{0_2}. Two CCS terms p and q are *equivalent* ($p \sim q$) if $SOS(p) \sim SOS(q)$.

TS_2 simulates TS_1 if a strong simulation $\mathcal{R}$ exists such that $(s_{01}, s_{02}) \in \mathcal{R}$.

Given a state s of a transition system $TS = (S, T, D, s_0)$, we say that $s \not\rightarrow$ if no $s' \in S$ and $\mu \in T$ exist such that $(s, \mu, s') \in D$.

CCS can be used to define a wide class of systems, that ranges from Turing machines to finite systems [24]; therefore, in general, CCS terms cannot be represented as finite state systems.

2.2 ACTL

We introduce now the action based branching temporal logic ACTL defined in [11]. This logic is suitable to express properties of reactive systems defined by means of TS's. ACTL is in agreement with the notion of bisimulation defined above. Before defining syntax and semantics of ACTL operators, let us introduce some notions and definitions which will be used in the sequel.

For $A \subseteq Act$, we let $D_A(s)$ denote the set $\{s'$: there exists $\alpha \in A$ such that $(s, \alpha, s') \in D\}$. We will also use the action name, instead of the corresponding singleton denotation, as subscript. Moreover, we let $D(s)$ denote in short $D_{Act}(s)$ and $D_{A_\tau}(s)$ denote $D_{A \cup \{\tau\}}(s)$.
For $A, B \subseteq Act$, we let A/B denote the set $A - (A \cap B)$.
Given a LTS TS=(S,T,D,s_0), we define:

- σ is a path from $r_0 \in S$ if either $\sigma = r_0$ (the empty path from r_0) or σ is a (possibly infinite) sequence $(r_0, \alpha_1, r_1)(r_1, \alpha_2, r_2) \ldots$ such that $(r_i, \alpha_{i+1}, r_{i+1}) \in D$ for each $i \geq 0$.

- A path σ is called maximal if either it is infinite or it is finite and its last state r has no successor states ($D(r) = \emptyset$). The set of maximal paths from r_0 will be denoted by $\Pi(r_0)$.

- If σ is infinite, then $|\sigma| = \omega$.
If $\sigma = r_0$, then $|\sigma| = 0$.

If $\sigma = (r_0, \alpha_1, r_1)(r_1, \alpha_2, r_2) \dots (r_n, \alpha_{n+1}, r_{n+1})$, $n \geq 0$, then $|\sigma| = n + 1$. Moreover, we will denote the ith state in the sequence, i.e. r_i, by $\sigma(i)$. □

To define the logic ACTL [11], an auxiliary logic of actions is introduced. The collection $\mathcal{AF}$ of *action formulae* over Vis is defined by the following grammar where χ, χ', range over action formulae, and $\alpha \in Vis$:

$\chi ::= \alpha | \neg\chi | \chi \wedge \chi$

We write $f\!f$ for $\alpha_0 \wedge \neg\alpha_0$, where α_0 is some chosen action, and $t\!t$ stands for $\neg f\!f$. Moreover, we will write $\chi \vee \chi'$ for $\neg(\neg\chi \wedge \neg\chi')$. An action formula permits the expression of constraints on the actions that can be observed (along a path or after next step); for instance, $\alpha \vee \beta$ says that the only possible observations are α or β, while $t\!t$ stands for "all actions are allowed" and $f\!f$ for "no actions can be observed", that is only silent actions can be performed.

The satisfaction of an action formula χ by an action α, $\alpha \models \chi$, is defined inductively by:

•$\alpha \models \beta$ iff $\alpha = \beta$; •$\alpha \models \neg\chi$ iff not $\alpha \models \chi$; •$\alpha \models \chi \wedge \chi'$ iff $\alpha \models \chi$ and $\alpha \models \chi'$

Given an action formula χ, the set of the actions satisfying χ can be given by the function $\kappa : \mathcal{AF}(Vis) \rightarrow 2^{Vis}$ as follows:

$$\kappa(\chi) = \{\alpha | \alpha \models \chi\}$$

The syntax of ACTL is defined by the state formulae generated by the following grammar:

$\phi ::= t\!t \mid \phi \wedge \phi \mid \neg\phi \mid E\gamma \mid A\gamma$

$\gamma ::= X_\chi \phi \mid X_\tau \phi \mid \phi\, {}_\chi U\, \phi \mid \phi\, {}_\chi U_{\chi'}\, \phi$

where χ, χ' range over action formulae, E and A are path quantifiers, X and U are *next* and *until* operators respectively.

Let $TS = (S, Act, D, s_0)$ be a LTS. *Satisfaction* of a state formula ϕ (path formula γ) by a state s (path σ), notation $s \models_{TS} \phi$ ($\sigma \models_{TS} \gamma$) is given inductively by :

$s \models_{TS} t\!t$		always;
$s \models_{TS} \phi \wedge \phi'$	iff	$s \models_{TS} \phi$ and $s \models_{TS} \phi'$;
$s \models_{TS} \neg\phi$	iff	not $s \models_{TS} \phi$;
$s \models_{TS} E\gamma$	iff	there exists a path $\sigma \in \Pi(s)$ such that $\sigma \models_{TS} \gamma$;
$s \models_{TS} A\gamma$	iff	for all maximal paths $\sigma \in \Pi(s)$, $\sigma \models_{TS} \gamma$;
$\sigma \models_{TS} X_\chi \phi$	iff	$\|\sigma\| \geq 1$ and $\sigma(2) \in D_{\kappa(\chi)}(\sigma(1))$ and $\sigma(2) \models_{TS} \phi$;

$\sigma \models_{TS} X_\tau \phi$ iff $|\sigma| \geq 1$ and $\sigma(2) \in D_{\{\tau\}}(\sigma(1))$ and $\sigma(2) \models_{TS} \phi$;
$\sigma \models_{TS} \phi\, _\chi U \phi'$ iff there exists $i \geq 1$ such that $\sigma(i) \models_{TS} \phi'$, and for all $1 \leq j \leq i-1$: $\sigma(j) \models_{TS} \phi$ and $\sigma(j+1) \in D_{\kappa(\chi)_\tau}(\sigma(j))$;
$\sigma \models_{TS} \phi\, _\chi U_{\chi'} \phi'$ iff there exists $i \geq 2$ such that $\sigma(i) \models_{TS} \phi'$ and $\sigma(i) \in D_{\kappa(\chi')}(\sigma(i-1))$, and for all $1 \leq j \leq i-1$: $\sigma(j) \models_{TS} \phi$ and $\sigma(j) \in D_{\kappa(\chi)_\tau}(\sigma(j-1))$.

Several useful modalities can be defined, starting from the basic ones. In particular, we will write:

- $A\widetilde{X}_\chi \phi$ for $\neg EX_\chi \neg\phi$ and $E\widetilde{X}_\chi \phi$ for $\neg AX_\chi \neg\phi$. These are called the *weak next* operators.
- $EF\phi$ for $E(tt\, _{tt}U\, \phi)$, and $AF\phi$ for $A(tt\, _{tt}U\, \phi)$; these are called the *eventually* operators.
- $EG\phi$ for $\neg AF \neg\phi$, and $AG\phi$ for $\neg EF\neg\phi$; these are called the *always* operators.

ACTL can be used to define *liveness* (something good eventually happen) and *safety* (nothing bad can happen) properties of reactive systems. In a branching time logic both liveness and safety properties could be divided into two classes: *universal* liveness (safety) properties and *existential* liveness (safety) properties. The former state that a condition holds at some (all) states of *all* computation paths. The latter state that a condition holds at some (all) states of *one* computation path. Moreover liveness properties can be better classified as in the following [19, 22]:
Termination properties: "a good thing happens at some states of a (all) computation(s)".
Recurrence properties: "a good thing happens at infinitely many states of a (all) computation(s)".
Persistence property: "a good thing happens at all but finitely many states of a (all) computation(s)".
We can also talk of *finite properties*, that state some condition on the finite initial part of the behaviour of the system.

2.3 Infinite state systems and logical properties

We know that all ACTL formulae are decidable on finite state transition systems and the linear time ACTL model checker [10] can be used to do this job. Hence, when we have a CCS description of a system and we want to prove on it ACTL properties, the labeled transition system associated to it needs to be built. This will be the model on which the satisfiability of the formulae will be checked. Problems, obviously, arise when the system to be modelled has an infinite state representation, due for example to the interplay between parallel composition and recursion operators.

As an example, let us consider the CCS definition of a bag containing two kinds of elements:

$$X = p1.(g1.nil|X) + p2.(g2.nil|X)$$

where p_1 and p_2 represent insertions and g_1 and g_2 deletions of the two kinds of elements, respectively. It is known that X is neither finite state nor context-free. Some typical properties of a bag could be requested to be checked on this specification, in order to validate it:
1) The bag is not a set, therefore it is possible to put twice the same value in the bag consecutively: $AFAX_{p_1}EX_{p_1}tt$.
2) It is possible, on all (but finitely many) states to do a *put* action immediately followed by a *get* action: $EFEG(EX_{p_1}EX_{g_1}tt)$.
3) There exists a computation path on which it is possible to do infinitely often *put* actions: $EGAF(EX_{p_1 \vee p_2}tt)$.
4) It is always possible to perform a put action: $AGEX_{p_1 \vee p_2}tt$.

3 Verification by approximations

Let us first present a syntactic characterization, as ACTL formulae, of the logical properties we will deal with. We then introduce the general notion of chain of finite approximations of the transition system of a term p. Finally, we introduce a notion of approximation suitable to prove liveness properties.

3.1 Temporal properties

Definition 3.1 (Positive formula) *We say that π' is a positive formula if it is an ACTL formula without negations.*

Definition 3.2 (Liveness property) *We say that ψ is a liveness property if one of the following holds, where π' is a positive formula:*

- $\psi = AF\pi'$ *or* $\psi = EF\pi'$ *(*termination property*)*
- $\psi = AFAG\pi'$, $\psi = EFAG\pi'$, $\psi = AFEG\pi'$ *or* $\psi = EFEG\pi'$ *(*persistence property*)*
- $\psi = AGAF\pi'$, $\psi = EGAF\pi'$, $\psi = AGEF\pi'$ *or* $\psi = EGEF\pi'$ *(*recurrence property*)*

Definition 3.3 (Finite property) *We say that σ is a finite property if it can be expressed by an ACTL formula defined by the following grammar:*
$\sigma ::= tt \mid \sigma \wedge \sigma \mid \sigma \vee \sigma \mid \neg\sigma \mid E\gamma \mid A\gamma$
$\gamma ::= X_\chi\sigma \mid X_\tau\sigma$

Note that the subset of ACTL defined by this grammar corresponds to the Hennessy-Milner logic [15].

Definition 3.4 (Positive finite property) *We say that π is a positive finite property if it is a finite property without negations.*

Definition 3.5 (Safety property) *We say that θ is a safety property if $\theta = AG\pi$ or $\theta = EG\pi$ and π is a positive finite property.*

The given syntactical presentation of liveness and safety properties does not obviously cover all the liveness and safety properties expressible by means of all the ACTL operators as the negation operator. Indeed, negation makes the syntactic classification of formulae difficult. Following this classification, we have that properties 1) to 3) of the bag example are liveness properties, while 4) is a safety one.

Finite, liveness and safety properties are decidable on a finite state LTS. In general, while finite properties are provable, liveness (including termination, persistence and recurrence) and safety properties can be undecidable for a non-finite state term p.

3.2 Approximation chains

Given a CCS term p, we define chains of finite LTSs which more and more accurately simulate the behaviour of SOS(p). Since each LTS in a chain is finite proof checking methodologies for finite LTSs can be used. First we define in the most general way the concept of approximation chain. In the following we denote, with $\mathcal{T}$ and T, the set of all LTSs and a generic LTS, respectively.

Definition 3.6 (Approximation chain) *Let $\preceq$ a preorder over $\mathcal{T}$. We say that T_1 approximates by $\preceq$ ($\preceq$-approximates) T_2 iff $T_1 \preceq T_2$. Given a term p, a chain $\{T_i(p) | i \geq 0\}$ on $(\mathcal{T}, \preceq)$ is called* approximation chain for p by *$\preceq$ ($\preceq$-approximation chain) iff:*

- *for each i, $T_i(p)$ is finite;*
- *for each i, $T_i(p) \preceq T_{i+1}(p)$;*
- *$SOS(p)$ is a least upper bound of $\{T_i(p)\}$.*

Note that, if we have a finite approximation chain $\{T_i(p) | r \geq i \geq 0\}$, then $T_r(p) \sim SOS(p)$.

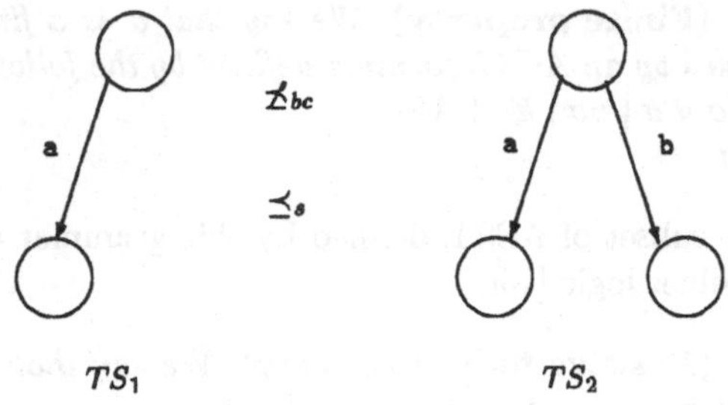

FIGURE 2. Simulation vs. BC-simulation.

Definition 3.7 (Properties preserved by $\preceq$) *A preorder $\preceq$ preserves a property ϕ if whenever T_1 verifies ϕ and $T_1 \preceq T_2$ then T_2 verifies ϕ.*

The above definitions allow us to define a procedure for proving the validity of a property on an infinite state-system, by checking the property on the elements of an approximation chain, starting from the first one, until we find that the property is verified. The procedure is sound if the chain preserves the property, i.e. it must happen that, if we are able to prove ϕ on an element of the chain, we can assert the validity of ϕ on $SOS(p)$. This means that the property must be monotonic on the preorder. The first result we show is that simulation, from now on denoted by $\preceq_s$, is not suitable to prove all liveness properties.

is possible to build different kinds of different sets of properties. and then gradually refine result holds.

Proposition 3.1 *$\preceq_s$ does not preserve all liveness properties.*
Proof *Let us consider the following liveness property:*
Each path contains a state from which all the outcoming arcs are labelled by *a, expressed by $(AFAX_a tt)$ and the transition systems TS_1 and TS_2 in Figure 2.*
We have that $TS_1 \preceq_s TS_2$, but TS_1 verifies the property and TS_2 does not.

In order to manage all liveness properties, we now introduce a stronger notion of simulation between transition systems. This notion, in contrast to simulation, permits the definition of approximation chains that *preserve* the branching structure, that is, for each approximation, if a node has been exploded, all its branches have been developed.

Definition 3.8 (Branching Complete Simulation) *Let $TS_1 = (S_1, T_1, D_1, s_{0_1})$ and $TS_2 = (S_2, T_2, D_2, s_{0_2})$ be transition systems and let $s_1 \in S_1$ and $s_2 \in S_2$.*
s_2 BC-simulates s_1 *if there exists a* strong BC-simulation *that relates s_1 and s_2. $\mathcal{R} \subseteq S_1 \times S_2$ is a strong BC-simulation if $\forall (s_1, s_2) \in \mathcal{R}$, $\mu \in T_1 \cup T_2$,*

- $s_1 \xrightarrow{\mu}_1 s_1'$ *implies* $\exists s_2' : s_2 \xrightarrow{\mu}_2 s_2'$ *and* $(s_1', s_2') \in \mathcal{R}$.

- $s_2 \xrightarrow{\mu}_2 s'_2$ *implies either* $s_1 \not\rightarrow_1$ *or* $s_1 \xrightarrow{\mu}_1 s'_1$ *and* $(s'_1, s'_2) \in \mathcal{R}$.

TS_2 BC-simulates TS_1 *($TS_1 \preceq_{bc} TS_2$) if a branching complete simulation* $\mathcal{R}$ *exists such that* $(s_{0_1}, s_{0_2}) \in \mathcal{R}$.

It is easy to see that $\preceq_{bc}$ is a preorder and that $TS_1 \preceq_{bc} TS_2$ implies $TS_1 \preceq_s TS_2$, but the converse is not true in general. For example, TS_2 does not BC-simulate TS_1 in Figure 2.

The notion of approximation chain based on BC-simulation preserves the branching structure of the transition systems all along the chain. This allow us to prove properties not provable on a chain based on simulation. One of the main results of the paper is the following:

Proposition 3.2 $\preceq_{bc}$ *preserves liveness properties.*
Proof sketch *By structural induction on the structure of the liveness formulae and taking into account that the liveness properties are defined on a positive fragment of ACTL and that the BC-simulation forces the simulating transition system to exactly maintain all the (bisimilar) branches of the simulated one, if any.*

It is now easy to relate approximation chains, based on BC-simulation, with liveness properties. The following proposition is the basis of our verification method.

Proposition 3.3 *Let p be a term and* $\{T_i(p)\}$ *a* $\preceq_{bc}$*-approximation chain for p. If* ϕ *is a liveness property, it holds that: if* $s_0 \models_{T_i(p)} \phi$ *for some i, then* $s_0 \models_{SOS(p)} \phi$.
Proof. *It follows by proposition 3.2.*

proving existential (*E*...) or universal (*A*...) due to the fact that BC-simulation preserves the

Let us now consider safety properties. It is easy to convince ourselves that we are not able to prove the satisfiability of a safety property by only using approximations of the given system. In fact, if we consider the syntax on which safety properties are defined, we note that each formula belonging to this ACTL subset is constituted by next modalities, with no negations, under a quantified always modality. Now, the evaluation of a next operator is false on all the states of a TS that have no successor. Therefore, the whole safety formula is false (consider for example the formula $AGAX_a tt$ on TS_1).
On the other hand, if a safety property is true on a $\preceq_{bc}$-approximation of a system, then such an approximation has at least one cyclic path that makes the formula true. This is enough to deduce that the formula is true on the SOS representation of the system. Indeed, the following proposition can be stated:

Proposition 3.4 *Safety properties are preserved by* $\preceq_{bc}$.

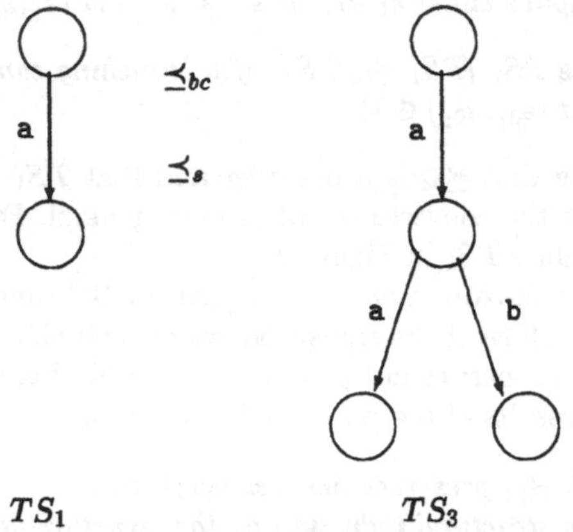

FIGURE 3. Simulation and BC-simulation.

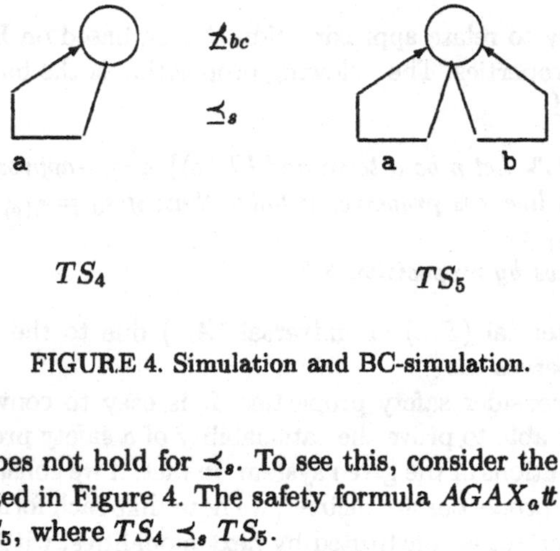

FIGURE 4. Simulation and BC-simulation.

The same does not hold for $\preceq_s$. To see this, consider the transition systems represented in Figure 4. The safety formula $AGAX_a tt$ is true on TS_4 but not on TS_5, where $TS_4 \preceq_s TS_5$.

preservazione corretto con questo esempio

A proof methodology can be derived for safety properties, starting from the above result. Unfortunately only a limited subclass of such properties are provable when finite approximations are considered for non-finite state systems: for example, on a non-finite state system we cannot prove any universal safety property. We can however define a proof methodology that takes into account the duality existing between liveness properties and safety ones. In this respect, we provide a method to prove the non-validity of a safety property on a finite approximation. To make this possible we need to forget that we are working on finite approximations in which there exist states with no successors and on which every safety formula is false.

This can be done considering a weaker version of the safety property under study, by substituting the next modalities with weak next modalities. Now, if this weak formula is false on one of the approximations p it will necessarily be false on $SOS(p)$. This idea is formalized by the following:

Definition 3.9 (Weak finite property) *We say that π is a weak finite property if it can be expressed by an ACTL formula defined by the following grammar:* $\sigma ::= tt \mid \sigma \wedge \sigma \mid \sigma \vee \sigma \mid E\gamma \mid A\gamma$
$\gamma ::= \widetilde{X}_\chi \sigma \mid \widetilde{X}_\tau \sigma$

Definition 3.10 (Weak safety property) *We say that θ is a weak safety property if $\theta = AG\pi$ or $\theta = EG\pi$ and π is a weak finite property.*

For weak safety properties, the following proposition holds :

Proposition 3.5 *Let p be a term and $\{T_i(p)\}$ a $\preceq_{bc}$-approximation chain for p. If ψ is a weak safety property, it holds that: if $s_0 \not\models_{T_i(p)} \psi$ for some i, then $s_0 \not\models_{SOS(p)} \psi$.*
Proof sketch *For duality from Prop. 3.3*

Let us now consider finite properties. The following holds:

Proposition 3.6 *$\preceq_s$ does not preserve all finite properties.*
Proof sketch *Consider the finite property:* Each path starts with an action *a ($AX_a tt$), with TS_1 and TS_2 of Figure 2. We have that $TS_1 \preceq_s TS_2$, but TS_1 verifies the property and TS_2 does not.*

Following the same reasoning of 3.2.

Since finite properties represent a particular class of liveness properties we have a semidecision procedure for testing the validity of these properties by using approximation chains based on $\preceq_{bc}$. We can do more, as one should have expected, and provide a decision procedure for finite properties. To this end, we furtherly constrain our chains. Let us consider, for example, the following finite property for $SOS(p)$ for some p:
All paths start with the action b and contain at least an action a as a second action ($AX_b EX_a tt$).
Approximation chains based on $\preceq_{bc}$ are not suitable to give a positive or negative answer if $SOS(p)$ is infinite: in fact a new path of length 2 may appear in whatever element of the chain. The property is decidable if, instead, each transition system $T_i(p)$ of the chain grows on all possible paths with respect to $T_{i-1}(p)$. This suggests the following notion:

Definition 3.11 (Transition system path-approximation) *Let TS_1 and TS_2 be transition systems. We say that TS_1 is an* n-path-approximation *of TS_2 ($TS_1 \preceq_n TS_2$) if*

- *$TS_1 \preceq_{bc} TS_2$;*
- *either $TS_1 \sim TS_2$ or the paths of length $\leq n$ of TS_1 and TS_2 coincide.*

We can now state the following:

Proposition 3.7 *Let π be a finite property of depth n, that is with only n nested next operators, and $\{T_i(p)\}$ a $\preceq_{bc}$-approximation chain for a term p such that $T_i(p) \preceq_i SOS(p)$ for each i. Then $s_0 \models_{SOS(p)} \pi$ iff $s_0 \models_{T_n(p)} \pi$.*
Proof sketch *We have that $T_n(p)$ has all the paths of length n of $SOS(p)$.*

4 How to build approximations

In this section, we present some ways of constructing approximation chains. In order to obtain correct approximations for a term p, the idea is to derive p using the operational semantics until some stopping condition, thus obtaining a partial transition system, which is furtherly expanded to obtain the successive elements of the chain. The first chain we present, described in the following sub-secton, is based on the standard SOS semantics. In order to obtain better approximations, we then introduce a second chain, which is based on a different semantics, able to produce "more expressive" transition systems.

4.1 SOS approximations

Definition 4.1 ($\{M_i(p)\}$) *Given a term p, the chain $\{M_i(p) = (S_{M_i}, Act, D_{M_i}, s_0)\}$ is inductively defined as follows:*

- $M_0(p) = (\{p\}, Act, \{\}, p)$
- $M_{i+1}(p) = (S_{M_{i+1}}, Act, D_{M_{i+1}}, p)$ *where*
  - $S_{M_{i+1}} = S_{M_i} \cup \{q | p \in S_{M_i}$ *and* $\exists \mu \in Act \ : \ p \xrightarrow{\mu}_{SOS} q\}$;
  - $D_{M_{i+1}} = D_{M_i} \cup \{(p, \mu, q) | p \in S_{M_i}$ *and* $\exists \mu \in Act \ : \ p \xrightarrow{\mu}_{SOS} q\}$.

Informally, $M_0(p)$ has the only state p without transitions and $M_{i+1}(p)$, $i \geq 0$, is obtained from $M_i(p)$, by adding to the states (and the related transitions) of $M_i(p)$ all those states reachable from them with only one action. The following proposition holds:

Proposition 4.1 *Given a term p, the chain $\{M_i(p)\}$ is a $\preceq_{bc}$-approximation chain for p.*
Proof sketch. *By induction on the length of the chain and by definig suitable BC-simulations.*

Actually, the chain $\{M_i(p)\}$ is the simplest chain derivable from SOS(p) which is a $\preceq_{bc}$-approximation chain. In fact the simpler approximation chain which at any step adds a single new transition to the previous element of the chain, is not a $\preceq_{bc}$-approximation chain.

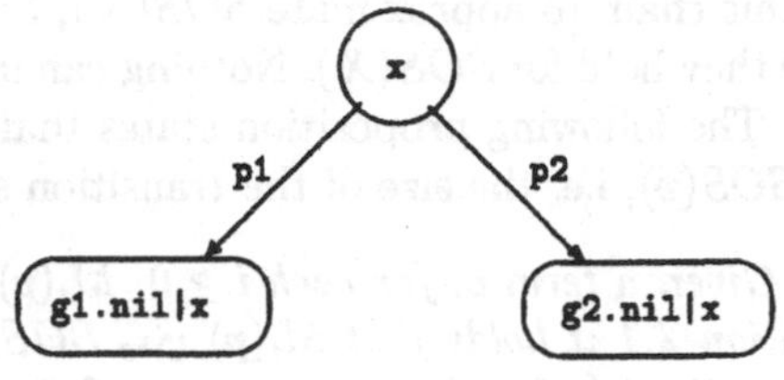

FIGURE 5. $M_1(X)$

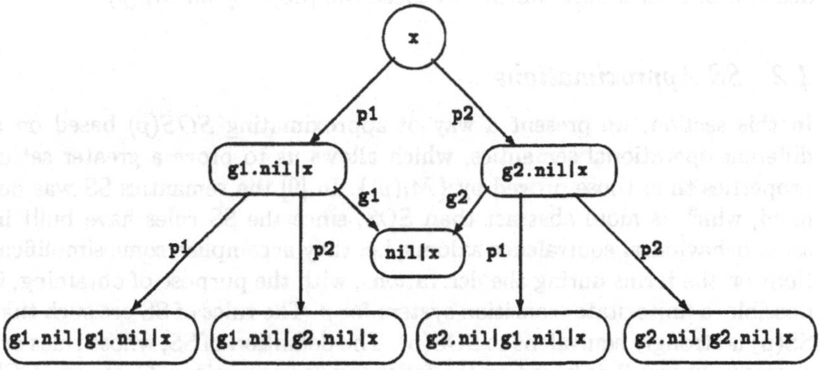

FIGURE 6. $M_2(X)$

Example 4.1 Let us now reconsider the bag example of section 2.3, and try to prove the properties on the chain $\{M_i(X)\}$. Since $\{M_i(X)\}$ is a $\preceq_{bc}$-approximation chain, it preserves all properties from 1) to 3) and does not preserve the safety property 4). Thus, if we find that an approximation $M_i(X)$ verifies a property among 1) and 3), we prove that the property holds for the bag (i.e. $SOS(X)$). $M_0(X)$ is given by a transition system with only one state, i.e. X itself, while $M_1(X)$ and $M_2(X)$ are represented in Figures 5 and 6 respectively.

We have that property 1) is not satisfied by $M_1(X)$, it is satisfied by $M_2(X)$ and thus it is true for the bag. Moreover, property 4) is not verified by $M_1(X)$ and $M_2(X)$; on the other hand, its weak version ($AGE\widetilde{X}_{p_1 \vee p_2} tt$) is verified by both $M_1(X)$ and $M_2(X)$; this does not allow us to deduce anything about the satisifiability of the safety property for the bag. Properties 2) and 3) are not verified by $M_1(X)$ neither by $M_2(X)$. It is easy to see that these properties are not verified by any $M_i(X)$, for each i. In fact their satisfiability implies detecting a cycle in the transition system: this cycle will never appear in the chain $\{M_i(X)\}$.

Thus, if we use this chain to approximate $SOS(X)$, these properties are not provable, while they hold for $SOS(X)$. Nothing can instead be asserted about property 4). The following proposition states that each M_i is a $\preceq_i$-approximation of $SOS(p)$, i.e. the size of the transition system grows.

Proposition 4.2 *Given a term p, for each $i \geq 0$, $M_i(p) \preceq_i SOS(p)$.*
Proof. *By proposition 4.1 it holds that $M_i(p) \preceq_{bc} SOS(p)$. Moreover, by induction on the length of $\{M_i(p)\}$, we have by definition that $M_i(p)$ has all the paths of length less or equal to i.*

As a consequence, using $\{M_i(p)\}$ we can decide any finite property of depth n of a term p: it sufficies to check the property on $M_n(p)$.

4.2 SS Approximations

In this section, we present a way of approximating $SOS(p)$ based on a different operational semantics, which allows us to prove a greater set of properties than those proved by $\{M_i(p)\}$. In [9] the semantics SS was defined, which is more abstract than SOS, since the SS rules have built in some behavioural equivalence axioms, i.e. they accomplish some simplifications on the terms during the derivations, with the purpose of obtaining, if possible, a finite-state transition system for p. The rules of SS are such that SS(p) is strongly equivalent to SOS(p). The definition of SS, whose rules are shown in Figure 7, is based on the following considerations. Given the CCS syntax, those operators that, in presence of recursion, would give rise to the derivation of growing terms (and therefore to an infinite number of derivations) are parallel composition, restriction and relabelling. For restriction and relabelling, in a language with finite action set, the unlimited growth of terms can be prevented by using suitable inference rules. In fact, successive, possibly intermixed, occurrences of restriction and relabelling can be reduced to only one restriction, followed by only one relabelling. Moreover, the parallel operator can be deleted as soon as one of the two arguments terminates, i.e. is equivalent to *nil*. The SS inference rules accomplish these strong equivalence preserving simplifications during the derivation. The following notation is used in the rules:

$p\backslash\backslash A =$

$$\begin{array}{l} p\backslash A, \text{ if } p \neq q\backslash B, p \neq q[f] \\ q\backslash A \cup B, \text{ if } p = q\backslash B \\ q\backslash f^1(A)[f], \text{ if } p = q[f], q \neq r\backslash B \\ q\backslash f^1(A) \cup B[f], \text{ if } p = q\backslash B[f] \end{array}$$

$p[[f]] =$

$$\begin{array}{l} p[f], \text{ if } p \neq q[g] \\ q[f \circ g], \text{ if } p = q[g] \end{array}$$

S-Act=Act S-Con=Con S-Sum=Sum

$$\textbf{S-Par}_1 \quad \frac{p \xrightarrow{\mu} p', \textit{not } p' \not\rightarrow}{p|q \xrightarrow{\mu} p'|q \text{ and } q|p \xrightarrow{\mu} q|p'}$$

$$\textbf{S-Par}_2 \quad \frac{p \xrightarrow{\mu} p',\ p' \not\rightarrow}{q|p \xrightarrow{\mu} q \text{ and } q|p \xrightarrow{\mu} q}$$

$$\textbf{S-Com}_1 \quad \frac{p \xrightarrow{\alpha} p',\ q \xrightarrow{\overline{\alpha}} q',\ \textit{not } p' \textit{ /rightarrow and not } q' \not\rightarrow}{p|q \xrightarrow{\tau} p'|q'}$$

$$\textbf{S-Com}_2 \quad \frac{p \xrightarrow{\alpha} p',\ q \xrightarrow{\overline{\alpha}} q',\ p' \not\rightarrow}{p|q \xrightarrow{\tau} q' \text{ and } q|p \xrightarrow{\tau} q'}$$

$$\textbf{S-Res} \quad \frac{p \xrightarrow{\mu} p', \mu, \overline{\mu} \notin A}{p\backslash A \xrightarrow{\mu} \textit{qackslash}\backslash A}$$

$$\textbf{S-Rel} \quad \frac{p \xrightarrow{\mu} q}{p[f] \xrightarrow{f(\mu)} q[[f]]}$$

FIGURE 7. The SS rules

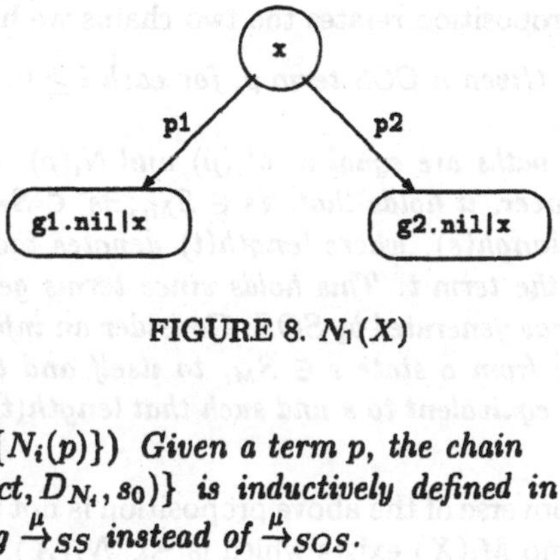

FIGURE 8. $N_1(X)$

Definition 4.2 ($\{N_i(p)\}$) *Given a term p, the chain* $\{N_i(p) = (S_{N_i}, Act, D_{N_i}, s_0)\}$ *is inductively defined in the same way as* $\{M_i(p)\}$, *but using* $\xrightarrow{\mu}_{SS}$ *instead of* $\xrightarrow{\mu}_{SOS}$.

If we reconsider the bag example, Figures 8, 9 show $N_1(X)$ and $N_2(X)$, respectively.

The following proposition holds:

Proposition 4.3 *Given a term p,*

- *the chain* $\{N_i(p)\}$ *is a* $\preceq_{bc}$*-approximation chain for p;*
- *for each* $i \geq 0$, $N_i(p) \preceq_i SOS(p)$

Proof sketch *Analogous to the proof of proposition 4.1 and 4.2 and since* $SOS(p) \sim SS(p)$.

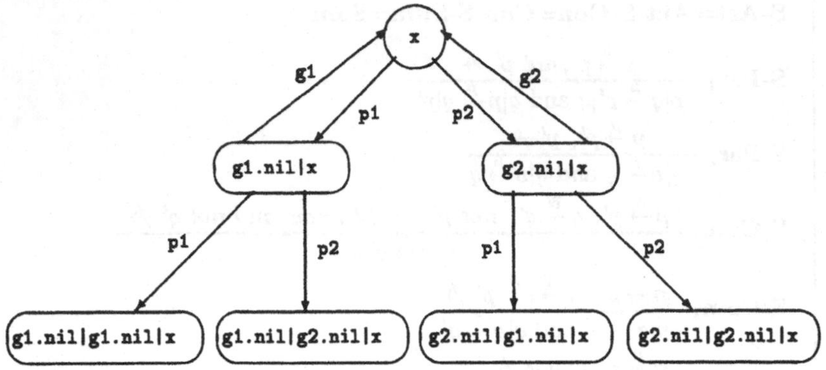

FIGURE 9. $N_2(X)$

If we check the properties 1) ... 4) on the chain $\{N_i(p)\}$, we have the same results as with $\{M_i(p)\}$ for 1) and 4), but $N_2(X)$ satisfies properties 2) and 3), which are then true for the bag, while their validity is not provable on the chain $\{M_i(X)\}$.

The following proposition relates the two chains we have introduced.

Proposition 4.4 *Given a CCS term p, for each $i \geq 0$, $\exists j$ such that $M_i(p) \preceq_{bc} N_j(p)$.*

Proof. *The finite paths are equal in $M_i(p)$ and $N_i(p)$, since they are both $\preceq_i SOS(p)$. Moreover, it holds that: $\forall s \in S_{M_i}, \exists s' \in S_{N_i}$ such that $s \sim s'$ and $length(s') \leq lengh(s)$, where $length(t)$ denotes the number of operators occurring in the term t. This holds since terms generated by SS are "shorter" than terms generated by SOS. Consider an infinite path in $M_i(p)$, i.e. a path leading from a state $s \in S_{M_i}$ to itself and take n equal to the number of terms t equivalent to s and such that $length(t) \leq lengh(s)$. Take $j = i + n$.*

Note that the converse of the above proposition is not true: if we consider the bag example, no $M_i(X)$ exists which is $\preceq_{bc} N_2(X)$.

5 Suitability of approximation chains

Let us consider a liveness property ϕ and a $\preceq_{bc}$-approximation chain $\{T_i(p)\}$ for a term p. Proposition 3.3 above ensures that, if we are able to prove ϕ on an element of the chain, we can assert the validity of ϕ on $SOS(p)$. Thus an algorithm to check the validity of a liveness property is that of checking it on the elements of the chain, starting from the first one, until we find that the property is verified. But the converse of proposition 3.3 is not true in general: if a liveness property ϕ is verified on $SOS(p)$, this does not imply that it is true for some $\{T_i(p)\}$. Thus, given an approximation chain, the above algorithm (which checks a liveness property on the elements of the chain) is not in general a semidecision procedure for the validity of a formula. This is the case of the chain $\{M_i(p)\}$ and the properties 2) and 3) of our example above. Moreover, different approximation chains for the same term can be used to check different sets of properties, in the sense that, given a property ϕ, it is possible that the above algorithm is a semidecision procedure for ϕ if using a chain, while it cannot be used to semidecide the validity ϕ with another chain. This suggests a comparison criterion on the suitability of approximation chains for proving liveness properties.

Definition 5.1 (Checkable properties) *Let be given a term p and a $\preceq_{bc}$ approximation chain $\{T_i(p)\}$. We say that a liveness property ϕ is checkable by $\{T_i(p)\}$ if*

- *either ϕ is not verified by $SOS(p)$ or*
- *$(T_r(p) \in \{T_i(p)\})$ exists such that $s_0 \models_{T_r(p)} \phi$.*

The set of checkable properties of p by $\{T_i(p)\}$ is denoted as $\mathcal{P}_{T_i}(p)$.

Thus $\mathcal{P}_{T_i}(p)$ includes the properties for whose validity there is a semidecision procedure using $\{T_i(p)\}$.

Definition 5.2 (Suitability of approximation chains) *Let be given a term p and two $\preceq_{bc}$ approximations chains $\{T_i(p)\}$ and $\{S_i(p)\}$. We say that $\{T_i(p)\}$ is more suitable or equal for p than $\{S_i(p)\}$ if $\mathcal{P}_{S_i}(p) \subseteq \mathcal{P}_{T_i}(p)$. Moreover, $\{T_i(p)\}$ is strictly more suitable for p than $\{S_i(p)\}$ if $\mathcal{P}_{S_i}(p) \subset \mathcal{P}_{T_i}(p)$.*

Note that the notion of suitability of approximation chains is different from a notion considering the "growing rate" of the chains. Given, for example, an approximation chain $\{T_i(p)\}$, let us consider the chain containing a subset of the elements of $\{T_i(p)\}$, for example the elements of even position, i.e. $\{S_i(p)\} = \{T_0(p), T_2(p), T_4(p), \cdots\}$. We have that $\{S_i(p)\}$ grows faster than $\{T_i(p)\}$, but it is not more suitable. As a consequence of the above definitions and propositions 4.4, we can state the following propositions:

Proposition 5.1 *For each term p, $\mathcal{P}_{M_i}(p) \subseteq \mathcal{P}_{N_i}(p)$.*
Proof sketch. *By proposition 4.4.*

The following proposition states that the converse of proposition 5.1 is not true in general.

Proposition 5.2 *Given a term p, $\mathcal{P}_{M_i}(p) \subset \mathcal{P}_{N_i}(p)$, i.e. $\{N_i(p)\}$ is strictly more suitable than $\{M_i(p)\}$.*
Proof sketch *Properties 2) and 3) in the bag example are checkable by $\{N_i(p)\}$ but not by $\{M_i(p)\}$.*

6 Implementation in the JACK environment

The JACK system [3] is a verification environment for process algebra description languages. It is able to cover a large extent of the formal software development process, such as rewriting techniques, behavioural equivalence proofs, graph transformations, and (ACTL) logic verification. In JACK a particular description format is used to represent TSs, the so called *format commun fc2*, that has been proposed as standard format for automata [20]. The ACTL model checker was built on the basis of an algorithm similar to that of the EMC model checker [5], so it guarantees model checking of an ACTL formula on a TS in a linear time complexity [10].

The JACK environment has been extended with a tool to build the chain $\{N_i(p)\}$. We now describe the methodology for proving properties. Let be given a CCS term p and a list of ACTL formulae to be checked on it. A verification session has the following steps:

1. The term is input to JACK. If the term satisfies the finiteness condition of the transition system generator inside JACK, a corresponding transition system TS is built and the list of ACTL formulae is checked on it. The session terminates.
2. If the syntactic finiteness conditions are not satisfied, then we call the chain generator of JACK. Once obtained the first approximation $N_1(p)$, we put $TS := N_1(p)$.
3. The list of ACTL formulae is input to the model checker which checks them on TS. If $N_{i+1}(p) = TS$, the session terminates, since $TS \sim SOS(p)$. Otherwise, the results of the model checker are analyzed according to propositions 3.3, 3.5 and 3.7. This means that, possibly, a new approximation is built, i.e. $TS := N_{i+1}(p)$ and we repeat step 3.

Acknowledgement

We wish to acknowledge Luigi Polverini and Salvatore Larosa for their work on the implementation of the NSS approximation generator, Rocco De Nicola and Gioia Ristori for interesting discussions about the topics of this paper.

7 References

[1] J. C. M. Baeten, J. A. Bergstra, J. W. Klop. Decidability of bisimulation equivalence for processes generating context-free languages. Journal of ACM 40,3,1993, pp. 653-682.

[2] G. Bruns. A practical technique for process abstraction. CONCUR'93, LNCS 715, pp. 37-49.

[3] A. Bouali, S. Gnesi, S. Larosa. The integration Project for the JACK Environment. Bulletin of the EATCS, n.54, October 1994, pp.207-223.

[4] O. Burkart, B. Steffen. Pushdown processes: Parallel Composition and Model Checking. Proceedings, CONCUR 94, LNCS 836, 1994, pp.98-113.

[5] E.M. Clarke, E.A. Emerson, A.P. Sistla. Automatic Verification of Finite State Concurrent Systems using Temporal Logic Specifications. ACM Toplas, 8 (2), 1986, pp. 244-263.

[6] E.M.Clarke, O.Grumberg, D.E.Long. Model Checking and Abstraction. ACM Toplas, 16 (5), 1994, pp.1512-1542.

[7] R. Cleaveland, J. Parrow, B. Steffen. The Concurrency Workbench. Proceedings of Automatic Verification Methods for Finite State Systems. Lecture Notes in Computer Science 407, Springer-Verlag, 1990, pp. 24-37.

[8] D.Dams, O.Grumberg, R.Gerth. Automatic Verification of Abstract Interpretation of Reactive Systems: Abstractions Preserving ∀CTL*, ∃CTL*, CTL*. IFIP working conference on Programming Concepts, Methods and Calculi (PROCOMET'94), 1994.

[9] N. De Francesco, P. Inverardi. Proving Finiteness of CCS Processes by Non-standard Semantics. Acta Informatica, 31 (1), 1994, pp. 55-80.

[10] R. De Nicola, A. Fantechi, S. Gnesi, G. Ristori. An action-based framework for verifying logical and behavioural properties of concurrent systems. Computer Network and ISDN systems, Vol. 25, No.7, 1993, pp 761-778.

[11] R. De Nicola, F. W. Vaandrager. Action versus State based Logics for Transition Systems. Proceedings Ecole de Printemps on Semantics of Concurrency. LNCS 469, 1990, pp. 407-419.

[12] J.C. Fernandez, H. Garavel, L. Mounier, A. Rasse, C. Rodriguez, J. Sifakis. A Toolbox for the Verification of LOTOS Programs. 14th ICSE, Melbourne, 1992, pp. 246-261.

[13] J.C. Fernandez, L. Mounier. Verifying Bisimulations "On the Fly". Formal Description Techniques, III, Elsevier Science Publisher, pp. 95-110, 1991.

[14] J. C. Godskesen, K. G. Larsen, M. Zeeberg. TAV Users Manual. Internal Report, Aalborg University Center, Denmark, 1989.

[15] M. Hennessy and R. Milner. Algebraic Laws for Nondeterminism and Concurrency. *Journal of ACM*, **32**, 1985, pp. 137-161.

[16] H. Hungar, B. Steffen. Local Model Checking for Context-Free Processes. Proceedings, ICALP 93, LNCS 700, 1993, pp.593-605.

[17] H. Hungar. Local Model Checking for Parallel Composition of Context-Free Processes. Proceedings, CONCUR 94, LNCS 836, 1994, pp.114-128.

[18] H. Huttel, C Stirling. Actions speak louder than words: Proving Bisimilarity for Context Free Processes. LICS 91, IEEE Computer Society Press, 1991, pp. 376-386.

[19] E. Kindler. Safety and Liveness Properties: A Survey. Bulletin of the EATCS, 53, 1994, pp.268-272.

[20] E. Madelaine. Verification Tools from the Concur Project. Bulletin of EATCS 47, 1992, pp. 110-120.

[21] E. Madelaine, D. Vergamini. AUTO: A Verification Tool for Distributed Systems Using Reduction of Finite Automata Networks. FORTE '89, North-Holland, 1990, pp. 61-66.

[22] Z. Manna, A. Pnueli. The Anchored Version of the Temporal Framework, Linear Time, Branching Time and Partial Order in Logics and Models for Concurrency. Lecture Notes in Computer Science 354, Springer-Verlag, 1989, pp. 201-284.

[23] R. Milner. Communication and Concurrency. Prentice Hall, 1989.

[24] D. Taubner. Finite Representations of CCS and TCSP Programs by Automata and Petri Nets. LNCS 369, 1989.

On Automatic and Interactive Design of Communicating Systems

Jürgen Bohn*†
Stephan Rössig*†

ABSTRACT This paper presents a transformational approach to the design of distributed systems where environment and concurrently running components communicate via synchronous message passing along directed channels. System specifications that combine trace-based with state-based reasoning are gradually modified by application of transformation rules until occam-like programs are achieved finally. We consider interactive and automatic aspects of such a design process and illustrate our approach by sketching the development of a shared register implementation.

1 Introduction

The design of provable correct software requires formal methods whose usage should be assisted by suitable tools. Following a transformational approach the design needs interactive user help when important design decisions have to be made. Nevertheless simple parts should be automated as far as possible. Ideally the user only guides the design process by indicating the design ideas which are then carried out automatically. Typically sequential implementations are more appropriate for automation while parallelization needs interaction to determine the intended program architecture.

Our approach deals with the transformational development of communicating systems in the mixed term language MIX which encompasses specification and programming notation. A formal refinement notion guarantees that starting from a specification of a desired system only correct implementations can be reached. As part of the ESPRIT Basic Research Action

*This research was partially supported by the CEC with the ESPRIT Basic Research Project No. 7071 ProCoS II, by the German Ministry of Research and Technology (BMFT) as part of the project KORSO under grant No. 01 IS 203 N and by the Deutsche Forschungsgemeinschaft under grant No. Ol 98/1-1.

†FB Informatik, C.v.O. Universität Oldenburg, Postfach 2503, 26111 Oldenburg, Germany, email: {bohn,roessig}@informatik.uni-oldenburg.de

ProCoS a refinement calculus for communicating systems was developed in order to provide a constructive and mathematically sound way for bridging the gap between specifications and programs [Old91, Rös94]. We consider communicating systems as an approach to distributed computing that integrates the state transformation aspect of iterative programs in the sense of UNITY [CM88] and action systems [Bac90] with the CSP paradigm of synchronous message passing along communication channels. When designing such systems several different aspects like concurrency, communication, nondeterminism, deadlock, termination, divergence and assignment to variables have to be considered. A state-trace-readiness semantics in a specification-oriented fashion provides the necessary power to express such properties and concepts. Additionally it induces immediately a refinement relation which is used to define correctness of system transformations.

The rest of this paper is structured as follows. Section 2 introduces our specification language SL and explains how SL constructs can be applied in order to specify a regular register with concurrent access. Section 3 considers basic aspects of a transformational approach to system design. Section 4 sketches major steps within the development process of a parallel architecture of sequential components implementing the regular register. Section 5 treats the derivations of sequential implementations by systematic exploitation of specifications. Section 6 deals with the automation of such systematic proceeding in order to decrease the degree of user interaction within the whole design process. A final section concludes this paper with a short discussion of the achieved results.

2 Specification Language SL

The specification language SL develops further the ProCoS specification language SL_0 [JROR90] that was designed to describe continuously running embedded systems communicating with their environment via synchronous message passing along directed channels. A communication along a channel takes place if both, system and environment, are ready for communication on that channel. A system is in a deadlock whenever it does not become ready for communication on at least one channel.

An SL specification provides several parts to describe such communicating systems in a constraint-oriented style. Syntactically a specification is a list of so-called basic items enclosed by **spec** – **end** brackets. The following sketches the basic ideas of these constructs using the general specification pattern given in figure 1. Afterwards a few more details are discussed in the context of an example specification (cf. figure 3).

The *interface* Δ stresses a static view of the intended system by listing all entities which may be used for interaction with the environment. It consists of optionally typed declarations of external channels with associated direc-

spec

dir_c c [of ty_c] $mode_x$ x [of ty_x]	Δ
$ta =$ **trace** α_{ta} **in** re_{ta}	TA
$ca =$ **com** na_{ca} **write** $\overline{w}_{ca}$ **read** $\overline{r}_{ca}$ **when** wh_{ca} **then** th_{ca}	CA
var v **of** ty_v	lV
chan c [**of** ty_c]	lC
$ini =$ **initial** p_{ini}	SR^{ini}
$sta =$ **stable** p_{sta} **for** $\overline{c}_{sta}$	SR^{sta}
$alw =$ **always** p_{alw}	SR^{alw}
$est =$ **establish** p_{est} **by** $\overline{c}_{est}$	SR^{est}

end

FIGURE 1. Specification format.

tion indication (`input` or `output`) and of global variables with assoicated access mode (`write` or `read-only`).

Essentially the description of the intended dynamic behaviour is split into two parts in SL. The *trace part TA* specifies in which order communications may take place on the various channels. A trace assertion $ta \in TA$ describes a sequencing constraint for the channels of alphabet α_{ta} by giving a regular expression[1] re_{ta} over these channels. Several ordering aspects can be specified in a modular fashion by stating different trace assertions. Technically the so-called *trace language* $\mathcal{L}[\![\Delta, TA]\!]$ of the specification is that regular language over all channels which obeys all sequencing constraints simultaneously. The trace part prevents any communication trace of which the channel order does not belong to $\mathcal{L}[\![\Delta, TA]\!]$.

The *state part CA* relates single communications with the current system state. A communication assertion $ca \in CA$ consists of a channel name na_{ca}, two disjoint lists $\overline{w}_{ca}$ and $\overline{r}_{ca}$ of write and read-only variables, respectively, and two predicates. The when-predicate wh_{ca} over free variables $\overline{w}_{ca}, \overline{r}_{ca}$ disables channel na_{ca} for communication whenever wh_{ca} does not hold in the current state. The value of a communication refered to by $@na_{ca}$ as well as its effect on the system state are specified by the then-predicate th_{ca} over free variables $\overline{w}_{ca}, \overline{r}_{ca}, \overline{w}'_{ca}, @na_{ca}$. In the style of TLA [Lam94] and Z

[1]of an extended format additionally using `pref` as prefix closure operator

[Spi89] the unprimed variables refer to the values in the before state while the primed ones to those in the after state in which read-only variables $\overline{r}_{ca}$ must not change their values. Giving empty lists as well as predicate **true** is optional. Several communcation assertions for the same channel must be obeyed all together.

The use of a more operational formalization approach to the behaviour specification is supported by declarations of local variables *lV* and local channels *lC*. The various state restrictions *SR* provide a good basis for the integrated reasoning with state-based arguments as invariance and stable properties and with control flow arguments as initial state and establish properties. Technically these latter constraints could be replaced by certain more or less complex combinations of other basic items of which intuitive understanding is then often lost. The same holds for the always possible replacement of the trace part by additional local variables and communications assertions.

REGISTER EXAMPLE

In [LG89] a good overview can be found about the various kinds of shared registers treated in the literature on distributed algorithms. According to the classification in [Lam86] we use as running example in this paper a regular register with a single reader and a single writer. In general a register stores values of a type *V* and the most recently written value shall be returned to the reader if its access does not overlap with a write. In the case of overlapping phases the regular behaviour guarantees that a read phase will return a value that was hold before or after one of write accesses. Figure 2 presents our view of a single-writer, single-reader register

FIGURE 2. Register as communicating system

as communicating system. The writer initiates a writing phase by sending the new value along the input channel *W*. This phase ends when a corresponding acknowledgment signal is output on channel *A*. Conversely, the reader initiates a reading phase by sending a request signal along the input channel *R*. This phase ends when a value is returned along the output channel *T*.

Figure 3 shows a complete SL specification of a regular register which is explained here shortly.[2] Here the interface consisting of the declarations of channels *W*, *A*, *R*, *T* together with the trace part consisting of trace as-

[2]Similar SL specifications of various registers are presented in [OR93, Rös94] together with a very detailed motivation of the single components.

```
        spec input W of V
             output A of signal
             input R of signal
             output T of V
        ta1: trace W, A in pref(W.A)*
        ta2: trace R, T in pref(R.T)*
             var new, old of V
             var C of set(V)
        caW: com W write new, C then new' = @W ∧ C' = C ∪ {@W}
        caA: com A write old read new then old' = new
        caR: com R write C read new, old then C' = {new, old}
        caT: com T read C then @T ∈ C
        end
```

FIGURE 3. Specification of a regular register.

sertions ta_1, ta_2 formalize the value independent aspects. Communications along channels of type `signal` are used for synchronization purposes only but do not pass any message value. The trace assertions guarantee that initiating and ending communications of write as well as read phases always occur in alternating order starting with channels W and R, respectively.

To specify the values that may be returned we use local variables to store certain pieces of information. Variables *old* and *new* shall hold the before and the after value when a write access is active and otherwise that unique value which is stored in the register. Therefore a communication on W updates *new* with the newly received value what is formalized by conjunct $new' = @W$ in the then-predicate of ca_W. Analogously $old' = new$ expresses that *old* gets the value of *new* whenever an A signal ends up a write phase. The idea of the set-valued variable C is to collect all possible return values for a read access. Thus the value $@T$ to be passed by an ending T communication can be easily chosen from C. Any write phase starting during a read phase overlaps this and thus every newly written value becomes a possible return value. Therefore each W communication enriches C by its communication value $@W$.

Outside of write phases both variables *old* and *new* hold the same value and hence the then-predicate $C' = \{new, old\}$ of ca_R describes a singlton set for variable C, resulting in a unique return value for a reader. Formally the equality of *old* and *new* outside write phases can be expressed in SL for the register specification by the state restrictions

$$\texttt{establish}\ new = old\ \text{by}\ A$$

$$\texttt{stable}\ new = old\ \texttt{for}\ R, T, A\ .$$

Intuitively the establish property says that *new* equals *old* after ending a write phase by an acknowledge signal on channel A, while the stable property guarantees that communications on R, T and A do not violate a given equality. Obviously the stable property holds because communications on channels R and T must not effect the values of *old* and *new* and those along channel A just establish this equality. By transformational reasoning we can prove that both state restrictions are redundant for the specification in figure 3, i.e. they do not strengthen the specified behaviour.

3 Transformational Implementation Design

To implement communicating systems we use an occam-like programming language PL [INM88]. Programs are terms constructed from the 0-ary operators **STOP**, **SKIP**, multiple assignments, input and output on channels, the unary operators **WHILE**, **var** and **chan** for describing loops and declaration of local variables and channels, and the operators **SEQ**, **IF**, **ALT** and **PAR** for sequential, conditional, alternative and parallel composition of lists of n arguments. Figure 4 shows a PL program which implements the register specification of figure 3. Analogously to specifications a program declares its

```
system input W of V
       output A of signal
       input R of signal
       output T of V
       chan u, d of V
       chan r of signal
       PAR[ var new of V
              WHILE true do SEQ[ W?new, u!new, A! ] od,
            var x of V
              WHILE true do ALT[ u?x-->SKIP, r?-->d!x ] od,
            var y of V
              WHILE true do SEQ[ R?, r!, d?y, T!y ] od          ]
   end
```

FIGURE 4. Register Implementation.

interface to the environment explicitly. The **system** – **end** brackets emphasize that programs represent implementations of communicating systems.

Semantically a communicating system is viewed as pair $\Delta : P$ where the interface Δ declares the communication channels and global variables. The predicate P characterizes the dynamic behaviour of the system as the set of possible observations in a state-trace-readiness model. This model integrates a purely event-based readiness approach [OH86] and a standard input/output semantics into a specification-oriented semantics of which details are presented in [Old91, Rös94]. A major reason for this semantics construction is the immediate presence of a refinement notion for communicating systems. A system $\Delta_1 : P_1$ ***refines*** a system $\Delta_2 : P_2$ if both ones have the same interface and if behaviour P_1 implies behaviour P_2:

$$\Delta_1 : P_1 \Rrightarrow \Delta_2 : P_2 \quad \text{iff} \quad \Delta_1 = \Delta_2 \text{ and } \models P_1 \Rightarrow P_2 .$$

This definition encompasses a correctness notion ***Prog*** $\Rrightarrow$ ***Spec*** since specifications and programs are special representations of communicating systems.

Figure 5 shows a design sequence of a transformational implementation approach. Starting from an SL specification ***Spec***, a PL implementation

$$\begin{array}{ccc} Spec \equiv & S_1 & \\ & \Uparrow & \\ & \vdots & \\ & \Uparrow & \\ & S_n & \equiv Prog \end{array}$$

FIGURE 5. Implementation design sequence.

Prog is derived in a top-down fashion by iterated application of transformation rules such that the specification notation is gradually replaced by programming language constructs. The intermediate system expressions S_i are so-called ***mixed terms*** of the language MIX. This language encompasses specifications and programs as disjoint subsets and extends the application of every programming operator to arbitrary mixed terms. Moreover, there exist additional MIX specific operators in order to express intermediate stages of a system design much more conveniently. E.g. the treatment of the semantically complex PL operator `PAR` can be reduced within MIX to a combination of the simpler operators `SYN` and `HIDE` dealing separately with the aspects of multiple synchronization and of divergence raised by infinite internal communication.

Typically a transition step from mixed term S_i to S_{i+1} is performed by replacing some specification expression S in S_i by a mixed term T where the refinement $T \Rrightarrow S$ is guaranteed by a transformation rule. Then the overall implementation correctness follows from the transitivity of $\Rrightarrow$ and the monotonicity of all operators.

In easy cases a transformation step will replace a specification by a basic PL statement as e.g. an input or output communication or an assignment. Figure 13 below shows appropriate equivalences of specification and programming constructs. But more often more complex specifications have to be decomposed into mixed terms applying some composition operator to several simpler arguments. As typical example supporting this later kind of refinements, figure 6 shows a transformation rule which introduces the

$$\textbf{spec } \Delta \; TA \; CA \; lV \textbf{ end}$$

$$\Uparrow$$

$$\texttt{SYN}[\,\textbf{spec } \Delta_1 \; TA_1 \; CA_1 \; lV_1 \textbf{ end}, \ldots, \textbf{spec } \Delta_n \; TA_n \; CA_n \; lV_n \textbf{ end}\,]$$

provided $\Delta = \bigcup_{||\, i=1}^{n} \Delta_i$, $TA = \bigcup_{i=1}^{n} TA_i$, $CA = \bigcup_{i=1}^{n} CA_i$, $lV = \biguplus_{i=1}^{n} lV_i$ and ...

FIGURE 6. Transformation rule SYN decomposition.

synchronization operator SYN. Generally a side condition "provided ..." restricts the applicability of the transformation rule and describes how the new mixed term is derived by syntactic modifications from the given one. In the example it is expressed that essentially the basic items of the given specification have to be shared out between the new argument specifications **spec** Δ_i TA_i CA_i lV_i **end** obeying some static semantic constraints.

For practical implementation designs a user needs guidance how to realize intuitive implementation ideas by application of such transformation rules. Here so-called design *strategies* provide recipes how to combine several rules in order to derive implementations in certain situations systematically or even mechanically. Data refinement, parallelization concepts or the development of specific sequential implementations are implementation concepts that can be supported by such strategies. As example we will later consider the automated synthesis of sequential programs based on the syntax directed transformation strategy SDT.

TOOL SUPPORT

An interesting consequence of basing all semantic reasoning on a uniform predicate language is that this reasoning comes close to what can be mechanically supported by higher order logic theorem provers. In the German national research project KORSO one of the goals was to provide tool support for formal methods in software design [BH94]. As part of this work a computer assisted validation of our semantical model was performed within the theorem prover LAMBDA [BR95]. To this end first the model was implemented in the higher order logic of LAMBDA [FM91, FFHM93] and various basic propositions about the model have been verified in the LAMBDA framework interactively. On the one hand this validation gives great confidence in soundness of the model as well as of its formalization in LAMBDA. On the other hand a basic transformation environment for communicating systems emerges from the verification of transformation rules since LAMBDA provides mechanisms for the representation of syntactic objects and supports their modification by rule applications. Particularly a transformational design processes is assisted by saving the design history, backtracking mechanisms, generation of proof obligations and a rule browser. Furthermore the tactics concept provides a possibility to perform algorithmic rule applications and automatic condition checking.

4 Parallel Register Architecture

Frequently specifications require that sometimes a system should be ready for communication on several channels. As in occam, the restriction to so-called input guards as arguments of the alternative operator ALT forces parallel implementations in such cases where an output channel must be together ready with at least one other channel.

In the regular register such a situation is present e.g. when a first communication took place. Initially the regular register must be ready for input channels *W* and *R*. Independently on the channel along which a communication is performed in the next situation common readiness is required for an input and an output channel. Hence an occam-like implementation of this register has to use concurrently running subcomponents which interact via internal communication. Obviously we shall choose one write manager component *WM* dealing with write access and a read manager *RM* serving the reader. Both these components require access to the value stored in the register. But PL does not provide shared variables and therefore a third component *SV* will play this role. Figure 7 indicates how these components

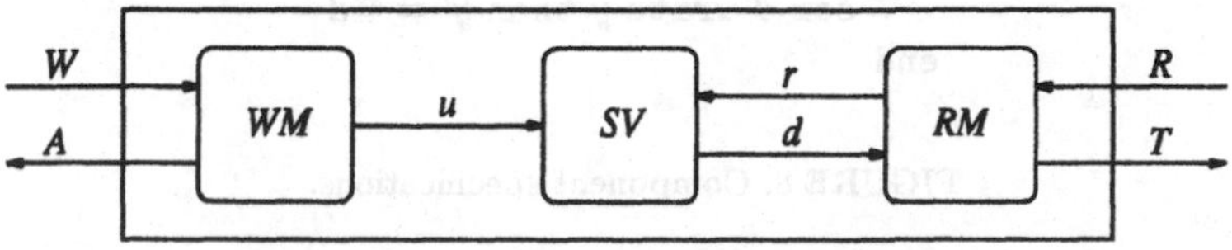

FIGURE 7. Intended process architecture.

are connected via local channels u, r, d of which usage is as follows. After having received a new value along *W* the *WM* component updates the current register value by sending the new value along channel *u* to *SV* before the external acknowledgment on *A* is offered. *RM* serves a read request along *R* by sending an internal request along *r* to *SV*. The shared variable process immediately answers by delivering its actual value along channel *d* to *RM* which then transmits this value along *T* to the reader.[3][4] The spec-

[3]The different treatment of write and read accesses to the shared variable process is necessary in order to allow a sequential implementation of *SV*. Otherwise the problem of output channels in non singleton readysets would only be delayed.

[4]Note that this register implementation refines the regular specification properly

ifications *WMspec*, *SVspec* and *RMspec* presented in figure 8 express this

$$
\begin{aligned}
WMspec = \texttt{spec}\ & \texttt{input}\ W\ \texttt{of}\ V\\
& \texttt{output}\ A\ \texttt{of signal}\\
& \texttt{output}\ u\ \texttt{of}\ V\\
& \texttt{trace}\ W, A, u\ \texttt{in pref}(W.u.A)^*\\
& \texttt{var}\ new\ \texttt{of}\ V\\
& \texttt{com}\ W\ \texttt{write}\ new\ \texttt{then}\ new' = @W\\
& \texttt{com}\ u\ \texttt{read}\ new\ \texttt{then}\ @u = new\\
\texttt{end}&\\
SVspec = \texttt{spec}\ & \texttt{input}\ u\ \texttt{of}\ V\\
& \texttt{input}\ r\ \texttt{of signal}\\
& \texttt{output}\ d\ \texttt{of}\ V\\
& \texttt{trace}\ u, r, d\ \texttt{in pref}(u + r.d)^*\\
& \texttt{var}\ x\ \texttt{of}\ V\\
& \texttt{com}\ u\ \texttt{write}\ x\ \texttt{then}\ x' = @u\\
& \texttt{com}\ d\ \texttt{read}\ x\ \texttt{then}\ @d = x\\
\texttt{end}&\\
RMspec = \texttt{spec}\ & \texttt{input}\ R\ \texttt{of signal}\\
& \texttt{output}\ T\ \texttt{of}\ V\\
& \texttt{output}\ r\ \texttt{of signal}\\
& \texttt{input}\ d\ \texttt{of}\ V\\
& \texttt{trace}\ R, T, r, d\ \texttt{in pref}(R.r.d.T)^*\\
& \texttt{var}\ y\ \texttt{of}\ V\\
& \texttt{com}\ T\ \texttt{read}\ y\ \texttt{then}\ @T = y\\
& \texttt{com}\ d\ \texttt{write}\ y\ \texttt{then}\ y' = @d\\
\texttt{end}&
\end{aligned}
$$

FIGURE 8. Component specifications.

intuitive description of *WM*, *SV* and *RM* formally. They are designed by systematic transformation from the original specification shown in figure 3. In the following we list the major transformation steps towards the parallel decomposition.[5] Essentially these steps are motivated by the intended architecture which reflects the overall design ideas.

1. The local channels u, r, d are declared and their global communication behaviour is restricted according to the indicated communication order by modification of the trace assertions ta_1, ta_2 to

because of a more deterministically chosen return value in the case of overlapping write and read accesses. Essentially this implementation realizes the stronger behaviour of an atomic register.

[5]In [OR93, Rös94] detailed explanations are given on the execution of such steps.

```
trace W, A, u in pref(W.u.A)*
trace R, T, r, d in pref(R.r.d.T)*
trace u, r, d in pref(u + r.d)*.
```

2. To store the register value in *SV* and to hold the return value in *RM*, respectively, the state space is extended by variable declaration

    var x, y **of** V.

3. The original variables *old* and *C* are removed. To this end they are made auxiliary variables by introduction of appropriate state restrictions and strengthening of communication effects.

4. The local channel declarations are moved in front of the specification and thus they become global ones for the body. Since the trace part prevents infinite communication on local channels *u*, *r*, *d* only, their hiding from the specification does not introduce divergence.

5. The communication assertions of channels *u* and *d* are split in order to enable the intended distribution of local variables *new*, *x*, *y* onto the components *WM*, *SV*, *RM*.

6. Now the synchronous decomposition rule shown in figure 6 is applied and we end up with the mixed term

```
chan u, d of V
chan r of signal
HIDE u, r, d in SYN[ WMspec, SVspec, RMspec ]
```

    with the component specifications of figure 8. Finally the operators **HIDE** and **SYN** are replaced by **PAR** because exactly all channels linking two argument systems of **SYN** are hidden.

The steps 2. and 3. perform a data refinement on the internal state space thereby proceeding quite systematically. A partial automation of this strategy would be very useful and seems to be possible. Generally executing the above steps and especially those performing the parallel decomposition requires a high degree of user interaction because the underlying rules allow various instantiations of their parameters leading to quite different refinements.

In contrast implementations of the three component specifications *WMspec*, *SVspec* and *RMspec* can be achieved by automatic synthesis of sequential programs. The conceptual basis of this automation and its implementation within LAMBDA are dealt with in the rest of this paper.

5 Designing Sequential Implementations

A notion of termination is essential when dealing with sequential implementations. In this section we present a suitable extension of SL to enable the description of termination. This new notion provides the basis for a transformational design of sequential implementations.

In order to refine a specification into a sequential composition of several specifications of reduced complexity, the circumstances have to be expressed, under which the control flow passes from one system to the next one. Therefore so-called *T-specifications* are introduced in SL. These are syntactically distinguished by **system** – **end** brackets instead of **spec** – **end** bracketed so-called S-specifications. Dependent on the trace part T-specifications may terminate in certain situations where the corresponding S-specifications would reach a deadlock. For a detailed comparison of S- and T-specifications see [Rös94]. A consequence of this differentiation is that an empty T-specification **system end** immediately terminates what is equivalent to the SKIP statement at the programming level. In contrast the empty S-specification **spec end** denotes an immediate deadlock which is represented in PL by STOP.

The following presents two transformation rules which relate S- and T-specifications. The first one in figure 9 allows in particular to switch from

$$\textbf{spec}\ \Delta\ TA\ CA\ \textbf{end}$$

$$\Uparrow$$

$$\texttt{SEQ[}\ \textbf{system}\ \Delta\ TA_1\ CA\ \textbf{end},\ \texttt{STOP}\ ]$$

provided $\mathcal{L}[\![\Delta, TA]\!] = pc\mathcal{L}[\![\Delta, TA_1]\!]$.

FIGURE 9. Linking S- and T-specifications

an S- to a T-specification which at most differs in the trace part. The trace language $\mathcal{L}[\![\Delta, TA]\!]$ of the S-specification must be equal to $pc\mathcal{L}[\![\Delta, TA_1]\!]$ which denotes the prefix closure of the trace language of the T-specification. When the refined system reaches the STOP it starves in a deadlock.

Figure 10 shows a more general rule for the sequential decomposition of S-specifications. The first condition of this rule links the trace languages of the different specifications. The other condition "$\mathcal{L}[\![\Delta, TA_1]\!]$ is prefix free" guarantees a unique transition of the control flow from the first to the second argument in the mixed term.

In the following we concentrate on the implemention of T-specifications. The introduction of while-loops within the implementation design process simplifies T-specifications of which trace languages are iterations of prefix-free base languages. The body of an achieved while-loop is built up from

$$\textbf{spec } \Delta\ TA\ CA \textbf{ end}$$

$$\Uparrow$$

$$\texttt{SEQ[system } \Delta\ TA_1\ CA \textbf{ end, spec } \Delta\ TA_2\ CA \textbf{ end]}$$

provided $\mathcal{L}[\![\Delta, TA]\!] = pc\mathcal{L}[\![\Delta, TA_1]\!] \cup \mathcal{L}[\![\Delta, TA_1]\!].\mathcal{L}[\![\Delta, TA_2]\!]$
and $\mathcal{L}[\![\Delta, TA_1]\!]$ is prefix free.

FIGURE 10. Transformation rule sequential decomposition.

the given specification by reducing the trace language to this base language as shown in the conditions of the while rule in figure 11. The termination

$$\textbf{system } \Delta\ TA\ CA \textbf{ end}$$

$$\Uparrow$$

$$\texttt{WHILE } \bigvee_{c \in first(\Delta, TA_1)} wh_c \textbf{ do system } \Delta\ TA_1\ CA \textbf{ end od}$$

provided $\mathcal{L}[\![\Delta, TA]\!] = \mathcal{L}[\![\Delta, TA_1]\!]^*$ and $\mathcal{L}[\![\Delta, TA_1]\!]$ is prefix free.

FIGURE 11. Transformation rule loop decomposition.

condition ($\bigvee_{c \in first(\Delta, TA_1)} wh_c$) is constructed from the when-predicates of those channels which are initially enabled by the trace language.

The decomposition of S-specifications into while-loops can be performed by an preparatory application of the rule in figure 9 and afterwards introducing a while-loop for the T-specification part. In case of a never terminating loop as first argument the sequential composition with STOP as second argument can be simplified using the rewriting rule:

$$\texttt{SEQ[WHILE true do } P \textbf{ od}, Q\ \texttt{]} \ \rightarrow\ \texttt{WHILE true do } P \textbf{ od} .$$

Another way of decomposing a specification into several ones with simpler trace languages are disjunctive decompositions thereby introducing an ALT or IF operator. Figure 12 shows a transformation rule for alternative decomposition which splits a T-specification into k subspecifications, where k is the number of that interface channels that occur as first element in at least one word of the trace language. Immediate termination is impossible due to the first rule condition. Each subspecification contains an additional trace assertion that marks one channel to precede each communication trace of that subsystem.

$$\texttt{system}\ \Delta\ TA\ CA\ \texttt{end}$$

$$\Uparrow$$

$$\texttt{ALT[}\ \texttt{system}\ \Delta\ TA\ \texttt{trace}\ \overline{c}\ \texttt{in}\ d_1.(c_1 + \cdots + c_n)^*\ \ CA\ \texttt{end},$$
$$\ldots,$$
$$\texttt{system}\ \Delta\ TA\ \texttt{trace}\ \overline{c}\ \texttt{in}\ d_k.(c_1 + \cdots + c_n)^*\ \ CA\ \texttt{end}\ \texttt{]}$$

provided $\varepsilon \notin \mathcal{L}[\![\Delta, TA]\!]$ and $first(\Delta, TA) = \{d_1, \ldots, d_k\} \neq \emptyset$
and $\overline{c} = Chans(\Delta)$.

FIGURE 12. Transformation rule alternative decomposition.

Using these decomposition rules and similiar ones a specification can be systematically refined into a mixed term where the trace languages of all occuring specifications are very simple. Here the languages consist of the empty word or of a single channel name. If furthermore the state part is also of a simple pattern then such specifications can be directly replaced by PL statements. Figure 13 shows that certain T-specifications are equivalent

$c?v \equiv$ **system input** c **write** v
  trace c **in** c
  com c **write** v **then** $v' = @c$
end

$c? \equiv$ **system input** c **of signal**
  trace c **in** c
end

$c!e \equiv$ **system output** c **read** $free\ (e)$
  trace c **in** c
  com c **read** $free(e)$ **then** $@c = e$
end

$c! \equiv$ **system output** c **of signal**
  trace c **in** c
end

FIGURE 13. Meaning of input and output communication statements in PL.

to input and output communications in PL. Other simple specifications can be transformed into these patterns and are therefore automatically implementable, as described in the next chapter.

TOOL SUPPORT FOR APPLICATION OF SINGLE RULES

A transformational design step based on one rule application can be supported by a tool with the generation of the modified system and the check of the side conditions. A single application of one transformation rule in a theorem prover like LAMBDA on the one hand modifies the current MIX term and on the other hand generates proof obligations from the rule conditions. To reduce the necessary interaction with the tool the proof programming language of tactics can be used. Tactics are based on possibly guided single rule applications and equational rewriting which are combined by tactical composition constructs like sequences, if-then-else statements and repetitions to proof searching algorithms.

Since most application conditions of our transformation rules are decidable their verification can be automated. For example all conditions concerning regular expressions are decidable. Many other conditions are provable by simple set operations. The tool only needs user guidance when a transformation rule modifies a MIX term in a way that cannot be generated from the context. For example the user should describe the desired subspecifications when applying the parallel decomposition of figure 10.

6 Automatic Program Synthesis

A transformational software design requires even with tool assistance user support to realize creative design decisions. Nevertheless, if the designer has made some decision a tool should perform all necessary transformation steps and check their correct execution. Thus we have started to implement design strategies thereby exploiting the LAMBDA implementations of the transformation rules which arose from a formal validation of our approach [BR95].

There are two ways how to integrate strategies inside LAMBDA. The first one is provided by tactics. Strategies can be realized by sequential combinations of tactics for single transformation rules. This method allows a flexible combination of previously defined tactics. But reasoning about the strategies is impossible in LAMBDA itself because tactics are expressed in a meta language. E.g. termination of tactic applications cannot be proven in LAMBDA.

The second way overcomes this disadvantage. Here strategies are formalized within LAMBDA as functions which implement algorithms that describe the design ideas. This integrated treatment allows us to prove properties of strategies as termination and applicability in certain situations in LAMBDA. While the correctness of tactical strategies follows immediately from the correctness of their underlying rules the correctness of strategy functions has to be proved itself, although these proofs are also reducible to easier rules or simple statements. The correctness of a function ***strat*** realizing a

$$\frac{S}{\overset{\Uparrow}{\equiv}\ \mathit{strat}(S)}$$

provided ...

FIGURE 14. Strategy as function.

certain strategy is easily expressed as transformation rule (cf. figure 14) where "..." characterize all side conditions of the strategy. The automated application of such a strategy in LAMBDA is then reduced to a call of a simple tactic which applies the corresponding rule and afterwards expands the definition of *strat*.

A tactical combination of several rules requires the explicit condition check for each rule application. Often in the context of a strategy similar conditions have to be checked for the various rules applications. Such overlapping checks can be avoided in the case of functional strategy implementation. Here all these checks are collected in the single strategy condition thereby removing redundant checks.

SCS: IMPLEMENTING SPECIFICATIONS OF SINGLE COMMUNICATIONS

In a last step of any transformation process simple specifications of communications and their effects to the systems state have to be implemented. Therefore the equivalences of input and output communications in figure 13 are extended to specifications with less restricted communication assertions. Figure 15 shows the implementation of a so-called SCS (*Single Communication System*) for an input channel. The new variable v_c is introduced to pass the received value from the input to the effect computation. An analogous rule with the sequence SEQ[$impl(th_c[v_c'/@c]), c\,!\,v_c$] holds in the case of an output channel. Here the communication value has to be computed before it can be offered to the environment.

The mixed term derived from an SCS rule applications is transformed further by replacing $impl(th_c[v_c/@c])$ and $impl(th_c[v_c'/@c])$, respectively. For a transition predicate p we use $impl(p)$ to denote any program that computes this state transition and afterwards terminates. Not every transition predicate is implementable, e.g. $false$. Thus the design process should yield then-predicates which can be treated by rules of the following kind:

Applying SCS and *impl*() rules recursively yields a little basic strategy which implements specifications of which the trace part cannot be further

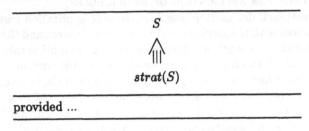

$$\begin{array}{l}\textbf{system input } c \textbf{ of } ty \textbf{ write } w \textbf{ read } r\\ \quad \textbf{trace } c \textbf{ in } c\\ \quad \textbf{com } c \textbf{ write } w \textbf{ read } r \textbf{ when } wh_c \textbf{ then } th_c\\ \textbf{end}\end{array}$$

$$\Uparrow$$

$$\texttt{IF[}\ wh_c \rightarrow \textbf{var } v_c \textbf{ of } ty\ \ \texttt{SEQ[}\ c?v_c, impl(th_c[v_c/@c])\ ]\ ]$$

provided v_c is a fresh variable

FIGURE 15. SCS transformation for input channel.

$$impl(x' = e)$$

$$\Uparrow$$

$$x := e$$

FIGURE 16. Implementing a transition predicate as assignment.

decomposed. Automating this SCS strategy as tactic would first apply the SCS rules and then repeatedly *impl*()-rules. A formalization as function in LAMBDA recursively walks through the structure of a mixed term and replaces SCS suitable systems by PL implementations as follows:

$$\begin{array}{lcl}\text{SCS}(\ \texttt{SEQ[}\ P,Q\ ]\ ) & = & \texttt{SEQ[}\ \text{SCS}(\ P\ ), \text{SCS}(\ Q\ )\ ]\\ \text{SCS}(\ \texttt{ALT[}\ P,Q\ ]\ ) & = & \texttt{ALT[}\ \text{SCS}(\ P\ ), \text{SCS}(\ Q\ )\ ]\\ \text{SCS}(\ \texttt{WHILE}\ b \text{ do } P \text{ od}\ ) & = & \texttt{WHILE}\ b \text{ do SCS}(\ P\ ) \text{ od}\\ \ldots & & \\ \multicolumn{3}{l}{\text{SCS}(\ \textbf{system ouput } c \textbf{ of } ty_c \ldots \textbf{trace } c \textbf{ in } c\ \textbf{ com } c \ldots \textbf{end}\ )}\\ & = & \texttt{IF[}\ wh_c \rightarrow \textbf{var } v_c \textbf{ of } ty_c\\ & & \qquad \texttt{SEQ[}\ impl(th_c[v'_c/@c]), c\,!\,v_c\ ]\ ]\\ \multicolumn{3}{l}{\text{SCS}(\ \textbf{system input } c \textbf{ of } ty_c \ldots \textbf{trace } c \textbf{ in } c\ \textbf{ com } c \ldots \textbf{end}\ )}\\ & = & \texttt{IF[}\ wh_c \rightarrow \textbf{var } v_c \textbf{ of } ty_c\\ & & \qquad \texttt{SEQ[}\ c?v_c, impl(th_c[v_c/@c])\ ]\ ]\end{array}$$

All other mixed terms remain unchanged by SCS. The corresponding strategy rule is presented in figure 18. In the following SDT strategy we will use this SCS implementation as basic strategy.

$$\frac{\begin{array}{c} \mathit{impl}(p \wedge q) \\ \Uparrow\!\!|||\\ \texttt{SEQ}[\ \mathit{impl}(p),\ \mathit{impl}(q[\mathit{Writes}(p)/\mathit{Writes}(p)'])\ ] \end{array}}{\text{provided } \mathit{Writes}(p) \cap \mathit{Reads}(q) = \emptyset}$$

FIGURE 17. Sequential decomposition of a transition predicate.

$$\frac{\begin{array}{c} S \\ \Uparrow\!\!|||\\ SCS(S) \end{array}}{\text{provided no local variable } v_c \text{ occurs free in } th_c}$$

FIGURE 18. SCS strategy rule

SDT: GENERATING SEQUENTIAL IMPLEMENTATIONS

For restricted classes of specifications it is possible to generate a program structure from the trace part automatically. The idea of the ***Syntax Directed Transformation*** strategy (SDT) is to drive the transformation process by the structure of the regular expression of the only trace assertion of a specification. A tactical automation of this strategy would recursively apply the decomposition rules presented in chapter 5. This tactic would perform many similar checks of application conditions which are avoided by the following functional implementation.

The function PCS formalizes in LAMBDA the inductive construction of a ***Program Control Structure*** from the operators of one regular expression and calls the SCS strategy to generate communication statements for channel names in the regular expression.

$$\begin{array}{lll}
\texttt{PCS}(\ \Delta, re1 + re2, CA\ ) & = & \texttt{ALT}[\ \texttt{PCS}(\ \Delta, re1, CA\ ), \texttt{PCS}(\ \Delta, re2, CA\ )\ ] \\
\texttt{PCS}(\ \Delta, re1.re2, CA\ ) & = & \texttt{SEQ}[\ \texttt{PCS}(\ \Delta, re1, CA\ ), \texttt{PCS}(\ \Delta, re2, CA\ )\ ] \\
\texttt{PCS}(\ \Delta, re*, CA\ ) & = & \texttt{WHILE ... do ... od} \\
\texttt{PCS}(\ \Delta, c, CA\ ) & = & \texttt{SCS}(\ \texttt{system}\ \Delta|_c, \texttt{trace}\ c\ \texttt{in}\ c\ , CA|_c\ \texttt{end}\ )
\end{array}$$

The interface Δ and communication assertions CA are used for calls of the SCS strategy where $\Delta|_c$ denotes the restriction of Δ and $CA|_c$ gives the communication assertion of channel c. Figure 19 shows the corresponding PCS rule which generates sequential programs for certain T-specifications.

Basically PCS uses the rules presented in chapter 5 and the SCS function.

$$\frac{\texttt{system}\ \Delta\ \texttt{trace}\ \bar{c}\ \texttt{in}\ re\ \ CA\ \ \texttt{end}}{\Uparrow_{|||}}$$

$$\texttt{system}\ \Delta\ \texttt{PCS(}\ \Delta, re, CA\ \texttt{)}\ \texttt{end}$$

provided *re* is SDT suitable
and $impl(th_c)$ is defined for all $c \in \bar{c} = Chans(\Delta)$.

FIGURE 19. PCS implementation of system specifications.

The conditions of the PCS rule guarantee that all application conditions corresponding to the intermediate transformation steps are satisfied. SDT suitable regular expressions contain no nested iterations (stars). Further more alternative regular expressions are restricted to input channels as first letters.

Now the *SDT strategy* is defined as follows: An S-specification is transformed by the rule in figure 9 into a T-specification with a following STOP. Then PCS and SCS are applied to this T-specification. Based on algebraic laws, the so far generated program is finally simplified by rewriting rules like those in figure 20.

SEQ[WHILE *true* do *P* od, *Q*]	$\rightarrow$	WHILE *true* do *P* od
ALT[ALT[...]]	$\rightarrow$	ALT[...]
IF[$b \rightarrow$ SEQ[$c?x, P$]]	$\rightarrow$	ALT[$b \& c?x \rightarrow P$]
IF[$true \rightarrow P$]	$\rightarrow$	P
SEQ[$c?v, x := v$]	$\rightarrow$	SEQ[$c?x, v := x$]
SEQ[$v := e, c!v$]	$\rightarrow$	SEQ[$v := e, c?e$]
var v of ty P	$\rightarrow$	P, if v is an auxiliary var. in P

FIGURE 20. Rewriting Rules for the SDT strategy

The SDT strategy can be applied to each of the component specifications *WMspec*, *RMspec* and *SVspec* (see figure 8) of the register example. The combined application of PCS, SCS, *impl*() and simplifying rewriting rules yield the implementations which are shown as the three arguments of the PAR operator in figure 4.

The three specifications *WMspec*, *SVspec* and *RMspec* satisfy the application conditions of the SDT strategy. Its application yields the following implementations of *WM*, *SV* and *RM*:

$$\begin{array}{lll} WM & = & \texttt{var } new \texttt{ of } V \\ & & \texttt{WHILE true do SEQ[} W?new, u!new, A! \texttt{] od} \\ SV & = & \texttt{var } x \texttt{ of } V \\ & & \texttt{WHILE true do ALT[} u?x \to \texttt{SKIP}, r? \to d!x \texttt{] od} \\ RM & = & \texttt{var } y \texttt{ of } V \\ & & \texttt{WHILE true do SEQ[} R?, r!, d?y, T!y \texttt{] od} \end{array}$$

FIGURE 21. Implementations of *WMspec*, *RMspec* and *SVspec*.

7 Discussion

We reported on a mixed term language MIX for the transformational design of communicating systems. Using the example of a register specification we demonstrated how to realize certain implementation ideas in a transformational design approach.

In the theorem prover LAMBDA the mixed terms and transformation rules have been formalized in order to validate the whole approach and prove the rules mechanically. At a first stage this embedding provides a simple tool for interactive execution of transformation steps.

In a transformational setting strategies systematically combine several rules in order to direct large transformation steps. To decrease the degree of user interaction in a design process the execution of such strategies has been automated in LAMBDA. Aspects of different realizations are discussed on the examples SCS and PCS. These strategies are used to generate implementations for the sequential components of the previously parallel decomposed register specification. A formal treatment of strategies inside LAMBDA allows to prove properties like correctness, termination and applicability to certain mixed terms.

Ideas for further strategies reveals in the context of parallel implementations concerning the systematic treatment of shared variables and methods of data refinement. Building up these strategies together with their integration in a design tool yields improved support of important design tasks.

8 References

[Bac90] R.J.R. Back. Refinement calculus, Part II: Parallel and Reactive Programs. In J.W. de Bakker, W.P. de Roever, and G. Rozenberg, editors, *Stepwise Refinement of Distributed Systems - Models, Formalisms, Correctness*, LNCS 430, pages 67–93. Springer-Verlag, 1990.

[BH94] J. Bohn and H. Hungar. Traverdi – Transformation and Verification of Distributed Systems. In M. Broy and S. Jänichen, editors,

KORSO Correct Software by Formal Methods, LNCS. Springer-Verlag, 1995. to appear.

[BR95] J. Bohn and S. Rössig. Towards a design assistant for communicating systems. ProCoS Doc. Id. OLD JB 2/1, Univ. Oldenburg - FB Informatik, 1995. URL: `ftp://ftp.informatik.uni-oldenburg.de/pub/procos/JB-2-1.ps.Z`

[CM88] K.M. Chandy and J. Misra. *Parallel Program Design - A Foundation*. Addison-Wesley, 1988.

[FFHM93] M. Francis, S. Finn, R.B. Hughes, and E. Mayger. *LAMBDA Version 4.3, Documentation Set*. Abstract Hardware Limited, London, 1993.

[FM91] M. Fourman and E. Mayger. Integration of formal methods with system design. In *Proc. VLSI'91, Edingburgh*, 1991.

[INM88] INMOS Ltd. *occam 2 Reference Manual*. Prentice Hall, 1988.

[JROR90] K.M. Jensen, H. Rischel, E.-R. Olderog, and S. Rössig. Syntax and informal semantics of the ProCoS specification language level 0. Technical Report ESPRIT Basic Research Action ProCoS, Doc. Id. ID/DTH KMJ 4/2, Technical University of Denmark, Lyngby, Dept. Comput. Sci., 1990.

[Lam86] L. Lamport. On interprocess communications Part II. *Distributed Comp.*, 1:86–101, 1986.

[Lam94] L. Lamport. The temporal logic of actions. *TOPLAS*, 16(3):872–923, 1994.

[LG89] N.A. Lynch and K.J. Goldman. Distributed algorithms. Technical Report MIT/LCS/RSS 5 6.852 Fall 1988, MIT, 1989.

[OH86] E.-R. Olderog and C.A.R. Hoare. Specification-oriented semantics for communicating processes. *Acta Inform.*, 23:9–66, 1986.

[Old91] E.-R. Olderog. Towards a Design Calculus for Communicating Programs. In J.C.M. Baeten and J.F. Groote, editors, *Proc. CONCUR '91*, LNCS 527, pages 61–77. Springer-Verlag, 1991.

[OR93] E.-R. Olderog and S. Rössig. A case study in transformational design of concurrent systems. In M.-C. Gaudel and J.-P. Jouannaud, editors, *TAPSOFT'93: Theory and Practice of Software Development*, LNCS 668, pages 90–104. Springer-Verlag, 1993.

[Rös94] S. Rössig. *A Transformational Approach to the Design of Communicating Systems.* PhD thesis, Tech. report 4-94, Univ. Oldenburg – FB Informatik, 1994. URL: `ftp://ftp.informatik.uni-oldenburg.de/pub/procos/PhD-roessig.ps.gz`

[Spi89] J.M. Spivey. *The Z Notation: A Reference Manual.* Prentice Hall, London, 1989.

Layers as Knowledge Transitions in the Design of Distributed Systems

Wil Janssen*†‡

ABSTRACT Knowledge based logics allow to give generic specifications of classes of network protocols. This genericity is combined with methods to derive sequentially structured or *layered* implementations of distributed algorithms. Knowledge based logic is used to specify layers in such algorithms as *knowledge transitions*. The resulting layered implementations are transformed to *distributed* algorithms by means a transformation rule based on the principle of *communication closed layers*.
In this way a class of solutions to a problem for different architectures can be derived along the same lines simultaneously. This design technique for distributed algorithms is applied to a number of examples including different versions of the Two-Phase Commit protocol.

1 Introduction

The design and analysis of distributed systems is a complicated task. Many different processes can be active simultaneously and communicate in a seemingly unstructured way, communication protocols are intertwined with the basic program, and different system architectures can result in completely different algorithms. Over the last few years there have been a number of attempts to solve these problems concerning the specification and design of distributed systems. One of the possible approaches is to remove all architectural decisions from the specification language, in order to be able to concentrate on the algorithmic aspects. This approach has been taken in, for example, *action systems* or *IO-automata* [5, 17, 3, 20, 19].
A second approach is the use of *knowledge-based* or *epistemic* logics and language constructs [11, 12, 21, 10]. The use of knowledge-based logics allows to express properties of systems and actions in a more global way,

*This work has partially been supported by Esprit/BRA Project 6021 (REACT).
†Most of the work reported on was done when the author was working at the University of Twente.
‡University of Oldenburg, Fachbereich Informatik, Postfach 2503, D-26111 Oldenburg, Germany. Phone: + 49 441 7982362; E-mail: Wil.Janssen@informatik.uni-oldenburg.de.

abstracting away from communication structures and architectural decisions.
Finally, there has been a considerable amount of attention to the use of ***layered methods*** in the design of distributed systems [8, 27, 28, 6, 18, 15, 31, 13]. It has been observed that in many protocols in distributed systems the logical structure of the system is basically a sequential one, whereas the actual structure is distributed and depends very much on the details of the implementation architecture. By viewing the algorithm as a sequentially structured system, analysis becomes much simpler and is more or less the same for larger classes of protocols, instead of being applicable to a single algorithm only.
In this paper we combine the above observations. We use the fact that many systems can be designed and analyzed in a layered fashion, plus the fact that knowledge-based logics allow for a specification of such layers at an appropriate level of abstraction, that is, as ***knowledge transitions***.

Knowledge concerns facts that we associate a ***location*** or ***distribution*** with. Facts can be known to a certain process or set of processes. Knowledge can exist in different ways: ***distributed knowledge*** is knowledge of the group of processes as a whole. It concerns facts that would be known if all processes would combine their information.
The strongest level of knowledge is ***common knowledge***, which informally corresponds to facts that are "publicly known." For example, in systems with reliable communication it is common knowledge that no messages are lost. States of knowledge are expressed using a set of modalities, K, D, S, E, and C. Let G be a group of processes, or ***agents*** as they are usually called in this context. The expression $K_i\varphi$ states that process i ***knows*** the proposition φ. $S_G\varphi$ states that ***somebody*** in the group G knows φ, and $E_G\varphi$ gives that ***everybody*** in G knows φ. Finally, $D_G\varphi$ states that it is ***distributed*** knowledge in G that φ holds, which means that if we combine the knowledge of every process $i \in G$ we can derive φ, and $C_G\varphi$ that it is ***common*** knowledge in G that φ holds. In this paper common knowledge will not play an important role and is not discussed further.

Protocols, distributed algorithms, and conceptual layers in them can often be described as transitions from one state of knowledge to another. A transition

$$\Phi \leadsto \Psi$$

states that if we start in a state satisfying Φ, on termination we will be in a state satisfying Ψ. Therefore, knowledge transitions can be viewed as a generalization of Hoare style preconditions and postconditions to knowledge based assertions. For example, broadcasting protocols can be specified as a transition from a state of knowledge where one process i (the broadcaster) knows a fact φ to a state where all processes in the set G of participating processes know the same fact. So it is a transition of the form

$$K_i\varphi \leadsto E_G\varphi.$$

If we do not know the identity of the broadcaster this would result in

$$S_G\varphi \rightsquigarrow E_G\varphi.$$

(In fact, this is a simplification. There must also be some common knowledge in the system for this to hold but this is beyond the scope of this paper. See Halpern and Moses [11] for details.) Often parts of protocols are used to gather information of all processes to a single coordinating process. This means that from a state where every process i knows some fact φ_i, the system evolves to a state where a single process c knows all these facts:

$$\wedge_{i\in G} K_i\varphi_i \quad \rightsquigarrow \quad K_c(\wedge_{i\in G}\varphi_i),$$

or stated differently:

$$D_G(\wedge_{i\in G}\varphi_i) \quad \rightsquigarrow \quad K_c(\wedge_{i\in G}\varphi_i).$$

Larger protocols can often also be specified in such a manner. Take for example *atomic commit* protocols for distributed databases (see Bernstein, Hadzilacos and Goodman [4] for an overview of this field). Informally speaking, the protocol has to make a decision for a set of participating processes, based on the internal state of those processes. Every process P_i can decide locally whether or not it can make the changes made in a transaction permanent. The protocol decides to commit iff all processes can do so. If one or more processes cannot, it should decide to abort in order to keep the data at the different processes consistent. The decision should be made known to all processes which will then take the appropriate actions. The internal state is reflected in a vote YES or NO for every process i, such that $vote_i = \text{YES}$ iff changes can be made permanent. Such a protocol can be specified as the following knowledge transition. Let $total\_vote = \text{YES}$ iff $\wedge_{i\in G} vote_i = \text{YES}$.

$$\bigwedge_{i\in G} K_i vote_i \rightsquigarrow \bigwedge_{i\in G} K_i(total\_vote \wedge (dec_i = \text{COMMIT} \Leftrightarrow total\_vote = \text{YES})).$$

Here, $K_i vote_i$ means that i knows the value of $vote_i$. This in fact abbreviates $K_i(vote_i = \text{YES}) \vee K_i(vote_i = \text{NO})$.

The approach we introduce in this paper is the following. Given a specification of a problem (using knowledge modalities), we refine this specification to a ***sequence of knowledge transitions***. For example, the above transition can be split into three simpler transitions are follows:

$$\begin{aligned} \bigwedge_{i\in G} K_i vote_i \quad &\rightsquigarrow \quad K_c total\_vote \\ &\rightsquigarrow \quad E_G total\_vote \\ &\rightsquigarrow \quad \bigwedge_{i\in G} K_i total\_vote \wedge (dec_i = \text{COMMIT} \Leftrightarrow total\_vote = \text{YES}). \end{aligned}$$

These knowledge transitions are then ***instantiated*** with protocol layers that are suited for the architecture under consideration and implement the knowledge transitions specified. The result of this is an algorithm that consists of a ***sequence of layers***.
Such an algorithm can then be ***transformed*** to a parallel or distributed algorithm, using the techniques developed by Janssen, Poel and Zwiers as discussed in, for example, [16, 25, 31, 13]. This transformation is based on the principle of ***communication closed layers*** as introduced by Elrad and Francez [8], translated to an algebraic setting. After some optimizations the transformed system results in an algorithm that solves the original problem and is tailored to a certain implementation architecture.
In order to be able to take this approach, we give a ***classification*** of knowledge transitions, and of the ways such transitions can be implemented for different architectures. As such, the knowledge transitions serve as a vehicle for the abstract specification of protocol layers. By taking different refinements of the problem specification using different transitions, different implementations of the problem can be obtained along the same lines, thus emphasizing the similarities and characteristics of the implementations.
The applicability of such layered approaches in general (not particularly using knowledge transitions) has been shown by numerous examples, such as distributed minimum weight spanning tree algorithms, parallel parsing, parts of a caching algorithm, pipelining, real-time mutual exclusion, and minimal distance algorithms.

The outline of this paper is as follows. We first discuss our process language and knowledge based logic with their semantics, and a transformation principle for programs. Thereafter we introduce knowledge transitions and classify well-known communication structures for different networks as knowledge transitions. Finally we explain how to derive algorithms as sequences of knowledge transitions and apply this to different versions of the Two-Phase Commit protocol and to so-called waves.

2 Programs, communication closedness and knowledge

Many protocols and distributed algorithms are given in a setting of asynchronous message passing. In this paper we restrict ourselves to this form of communication, in order to simplify technical details that would divert the attention from the main issues of this paper. We use a normal process language with choice, sequential composition and parallel composition, and asynchronous message passing. This language is extended with the notions of ***layers*** and ***layer composition***.

Systems consist of a number of components with local variables that communicate using $send(c, e)$ and $receive(c, x)$ actions, where c is a chan-

nel, e is an expression and x is a variable. Channels connect two unique processes and are unidirectional. Often a channel is therefore represented as a pair (v, v') of nodes or processes. Channels are viewed as *single place* buffers.
Besides communication actions and assignments $x := e$ to local variables, our programming language includes conditionals of the form **if** b **then** S **else** T **fi**. If T is omitted it is assumed to be **skip** (do nothing). Actions can be composed by means of parallel composition "$\|$" and sequential composition " ; ".

Any process that is composed out of the constructs above is called a *layer*. Layers can be composed by means of *layer composition* "$\bullet$". Informally speaking, when we compose two layers S and T by means of layer composition the resulting process $S \bullet T$ executes actions a of S before actions b of T iff a and b are *dependent*. Two actions are dependent, denoted by $a \leftrightsquigarrow b$, iff they access the same (local) variables, or access the same channel. So layer composition can be seen as an intermediate between sequential composition, where full ordering between S and T would be specified, and parallel composition, where ordering between dependent actions of S and T can be in an arbitrary direction, not necessarily from S to T. As such, layer composition cannot directly be translated into well-known program constructs, but it serves as a specification construct in the initial and intermediate design stages. Moreover, layer composition has nice algebraic properties that make it well-suited for a transformational style of program derivation. Please refer to the work by Janssen, Poel and Zwiers, for example [15, 31, 13], for detailed discussions thereof.

Layered programs and communication closed layers

One of the most important algebraic properties that relies on the use of layer composition is the so-called *communication closed layers law* CCL. It is based on the principle of communication closed layers as introduced by Elrad and Francez [8]. This law states that under a certain side condition, a *layered* or sequentially structured system $(P \| R) \bullet (Q \| S)$ behave the same (has the same semantics) as the *parallel* system $(P \bullet Q) \| (R \bullet S)$. The side condition is that there exist no "cross-dependencies" between components in different layers. Formally, assume for processes P, Q, R, and S, that P and S are independent, and that Q and R are independent ($P \not\leftrightsquigarrow S$ and $Q \not\leftrightsquigarrow R$). Under this assumption we have

$$(P \| R) \bullet (Q \| S) \quad = \quad (P \bullet Q) \| (R \bullet S) \qquad \text{(CCL)}$$

This law can be generalized to more processes and more layers of course.

The idea is to derive layered implementations that satisfy this side condition, and to transform these to distributed implementations. In general this side condition does not hold for systems consisting of a number of layers, as different layers can have common channels leading to cross-dependencies. In order to circumvent these problems, we temporarily introduce ***virtual channels*** per layer, for example by replacing every channel C in layer l by a channel C_l. The resulting process is equivalent to the original one. Thereafter the CCL law trivially applies, as all dependencies are either within a single layer or between different layers but within the same process.

After transforming the renamed system to a parallel system, we can replace the layer composition by sequential composition and replace the virtual channels by again a single channel per edge by means of ***multiplexing techniques*** (see [13, 31]). These multiplexing techniques do not always apply. In this setting a sufficient condition is to ensure that in every layer every *send* is matched by a *receive* action for the same channel for every possible evaluation of conditionals. Informally speaking this implies that channels are empty at the end of a layer, and therefore *receive* actions in other layers will read the values sent in the layer they belong to. Multiplexing and replacing layer composition by sequential composition do not preserve semantic equality. They do however preserve the input/output behavior of systems, that is, if viewed as pairs of initial and final states the systems are the same. This is called ***IO-equivalence***.

The combined result of the above steps is summarized by the following transformation principle.

> Let S be a system consisting of a number of layers
>
> $$S \triangleq L(0) \bullet L(1) \bullet \cdots \bullet L(n),$$
>
> where every layer is of the form
>
> $$L(l) \triangleq \textbf{for } i \in G \textbf{ par } P(i,l) \textbf{ rof},$$
>
> with every *send* action matched by a *receive* action, for all possible evaluations of the conditionals. Assume all components communicate by means of asynchronous message passing only. Then S is IO-equivalent to the system S'
>
> $$S' \triangleq \textbf{for } i \in G \textbf{ par } P(i) \textbf{ rof},$$
>
> where
>
> $$P(i) \triangleq P(i,0)\,;\, P(i,1)\,;\, \cdots\,;\, P(i,n).$$

Knowledge based logic

Knowledge based or epistemic logic [11, 10, 21] is a class of modal logics that allow to add some notion of locality to formulae. We cannot only say that φ holds, but also that φ holds for a process or agent i, or is a fact that holds for the combined states of a group G of processes, so-called ***distributed*** or *group* knowledge.

The basic modality is K, which stands for knowledge. The formula $K_i\varphi$ states that process i knows φ. $K_i\varphi$ holds in a states s such that the local state part s_i of s for process i satisfies φ. Knowledge of different processes can be combined. We say that φ is distributed knowledge for a group of processes G iff φ holds for the combined states of all processes $i \in G$. For example, if $K_i x = 1$ and $K_j y = 2$, then $D_{\{i,j\}} y = x + 1$.
Formally speaking, we use the following logic. Assume a given non-empty set P of propositional constants and let A be a finite set of agents or processes. The set $L_A(P)$ of epistemic formulae $\varphi, \psi, \ldots$ is the smallest set closed under

- If $p \in P$ then $p \in L_A(P)$;
- If $\varphi, \psi \in L_A(P)$, then $\varphi \wedge \psi \in L_A(P)$ and $\neg\varphi \in L_A(P)$;
- If $G \subseteq A, i \in A, \varphi \in L_A(P)$, then $K_i\varphi \in L_A(P), D_G\varphi \in L_A(P)$.

As usual, we define implication "$\Rightarrow$" and disjunction "$\vee$" as abbreviations. Also, *true* and *false* abbreviate $p_0 \vee \neg p_0$ and $p_0 \wedge \neg p_0$ for some constant $p_0 \in P$ respectively. Finally the modalities "E" and "S" are defined as abbreviations as well. The modality E_G states that *everybody* in G knows a certain proposition, and the modality S_G states that *somebody* in G knows a certain proposition. They are defined as

$$E_G\varphi \equiv \bigwedge_{i \in G} K_i\varphi,$$

$$S_G\varphi \equiv \bigvee_{i \in G} K_i\varphi.$$

The basic modalities are characterized by a number of axioms and rules. (See, for example, Meyer, van der Hoek and Vreeswijk [21] or Fagin et al. [10] for detailed discussions.)

$$K_i\varphi \Rightarrow \varphi$$
$$D_G\varphi \Rightarrow \varphi \qquad \text{knowledge axioms}$$

$$(K_i\varphi \wedge K_i(\varphi \Rightarrow \psi)) \Rightarrow K_i\psi$$
$$(D_G\varphi \wedge D_G(\varphi \Rightarrow \psi)) \Rightarrow D_G\psi \qquad \text{consequence closure}$$

$$K_i\varphi \Rightarrow K_iK_i\varphi$$
$$D_G\varphi \Rightarrow D_GD_G\varphi \qquad \text{positive introspection}$$

$$\neg K_i\varphi \Rightarrow K_i\neg K_i\varphi$$
$$\neg D_G\varphi \Rightarrow D_G\neg D_G\varphi \qquad \text{negative introspection}$$

$$\frac{\varphi}{K_i\varphi, \quad D_G\varphi} \qquad \text{knowledge generalization}$$

In the following we use a number of properties of the logic. Let $i \in G$, and let G be a subset of G'. Then

$$\begin{array}{rcl} K_i\varphi & \Rightarrow & D_G\varphi, \\ K_i\varphi & \Rightarrow & S_G\varphi, \\ D_G\varphi & \Rightarrow & D_{G'}\varphi, \\ E_{G'}\varphi & \Rightarrow & E_G\varphi, \\ E_G\varphi & \Rightarrow & S_G\varphi, \\ K_i(\varphi \wedge \psi) & \Leftrightarrow & K_i\varphi \wedge K_i\psi, \\ D_G(\varphi \wedge \psi) & \Leftrightarrow & D_G\varphi \wedge D_G\psi, \\ K_i(\varphi \vee \psi) & \Leftarrow & K_i\varphi \vee K_i\psi. \end{array}$$

Note that the latter implication is not an equivalence. As a counter example that K_i*true*, which obviously holds. However, $K_i\varphi \vee K_i\neg\varphi$ is *not* a tautology. Process i need not know whether φ holds or whether its negation holds.

We use $K_i x$ to state that i knows the value of x, which abbreviates $\bigvee_{v \in Val} K_i x = v$, if x takes its value from *Val*.

In the next two paragraphs we define the semantics of processes and the semantics of the logic. Knowledge thereof is not needed to understand what follows and they can be skipped on first reading.

Semantics of processes

Any run h of the system can be represented as a partially ordered set of events $h = (V, \rightarrow)$, where events are different occurrences of actions. Every event e has as an attribute its process identity $Id(e)$. Furthermore, events have a ***read set*** $R(e)$ and a write set $W(e)$, consisting of the variables read and written plus their values respectively. Two events e, e' are ***dependent***, denoted by $e \leftrightsquigarrow e'$, iff one event writes a variable the other accesses as well.

Every run should be ***dependency closed***, that is, for events $e, e' \in V$, if $e \leftrightsquigarrow e'$ then either $e \rightarrow e'$ or $e' \rightarrow e$. Cycles in the ordering are not allowed, as $(V, \rightarrow)$ is an (irreflexive) partial order.

Channels also fit into this framework: A channel c is modeled by a pair $(c.flag, c.val)$, where $c.flag$ is a boolean variable, and $c.val$ is a variable of the same type as the messages to be sent. A send $send(c, e)$ of message e along channel c and a $receive(c, x)$ can be defined as abbreviations of the following (guarded) assignments.

$$\begin{array}{rcl} send(c, f) & \triangleq & \textbf{await } \neg c.flag \textbf{ do } c.flag, c.val := true, f, \\ receive(c, x) & \triangleq & \textbf{await } c.flag \textbf{ do } c.flag, x := false, c.val. \end{array}$$

In this paper we do not take deadlock into account. Moreover we give only a short overview of the semantics. For a detailed account see [13, 31].

The semantics of processes is given by a function $[\![\cdot]\!] : S \longrightarrow \mathcal{H}$, where $\mathcal{H}$ is the domain of sets of partially ordered event sets. The **skip** action results in the empty run $(\emptyset, \emptyset)$, also denoted as "$\oslash$". Therefore

$$[\![\ \mathbf{skip}\ ]\!] \stackrel{\text{def}}{=} \{\oslash\}.$$

The semantics of (guarded) assignments is the set of runs $\{(\{e\}, \emptyset)\}$ where e is an event that reads the variables in the guards and the expression such that the guard evaluates to *true*, and writes the variables in the assignment. As an example, events e corresponding to $receive(c, x)$ have

$$R(e) = \{(c.flag, true), (c.val, n)\},$$

and

$$W(e) = \{(c.flag, false), (x, n)\},$$

for some value of n. Obviously, events accessing the same channel are dependent. Conditionals **if** b **then** S **else** T **fi** result in a choice between either $b\ ;\ S$ or $\neg b\ ;\ T$, where b is an empty assignment guarded by b.

Sequential composition of two runs is obtained by taking the disjoint union of the sets of events, and augmenting the order correspondingly.

$$(V_0, \rightarrow_0)\ ;\ (V_1, \rightarrow_1) \stackrel{\text{def}}{=} (V_0 \uplus V_1, \rightarrow_0 \uplus \rightarrow_1 \uplus (V_0 \times V_1)).$$

The sequential composition of two sets of runs is obtained by pointwise extension. Therefore the semantics of a sequentially composed term is obtained by the sequential composition of the semantics of the components. Note that we do not require that the states of the corresponding runs match in some sense. This in order to allow events from other components to "interfere".

For layer composition only *minimal* order to obtain dependency closedness is added.

$$(V_0, \rightarrow_0) \bullet (V_1, \rightarrow_1) \stackrel{\text{def}}{=} (V_0 \uplus V_1, \rightarrow_0 \uplus \rightarrow_1 \uplus ((V_0 \times V_1) \cap \leadsto)).$$

Parallel composition is similar to layer composition in that is requires minimal extension of ordering only, but ordering can be chosen arbitrarily. Therefore it results in a *set of runs*.

For *closed systems*, that is, systems without any processes running in its environment, we require that they are *state consistent*. This means that any event should read the last value that was written before it for any variable x, and that all initial reads should be consistent as well. Note that events writing into the same variable are dependent and therefore ordered. Thus the last written value is well-defined. Let

$$[\![S]\!]_S \stackrel{\text{def}}{=} \{h \in [\![S]\!] \mid h \text{ is state consistent }\}.$$

With any process i we associate a set of variables Var_i consisting of the local variables of i and the channels it is connected to. Let Var be the set of all variables and channels. A state s is a mapping from Var to values. It can be represented as a tuple $(s_1, s_2, \ldots, s_n)$ of local states of processes, where we require that if $c \in Var_i \cap Var_j$, then $s_i(c) = s_j(c)$, that is, the local states are consistent for shared variables. (In this case, the only variables shared are the channels.)
With any state-consistent run h we can associate a final state, given an initial global state s that is consistent with h. This is represented by $state(s, h)$. Informally speaking, this states gives the final values read or written in h, or the value a variable has in the initial state s if it is not accessed in h.

Semantics of the logic

The semantics we give in this section is a straightforward adaptation of the semantics given by, for example, Fagin et al. in [10], to our partial order framework.

As basic assertions Φ we use are first order formulae over Var. We could extend this with propositions of the form "i received a value from j" etcetera, but in the context of this paper this is not needed. The only special assertions we use are $full(c)$ and $val(c)$, denoting that channel c stores a message and the value of that message, respectively. These can be viewed as abbreviations of basic assertions, as channels are implemented as pairs of shared variables. We assume a given interpretation π mapping states plus assertions to $\{true, false\}$.

Let S be a system with $[\![S]\!]_S = H$. Given H and π we define an equivalence relation "$\sim_i$" on states for every process i as follows

$$s \sim_i s' \text{ iff } s_i = s'_i,$$

where we view s and s' as tuples. This equivalence partitions the states of the processes in classes such that two states are in the same class iff process i cannot distinguish between them.
We now define the semantics of the logic inductively. Formally speaking, the equivalence relations "$\sim_i$" will act as the accessibility relations $\mathcal{K}_i$ in a Kripke Structure

$$(S, \pi, \mathcal{K}_1, \ldots, \mathcal{K}_n),$$

where S is the set of states of the system. Let $p \in \Phi$, and let s be a global state.

$$((H, \pi), s) \models p \quad \stackrel{\text{def}}{=} \quad \pi(s)(p),$$

$$((H, \pi), s) \models K_i\varphi \quad \stackrel{\text{def}}{=} \quad \forall h \in H, s' \text{ consistent with } h. \quad state(s', h) \sim_i s \Rightarrow ((H, \pi), state(s', h)) \models \varphi,$$

$$((H,\pi),s) \models D_G\varphi \stackrel{\text{def}}{=} \forall h \in H, s' \text{ consistent with } h. \\ (\forall i \in G.\ state(s',h) \sim_i s) \Rightarrow \\ ((H,\pi), state(s',h)) \models \varphi.$$

As usual, let $(H,\pi) \models \varphi$ be defined as

$$\forall s.\ ((H,\pi),s) \models \varphi,$$

and $\models \varphi \stackrel{\text{def}}{=} \forall (H,\pi).\ (H,\pi) \models \varphi$.

3 Knowledge transitions and communication structures

We have discussed our process language and knowledge based logic. In the introduction we have argued informally that protocols or protocol layers can sometimes be viewed as transitions from one state of knowledge to another. In this section we give an overview of possible knowledge transitions and classify well-known communication structures as knowledge transitions.

Not all knowledge transitions make equally much sense. The transition $K_i\varphi \rightsquigarrow E_G\varphi$ intuitively corresponds a broadcast-like protocol where φ is sent to all processes. A transition such as $K_i\varphi \rightsquigarrow D_G\varphi$ however makes less sense: if $i \in G$ this is immediately fulfilled without any communication.
In table .1 the transitions are summarized. Every entry in the table gives the relation between φ and ψ for which that knowledge transition makes sense for different relations between i, j, G and G'. In the general case, protocol layers can also lead to an increase in knowledge due to the fact that, for example, a process knows from whom it has received messages. This increase in knowledge is not reflected in this table, only the way φ directly relates to ψ is given. Transitions that have a non-trivial implementation are named in this table. The entry "skip" means that the transition is trivially satisfied by doing nothing.

The roles of $\wedge K_i$ and of E_G are often similar, due to the similarities in their definitions. Furthermore, there is a correspondence between D_G and $\wedge K_i$, as we can observe in the table. We can roughly distinguish four different types of transitions:

- ***Broadcast, distribute*** or ***notify*** transitions. These distribute information that is known for a certain process or set of processes to a larger set of processes.
- ***Centralize*** or ***search*** transitions. In this case information from different processes is gathered to a single process or different set of processes.

$\rightsquigarrow$	$K_j\psi$	$S_{G'}\psi$	$\bigwedge_{G'} K_i\psi_i$	$E_{G'}\psi$	$D_{G'}\psi$
$K_i\varphi$	$i = j : \varphi \Rightarrow \psi$, skip $i \neq j : \varphi \Rightarrow \psi$, notify	$i \in G'$: $\varphi \Rightarrow \psi$, skip	$\varphi \Rightarrow \psi_i$, broadcast	$\varphi \Rightarrow \psi$, broadcast	$i \in G'$: $\varphi \Rightarrow \psi$, skip
$S_G\varphi$	$\varphi \Rightarrow \psi$, search	$G \subseteq G'$: $\varphi \Rightarrow \psi$, skip	$\varphi \Rightarrow \psi_i$, broadcast	$G \subseteq G'$: $\varphi \Rightarrow \psi$, broadcast	$G \subseteq G'$: $\varphi \Rightarrow \psi$, skip
$\bigwedge_G K_i\varphi_i$	$(\wedge\varphi_i) \Rightarrow \psi$, centralize	$(\wedge\varphi_i) \Rightarrow \psi$, elect	$G \subseteq G'$: $(\wedge\varphi_i) \Rightarrow \psi_i$, confer	$G \subseteq G'$: $(\wedge\varphi_i) \Rightarrow \psi$, confer	$G \subseteq G'$: $(\wedge\varphi_i) \Rightarrow \psi$, skip
$E_G\varphi$	$j \in G$: $\varphi \Rightarrow \psi$, skip $j \notin G$: $\varphi \Rightarrow \psi$, notify	$G \cap G' \neq \emptyset$: $\varphi \Rightarrow \psi$, skip $G \cap G' = \emptyset$: $\varphi \Rightarrow \psi$, notify	$G' \subseteq G$: $\varphi \Rightarrow \psi_i$, skip $G' \not\subseteq G$: $\varphi \Rightarrow \psi_i$, distribute	$G' \subseteq G$: $\varphi \Rightarrow \psi$, skip $G' \not\subseteq G$: $\varphi \Rightarrow \psi$, distribute	$G \cap G' \neq \emptyset$: $\varphi \Rightarrow \psi$, skip
$D_G\varphi$	$\varphi \Rightarrow \psi$, centralize	$\varphi \Rightarrow \psi$, elect	$G \subseteq G'$: $\varphi \Rightarrow \psi_i$, confer	$\varphi \Rightarrow \psi$, confer	$G \subseteq G'$: $\varphi \Rightarrow \psi$, skip $G \not\subseteq G'$: $\varphi \Rightarrow \psi$, centralize

TABLE .1. Knowledge transitions

- *Elect* transitions. In this case again distributed information is gathered, but resulting not towards a certain process or set of processes, but leading to an in general unknown "winner."
- *Confer* transitions. For confer transitions distributed information is made known to all or to a larger set of processes.

We would like to give instantiations of all non-trivial knowledge transitions with layers that implement that transition for a certain architecture. Some transitions are more difficult to implement than others for certain architectures. Take, for example, the transition $K_i\varphi \rightsquigarrow E_G\varphi$. In a fully connected network a single round of send actions suffices. In an arbitrary network one needs message diffusion or other more complicated algorithms. Also, some knowledge transitions can be built up from other transitions. In order to confer one can, for example, combine a centralizing phase with a distribution phase. Here we restrict ourselves to a few characteristic transitions, needed in the examples.

From the literature many communication structures are known. Broadcasts, waves, phases, heartbeats, logic pulsing, rooted tree communication, message diffusion all correspond to certain types of protocols for different network architectures. (See Raynal and Helary [26] and Andrews [1] for overviews.) Such protocols or protocol layers correspond to (sequences of) knowledge transitions. We give a classification of such layers for different architectures. This classification is by no means complete; not all communication structures are discussed. It should however be possible to classify other communication structures along the same lines. A proof rules for doing so is given at the end of this section.

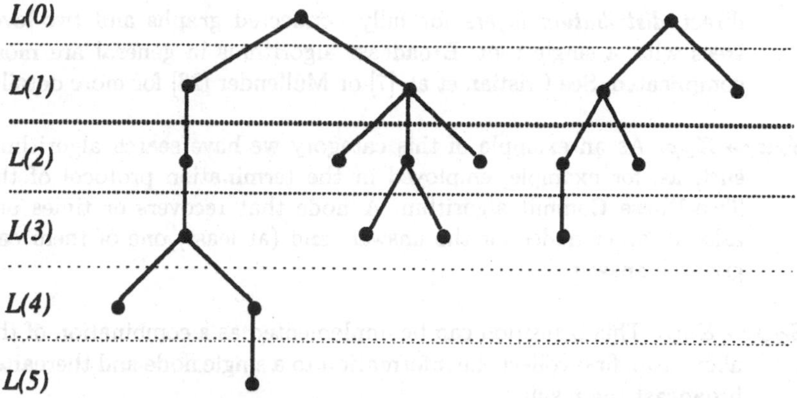

FIGURE 1. Levels of nodes in a tree structured network

We discuss two different types of network architectures: rooted trees or sets of rooted trees, and connected graphs. Other architectures, such as linear lists or fully connected graphs, are special cases of these two.
Assume we have a finite set of nodes V, and a subset $Root \subseteq V$ of root nodes. Let $root(v) \equiv v \in Root$. Every node v has a set of directed downward edges $down(v)$, and a set of successor nodes $S(v)$, and every non-root node v has an upward edge $up(v)$ pointing towards its root node. Every node in a tree is at a certain level, that is, it has a certain distance to its root. The set $L(l)$ is the set of nodes at level l (see figure 1).
A graph $\mathcal{G}$ is represented as a pair $\mathcal{G} = (V, E)$, where V is the set of nodes and E is a set of undirected edges. For every edge $j \in E$ we assume two directed unidirectional channels. For any node $v \in V$ let $out(v)$ denote the set of edges incident to v, that is,

$$out(v) \stackrel{\text{def}}{=} \{(v, u) \in E\}.$$

Furthermore, let $adj(v)$ be the set of nodes adjacent to v. We have the following generic instantiations of knowledge transitions, going from top-left to bottom-right in the table.

$K_i\varphi \rightsquigarrow K_j\varphi$. This is the most elementary transition. A process i notifies some process j of a certain fact known to i. If i and j are adjacent, it can be implemented by a pair of communication actions. If not, some kind of relaying or forwarding protocol is to be used. We omit details.
In general, this transition can be implemented abstractly by a so-called notify action as proposed by Moses and Kislev [22]. An action notify(j, φ) by process i ensures that eventually j knows φ.

$K_v\varphi \rightsquigarrow E_V\varphi$. This coincides with $K_v\varphi \rightsquigarrow \wedge K_v\psi_v$ for $\varphi \Rightarrow \psi_v$. Under this category fall *broadcast* protocols for arbitrary graphs, and simple direct ***distribution layers*** for fully connected graphs and two-level trees with a single root. Broadcast algorithms in general are more complicated. See Cristian et al. [7] or Mullender [23] for more details.

$S_V\varphi \rightsquigarrow K_v\varphi$. As an example of this category we have search algorithms such as, for example, employed in the termination protocol of the Two-Phase Commit algorithm. A node that recovers or times out asks all other nodes for the answer, and (at least) one of them can give the answer.

$S_G\varphi \rightsquigarrow E_G\varphi$. This transition can be implemented as a combination of the above two: first collect the information to a single node and thereafter broadcast the result.
A simpler solution can be given is the case of a fully connected network: the node that knows φ sends the value to all other nodes. Other nodes can either send a default message or do nothing, depending on the context of the algorithm.

$\bigwedge_G K_i\varphi_i \rightsquigarrow K_j\psi$. Centralizers captured by the transition above occur frequently in protocols. Information that is located at different nodes is to be gathered to a single node. For tree-structured networks this can be done by means of the so-called *wave concept.* (See Raynal and Helary, [26].) The root node initiates a request wave down the tree, which is returned from the leaves upwards, gathering the information. If all nodes know that the information is to be sent, the request part can be omitted. The downward part, upward part, and the full wave are given in figure 2. We assume that $\wedge\varphi_v \Rightarrow \psi$. Fully connected networks can handled similarly, as if they were two-level trees.

$\bigwedge_G K_i\varphi_i \rightsquigarrow E_G\psi$. This transition can be implemented by adding the downward part of a wave to a full wave for tree-structured networks. For fully connected graphs this can be implemented much simpler: every node sends its information to every other node. This is, for example, used in decentralized Two-Phase Commit algorithms.

$E_G\varphi \rightsquigarrow E_{G'}\varphi$. For $G \subseteq G'$ this transition models that knowledge is distributed to a larger set of nodes. The transition $K_i\varphi \rightsquigarrow E_{G'}\varphi$ is a special case. Such transitions (conceptually) occur in tree-structured networks where the information is distributed from nodes at one level to nodes at the next level, or in networks that use ***message diffusion*** to broadcast messages over an arbitrary connected network (see, for example, Cristian et al. [7]).
In fact, message diffusion and downward wave parts can be viewed as sequences of transitions of this type themselves. We come back to this later.

```
Downward ≜
  for v ∈ V par
    if ¬root(v) then receive(up(v), req_v) fi ;
    for j ∈ down(v) par send(j, req_v) rof
  rof,
Upward ≜
  for v ∈ V par
    for j = (v, v') ∈ down(v) par receive(j, φ_v') rof ;
    "Compute ψ_v from ⋀_{v'∈S(v)} φ_v' ∧ φ_v" ;
    if ¬root(v) then send(up(v), ψ_v) fi
  rof,
Wave ≜
  for v ∈ V par
    if ¬root(v) then receive(up(v), req_v) fi ;
    for j ∈ down(v) par send(j, req_v) rof ;
    for j = (v, v') ∈ down(v) par receive(j, φ_v') rof ;
    "Compute ψ_v from ⋀_{v'∈S(v)} φ_v' ∧ φ_v" ;
    if ¬root(v) then send(up(v), ψ_v) fi
  rof.
```

FIGURE 2. Waves in tree-structured networks

$D_G\varphi \rightsquigarrow K_j\varphi$. This transition is a special case of the centralizer transition $\wedge_G K_i\varphi_i \rightsquigarrow K_j\psi$ if φ_i is the information of node i to compute φ. It should therefore be known in what way the information to compute φ is distributed over the nodes.

$D_G\varphi \rightsquigarrow E_G\varphi$. Again this case is similar to the case for $\wedge_G K_i\varphi_i \rightsquigarrow E_G\psi$.

$D_G\varphi \rightsquigarrow D_{G'}\varphi$. For $G' \subseteq G$ this can correspond to a level transition in the upward part of a wave. When the information from one level is gather to a higher level, only the information of the higher levels is needed to compute the over all result. So again, an upward wave can be viewed as a sequence of these transitions.

This list is by no means complete. It simply presents a number of generic implementations of knowledge transitions for two types of networks.

How to classify layers?

Above we have given a classification of certain layers as knowledge transitions. An intuitive explanation has been given of why those layers belong to that transition class. In principle we have to *prove* that an algorithm satisfies a certain specification or knowledge transition.

To give such a prove we would like stay as much as possible within the limits of well-known proof systems for parallel algorithms, such as Owicki-Gries style proofs [24, 2]. The programs we use in this paper can be treated as programs with an **await** construct to implement *send* and *receive* actions, and channels plus disjoint sets of variables. Thus we can give (non-knowledge based) proof outlines for programs in the usual way (see Apt and Olderog [2] for a extensive overview). In order to be able to prove knowledge based properties of programs we add the following rule, based on proof outlines for parallel programs, the rule for knowledge generalization, and the definition of $K_i\varphi$. Let φ_i and ψ_i be basic assertions, not using the knowledge modalities, and let $S \vdash \Phi \rightsquigarrow \Psi$ denote that program S satisfies the knowledge transition $\Phi \rightsquigarrow \Psi$. We have the following proof rule.

$$\frac{\begin{array}{l}\{\varphi_i\}S_i\{\psi_i\},\ \text{for all } 1 \leq i \leq n,\\ \text{There exist valid proof outlines } \{\varphi_i\}S_i^{\dagger}\{\psi_i\} \text{ that}\\ \text{are interference free,}\end{array}}{S_1 \parallel \cdots \parallel S_n \quad \vdash \quad \bigwedge_{1\leq i\leq n} K_i\varphi_i \quad \rightsquigarrow \quad \bigwedge_{1\leq i\leq n} K_i\psi_i}$$

Using rules for disjunction and conjunction, and the properties of our modalities, we can give derived rules for the other modalities, such as D_G and S_G. Soundness of the knowledge based rule follows in a rather straightforward way from the soundness of the Owicki/Gries rule for parallelism and the definition of validity of K_i (see [14] for a proof).

4 Deriving distributed algorithms

In this section we give a number of examples of derivations using the approach sketched above. We start with a class of Two-Phase Commit implementations and end with waves. The same derivation style can be applied to other systems that have an underlying logical structure that is layered. In [14] some other examples are discussed as well, such as a distributed algorithm for computing minimal distances in networks.

4.1 Two-Phase Commit

The Two-Phase Commit protocol is an example of *atomic commit protocols* that are used in distributed databases to guarantee *consistency* of the database. A distributed database consists of a number of sites connected by some network, where every site has a local database. Data are distributed over a number of sites. In such a distributed database system *transactions*, consisting of a series of read and write actions, are executed. Reading and writing database items is be done by forwarding the action to the site where the item is stored. Terminating the transaction however involves *all* sites accessed in the transaction, as all sites must agree on the decision to be taken—which is either to *commit* or to *abort*—in order to guarantee consistency. In the case of an abort all changes made by the transaction are discarded, in the case of a commit they are made permanent. A protocol that guarantees such consistency is called an atomic commit protocol (ACP). We refer to Bernstein, Hadzilacos and Goodman [4] for more details.

In an ACP every participating process has one vote: YES or NO, and every process can reach one out of two decisions: COMMIT or ABORT. Here we do not take into account the possibility of communication failures or site failures, that is, we assume that every message sent is eventually delivered and that sites are working correctly.

First of all we should give a specification of the atomic commit problem as a knowledge transition. Thereafter we refine this transition to a sequence of (simpler) transitions. As we do not take failures into account the requirements can be phrased as follows: *Given the votes of every participating process, each process should decide to* COMMIT *iff every process has voted* YES. This is represented by the following knowledge transition. Let G be the set of participating processes and define $total\_vote = \textsc{yes}$ iff $\bigwedge_{i \in G} vote_i = \textsc{yes}$. So *total_vote* is not a variable but represents the combined values of all local variables $vote_i$.

$$\bigwedge_{i \in G} K_i vote_i \rightsquigarrow \bigwedge_{i \in G} K_i(total\_vote \wedge (dec_i = \textsc{commit} \Leftrightarrow total\_vote = \textsc{yes})).$$

Using the definitions of D_G and *total_vote* (given the distribution of the variables over the processes) this can be rewritten to

$$D_G total\_vote \rightsquigarrow \bigwedge_{i \in G} K_i(total\_vote \wedge (dec_i = \textsc{commit} \Leftrightarrow total\_vote = \textsc{yes})).$$

Deriving layered implementations

To derive implementations for knowledge transitions the following strategy is employed. We first check whether the transition under consideration has an immediate implementation for a certain network architecture. If this is the case, we're done. If not so we split the transition into two or more smaller transitions and continue with them. This "transition splitting" is in fact a real design step which can have consequences for the eventual implementation. The resulting *layered* algorithm is thereafter transformed to a *distributed* system using the transformation principle discussed in section 2.

In order to simplify matters, we first split of a transition "$\overset{2}{\rightsquigarrow}$," to be implemented by a final layer TPC_2 from the transition specified, where the decision is "executed," from the rest. In this final layer only local changes need to be performed, so its implementation is straightforward. This results in the following two transitions.

$$D_G total\_vote \overset{1}{\rightsquigarrow} E_G total\_vote \overset{2}{\rightsquigarrow}$$
$$\bigwedge_{i \in G} K_i(total\_vote \wedge (dec_i = \text{COMMIT} \Leftrightarrow total\_vote = \text{YES})).$$

The first transition is a *confer transition* (see table .1), and can immediately be implemented for fully connected networks by means of sending the votes to all other nodes, as was mentioned in the previous section. This would result in the following layer implementing "$\overset{1}{\rightsquigarrow}$."

$TPC_1 \triangleq$
  $\{D_G total\_vote\}$
  for $i \in G$ **par**
    for $i' \in G - \{i\}$ **par** $send((i, i'), vote_i)$ **rof** ;
    for $i' \in G - \{i\}$ **par** $receive((i, i'), vote_{ii'})$ **rof**
  rof
  $\{E_G total\_vote\}$

A second possibility is that we do *not* have a fully connected network, but some kind of tree structured network. In that case there is no apparent immediate solution to the above transition. So we split the transition again, and do so in the following way. Let $c \in G$ be some participating process.

$$D_G total\_vote \overset{3}{\rightsquigarrow} K_c total\_vote \overset{4}{\rightsquigarrow} E_G total\_vote.$$

The question now is what a sensible choice for c would be. Under the given assumption that we have a tree structured network an obvious choice is to take for c the root of the tree. There is however—under additional conditions—a second possibility. For a *linear tree* or chain, that is, a tree where every node has at most one downward edge, we can also take the (unique) leaf of the tree! We assume that the tree has at least two nodes. We first discuss the former possibility.
To obtain a $D_G total\_vote \rightsquigarrow K_c total\_vote$ transition, which is a *centralize transition*, we can use a full wave as discussed in the previous section. This would result in the following implementation.

$TPC_3 \triangleq$
  $\{D_G total\_vote\}$
  for $i \in G$ **par**
    if $\neg root(i)$ **then** $receive(up(i), req_i)$ **fi** ;
    for $j \in down(i)$ **par** $send(j, req_i)$ **rof** ;
    for $j = (i, i') \in down(i)$ **par** $receive(j, vote_{ii'})$ **rof** ;
    if $(\forall i' \neq i \in S(i).\ vote_{ii'} = \text{YES}) \wedge vote_i = \text{YES}$ **then** $rep_i := \text{YES}$
        else $rep_i := \text{NO}$ **fi** ;
    if $\neg root(i)$ **then** $send(up(i), rep_i)$ **fi**
  rof
  $\{K_c total\_vote\}$

The value of *total_vote* is stored in rep_c.

In the linear case we have the following implementation. Let $down(i)$ denote the unique edge downward for every node i in this case. For the leaf of the linear tree this is *nil*, and $send(nil, e) \stackrel{\text{def}}{=}$ **skip** .

$TPC_{3'} \triangleq$
  $\{D_G\, total\_vote\}$
  for $i \in G$ **par**
    if $\neg root(i)$ **then** $receive(up(i), v_i)$ **fi** ;
    if $(root(i) \wedge vote_i = \text{YES}) \vee (v_i = \text{YES} \wedge vote_i = \text{YES})$
      then $send(down(i), \text{YES})$ **else** $send(down(i), \text{NO})$ **fi**
  rof
  $\{K_c\, total\_vote\}$

The *total_vote* follows in this case from the values of v_c and $vote_c$.

To implement the second transition in this layer, "$\overset{4}{\leadsto}$", we can use a downward wave for the first case, and an upward wave in the linear case, as it is a *broadcast transition*, leading to the following implementations:

$TPC_4 \triangleq$
  $\{K_c\, total\_vote\}$
  for $i \in G$ **par**
    if $\neg root(i)$ **then** $receive(up(i), rep_i)$ **fi** ;
    for $j \in down(i)$ **par** $send(j, rep_i)$ **rof**
  rof,
  $\{E_G\, total\_vote\}$,
$TPC_{4'} \triangleq$
  $\{K_c\, total\_vote\}$
  (**if** $v_c = \text{YES} \wedge vote_c = \text{YES}$ **then** $rep_c := \text{YES}$ **else** $rep_c := \text{NO}$ **fi** ;
  $send(up(c), rep_c)$) $\|$
  for $i \in G - \{c\}$ **par**
    $receive(down(i), rep_i)$;
    $send(up(i), rep_i)$
  rof
  $\{E_G\, total\_vote\}$.

The first two lines of $TPC_{4'}$ correspond to the process for the leaf node. A third possible network configuration is a special case of general networks: the ring. In this case we could again take a similar approach as in the previous case by appointing one node to gather all votes, and send the result through the ring (see [14]).

Transforming sequences of layers to parallel processes

We have derived a number of layered implementations for the Two-Phase Commit protocol consisting of two or three layers, where every layer is a parallel composition over all participants. The actual implementation we should arrive at must be of the form **for** $i \in G$ **par** $P(i)$**rof**, that is, a single (sequential) process for every participant. The transformation from the layered to the distributed structure can be carried out using the CCL law, or more precisely, the transformation principle discussed in section 2. Using this principle we transform the layered implementations given above. As an example take the layered implementation for tree-structured networks. This layered implementation is

$$TPC_l \triangleq TPC_3 \bullet TPC_4 \bullet TPC_2.$$

Transforming this system immediately results in the distributed process *TPC* given below, which is IO-equivalent to the layered implementation. Therefore it satisfies the same initial knowledge transition specification.

$TPC \triangleq$
for $i \in G$ **par**
  if $\neg root(i)$ **then** $receive(up(i), req_i)$ **fi** ;
  for $j \in down(i)$ **par** $send(j, req_i)$ **rof** ;
  for $j = (i, i') \in down(i)$ **par** $receive(j, vote_{ii'})$ **rof** ;
  if $(\forall i' \neq i \in S(i).\ vote_{ii'} = \text{YES}) \wedge vote_i = \text{YES}$ **then** $rep_i := \text{YES}$
    else $rep_i := \text{NO}$ **fi** ;
  if $\neg root(i)$ **then** $send(up(i), rep_i)$ **fi** ;
  if $\neg root(i)$ **then** $receive(up(i), rep_i)$ **fi** ;
  for $j \in down(i)$ **par** $send(j, rep_i)$ **rof** ;
  if $rep_i = \text{YES}$ **then** $dec_i := \text{COMMIT}$ **else** $dec_i := \text{ABORT}$ **fi**
rof.

This algorithm can be optimized by combining the two conditionals in the sixth and seventh line, but the basic structure remains the above.

Similarly, we can transform the layered implementation of the linear algorithm TPC'_l using the transformation rule to the following distributable algorithm TPC'.

$TPC' \triangleq C \parallel \textbf{for } i \in G - \{c\} \textbf{ par } P(i) \textbf{ rof},$

$C \triangleq$

$\quad \textbf{if } \neg root(c) \textbf{ then } receive(up(c), v_c) \textbf{ fi };$

$\quad \textbf{if } v_c = \text{YES} \wedge vote_c = \text{YES} \textbf{ then } rep_c := \text{YES} \textbf{ else } rep_c := \text{NO} \textbf{ fi };$

$\quad send(up(c), rep_c);$

$\quad \textbf{if } rep_c = \text{YES} \textbf{ then } dec_i := \text{COMMIT} \textbf{ else } dec_i := \text{ABORT} \textbf{ fi},$

$P(i) \triangleq$

$\quad \textbf{if } \neg root(i) \textbf{ then } receive(up(i), v_i) \textbf{ fi };$

$\quad \textbf{if } (root(i) \wedge vote_i = \text{YES}) \vee (v_i = \text{YES} \wedge vote_i = \text{YES})$

$\qquad \textbf{then } send(down(i), \text{YES}) \textbf{ else } send(down(i), \text{NO}) \textbf{ fi };$

$\quad receive(down(i), rep_i);$

$\quad send(up(i), rep_i);$

$\quad \textbf{if } rep_i = \text{YES} \textbf{ then } dec_i := \text{COMMIT} \textbf{ else } dec_i := \text{ABORT} \textbf{ fi}.$

Note that for the networks under consideration, which have at least two participants, the first guard ($\neg root(c)$) always evaluates to *true* and can therefore be removed.

These protocols correspond to a generalization of the *decentralized Two-Phase Commit* and the *linear Two-Phase Commit* as they are known from the literature. The result for the fully connected network is known as *centralized Two-Phase Commit.*

Finally, we have the case of arbitrary network structures. To obtain the knowledge transition we can do two things: either we use some broadcast algorithm for networks, for example based on message diffusion, or we first construct a spanning tree in one layer and then apply tree based communication protocols. In the former case this is similar to the fully connected network case but with broadcast instead of send, and in the latter it is the same as for tree-based networks with an additional layer. We do not discuss these cases in any detail.

4.2 Waves as sequences of layers

The same principles as applied above can be used to derive certain knowledge transitions from more elementary ones. We can, for example, derive the protocol for (upward or downward) waves as a sequence of layers corresponding to levels in the tree. In a similar way we can derive the protocol for rings.

Take for example the downward part of a wave. It is characterized by the knowledge transition

$$\bigwedge_{v \in Root} K_v \varphi \;\leadsto\; \bigwedge_{v \in V} K_v \varphi.$$

With every node $v \in V$ a level number l is associated, giving the distance to the root it belongs to. Recall that $L(l)$ is the set of nodes at level l (see section 3, figure 1). Let $Upto(l) \stackrel{\text{def}}{=} \cup\{L(l') \mid 0 \leq l' \leq l\}$, and let n be the maximal level number of any node. We can now split the above transition in n transitions "$\stackrel{l}{\rightsquigarrow}$" for $0 \leq l < n$, where

$$E_{Upto(l)}\varphi \quad \stackrel{l}{\rightsquigarrow} \quad E_{Upto(l+1)}\varphi.$$

As $Upto(1) = Root$ and $Upto(n+1) = V$ this sequence refines the original transition. Every transition $E_{Upto(l)} \stackrel{l}{\rightsquigarrow} E_{Upto(l+1)}$ can be implemented as follows:

Down$(l) \triangleq$
  $\{E_{Upto(l)}\varphi\}$
  for $i \in L(l)$ **par**
    for $j \in down(i)$ **par** $send(j, \varphi)$ **rof**
  rof $\|$
  for $i \in L(l+1)$ **par** $receive(up(i), \varphi)$ **rof**
  $\{E_{Upto(l+1)}\varphi\}$

Note that for $down(i) = \emptyset$ the parallel statement

for $j \in down(i)$ **par** ... **rof**

reduces to **skip**.

This layered system we would like to transform to a distributed system. At first it seems however that the transformation principle we applied above does not apply here: the layers are not of the form **for** $v \in V$ **par** $P(v)$ **rof**. But fortunately, we can add **skip** components for any process that does not occur in the parallel composition in a layer. Moreover, after transformation these **skip** components can be removed, as (P ; **skip**) = (**skip** ; P) = P.
The result is the following algorithm.

Down $\triangleq$
  for $i \in Root$ **par**
    for $j \in down(i)$ **par** $send(j, \varphi)$ **rof**
  rof $\|$
  for $i \in V - Root$ **par**
    $receive(up(i), \varphi)$;
    for $j \in down(i)$ **par** $send(j, \varphi)$ **rof**
  rof.

Merging the code for the root nodes and the non-root nodes using a conditional statement results in the *Downward* layer given in section 3.

5 Concluding remarks

In this paper we have discussed how to use knowledge based logics in the layered design of distributed systems. The contribution of this paper is twofold. First of all we have given a classification scheme for protocol layers as knowledge transitions. Secondly we have shown how such knowledge transitions can be used to derive layered implementations of protocols. Thus we have used knowledge based logics to give generic specifications of program layers and protocols.

We have shown that this design principle applies to a number of algorithms. In principle, any algorithm that can be viewed as a layered system should fit in this framework, which concerns a substantial class of algorithms. There exist however algorithms that cannot be written as layered systems, for example, highly interactive systems such as memories, or so-called retroactive systems (see Janssen [13] for a discussion of these problems).

The role of knowledge based logic has been limited to the specification of knowledge transitions. It would be interesting to use that logic to prove the layers correct themselves, possible in the style of van Hulst and Meyer [29]. Possibly such ideas would allow the approach presented to be extended to non-layered systems as well. The advantage of the approach presented here however is that the extensions to well-known techniques for program verification needed in this approach are rather limited.

We have used epistemic logic primarily as a logic to express locality of information. In [30] Wieczorek proposes a logic with modalities that directly express location. This logic however is weaker in the sense that it does not allow to combine information of different locations using the properties of the knowledge modalities.

Another interesting approach using knowledge based logics is to use program constructs that allow for the use of knowledge based expressions. The notify construct as introduced by Moses and Kislev [22] is an example thereof. Furthermore one can use actions guarded by knowledge based expressions instead of normal boolean guards. Such programs are discussed by Fagin et al. in [10, 9]. One of the difficulties with these programs is however that the transition of a knowledge based program to an ordinary program has not yet been formalized. Possibly classification schemes as introduced here combined with layered derivation can be of help to formalize this transition.

Acknowledgements. The author would like to thank Mannes Poel for detailed reading of the manuscript, and Yoram Moses, Wim Koole and John-Jules Meyer for useful comments on this work.

6 References

[1] G. Andrews. *Concurrent Programming — Principles and Practice.* The Benjamin/Cummings Publishing Company, 1991.

[2] K. Apt and E.-R. Olderog. *Verification of sequential and concurrent programs.* Springer-Verlag, 1991.

[3] R. Back and K. Sere. Stepwise refinement of action systems. *Structured Programming*, 12:17–30, 1991.

[4] P. Bernstein, V. Hadzilacos, and N. Goodman. *Concurrency Control and Recovery in Database Systems.* Addison-Wesley, 1987.

[5] R. Chandy and J. Misra. *Parallel Program Design: A Foundation.* Addison-Wesley, 1988.

[6] C. Chou and E. Gafni. Understanding and verifying distributed algorithms using stratified decomposition. In *Proceeding 7th ACM Symposium on Principles of Distributed Computing*, 1988.

[7] F. Cristian, H. Aghili, R. Strong, and D. Dolev. Atomic broadcast: From simple message diffusion to byzantine agreement. In *Proceedings 15th International Symposium on Fault-Tolerant Computing*, 1985.

[8] T. Elrad and N. Francez. Decomposition of distributed programs into communication closed layers. *Science of Computer Programming*, 2:155–173, 1982.

[9] R. Fagin, J. Halpern, Y. Moses, and M. Vardi. Knowledge-based programs. In *Proceedings ACM Symposium on Principles of Distributed Computing.* ACM, 1995.

[10] R. Fagin, J. Halpern, Y. Moses, and M. Vardi. *Reasoning About Knowledge.* MIT Press, 1995. To appear.

[11] J. Halpern and Y. Moses. Knowledge and common knowledge in a distributed environment. *Journal of the ACM*, 37(3):549–587, 1990.

[12] J. Halpern and L. Zuck. A little knowledge goes a long way: Knowledge-based derivations and correctness proofs for a family of protocols. *Journal of the ACM*, 39(3):449–478, 1992.

[13] W. Janssen. *Layered Design of Parallel Systems.* PhD thesis, University of Twente, 1994.

[14] W. Janssen. Layers as knowledge transitions in the design of distributed systems. Technical Report 94-71, University of Twente, 1994.

[15] W. Janssen, M. Poel, and J. Zwiers. Action systems and action refinement in the development of parallel systems. In *Proceedings of CONCUR '91, LNCS 527*, pages 298–316. Springer-Verlag, 1991.

[16] W. Janssen and J. Zwiers. Protocol design by layered decomposition, a compositional approach. In J. Vytopil, editor, *Proceedings Formal Techniques in Real-Time and Fault-Tolerant Systems, LNCS 571*, pages 307–326. Springer-Verlag, 1992.

[17] B. Jonsson. Modular verification of asynchronous networks. In *Proceedings 6th ACM Symposium on Principles of Distributed Computing*, pages 152–166, 1987.

[18] S. Katz and D. Peled. Verification of distributed programs using representative interleaving sequences. *Distributed Computing*, 6(2), 1992.

[19] N. Lynch, M. Merritt, W. Weihl, and A. Fekete. *Atomic Transactions*. Morgan Kaufman Publishers, 1994.

[20] N. Lynch and M. Tuttle. Hierarchical correctness proofs for distributed algorithms. In *Proceedings 6th ACM Symposium on Principles of Distributed Computing*, pages 137–151, 1987.

[21] J.-J. Meyer, W. van der Hoek, and G. Vreeswijk. Epistemic logic for computer science: A tutorial. *Bulletin of the EATCS, numbers 44 and 45*, 1991.

[22] Y. Moses and O. Kislev. Knowledge-oriented programming, (extended abstract). In *Proceedings 12th ACM Symposium on Principles of Distributed Computing*, pages 261–270. ACM, 1993.

[23] S. Mullender, editor. *Distributed Systems*. Addison-Wesley, second edition, 1993.

[24] S. Owicki and D. Gries. An axiomatic proof technique for parallel programs. *Acta Informatica*, 6:319–340, 1976.

[25] M. Poel and J. Zwiers. Layering techniques for development of parallel systems. In G. v. Bochmann and D. Probst, editors, *Proceedings Computer Aided Verification, LNCS 663*, pages 16–29. Springer–Verlag, 1992.

[26] M. Raynal and J.-M. Helary. *Synchronization and control of distributed systems and programs*. John Wiley & Sons, 1990.

[27] F. Stomp and W.-P. de Roever. A correctness proof of a distributed minimum-weight spanning tree algorithm (extended abstract). In *Proceedings of the 7th ICDCS*, 1987.

[28] F. Stomp and W.-P. de Roever. A principle for sequential reasoning about distributed systems. *Formal Aspects of Computing*, 6(6):716–737, 1994.

[29] M. van Hulst and J.-J. Meyer. An epistemic proof system for parallel processes. In R. Fagin, editor, *Proceedings 5th TARK*, pages 243–254. Morgan Kaufmann, 1994.

[30] M. Wieczorek. *Locative Temporal Logic and Distributed Real-Time Systems*. PhD thesis, Catholic University of Nijmegen, 1994.

[31] J. Zwiers and W. Janssen. Partial order based design of concurrent systems. In J. de Bakker, W.-P. de Roever, and G. Rozenberg, editors, *Proceedings of the REX School/Symposium "A Decade of Concurreny", Noordwijkerhout, 1993, LNCS 803*, pages 622–684. Springer-Verlag, 1994.

Parallelism for Free: Bitvector Analyses ⇒ No State Explosion!

Jens Knoop*
Bernhard Steffen*
Jürgen Vollmer†‡

ABSTRACT One of the central problems in the automatic analysis of distributed or parallel systems is the combinatorial state explosion leading to models, which are exponential in the number of their parallel components. The only known cure for this problem are application specific techniques, which avoid the state explosion problem under special frame conditions. In this paper we present a new such technique, which is tailored to bitvector analyses, which are very common in data flow analysis. In fact, our method allows to adapt most of the practically relevant optimizations for sequential programs, for a parallel setting with shared variables and arbitrary interference between parallel components.

1 Motivation

Parallel systems are of growing interest, as they are more and more supported by modern hardware environments. However, it is very difficult to guarantee their reliability (cf. [MP]): the adaptation of the successful techniques for sequential systems seems inevitably be tied to the combinatorial explosion of the systems' state space leading to models, which are exponential in the number of the parallel components. As a consequence, also classical data flow analysis for parallel programming languages was considered too expensive to be implemented in real programming environments. The only known cure for this problem are application specific techniques, which avoid the state explosion problem under usually very specific frame condi-

*Fakultät für Mathematik und Informatik, Universität Passau, Innstrasse 33, D-94032 Passau, Germany. E-mail: {knoop,steffen}@fmi.uni-passau.de

†Fakultät für Informatik, Institut für Programmstrukturen und Datenorganisation (IPD), Universität Karlsruhe, Vincenz-Prießnitz-Straße 3, D-76128 Karlsruhe, Germany. E-mail: vollmer@ipd.info.uni-karlsruhe.de

‡A preliminary version of this article was published in the preliminary proceedings of TACAS'95 (cf. [KSV1]).

tions. For data flow analysis, this ranges from special heuristics (cf. [McD]) and approaches which require data independence of the parallel components (cf. [GS]) or exclude shared variables (cf. [LC]) over approaches tailored for specific analyses like mutual exclusion or data races (cf. [DC]) to approaches that are based on state space reductions (cf. [CH1, CH2, DBDS, GW, Va]). The latter allow general synchronization mechanisms, but still require the investigation of an appropriately reduced version of the global state space, which is often still unmanageable.

In this paper we show how to construct for unidirectional bitvector analysis problems (which are most prominent in practice) algorithms for parallel programs with shared memory and interleaving semantics that

1. optimally cover the phenomenon of *interference*
2. are as *efficient* as their sequential counterparts and
3. easy to implement.

The first property is a consequence of a Kam/Ullman-style ([KU]) Coincidence Theorem for bitvector analyses stating that the ***parallel meet over all paths (PMOP)*** solution, which specifies the desired properties, coincides with our ***parallel bitvector maximal fixed point (PMFP$_{BV}$)*** solution, which is the basis of our algorithm. This result is rather surprising, as it states that although the various interleavings of the executions of parallel components are semantically different, they need not be considered during bitvector analysis, which is the key observation of this paper.

The second property is a simple consequence of the fact that our algorithms behave like standard bitvector algorithms. In particular, they do ***not*** require the consideration of any kind of global state space. This is important, as even the corresponding reduced state spaces would usually still be exponential in size.

The third property is due to the fact, that only a minor modification of the sequential bitvector algorithm needs to be applied after a preprocess consisting of a single fixed point routine (cf. Section 3.3).

Thus, using our methods all the well-known algorithms for unidirectional bitvector analysis problems can be adapted for parallel programs at almost no cost on the runtime and the implementation side. This is highly relevant in practice as this class of bitvector problems has a broad scope of applications ranging from simple analyses like liveness, availability, very business, reaching definitions, and definition-use chains (cf. [He]) to more sophisticated and powerful program optimizations like code motion (cf. [DS, DRZ, KRS1, KRS2]), partial dead code elimination (cf. [KRS3]), assignment motion (cf. [KRS4]), and strength reduction (cf. [KRS5]). All these techniques, which only require unidirectional bitvector analyses, are now available for parallel programs. In Section 4 this is demonstrated by presenting a code motion algorithm, which evolves from the ***busy code motion*** transformation of [KRS2], and is unique in placing the computations of a parallel program computationally optimally.

Structure of the Paper

The next section will recall the sequential situation, while Section 3 develops the corresponding notions for parallel programs. Subsequently, Section 4 presents an application of our algorithm, and Section 5 contains the conclusions. The Appendix contains the detailed generic algorithm.

2 Sequential Programs

In this section we summarize the sequential setting of data flow analysis.

2.1 Representation: Program Models

In the sequential setting procedures are usually represented by ***directed flow graphs*** $G = (N, E, \mathbf{s}, \mathbf{e})$ with node set N and edge set E, where the nodes $n \in N$ represent the statements, and the edges $(n, m) \in E$ the ***nondeterministic*** branching structure of the procedure under consideration, while $\mathbf{s}$ and $\mathbf{e}$ denote the unique ***start node*** and ***end node*** of G. Without loss of generality, it is assumed that $\mathbf{s}$ and $\mathbf{e}$ do not have any predecessors and successors, respectively. Figure 1 shows the flow graph of some procedure for illustration.

However, similar to [St], we use here a different, transition system-like representation of a procedure, which we call a ***program model***. Like a flow graph, also a program model is a directed graph $T = (N, E, \mathbf{s}, \mathbf{e})$ with node set N, edge set E, and a unique ***start node*** $\mathbf{s}$ and ***end node*** $\mathbf{e}$ that are assumed to have no predecessors and successors, respectively. In contrast to a flow graph, however, the edges of T represent both the statements and the nondeterministic control flow of the underlying procedure, while the nodes only represent program points. This gives a program model the flavour of a transition system, and therefore, we will use the notions 'nodes' and 'states', and 'edges' and 'transitions' of a program model T synonymously.

Given a flow graph G the corresponding program model T results from the following simple transformation: For every node n of G do:

- introduce a new node n', and an edge e from n to n',
- label e with the assigment node n is labelled with in G, and remove the labelling of node n,

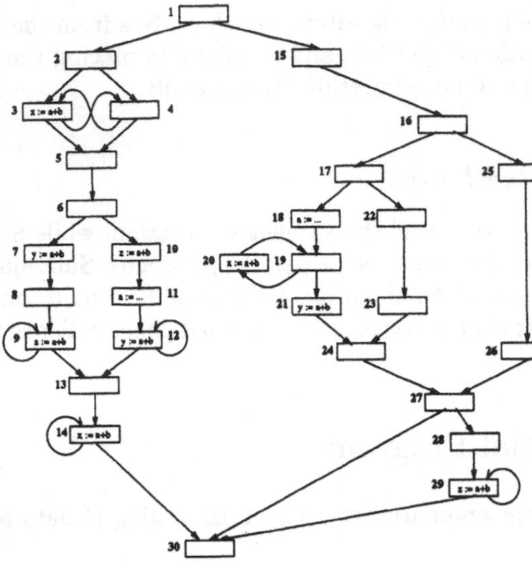

FIGURE 1. The Flow Graph G

- replace every edge starting in n (except for the one inserted in the first step) by a corresponding edge starting in n'.

Figure 2 shows the result of this transformation for the flow graph of Figure 1. It is worth noting that the two states of a program model corresponding to a node n of the underlying flow graph explicitly represent the usual distinction between the *entry point* and the *exit point* of n. This simplifies the formal development of the theory, as the implicit treatment of this distinction, which, unfortunately is usually necessary for the traditional flow graph representation, is obsolete here.

Given a program model T, then $pred_T(n)=_{df} \{ m \mid (m,n) \in E \}$ denotes the set of all immediate predecessors of a state n, and *source*(e) and *dest*(e) denote the source and the destination state of a transition e. A ***finite path*** in T is a sequence $(e_1, \ldots, e_q)$ of transitions such that $dest(e_j) = source(e_{j+1})$ for $j \in \{1, \ldots, q-1\}$; it is a path from m to n, if $source(e_1) = m$ and $dest(e_q) = n$. Moreover, $\mathbf{P}_T[m,n]$ denotes the set of all finite paths from m to n, and ε denotes the empty path containing no transition. Finally, without loss of generality we assume that every state $n \in N$ lies on a path from $\mathbf{s}$ to $\mathbf{e}$.

2.2 Data Flow Analysis

Data flow analysis (DFA) is concerned with the static analysis of programs in order to support the generation of efficient object code by "optimizing" compilers (cf. [He, MJ]). For imperative languages, DFA provides informa-

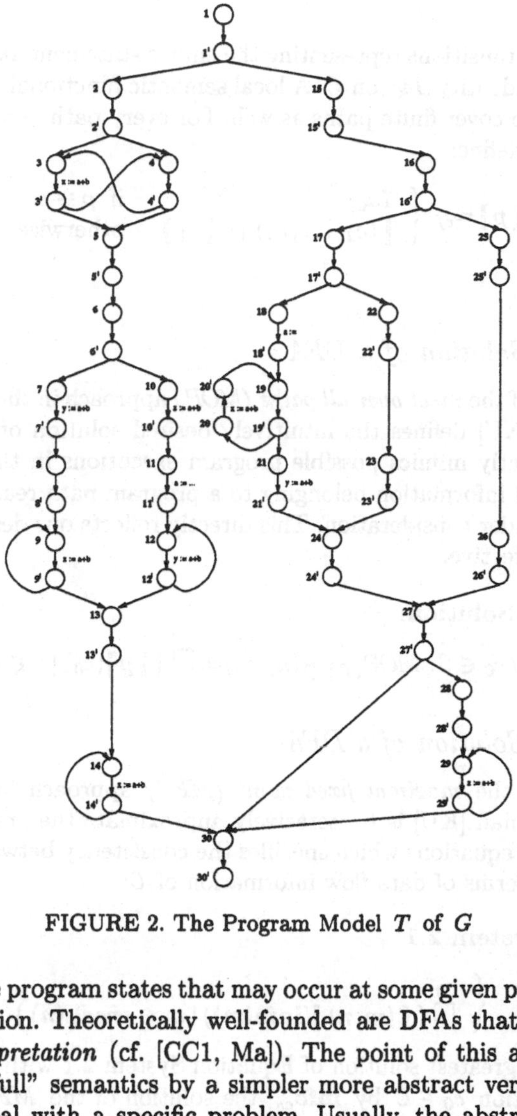

FIGURE 2. The Program Model T of G

tion about the program states that may occur at some given program points during execution. Theoretically well-founded are DFAs that are based on *abstract interpretation* (cf. [CC1, Ma]). The point of this approach is to replace the "full" semantics by a simpler more abstract version, which is tailored to deal with a specific problem. Usually, the abstract semantics is specified by a *local semantic functional*, which gives abstract meaning to every statement in terms of a transformation function on a complete lattice. Thus considering program models, the abstract semantics gives abstract meaning to every transition by means of a functional

$$[\![\ ]\!] : E \rightarrow (\mathcal{C} \rightarrow \mathcal{C})$$

where $(\mathcal{C}, \sqcap, \sqsubseteq, \perp, \top)$ denotes a complete lattice with least element $\perp$ and greatest element $\top$, whose elements express the data flow information of interest.[1]

Unlabelled transitions representing the empty statement **skip** are associated with the identity $Id_{\mathcal{C}}$ on $\mathcal{C}$. A local semantic functional $[\![\ ]\!]$ can easily be extended to cover finite paths as well. For every path $p = (e_1, \ldots, e_q) \in \mathbf{P}_G[m,n]$, we define:

$$[\![p]\!] =_{df} \begin{cases} Id_{\mathcal{C}} & \text{if } p \equiv \varepsilon \\ [\![(e_2, \ldots, e_q)]\!] \circ [\![e_1]\!] & \text{otherwise} \end{cases}$$

The MOP-Solution of a DFA

The solution of the *meet over all paths (MOP)* approach in the sense of Kam and Ullman [KU] defines the intuitively desired solution of a DFA. This approach directly mimics possible program executions in that it "meets" (intersects) all information belonging to a program path reaching the program point under consideration. This directly reflects our desires, but is in general not effective.

The *MOP*-Solution:

$$\forall n \in N \ \forall c_0 \in \mathcal{C}.\ MOP_{(T,[\![\ ]\!])}(n)(c_0) = \bigsqcap \{ [\![p]\!](c_0) \mid p \in \mathbf{P}_T[\mathbf{s}, n] \}$$

The MFP-Solution of a DFA

The point of the *maximal fixed point (MFP)* approach in the sense of Kam and Ullman [KU] is to iteratively approximate the greatest solution of a system of equations which specifies the consistency between conditions expressed in terms of data flow information of $\mathcal{C}$:

Equation System 2.1

$$\mathbf{info}(n) \quad = \quad \begin{cases} c_0 & \text{if } n = \mathbf{s} \\ \bigsqcap \{ [\![(m,n)]\!](\mathbf{info}(m)) \mid m \in pred_T(n) \} & \text{otherwise} \end{cases}$$

Denoting the greatest solution of Equation System 2.1 with respect to the start information $c_0 \in \mathcal{C}$ by $\mathbf{info}_{c_0}$, the solution of the *MFP*-approach is defined by:

The *MFP*-Solution: $\forall n \in N \ \forall c_0 \in \mathcal{C}.\ MFP_{(T,[\![\ ]\!])}(n)(c_0) = \mathbf{info}_{c_0}(n)$

For monotonic functionals,[2] this leads to a suboptimal but algorithmic description (cf. [KU]). The question of optimality of the *MFP*-solution

[1] In the following $\mathcal{C}$ will always denote a complete lattice.

[2] A function $f : \mathcal{C} \to \mathcal{C}$ is called *monotonic* iff $\forall c, c' \in \mathcal{C}.\ c \sqsubseteq c'$ implies $f(c) \sqsubseteq f(c')$.

was elegantly answered by the Coincidence Theorem of Kildall [Ki1, Ki2], and Kam and Ullman [KU], which we reformulate here for program models:

Theorem 2.2 (The (Sequential) Coincidence Theorem)
Given a program model $T=(N,E,\mathbf{s},\mathbf{e})$, the MFP-solution and the MOP-solution coincide, i.e. $\forall\, n \in N.\ MOP_{(T,[\![\ ]\!])}(n) = MFP_{(T,[\![\ ]\!])}(n)$, whenever all the semantic functions $[\![\, e \,]\!]$, $e \in E$, are distributive.[3]

The Functional Characterization of the MFP-Solution

From interprocedural DFA, it is well-known that the *MFP*-solution can alternatively be defined by means of a functional approach [SP]. Here, one iteratively approximates the greatest solution of a system of equations specifying consistency between functions $[\![\, n \,]\!]$, $n \in N$. Intuitively, a function $[\![\, n \,]\!]$ transforms data flow information that is assumed to be valid at the start node of the program into the data flow information being valid at n.

Definition 2.3 (The Functional Approach)
The functional $[\![\ ]\!] : N \to (\mathcal{C} \to \mathcal{C})$ is defined as the greatest solution of the equation system given by:

$$[\![\, n \,]\!] = \begin{cases} Id_{\mathcal{C}} & \text{if } n = \mathbf{s} \\ \bigsqcap\{[\![\,(m,n)\,]\!] \circ [\![\, m \,]\!] \mid m \in pred_T(n)\} & \text{otherwise} \end{cases}$$

The following equivalence result is important [KS]:

Theorem 2.4 $\forall n \in N\ \forall c_0 \in \mathcal{C}.\ MFP_{(T,[\![\ ]\!])}(n)(c_0) = [\![\, n \,]\!](c_0)$

The functional characterization of the *MFP*-solution will be the (intuitive) key for computing the parallel version of the maximal fixed point solution. As we are only dealing with Boolean values later on, the functional form can be dealt with without performance penalty.

3 Parallel Programs

As usual, we consider a parallel imperative programming language with an ***interleaving semantics***. Formally, this means that we view parallel programs semantically as 'abbreviations' for nondeterministic programs, which result from a product construction between parallel components (cf. [CC2,

[3]A function $f : \mathcal{C} \to \mathcal{C}$ is called ***distributive*** iff $\forall\, \mathcal{C}' \subseteq \mathcal{C}.\ f(\bigsqcap \mathcal{C}') = \bigsqcap\{f(c) \mid c \in \mathcal{C}'\}$. It is well-known that distributivity is a stronger requirement than monotonicity in the following sense: A function $f : \mathcal{C} \to \mathcal{C}$ is monotonic iff $\forall\, \mathcal{C}' \subseteq \mathcal{C}.\ f(\bigsqcap \mathcal{C}') \sqsubseteq \bigsqcap\{f(c) \mid c \in \mathcal{C}'\}$.

CH1, CH2]). In fact, the size of the nondeterministic 'product' program may grow exponentially in the number of parallel components of the corresponding parallel program. This immediately clarifies the dilemma of data flow analysis for parallel programs: even though it can be reduced to standard data flow analysis on the corresponding nondeterministic program, this approach is unacceptable in practice for complexity reasons. Fortunately, as we will see in Section 3.3, unidirectional bitvector analyses, which are most relevant in practice, can be performed as efficiently on parallel programs as on sequential programs.

The following section establishes the notational background for the formal development and the proofs.

3.1 Representation: Parallel Program Models

Syntactically, we express parallelism by means of a **par** statement whose components are assumed to be executed in parallel on a shared memory. As usual, we assume that there are neither jumps leading into a component of a **par** statement from outside nor vice versa. This already introduces the phenomena of interference and synchronization, and allows us to concentrate on the central features of our approach which, however, is not limited to this setting. For example, a replicator statement in order to allow a dynamical process creation can be integrated along the lines of [CH2, Vo1, Vo2].

Following [SHW] and [GS], the standard representation of a parallel program is a nondeterministic *parallel flow graph* $G^* = (N^*, E^*, \mathbf{s}^*, \mathbf{e}^*)$ with node set N^* and edge set E^* as illustrated in Figure 3. This figure shows the flow graph of Figure 1, where some of the branch instructions have been replaced by parallel statements.[4] The components of a parallel statement are encapsulated by a `ParBegin` and a `ParEnd` node, which are represented by ellipses. For clarity we additionally separate the parallel components by two parallels.

In anology to Section 2, we represent parallel programs as *parallel program models*, which are a straightforward extension of program models to the parallel setting. Except for subgraphs representing **par** statements a parallel program model is a program model in the sense of Section 2, and in fact, all the standard notation can be transferred. Also the transformation from flow graphs to program models is the same, except that `ParBegin` and `ParEnd` nodes are not duplicated. Figure 4 displays the parallel program model of the parallel flow graph of Figure 3.

A **par** statement and each of its components are also considered parallel program models. The graph T_{par} representing a complete **par** statement arises from linking its component graphs by means of a `ParBegin` and a

[4] Of course, this replacement is not assumed to be semantics preserving.

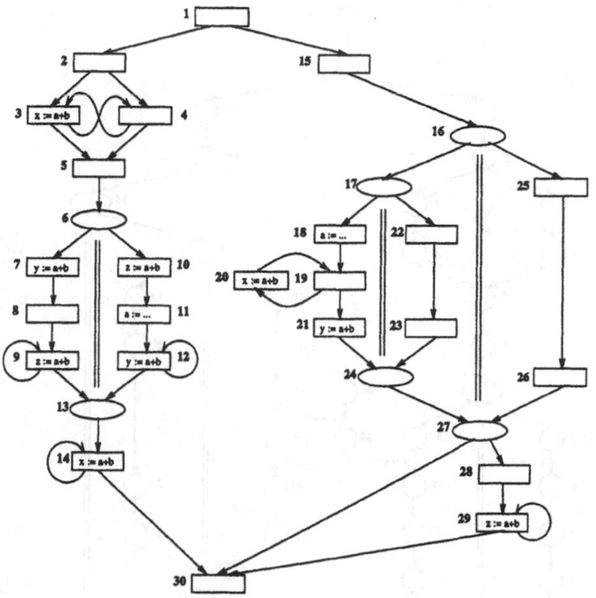

FIGURE 3. The Parallel Flow Graph G^*

ParEnd node which have the start nodes and the end nodes of the component graphs as their only successors and predecessors, respectively. The **ParBegin** node and the **ParEnd** node are the unique start node and end node of T_{par}. They form the entry and the exit to program regions whose subgraph components are assumed to be executed in parallel making the synchronization points in the program explicit. As in a parallel flow graph, we represent the states corresponding to a **ParBegin** node or a **ParEnd** node of a parallel flow graph by ellipses and additionally separate the corresponding component graphs by two parallels as shown in Figure 4.

Moreover, $\mathcal{T}_\mathcal{P}(T^*)$ and $\mathcal{T}_\mathcal{P}^{max}(T^*)$ denote the set of all subgraphs and of all maximal subgraphs of T^* representing a **par** statement, i.e.,[5]

$$\mathcal{T}_\mathcal{P}^{max}(T^*) =_{df} \{ T \in \mathcal{T}_\mathcal{P}(T^*) \mid \forall T' \in \mathcal{T}_\mathcal{P}(T^*).\ T \subseteq T' \Rightarrow T = T' \}$$

Additionally, $\mathcal{T}_\mathcal{C}(T')$, $T' \in \mathcal{T}_\mathcal{P}(T^*)$, denotes the set of component program models of T', and $\mathcal{T}_\mathcal{C}(T^*)$ is an abbreviation for $\bigcup \{ \mathcal{T}_\mathcal{C}(T') \mid T' \in \mathcal{T}_\mathcal{P}(T^*) \}$. It is worth noting that every graph $T \in \mathcal{T}_\mathcal{P}(T^*)$ and all of its component program models $T' \in \mathcal{T}_\mathcal{C}(T)$ are single-entry/single-exit regions of T^*. Moreover, for technical reasons (see Section 'Interleaving Predecessors') we assume that the unique transitions ending in the start state or starting in the end state of a graph $T \in \mathcal{T}_\mathcal{C}(T^*)$ are edges of T.

[5]For parallel program models T and T' we define: $T \subseteq T'$ if and only if $N \subseteq N'$ and $E \subseteq E'$.

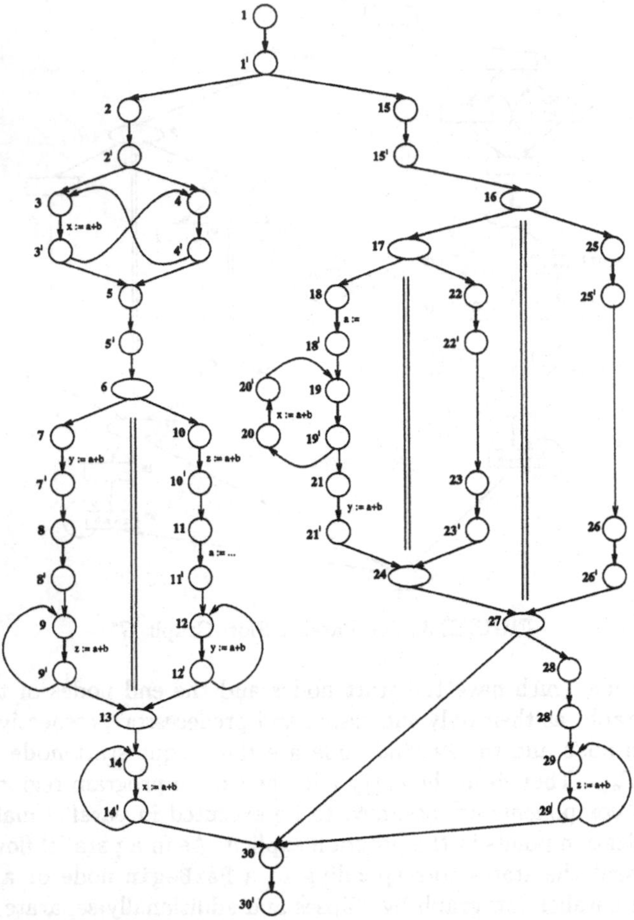

FIGURE 4. The Parallel Program Model T^* of G^*

Additionally, we need the functions *States*, *Trans*, *start*, and *end*, which map a parallel program model to its state set, its transition set, its start state, and its end state, respectively. Moreover, we need the polymorphic functions *ppm* and *cpm*, where *ppm* is defined for the states of graphs of $\mathcal{T}_{\mathcal{P}}(T^*)$ and for the graphs of $\mathcal{T}_{\mathcal{C}}(T^*)$, and *cpm* is defined for the states and the transitions of T^*. *ppm* maps its argument x to the smallest parallel program model of $\mathcal{T}_{\mathcal{P}}(T^*)$ containing x, i.e.,

$$ppm(x) =_{df} \begin{cases} \bigcap\{\, T' \in \mathcal{T}_{\mathcal{P}}(T^*) \mid x \in States(T') \,\} & \text{if } x \in States(\mathcal{T}_{\mathcal{P}}(T^*)) \\ \bigcap\{\, T' \in \mathcal{T}_{\mathcal{P}}(T^*) \mid x \subseteq T' \,\} & \text{if } x \in \mathcal{T}_{\mathcal{C}}(T^*) \end{cases}$$

Similarly, the polymorphic function *cpm* maps its argument x, which is a state or a transition of T^* to the smallest parallel component model containing x, if it lies in a graph $T \in \mathcal{T}_C(T^*)$, and to T^* itself otherwise, i.e.,[6]

$$cpm(x) =_{df} \begin{cases} \bigcap\{ T' \in \mathcal{T}_C(T^*) \mid x \in T' \} & \text{if } x \in \mathcal{T}_C(T^*) \\ T^* & \text{otherwise} \end{cases}$$

Note that both *ppm* and *cpm* are well-defined because **par** statements in a program are either unrelated or properly nested.

Additionally, we introduce the following abbreviations for the sets of start nodes (i.e., **ParBegin** nodes) and end nodes (i.e., **ParEnd** nodes) of graphs of $\mathcal{T}_\mathcal{P}(T^*)$:

$$N_N^* =_{df} \{ start(T) \mid T \in \mathcal{T}_\mathcal{P}(T^*) \} \quad \text{and} \quad N_X^* =_{df} \{ end(T) \mid T \in \mathcal{T}_\mathcal{P}(T^*) \}$$

Finally, given a parallel program model T, we define an associated sequential program model T_{seq}, which results from T by replacing all states belonging to a component parallel model of some graph $T' \in \mathcal{T}_\mathcal{P}^{max}(T)$ together with all transitions starting or ending in such a state by a transition leading from $start(T')$ to $end(T')$. Note that T_{seq} is a sequential program model in the sense of Section 2. This is illustrated in Figure 5, which shows the sequentialized version of the parallel program model encapsulated by the nodes **16** and **27** of Figure 4.

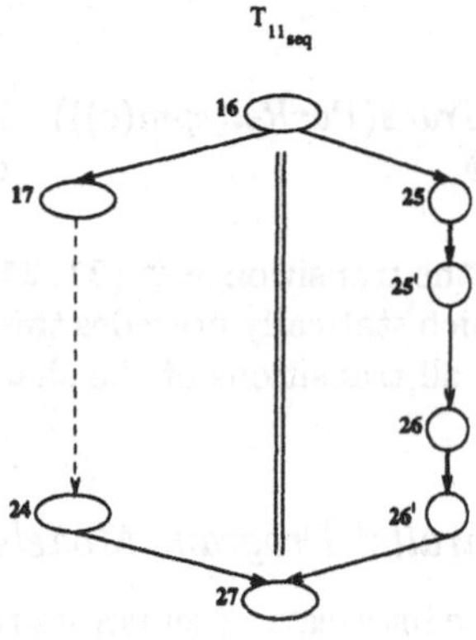

FIGURE 5. A Sequentialized Program Model

Interleaving Predecessors

Given a sequential program model T, the set of transitions that might precede a transition e at run-time is precisely given by the set of *static*

[6] $x \in \mathcal{T}_C(T^*)$ is an abbreviation for $x \in States(\mathcal{T}_C(T^*)) \cup Trans(\mathcal{T}_C(T^*))$.

predecessors, the incoming transitions of *source*(e). For parallel program models, however, the interleaving of parallel components must also be taken into account: here each transition occurring in a component of some **par** statement can dynamically also be preceded by any transition of another component of this **par** statement.

We denote this kind of predecessors as *interleaving predecessors*. This notion can easily be defined by means of the function *ParRel* mapping a graph of $\mathcal{T}_\mathcal{C}(T^*)$ to the set of its *parallel relatives*, i.e., the set of component graphs which are executed in parallel, i.e.,

$$ParRel : \mathcal{T}_\mathcal{C}(T^*) \rightarrow \mathcal{P}(\mathcal{T}_\mathcal{C}(T^*))$$

is defined by

$$ParRel(T) =_{df}$$

$$\mathcal{T}_\mathcal{C}(ppm(T)) \backslash T \;\cup\; \begin{cases} \emptyset & \text{if } ppm(T) \in \mathcal{T}_\mathcal{P}^{max}(T^*) \\ ParRel(ppm(T)) & \text{otherwise} \end{cases}$$

where $\mathcal{P}$ denotes the power set operator.

Based on this function, the set of interleaving predecessors of a transition $e \in E^*$ is given by the function $ItlvgPred_{T^*} : E^* \rightarrow \mathcal{P}(E^*)$ defined by:

$$ItlvgPred_{T^*}(e) =_{df} \begin{cases} Trans(ParRel(cpm(e))) & \text{if } e \in Trans(\mathcal{T}_\mathcal{P}(T^*)) \\ \emptyset & \text{otherwise} \end{cases}$$

For illustration consider the transition $\mathbf{e} \equiv (\mathbf{21}, \mathbf{21'})$ of Figure 6. While $\mathbf{e_0}$ is the only transition, which statically precedes this transition, its execution may be interleaved with all transitions of the shadowed components.

Program Paths of Parallel Program Models

As mentioned already, the interleaving semantics reduces parallel programs to (much larger) nondeterministic sequential programs representing all the possible interleavings explicitly (cf. [HU]). Paths in these nondeterministic 'product programs' model the possible executions of a parallel program model. We therefore define that an edge sequence of a parallel program model is a *parallel path* iff it is a path in the corresponding nondeterministic sequential product program, and we denote the set of all parallel paths from m to n by $\mathbf{PP}_{T^*}[m, n]$.[7]

[7] In [KSV1] an alternative and technically much more complicated definition was given for parallel flow graphs.

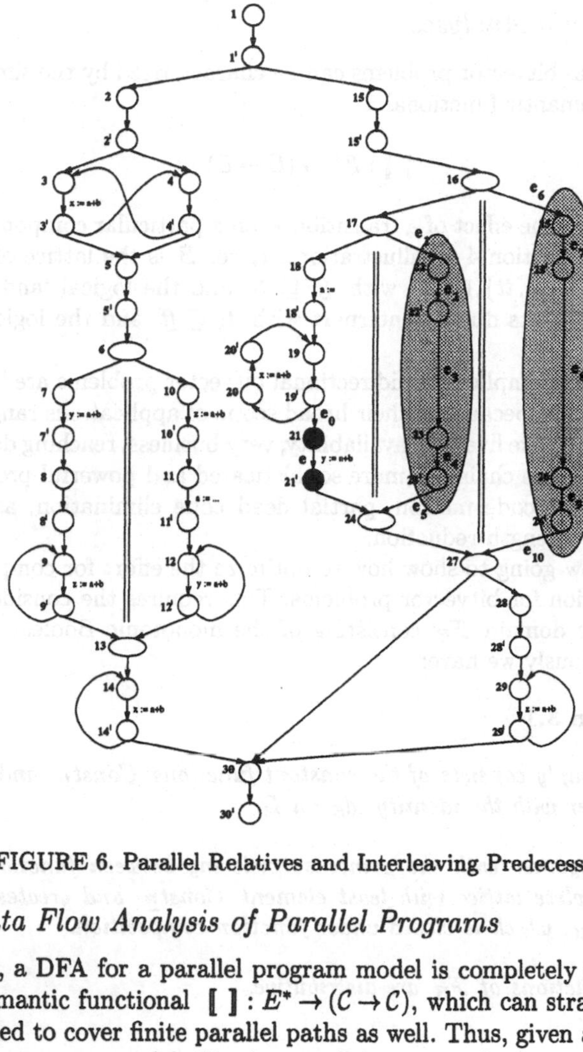

FIGURE 6. Parallel Relatives and Interleaving Predecessors

3.2 Data Flow Analysis of Parallel Programs

As before, a DFA for a parallel program model is completely specified by a local semantic functional $[\![\ ]\!] : E^* \rightarrow (\mathcal{C} \rightarrow \mathcal{C})$, which can straightforward be extended to cover finite parallel paths as well. Thus, given a state n of a parallel program model T^*, the parallel version of the 'desired' *MOP*-solution is given by:

The *PMOP*-Solution:

$$\forall n \in N^* \ \forall c_0 \in \mathcal{C}.\ PMOP_{(T^*, [\![\ ]\!])}(n)(c_0) = \bigsqcap \{ [\![p]\!](c_0) \mid p \in \mathbf{PP}_{T^*}[\mathbf{s}^*, n] \}$$

Note that the corresponding nondeterministic product program would allow us to straightforward adapt the sequential situation with all its results. However, the involved potentially exponential product construction is unacceptable in practice. Fortunately, as we will see in the next section, for bitvector problems there exists an elegant and efficient way out.

3.3 Bitvector Analyses

Unidirectional bitvector problems can be characterized by the simplicity of their local semantic functional

$$[\![\ ]\!] : E^* \to (\mathcal{B} \to \mathcal{B})$$

which specifies the effect of a transition e on a particular component of the bitvector (cf. Section 4 for illustration). Here, $\mathcal{B}$ is the lattice of Boolean truth values $(\{ff, tt\}, \sqcap, \sqsubseteq)$ with $ff \sqsubseteq tt$ and the logical 'and' as meet operation $\sqcap$, or its dual counterpart with $tt \sqsubseteq ff$ and the logical 'or' as meet operation $\sqcap$.

Despite their simplicity, unidirectional bitvector problems are highly relevant in practice because of their broad scope of applications ranging from simple analyses like liveness, availability, very business, reaching definitions, and definition-use chains to more sophisticated and powerful program optimizations like code motion, partial dead code elimination, assignment motion, and strength reduction.

We are now going to show how to optimize the effort for computing the *PMOP*-solution for bitvector problems. This requires the consideration of the semantic domain $\mathcal{F}_\mathcal{B}$ consisting of the monotonic Boolean functions $\mathcal{B} \to \mathcal{B}$. Obviously we have:

Proposition 3.1

1. *$\mathcal{F}_\mathcal{B}$ simply consists of the constant functions $Const_{tt}$ and $Const_{ff}$, together with the identity $Id_\mathcal{B}$ on $\mathcal{B}$.*

2. *$\mathcal{F}_\mathcal{B}$, together with the pointwise ordering between functions, forms a complete lattice with least element $Const_{ff}$ and greatest element $Const_{tt}$, which is closed under function composition.*

3. *All functions of $\mathcal{F}_\mathcal{B}$ are distributive.*

The key to the efficient computation of the 'interleaving effect' is based on the following simple observation, which pinpoints the specific nature of a domain of functions that only consists of constant functions and the identity on an arbitrary set M.

Lemma 3.2 (Main-Lemma)
Let $f_i : \mathcal{F}_\mathcal{B} \to \mathcal{F}_\mathcal{B}$, $1 \leq i \leq q$, $q \in \mathbb{N}$, be functions from $\mathcal{F}_\mathcal{B}$ to $\mathcal{F}_\mathcal{B}$. Then we have:

$$\exists k \in \{1, \ldots, q\}.\ f_q \circ \ldots \circ f_2 \circ f_1 = f_k \ \wedge\ \forall j \in \{k+1, \ldots, q\}.\ f_j = Id_\mathcal{B}$$

Interference

The relevance of this lemma for our application is that it restricts the way of possible interference within a parallel program model: each possible interference is due to a single transition within a parallel component. Combining this observation with the fact that for $e' \in \mathit{ItlvgPred}_{T^*}(e)$, there exists a parallel path, where e' is directly executed after e, we obtain that the potential of interference, which in general would be given in terms of paths, is fully characterized by the set $\mathit{ItlvgPred}_{T^*}(e)$. In fact, considering the computation of universal properties that are described by maximal fixed points (the computation of minimal fixed points requires the dual argument), the obvious existence of a path to *dest*(e) that does not require the execution of any transition of $\mathit{ItlvgPred}_{T^*}(e)$ implies that the only effect of interference is 'destruction'. This motivates the introduction of the predicate *NotKilled*, which we derive from a predicate *Kills* defined for graphs of $\mathcal{T}_C(T^*)$, which is true for such a graph if it contains a transition e with $[\![e]\!] = \mathit{Const}_{\mathit{ff}}$. Note that this predicate can easily be computed by a statical examination of T^*. Based on *Kills*, we now define the desired:

$$\mathit{NotKilled}(n) =_{df} \begin{cases} \bigwedge\{ \neg \mathit{Kills}(T') \mid T' \in \mathit{ParRel}(\mathit{cpm}(n)) \} & \\ \qquad\qquad\qquad \text{if } \mathit{cpm}(n) \in \mathcal{T}_C(T^*) & \\ \mathit{tt} \qquad\qquad\quad \text{otherwise} \end{cases}$$

Intuitively, *NotKilled* indicates that no transition of a parallel relative destroys the property under consideration, i.e. $[\![e']\!] \neq \mathit{Const}_{\mathit{ff}}$ for all $e' \in \mathit{ItlvgPred}_{T^*}(e)$, $e \in \mathit{Trans}(\mathit{cpm}(n))$. Note that only the constant function given by the precomputed value of this predicate is used in Definition 3.5 to model interference, and in fact, Theorem 3.6 guarantees that this modelling is sufficient. Obviously, this predicate is easily and efficiently computable. Algorithm 1.1 computes it as a side result.

Synchronization

Besides taking care of possible interference, we also need to take care of the synchronization required at nodes in N_X^*: control may only leave a parallel statement after all parallel components terminated. The corresponding information can be computed by a hierarchical algorithm that only considers purely sequential program models. The underlying idea coincides with that of interprocedural analysis [KS]: we need to compute the effect of complete subgraphs or in this case of complete parallel components. This information is computed in an 'innermost' fashion and then propagated to the next surrounding parallel statement.[8] The following definition, which is illustrated in Section 4, describes the complete three-step procedure:

[8] Also in [SHW] parallel statements are investigated in an innnermost fashion.

1. Terminate, if T does not contain any parallel statement. Otherwise, select successively all maximal program models T' occurring in a graph of $\mathcal{T_P}(T)$ that do not contain any parallel statement, and determine the effect $[\![T']\!]$ of this (purely sequential) graph according to the equational system of Definition 2.3.

2. Compute the effect $[\![T'']\!]^*$ of the innermost parallel statements T'' of T by

$$[\![T'']\!]^* = \begin{cases} Const_{ff} & \text{if } \exists T' \in \mathcal{T_C}(T'').\ [\![end(T')]\!] = Const_{ff} \\ Id_{\mathcal{B}} & \text{if } \forall T' \in \mathcal{T_C}(T'').\ [\![end(T')]\!] = Id_{\mathcal{B}} \\ Const_{tt} & \text{otherwise} \end{cases}$$

3. Transform T by replacing all innermost parallel statements $T'' = (N'', E'', \mathbf{s}'', \mathbf{e}'')$ by $(\{\mathbf{s}'', \mathbf{e}''\}, \{(\mathbf{s}'', \mathbf{e}'')\}, \mathbf{s}'', \mathbf{e}'')$, define the local semantics of $(\mathbf{s}'', \mathbf{e}'')$ by $[\![T'']\!]^*$, and set the predicate $Kills(\mathbf{s}'')$ to tt, if one of the start nodes of the parallel components of T'' satisfies the predicate *Kills*, and to ff otherwise. Continue with step 1.

This three-step algorithm is a straightforward hierarchical adaptation of the algorithm for computing the functional version of the *MFP*-solution for the sequential case. Only the second step realizing the synchronization at nodes in N_X^* needs some explanation, which is summarized in the following lemma.

Lemma 3.3 *The PMOP-solution of a parallel program model $T \in \mathcal{T_P}(T^*)$ that only consists of purely sequential parallel components $T_1, \ldots, T_k$ is given by:*

$$PMOP_{(T,[\![\ ]\!])}(end(T)) = \begin{cases} Const_{ff} & \text{if } \exists 1 \le i \le k.\ [\![end(T_i)]\!] = Const_{ff} \\ Id_{\mathcal{B}} & \text{if } \forall 1 \le i \le k.\ [\![end(T_i)]\!] = Id_{\mathcal{B}} \\ Const_{tt} & \text{otherwise} \end{cases}$$

Also the proof of this lemma is a consequence of Main Lemma 3.2. As a single transition is responsible for the entire effect of a path, the effect of each complete path through a parallel statement is already given by the projection of this path onto the parallel component containing the vital transition. Thus in order to model the effect (or *PMOP*-solution) of a parallel statement, it is sufficient to combine the effects of all paths local to the components, a fact, which is formalized in Lemma 3.3.

Now the following theorem can be proved by means of a straightforward inductive extension of the functional version of the sequential Coincidence Theorem 2.2, which is tailored to cover complete paths, i.e. paths going from the start to the end of a parallel statement:

Theorem 3.4 (The Hierarchical Coincidence Theorem)
Let $T \in \mathcal{T}_{\mathcal{P}}(T^*)$ be a parallel program model, and $[\![\ ]\!] : E^* \to \mathcal{F}_{\mathcal{B}}$ a local semantic functional. Then we have:

$$PMOP_{(T,[\![\ ]\!])}(end(T)) = [\![\, T \,]\!]^*$$

After this hierarchical preprocess the following modification of the equation system for sequential bitvector analyses leads to optimal results:

Definition 3.5 *The functional $[\![\ ]\!] : N^* \to \mathcal{F}_{\mathcal{B}}$ is defined as the greatest solution of the equation system given by:*[9]

$$[\![\, n \,]\!] = \begin{cases} Id_{\mathcal{B}} & \text{if } n = \mathbf{s}^* \\ [\![\, ppm(n) \,]\!]^* \circ [\![\, start(ppm(n)) \,]\!] \sqcap Const_{NotKilled(n)} & \text{if } n \in N^*_X \\ \bigsqcap \{ [\![\, (m,n) \,]\!] \circ [\![\, m \,]\!] \mid m \in pred_{T^*}(n) \} \sqcap Const_{NotKilled(n)} & \text{otherwise} \end{cases}$$

This allows us to define the $PMFP_{BV}$-solution, a fixed point solution for the bitvector case, in the following fashion:

The $PMFP_{BV}$-Solution:

$PMFP_{BV(T^*,[\![\ ]\!])} : N^* \to \mathcal{F}_{\mathcal{B}}$ defined by

$$\forall n \in N^*\ \forall b \in \mathcal{B}.\ PMFP_{BV(T^*,[\![\ ]\!])}(n)(b) = [\![\, n \,]\!](b)$$

As in the sequential case the $PMFP_{BV}$-solution is practically relevant, because it can efficiently be computed (see Algorithm 1.1 in Appendix 1). The following theorem now establishes that it coincides with the desired *PMOP*-solution.

Theorem 3.6 (The Parallel Bitvector Coincidence Theorem)
Let $T^* = (N^*, E^*, \mathbf{s}^*, \mathbf{e}^*)$ be a parallel program model, and $[\![\ ]\!] : E^* \to \mathcal{F}_{\mathcal{B}}$ a local semantic functional. Then we have that the PMOP-solution and the $PMFP_{BV}$-solution coincide, i.e.,

$$\forall n \in N^*.\ PMOP_{(T^*,[\![\ ]\!])}(n) = PMFP_{BV(T^*,[\![\ ]\!])}(n)$$

---

[9] Note that $[\![\ ]\!]$ is the straightforward extension of the functional defined in Definition 2.3. Thus the overloading of notation is harmless, as no reference to the sequential version is made in this definition.

Intuitively, the (sequential) Coincidence Theorem 2.2 can be read as that unidirectional distributive data flow analysis problems allow to model the confluence of control flow by merging the corresponding data flow informations during the iterative computation of the *MFP*-solution without losing accuracy. The intuition behind the Parallel Bitvector Coincidence Theorem 3.6 is the same, only the correspondence between control flow and program representation is more complicated due to the interleaving and synchronization effects.

4 Application: Code Motion

In this section we demonstrate the practicality of our framework by sketching a *code motion* algorithm, which is unique in placing the computations of a parallel program ***computationally optimally***. The power of this algorithm, which evolves as the straightforward extension of its sequential counterpart, the ***busy code motion*** transformation of [KRS2], is illustrated by means of the example of Figure 3, where our algorithm achieves the optimization result of Figure 7. It eliminates the partially redundant computations of $a+b$ at the nodes **3**, **10**, **12**, **14**, **20**, **21**, **29** by moving them to the nodes **2**, **11** and **18**, but it does not touch the partially redundant computations of $a+b$ at the nodes **7** and **9**, which cannot safely be eliminated.

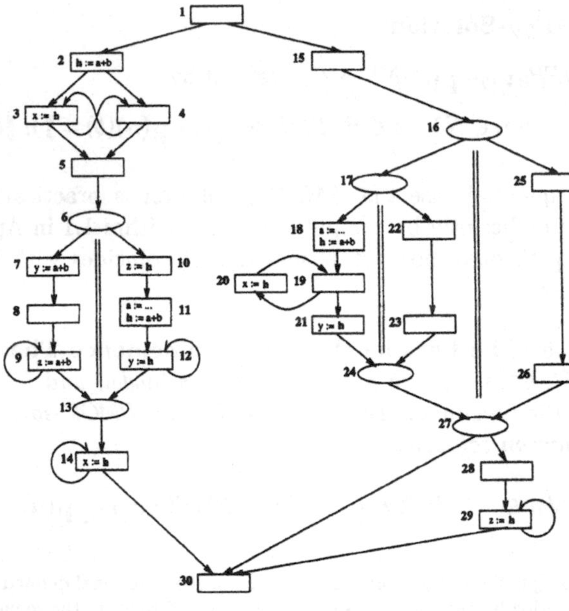

FIGURE 7. The Result of the BCM_{PP}-Transformation

Intuitively, code motion improves the run-time efficiency of a program by avoiding unnecessary recomputations of values at run-time. This is achieved by replacing the original computations of a program by temporaries that are initialized at certain program points. For sequential programs it is well-known that placing the computations ***as early as possible*** in a program, while maintaining its semantics, leads to computationally optimal results (cf. [KRS1, KRS2]). This carries over to the parallel setting.

As in the sequential case the as-early-as-possible placement of computations requires the computation of the set of program points where a computation is *up-safe* and *down-safe*, i.e., where it has been computed on every program path reaching the program point under consideration, and where it will be computed on every program continuation reaching the program's end node.[10] For the ease of presentation we assume here that parallel statements of the argument program are free of 'recursive' assignments, i.e., assignments whose left hand side variable occurs in its right hand side term.[11] The DFA-problems for up-safety and down-safety are then specified by the local semantic functionals $[\![\ ]\!]_{us}$ and $[\![\ ]\!]_{ds}$, where *Comp* and *Transp* are two local predicates, which are true for a transition e with respect to a computation t, if t occurs in the right hand side term of the statement of e, and if no operand of t is modified by it, respectively.

$$[\![e]\!]_{us} =_{df} \begin{cases} Const_{tt} & \text{if } Transp(e) \wedge Comp(e) \\ Id_{\mathcal{B}} & \text{if } Transp(e) \wedge \neg Comp(e) \\ Const_{ff} & \text{otherwise} \end{cases}$$

$$[\![e]\!]_{ds} =_{df} \begin{cases} Const_{tt} & \text{if } Comp(e) \\ Id_{\mathcal{B}} & \text{if } \neg Comp(e) \wedge Transp(e) \\ Const_{ff} & \text{otherwise} \end{cases}$$

It is worth noting that these are the very same functionals as in the sequential case because the effect of interference is completely taken care of by the corresponding versions of the predicate *NotKilled*, which are automatically derived from the definitions of the local semantic functionals.

Moreover, the functionals can directly be fed into the generic Algorithm 1.1 for computing the *PMFP*-solutions of down-safety and up-safety, as illustrated in Figure 8. As in the sequential case, down-safe start states are 'earliest', as well as other down-safe but not not up-safe states that

---

[10] Up-safety and down-safety are also known as ***availability*** and ***anticipability (very business)***, respectively.

[11] Recursive assignments can also be handled but require a slightly refined treatment.

either possess an 'unsafe' predecessor (see node **2**) or an incoming transition modifying an operand of the computation under consideration (see nodes **11′** and **18′**).

After inserting an initialization statement at each earliest state, all original computations belonging to transitions with a safe source state can be *replaced* by the corresponding temporary, as illustrated in Figure 8. This transformation results in the promised parallel program of Figure 7, which is indeed computationally optimal with respect to $a + b$.

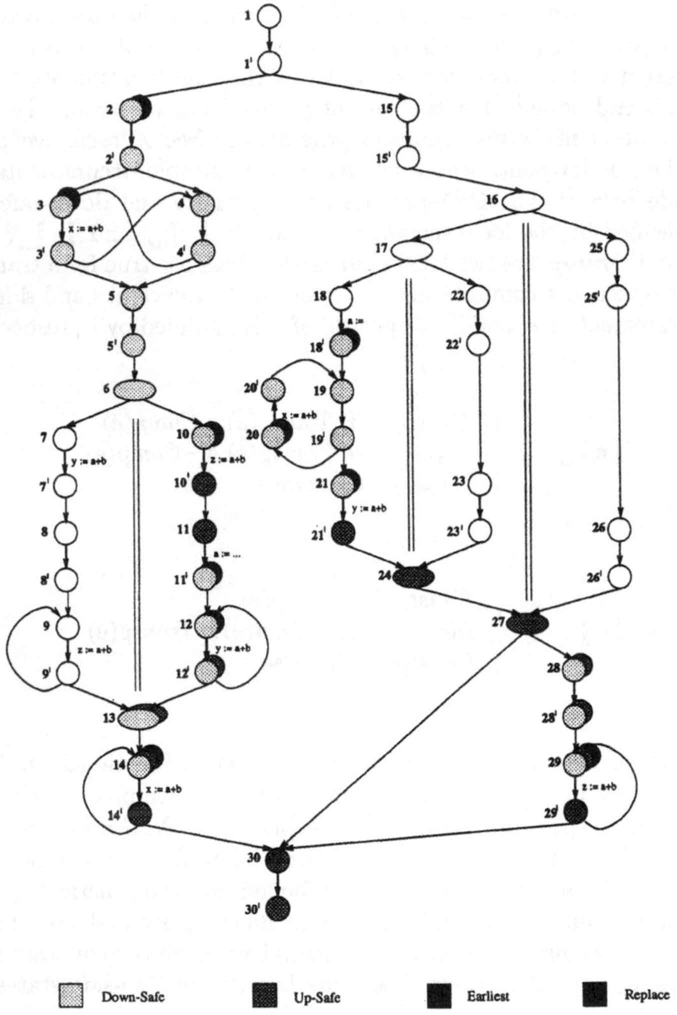

FIGURE 8. Down-Safe, Up-Safe, Earliest, and Replacement Points of $a + b$

5 Conclusions

We have shown how to construct for unidirectional bitvector problems optimal analysis algorithms for parallel programs with shared memory that are as efficient as their purely sequential counterparts, and which can easily be implemented. At the first sight, the existence of such an algorithm is rather surprising, as the interleaving semantics underlying our programming language is an indication for an exponential effort. However, the restriction to bitvector analysis constrains the possible ways of interference in such a way, that we could construct a generic fixed point algorithm that directly works on the parallel program without taking any interleavings into account. This algorithm is implemented on the *Fixpoint Analysis Machine* of [SCKKM]. Moreover, the 'lazy' variant (cf. [KRS1, KRS2]) of the code motion transformation of Section 4 is implemented in the ESPRIT project COMPARE #5933 [Vo1, Vo2].

6 References

[CC1] Cousot, P., and Cousot, R. Abstract interpretation: A unified lattice model for static analysis of programs by construction or approximation of fixpoints. In *Conference Record of the 4th International Symposium on Principles of Programming Languages (POPL'77)*, Los Angeles, California, 1977, 238 - 252.

[CC2] Cousot, P., and Cousot, R. Invariance proof methods and analysis techniques for parallel programs. In *Biermann, A. W., Guiho, G., and Kodratoff, Y. (eds.) Automatic Program Construction Techniques*, chapter 12, 243 - 271, Macmillan Publishing Company, 1984.

[CH1] Chow, J.-H., and Harrison, W. L. Compile time analysis of parallel programs that share memory. In *Conference Record of the 19th International Symposium on Principles of Programming Languages (POPL'92)*, Albuquerque, New Mexico, 1992, 130 - 141.

[CH2] Chow, J.-H., and Harrison, W. L. State Space Reduction in Abstract Interpretation of Parallel Programs. In *Proceedings of the International Conference on Computer Languages, (ICCL'94)*, Toulouse, France, May 16-19, 1994, 277-288.

[DBDS] Duri, S., Buy, U., Devarapalli, R., and Shatz, S. M. Using state space methods for deadlock analysis in Ada tasking. In *Proceedings of the ACM SIGSOFT'93 International Symposium on Software Testing and Analysis, Software Engineering Notes 18*, 3 (1993), 51 - 60.

[DC] Dwyer, M. B., and Clarke, L. A. Data flow analysis for verifying properties of concurrent programs. In *Proceedings of the 2nd ACM SIGSOFT'94 Symposium on Foundations of Software Engineering (SIGSOFT'94)*, New Orleans, Lousiana, *Software Engineering Notes 19*, 5 (1994), 62 - 75.

[DRZ] Dhamdhere, D. M., Rosen, B. K., and Zadeck, F. K. How to analyze large programs efficiently and informatively. In *Proceedings of the ACM*

SIGPLAN'92 Conference on Programming Language Design and Implementation (PLDI'92), San Francisco, California, *SIGPLAN Notices 27*, 7 (1992), 212 - 223.

[DS] Drechsler, K.-H., and Stadel, M. P. A variation of Knoop, Rüthing and Steffen's LAZY CODE MOTION. *SIGPLAN Notices 28*, 5 (1993), 29 - 38.

[GS] Grunwald, D., and Srinivasan, H. Data flow equations for explicitely parallel programs. In *Proceedings of the ACM SIGPLAN Symposium on Principles of Parallel Programming (PPOPP'93)*, *SIGPLAN Notices 28*, 7 (1993).

[GW] Godefroid, P., and Wolper, P. Using partial orders for the efficient verification of deadlock freedom and safety properties. In *Proceedings of the 3rd International Workshop on Computer Aided Verification (CAV'91)*, Aalborg, Denmark, Springer-Verlag, LNCS 575 (1991), 332 - 342.

[He] Hecht, M. S. Flow analysis of computer programs. Elsevier, North-Holland, 1977.

[HU] Hopcroft, J. E., and Ullman, J. E. Introduction to automata theory, languages, and computation. Addison-Wesley, Reading, Massach., 1979.

[Ki1] Kildall, G. A. Global expression optimization during compilation. Ph.D. dissertation, Technical Report No. 72-06-02, University of Washington, Computer Science Group, Seattle, Washington, 1972.

[Ki2] Kildall, G. A. A unified approach to global program optimization. In *Conference Record of the 1st ACM Symposium on Principles of Programming Languages (POPL'73)*, Boston, Massachusetts, 1973, 194 - 206.

[KRS1] Knoop, J., Rüthing, O., and Steffen, B. Lazy code motion. In *Proceedings of the ACM SIGPLAN'92 Conference on Programming Language Design and Implementation (PLDI'92)*, San Francisco, California, *SIGPLAN Notices 27*, 7 (1992), 224 - 234.

[KRS2] Knoop, J., Rüthing, O., and Steffen, B. Optimal code motion: Theory and practice. *Transactions on Programming Languages and Systems 16*, 4 (1994), 1117 - 1155.

[KRS3] Knoop, J., Rüthing, O., and Steffen, B. Partial dead code elimination. In *Proceedings of the ACM SIGPLAN'94 Conference on Programming Language Design and Implementation (PLDI'94)*, Orlando, Florida, *SIGPLAN Notices 29*, 6 (1994), 147 - 158.

[KRS4] Knoop, J., Rüthing, O., and Steffen, B. The power of assignment motion. In *Proceedings of the ACM SIGPLAN'95 Conference on Programming Language Design and Implementation (PLDI'95)*, La Jolla, California, *SIGPLAN Notices 30*, 6 (1995), 233 - 245.

[KRS5] Knoop, J., Rüthing, O., and Steffen, B. Lazy strength reduction. *Journal of Programming Languages 1*, 1 (1993), 71 - 91.

[KS] Knoop, J., and Steffen, B. The interprocedural coincidence theorem. In *Proceedings of the 4th International Conference on Compiler Construction (CC'92)*, Paderborn, Germany, Springer-Verlag, LNCS 641 (1992), 125 - 140.

[KSV1] Knoop, J., Steffen, B., and Vollmer, J. Parallelism for free: Efficient and optimal bitvector analyses for parallel programs. In *Preliminary Proceedings of the 1st International Workshop on Tools and Algorithms for the Construction and Analysis of Systems (TACAS'95)*, Aarhus, Denmark, BRICS Notes Series NS-95-2 (1995), 319 - 333.

[KSV2] Knoop, J., Steffen, B., and Vollmer, J. Optimal code motion for parallel programs. Fakultät für Mathematik und Informatik, Universität Passau, Germany, MIP-Bericht 9511 (1995), 30 pages.

[KU] Kam, J. B., and Ullman, J. D. Monotone data flow analysis frameworks. *Acta Informatica 7*, (1977), 309 - 317.

[LC] Long, D., and Clarke, L. A. Data flow analysis of concurrent systems that use the rendezvous model of synchronization. In *Proceedings of the ACM SIGSOFT'91 Symposium on Testing, Analysis, and Verification (TAV4)*, Victoria, British Columbia, *Software Engineering Notes 16*, (1991), 21- 35.

[Ma] Marriot, K. Frameworks for abstract interpretation. *Acta Informatica 30*, (1993), 103 - 129.

[McD] McDowell, C. E. A practical algorithm for static analysis of parallel programs. *Journal of Parallel and Distributed Computing 6*, 3 (1989), 513 - 536.

[MJ] Muchnick, S. S., and Jones, N. D. (Eds.). Program flow analysis: Theory and applications. Prentice Hall, Englewood Cliffs, New Jersey, 1981.

[MP] Midkiff, S. P., and Padua, D. A. Issues in the optimization of parallel programs. In *Proceedings of the International Conference on Parallel Processing, Volume II*, St. Charles, Illinois, (1990), 105 - 113.

[St] Steffen, B. Generating data flow analysis algorithms from modal specifications. *Science of Computer Programming 21*, (1993), 115 - 139.

[SCKKM] Steffen, B., Claßen, A., Klein, M., Knoop, J., and Margaria, T. The fixpoint-analysis machine. In *Proceedings of the 6th International Conference on Concurrency Theory (CONCUR'95)*, Philadelphia, Pennsylvania, Springer-Verlag, LNCS 962 (1995), 72 - 87.

[SHW] Srinivasan, H., Hook, J., and Wolfe, M. Static single assignment form for explicitly parallel programs. In *Conference Record of the 20th ACM SIGPLAN Symposium on Principles of Programming Languages (POPL'93)*, Charleston, South Carolina, 1993, 260 - 272.

[SP] Sharir, M., and Pnueli, A. Two approaches to interprocedural data flow analysis. In [MJ], 1981, 189 - 233.

[SW] Srinivasan, H., and Wolfe, M. Analyzing programs with explicit parallelism. In *Proceedings of the 4th International Conference on Languages and Compilers for Parallel Computing*, Santa Clara, California, Springer-Verlag, LNCS 589 (1991), 405 - 419.

[Va] Valmari, A. A stubborn attack on state explosion. In *Proceedings of the 2nd International Conference on Computer Aided Verification*, New Brunswick, New Jersey, Springer-Verlag, LNCS 531 (1990), 156 - 165.

[Vo1] Vollmer, J. Data flow equations for parallel programs that share memory. Tech. Rep. 2.11.1 of the ESPRIT Project COMPARE #5933, Fakultät für Informatik, Universität Karlsruhe, Germany, (1994).

[Vo2] Vollmer, J. Data flow analysis of parallel programs. In *Proceedings of the IFIP WG 10.3 Working Conference on Parallel Architectures and Compilation Techniques (PACT'95)*, Limassol, Cyprus, 1995, 168 - 177.

[WS] Wolfe, M, and Srinivasan, H. Data structures for optimizing programs with explicit parallelism. In *Proceedings of the 1st International Conference of the Austrian Center for Parallel Computation*, Salzburg, Austria, Springer-Verlag, LNCS 591 (1991), 139 - 156.

1 Computing the $PMFP_{BV}$-Solution

Algorithm 1.1 (Computing the $PMFP_{BV}$-Solution)

Input: *A parallel program model $T^* = (N^*, E^*, \mathbf{s}^*, \mathbf{e}^*)$, a local semantic functional $[\![\ ]\!] : E^* \rightarrow \mathcal{F}_{\mathcal{B}}$, a function $f_{init} \in \mathcal{F}_{\mathcal{B}}$ and a Boolean value $b_{init} \in \mathcal{B}$, where f_{init} and b_{init} reflect the assumptions on the context in which the program model under consideration is called. Usually, f_{init} and b_{init} are given by $Id_{\mathcal{B}}$ and $f\!f$, respectively.*

Output: *An annotation of T^* with functions $[\![T]\!]^* \in \mathcal{F}_{\mathcal{B}}$, $T \in \mathcal{T}_{\mathcal{P}}(T^*)$, representing the semantic functions computed in step 2 of the three-step procedure of Section 3.3, and with functions $[\![n]\!] \in \mathcal{F}_{\mathcal{B}}$, $n \in N^*$, representing the greatest solution of the equation system of Definition 3.5. In fact, after the termination of the algorithm the functional $[\![\ ]\!]$ satisfies:*

$$\forall\, n \in N^*.\ [\![n]\!] = PMFP_{BV\,(T^*,[\![\ ]\!])}(n) = PMOP_{(T^*,[\![\ ]\!])}(n)$$

Remark: *The global variables $[\![T]\!]^*$, $T \in \mathcal{T}_{\mathcal{C}}(T^*)$, each of which is storing a function of $\mathcal{F}_{\mathcal{B}}$, are used for storing the global effects of component graphs of graphs $T \in \mathcal{T}_{\mathcal{P}}(T^*)$ during the hierarchical computation of the $PMFP_{BV}$-solution. The global variables $Kills(start(T))$, $T \in \mathcal{T}_{\mathcal{C}}(T^*)$, store whether T contains a transition e with $[\![e]\!] = Const_{f\!f}$. These variables are used to compute the value of the predicate NotKilled of Section 3.3. Moreover, every program model $T \in \mathcal{T}_{\mathcal{P}}(T^*)$ is assumed to have a* rank, *which is recursively defined by:*

$$rank(T) =_{df} \begin{cases} 0 & \text{if } T \in \mathcal{T}_{\mathcal{P}}^{min}(T^*) \\ max\{\, rank(T') \mid T' \in \mathcal{T}_{\mathcal{P}}(T^*) \wedge T' \subset T \,\} + 1 & \text{otherwise} \end{cases}$$

where $\mathcal{T}_{\mathcal{P}}^{min}(T^*) =_{df} \{\, T \in \mathcal{T}_{\mathcal{P}}(T^*) \mid \forall T' \in \mathcal{T}_{\mathcal{P}}(T^*).\ T' \subseteq T \Rightarrow T' = T \,\}$ denotes the set of minimal *graphs of $\mathcal{T}_{\mathcal{P}}(T^*)$. Finally, $succ_T(n) =_{df} \{\, m \mid (n, m) \in E^* \,\}$*

denotes the set of all immediate successors of a state n of a parallel program model T, and MFP denotes the standard procedure for computing the MFP-solution in the sequential case.

```
BEGIN
  ( Synchronization: Computing [[T]]* for all T ∈ T_P(T*) )
  GLOBEFF(T*, [ ]);

  ( Interleaving: Computing the PMFP_BV-Solution [[n]] for all n ∈ N* )
  PMFP_BV(T*, [ ], f_init, b_init)
END.

where

PROCEDURE GLOBEFF (T = (N, E, s, e) : ParallelProgramModel;
                   [ ] : E → F_B  : LocalSemanticFunctional);
VAR i : integer;
BEGIN
  FOR i := 0 TO rank(T) DO
    FORALL T' ∈ {T'' | T'' ∈ T_P(T) ∧ rank(T'') = i} DO
      FORALL T'' ≡ (N'', E'', s'', e'') ∈ {T'''_seq | T''' ∈ T_C(T')} DO
        LET ∀e ∈ E''. [e]'' = { [[ppm(dest(e))]]*   if e ∈ N*_N × N*_X
                              { [e]                 otherwise
          BEGIN
            Kills(start(T'')) := ( |{n ∈ N'' | Kills(n)}| ≥ 1 ) ∨
                                 ( |{e ∈ E'' | [e]'' = Const_ff}| ≥ 1 );
            MFP(T'', [ ]'', Id_B);
            [[T'']]* := [[end(T'')]]
          END
      OD;
                   { Const_ff   if ∃T'' ∈ T_C(T'). [[T''_seq]]* = Const_ff
      [[T']]* :=   { Id_B       if ∀T'' ∈ T_C(T'). [[T''_seq]]* = Id_B
                   { Const_tt   otherwise
    OD
  OD
END.

PROCEDURE PMFP_BV (T = (N, E, s, e) : ParallelProgramModel;
                   [ ] : E → F_B  : LocalSemanticFunctional;
                   f_start : F_B;  IsKilled : B);
VAR f : F_B;
BEGIN
  IF IsKilled THEN FORALL n ∈ N DO [[n]] := Const_ff OD
  ELSE
    (Initialization of the annotation arrays [[ ]] and the variable workset)
    FORALL n ∈ States(T_seq)\{s} DO
              { Const_ff   if ∃e ∈ E. dest(e) = n ∧ [e] = Const_ff
      [[n]] := { Const_tt   otherwise
    OD;
```

```
[[ s ]] := f_start;
workset := { n ∈ States(T_seq) | n ∈ N*_N ∪ {s} ∨ [[ n ]] = Const_ff };

(Iterative fixed point computation)
WHILE workset ≠ ∅ DO
    LET n ∈ workset
        BEGIN
            workset := workset\{ n };
            IF n ∈ N\N*_N
                THEN
                    FORALL m ∈ succ_T(n) DO
                        f := [[ (n,m) ]]‾ ∘ [[ n ]];
                        IF [[ m ]] ⊐ f
                            THEN
                                [[ m ]] := f;
                                workset := workset ∪ { m }
                        FI
                    OD
                ELSE
                    FORALL T' ∈ T_C(ppm(n)) DO
                      PMFP_BV(T', [[ ]]‾, [[ n ]],     Σ_{T'' ∈ T_C(ppm(n))\{T'}} Kills(start(T'')) )
                    OD;
                    f := [[ ppm(n) ]]* ∘ [[ n ]];
                    IF [[ end(ppm(n)) ]] ⊐ f
                        THEN
                            [[ end(ppm(n)) ]] := f;
                            workset := workset ∪ { end(ppm(n)) }
                    FI
            FI
        END
    OD
  FI
END.
```

Let $[\![n]\!]_{alg}$, $n \in N^*$, denote the final values of the corresponding variables after the termination of Algorithm 1.1, and $[\![n]\!]$, $n \in N^*$, the greatest solution of the equation system of Definition 3.5, then we have:

Theorem 1.2 $\forall n \in N^*.\ [\![n]\!]_{alg} = [\![n]\!]$

Author Index

Lecture Notes in Computer Science

For information about Vols. 1–945

please contact your bookseller or Springer-Verlag

Vol. 946: C. Froidevaux, J. Kohlas (Eds.), Symbolic and Quantitative Approaches to Reasoning and Uncertainty. Proceedings, 1995. X, 420 pages. 1995. (Subseries LNAI).

Vol. 947: B. Möller (Ed.), Mathematics of Program Construction. Proceedings, 1995. VIII, 472 pages. 1995.

Vol. 948: G. Cohen, M. Giusti, T. Mora (Eds.), Applied Algebra, Algebraic Algorithms and Error-Correcting Codes. Proceedings, 1995. XI, 485 pages. 1995.

Vol. 949: D.G. Feitelson, L. Rudolph (Eds.), Job Scheduling Strategies for Parallel Processing. Proceedings, 1995. VIII, 361 pages. 1995.

Vol. 950: A. De Santis (Ed.), Advances in Cryptology - EUROCRYPT '94. Proceedings, 1994. XIII, 473 pages. 1995.

Vol. 951: M.J. Egenhofer, J.R. Herring (Eds.), Advances in Spatial Databases. Proceedings, 1995. XI, 405 pages. 1995.

Vol. 952: W. Olthoff (Ed.), ECOOP '95 - Object-Oriented Programming. Proceedings, 1995. XI, 471 pages. 1995.

Vol. 953: D. Pitt, D.E. Rydeheard, P. Johnstone (Eds.), Category Theory and Computer Science. Proceedings, 1995. VII, 252 pages. 1995.

Vol. 954: G. Ellis, R. Levinson, W. Rich, J.F. Sowa (Eds.), Conceptual Structures: Applications, Implementation and Theory. Proceedings, 1995. IX, 353 pages. 1995. (Subseries LNAI).

Vol. 955: S.G. Akl, F. Dehne, J.-R. Sack, N. Santoro (Eds.), Algorithms and Data Structures. Proceedings, 1995. IX, 519 pages. 1995.

Vol. 956: X. Yao (Ed.), Progress in Evolutionary Computation. Proceedings, 1993, 1994. VIII, 314 pages. 1995. (Subseries LNAI).

Vol. 957: C. Castelfranchi, J.-P. Müller (Eds.), From Reaction to Cognition. Proceedings, 1993. VI, 252 pages. 1995. (Subseries LNAI).

Vol. 958: J. Calmet, J.A. Campbell (Eds.), Integrating Symbolic Mathematical Computation and Artificial Intelligence. Proceedings, 1994. X, 275 pages. 1995.

Vol. 959: D.-Z. Du, M. Li (Eds.), Computing and Combinatorics. Proceedings, 1995. XIII, 654 pages. 1995.

Vol. 960: D. Leivant (Ed.), Logic and Computational Complexity. Proceedings, 1994. VIII, 514 pages. 1995.

Vol. 961: K.P. Jantke, S. Lange (Eds.), Algorithmic Learning for Knowledge-Based Systems. X, 511 pages. 1995. (Subseries LNAI).

Vol. 962: I. Lee, S.A. Smolka (Eds.), CONCUR '95: Concurrency Theory. Proceedings, 1995. X, 547 pages. 1995.

Vol. 963: D. Coppersmith (Ed.), Advances in Cryptology - CRYPTO '95. Proceedings, 1995. XII, 467 pages. 1995.

Vol. 964: V. Malyshkin (Ed.), Parallel Computing Technologies. Proceedings, 1995. XII, 497 pages. 1995.

Vol. 965: H. Reichel (Ed.), Fundamentals of Computation Theory. Proceedings, 1995. IX, 433 pages. 1995.

Vol. 966: S. Haridi, K. Ali, P. Magnusson (Eds.), EURO-PAR '95 Parallel Processing. Proceedings, 1995. XV, 734 pages. 1995.

Vol. 967: J.P. Bowen, M.G. Hinchey (Eds.), ZUM '95: The Z Formal Specification Notation. Proceedings, 1995. XI, 571 pages. 1995.

Vol. 968: N. Dershowitz, N. Lindenstrauss (Eds.), Conditional and Typed Rewriting Systems. Proceedings, 1994. VIII, 375 pages. 1995.

Vol. 969: J. Wiedermann, P. Hájek (Eds.), Mathematical Foundations of Computer Science 1995. Proceedings, 1995. XIII, 588 pages. 1995.

Vol. 970: V. Hlaváč, R. Šára (Eds.), Computer Analysis of Images and Patterns. Proceedings, 1995. XVIII, 960 pages. 1995.

Vol. 971: E.T. Schubert, P.J. Windley, J. Alves-Foss (Eds.), Higher Order Logic Theorem Proving and Its Applications. Proceedings, 1995. VIII, 400 pages. 1995.

Vol. 972: J.-M. Hélary, M. Raynal (Eds.), Distributed Algorithms. Proceedings, 1995. XI, 333 pages. 1995.

Vol. 973: H.H. Adelsberger, J. Lažanský, V. Mařík (Eds.), Information Management in Computer Integrated Manufacturing. IX, 665 pages. 1995.

Vol. 974: C. Braccini, L. DeFloriani, G. Vernazza (Eds.), Image Analysis and Processing. Proceedings, 1995. XIX, 757 pages. 1995.

Vol. 975: W. Moore, W. Luk (Eds.), Field-Programmable Logic and Applications. Proceedings, 1995. XI, 448 pages. 1995.

Vol. 976: U. Montanari, F. Rossi (Eds.), Principles and Practice of Constraint Programming — CP '95. Proceedings, 1995. XIII, 651 pages. 1995.

Vol. 977: H. Beilner, F. Bause (Eds.), Quantitative Evaluation of Computing and Communication Systems. Proceedings, 1995. X, 415 pages. 1995.

Vol. 978: N. Revell, A M. Tjoa (Eds.), Database and Expert Systems Applications. Proceedings, 1995. XV, 654 pages. 1995.

Vol. 979: P. Spirakis (Ed.), Algorithms — ESA '95. Proceedings, 1995. XII, 598 pages. 1995.

Vol. 980: A. Ferreira, J. Rolim (Eds.), Parallel Algorithms for Irregularly Structured Problems. Proceedings, 1995. IX, 409 pages. 1995.

Lecture Notes in Computer Science

For information about Vols. 1–945

please contact your bookseller or Springer-Verlag

Vol. 946: C. Froidevaux, J. Kohlas (Eds.), Symbolic and Quantitative Approaches to Reasoning and Uncertainty. Proceedings, 1995. X, 420 pages. 1995. (Subseries LNAI).

Vol. 947: B. Möller (Ed.), Mathematics of Program Construction. Proceedings, 1995. VIII, 472 pages. 1995.

Vol. 948: G. Cohen, M. Giusti, T. Mora (Eds.), Applied Algebra, Algebraic Algorithms and Error-Correcting Codes. Proceedings, 1995. XI, 485 pages. 1995.

Vol. 949: D.G. Feitelson, L. Rudolph (Eds.), Job Scheduling Strategies for Parallel Processing. Proceedings, 1995. VIII, 361 pages. 1995.

Vol. 950: A. De Santis (Ed.), Advances in Cryptology - EUROCRYPT '94. Proceedings, 1994. XIII, 473 pages. 1995.

Vol. 951: M.J. Egenhofer, J.R. Herring (Eds.), Advances in Spatial Databases. Proceedings, 1995. XI, 405 pages. 1995.

Vol. 952: W. Olthoff (Ed.), ECOOP '95 - Object-Oriented Programming. Proceedings, 1995. XI, 471 pages. 1995.

Vol. 953: D. Pitt, D.E. Rydeheard, P. Johnstone (Eds.), Category Theory and Computer Science. Proceedings, 1995. VII, 252 pages. 1995.

Vol. 954: G. Ellis, R. Levinson, W. Rich. J.F. Sowa (Eds.), Conceptual Structures: Applications, Implementation and Theory. Proceedings, 1995. IX, 353 pages. 1995. (Subseries LNAI).

VOL. 955: S.G. Akl, F. Dehne, J.-R. Sack, N. Santoro (Eds.), Algorithms and Data Structures. Proceedings, 1995. IX, 519 pages. 1995.

Vol. 956: X. Yao (Ed.), Progress in Evolutionary Computation. Proceedings, 1993, 1994. VIII, 314 pages. 1995. (Subseries LNAI).

Vol. 957: C. Castelfranchi, J.-P. Müller (Eds.), From Reaction to Cognition. Proceedings, 1993. VI, 252 pages. 1995. (Subseries LNAI).

Vol. 958: J. Calmet, J.A. Campbell (Eds.), Integrating Symbolic Mathematical Computation and Artificial Intelligence. Proceedings, 1994. X, 275 pages. 1995.

Vol. 959: D.-Z. Du, M. Li (Eds.), Computing and Combinatorics. Proceedings, 1995. XIII, 654 pages. 1995.

Vol. 960: D. Leivant (Ed.), Logic and Computational Complexity. Proceedings, 1994. VIII, 514 pages. 1995.

Vol. 961: K.P. Jantke, S. Lange (Eds.), Algorithmic Learning for Knowledge-Based Systems. X, 511 pages. 1995. (Subseries LNAI).

Vol. 962: I. Lee, S.A. Smolka (Eds.), CONCUR '95: Concurrency Theory. Proceedings, 1995. X, 547 pages. 1995.

Vol. 963: D. Coppersmith (Ed.), Advances in Cryptology - CRYPTO '95. Proceedings, 1995. XII, 467 pages. 1995.

Vol. 964: V. Malyshkin (Ed.), Parallel Computing Technologies. Proceedings, 1995. XII, 497 pages. 1995.

Vol. 965: H. Reichel (Ed.), Fundamentals of Computation Theory. Proceedings, 1995. IX, 433 pages. 1995.

Vol. 966: S. Haridi, K. Ali, P. Magnusson (Eds.), EURO-PAR '95 Parallel Processing. Proceedings, 1995. XV, 734 pages. 1995.

Vol. 967: J.P. Bowen, M.G. Hinchey (Eds.), ZUM '95: The Z Formal Specification Notation. Proceedings, 1995. XI, 571 pages. 1995.

Vol. 968: N. Dershowitz, N. Lindenstrauss (Eds.), Conditional and Typed Rewriting Systems. Proceedings, 1994. VIII, 375 pages. 1995.

Vol. 969: J. Wiedermann, P. Hájek (Eds.), Mathematical Foundations of Computer Science 1995. Proceedings, 1995. XIII, 588 pages. 1995.

Vol. 970: V. Hlaváč, R. Šára (Eds.), Computer Analysis of Images and Patterns. Proceedings, 1995. XVIII, 960 pages. 1995.

Vol. 971: E.T. Schubert, P.J. Windley, J. Alves-Foss (Eds.), Higher Order Logic Theorem Proving and Its Applications. Proceedings, 1995. VIII, 400 pages. 1995.

Vol. 972: J.-M. Hélary, M. Raynal (Eds.), Distributed Algorithms. Proceedings, 1995. XI, 333 pages. 1995.

Vol. 973: H.H. Adelsberger, J. Lažanský, V. Mařík (Eds.), Information Management in Computer Integrated Manufacturing. IX, 665 pages. 1995.

Vol. 974: C. Braccini, L. DeFloriani, G. Vernazza (Eds.), Image Analysis and Processing. Proceedings, 1995. XIX, 757 pages. 1995.

Vol. 975: W. Moore, W. Luk (Eds.), Field-Programmable Logic and Applications. Proceedings, 1995. XI, 448 pages. 1995.

Vol. 976: U. Montanari, F. Rossi (Eds.), Principles and Practice of Constraint Programming — CP '95. Proceedings, 1995. XIII, 651 pages. 1995.

Vol. 977: H. Beilner, F. Bause (Eds.), Quantitative Evaluation of Computing and Communication Systems. Proceedings, 1995. X, 415 pages. 1995.

Vol. 978: N. Revell, A M. Tjoa (Eds.), Database and Expert Systems Applications. Proceedings, 1995. XV, 654 pages. 1995.

Vol. 979: P. Spirakis (Ed.), Algorithms — ESA '95. Proceedings, 1995. XII, 598 pages. 1995.

Vol. 980: A. Ferreira, J. Rolim (Eds.), Parallel Algorithms for Irregularly Structured Problems. Proceedings, 1995. IX, 409 pages. 1995.

Vol. 981: I. Wachsmuth, C.-R. Rollinger, W. Brauer (Eds.), KI-95: Advances in Artificial Intelligence. Proceedings, 1995. XII, 269 pages. (Subseries LNAI).

Vol. 982: S. Doaitse Swierstra, M. Hermenegildo (Eds.), Programming Languages: Implementations, Logics and Programs. Proceedings, 1995. XI, 467 pages. 1995.

Vol. 983: A. Mycroft (Ed.), Static Analysis. Proceedings, 1995. VIII, 423 pages. 1995.

Vol. 984: J.-M. Haton, M. Keane, M. Manago (Eds.), Advances in Case-Based Reasoning. Proceedings, 1994. VIII, 307 pages. 1995.

Vol. 985: T. Sellis (Ed.), Rules in Database Systems. Proceedings, 1995. VIII, 373 pages. 1995.

Vol. 986: Henry G. Baker (Ed.), Memory Management. Proceedings, 1995. XII, 417 pages. 1995.

Vol. 987: P.E. Camurati, H. Eveking (Eds.), Correct Hardware Design and Verification Methods. Proceedings, 1995. VIII, 342 pages. 1995.

Vol. 988: A.U. Frank, W. Kuhn (Eds.), Spatial Information Theory. Proceedings, 1995. XIII, 571 pages. 1995.

Vol. 989: W. Schäfer, P. Botella (Eds.), Software Engineering — ESEC '95. Proceedings, 1995. XII, 519 pages. 1995.

Vol. 990: C. Pinto-Ferreira, N.J. Mamede (Eds.), Progress in Artificial Intelligence. Proceedings, 1995. XIV, 487 pages. 1995. (Subseries LNAI).

Vol. 991: J. Wainer, A. Carvalho (Eds.), Advances in Artificial Intelligence. Proceedings, 1995. XII, 342 pages. 1995. (Subseries LNAI).

Vol. 992: M. Gori, G. Soda (Eds.), Topics in Artificial Intelligence. Proceedings, 1995. XII, 451 pages. 1995. (Subseries LNAI).

Vol. 993: T.C. Fogarty (Ed.), Evolutionary Computing. Proceedings, 1995. VIII, 264 pages. 1995.

Vol. 994: M. Hebert, J. Ponce, T. Boult, A. Gross (Eds.), Object Representation in Computer Vision. Proceedings, 1994. VIII, 359 pages. 1995.

Vol. 995: S.M. Müller, W.J. Paul, The Complexity of Simple Computer Architectures. XII, 270 pages. 1995.

Vol. 996: P. Dybjer, B. Nordström, J. Smith (Eds.), Types for Proofs and Programs. Proceedings, 1994. X, 202 pages. 1995.

Vol. 997: K.P. Jantke, T. Shinohara, T. Zeugmann (Eds.), Algorithmic Learning Theory. Proceedings, 1995. XV, 319 pages. 1995.

Vol. 998: A. Clarke, M. Campolargo, N. Karatzas (Eds.), Bringing Telecommunication Services to the People – IS&N '95. Proceedings, 1995. XII, 510 pages. 1995.

Vol. 999: P. Antsaklis, W. Kohn, A. Nerode, S. Sastry (Eds.), Hybrid Systems II. VIII, 569 pages. 1995.

Vol. 1000: J. van Leeuwen (Ed.), Computer Science Today. XIV, 643 pages. 1995.

Vol. 1002: J.J. Kistler, Disconnected Operation in a Distributed File System. XIX, 249 pages. 1995.

Vol. 1004: J. Staples, P. Eades, N. Katoh, A. Moffat (Eds.), Algorithms and Computation. Proceedings, 1995. XV, 440 pages. 1995.

Vol. 1005: J. Estublier (Ed.), Software Configuration Management. Proceedings, 1995. IX, 311 pages. 1995.

Vol. 1006: S. Bhalla (Ed.), Information Systems and Data Management. Proceedings, 1995. IX, 321 pages. 1995.

Vol. 1007: A. Bosselaers, B. Preneel (Eds.), Integrity Primitives for Secure Information Systems. VII, 239 pages. 1995.

Vol. 1008: B. Preneel (Ed.), Fast Software Encryption. Proceedings, 1994. VIII, 367 pages. 1995.

Vol. 1009: M. Broy, S. Jähnichen (Eds.), KORSO: Methods, Languages, and Tools for the Construction of Correct Software. X, 449 pages. 1995. Vol.

Vol. 1010: M. Veloso, A. Aamodt (Eds.), Case-Based Reasoning Research and Development. Proceedings, 1995. X, 576 pages. 1995. (Subseries LNAI).

Vol. 1011: T. Furuhashi (Ed.), Advances in Fuzzy Logic, Neural Networks and Genetic Algorithms. Proceedings, 1994. (Subseries LNAI).

Vol. 1012: M. Bartošek, J. Staudek, J. Wiedermann (Eds.), SOFSEM '95: Theory and Practice of Informatics. Proceedings, 1995. XI, 499 pages. 1995.

Vol. 1013: T.W. Ling, A.O. Mendelzon, L. Vieille (Eds.), Deductive and Object-Oriented Databases. Proceedings, 1995. XIV, 557 pages. 1995.

Vol. 1014: A.P. del Pobil, M.A. Serna, Spatial Representation and Motion Planning. XII, 242 pages. 1995.

Vol. 1015: B. Blumenthal, J. Gornostaev, C. Unger (Eds.), Human-Computer Interaction. Proceedings, 1995. VIII, 203 pages. 1995.

Vol. 1017: M. Nagl (Ed.), Graph-Theoretic Concepts in Computer Science. Proceedings, 1995. XI, 406 pages. 1995.

Vol. 1018: T. Little, R. Gusella (Eds.), Network and Operating Systems Support for Digital Audio and Video. Proceedings, 1995. XI, 357 pages. 1995.

Vol. 1019: E. Brinksma, W.R. Cleaveland, K.G. Larsen, T. Margaria, B. Steffen (Eds.), Tools and Algorithms for the Construction and Analysis of Systems. Selected Papers, 1995. VII, 291 pages. 1995.

Vol. 1020: I.D. Watson (Ed.), Progress in Case-Based Reasoning. Proceedings, 1995. VIII, 209 pages. 1995. (Subseries LNAI).

Vol. 1021: M.P. Papazoglou (Ed.), OOER '95: Object-Oriented and Entity-Relationship Modeling. Proceedings, 1995. XVII, 451 pages. 1995.

Vol. 1022: P.H. Hartel, R. Plasmeijer (Eds.), Functional Programming Languages in Education. Proceedings, 1995. X, 309 pages. 1995.

Vol. 1023: K. Kanchanasut, J.-J. Lévy (Eds.), Algorithms, Concurrency and Knowlwdge. Proceedings, 1995. X, 410 pages. 1995.

Vol. 1024: R.T. Chin, H.H.S. Ip, A.C. Naiman, T.-C. Pong (Eds.), Image Analysis Applications and Computer Graphics. Proceedings, 1995. XVI, 533 pages. 1995.

Vol. 1025: C. Boyd (Ed.), Cryptography and Coding. Proceedings, 1995. IX, 291 pages. 1995.

Lecture Notes in Computer Science

This series reports new developments in computer science research and teaching, quickly, informally, and at a high level. The timeliness of a manuscript is more important than its form, which may be unfinished or tentative. The type of material considered for publication includes

- drafts of original papers or monographs,
- technical reports of high quality and broad interest,
- advanced-level lectures,
- reports of meetings, provided they are of exceptional interest and focused on a single topic.

Publication of Lecture Notes is intended as a service to the computer science community in that the publisher Springer-Verlag offers global distribution of documents which would otherwise have a restricted readership. Once published and copyrighted they can be cited in the scientific literature.

Manuscripts

Lecture Notes are printed by photo-offset from the master copy delivered in camera-ready form. Manuscripts should be no less than 100 and preferably no more than 500 pages of text. Authors of monographs and editors of proceedings volumes receive 50 free copies of their book. Manuscripts should be printed with a laser or other high-resolution printer onto white paper of reasonable quality. To ensure that the final photo-reduced pages are easily readable, please use one of the following formats:

Font size	Printing area		Final size
(points)	(cm)	(inches)	(%)
10	12.2 x 19.3	4.8 x 7.6	100
12	15.3 x 24.2	6.0 x 9.5	80

On request the publisher will supply a leaflet with more detailed technical instructions or a TEX macro package for the preparation of manuscripts.

Manuscripts should be sent to one of the series editors or directly to:

Springer-Verlag, Computer Science Editorial I, Tiergartenstr. 17,
D-69121 Heidelberg, Germany